COMMENTARY ON MATTHEW 5

PART 2

COMMENTARY ON MATTHEW 5

PART 2

STEPHEN MANLEY

COMMENTARY ON MATTHEW 5 (PART 2)
© 2020 by Stephen Manley

Published by Cross Style Press
Lebanon, Tennessee
CrossStyle.org

All rights reserved. No part of this book may be reproduced in any form without prior permission from the publisher, except for brief quotations.

Scripture taken from the New King James Version®. Copyright © 1982 by Thomas Nelson, Inc. Used by permission. All rights reserved.

Edited by Delphine Manley

ISBN-13: 978-0-9987265-9-5

Printed in the United States of America.

CrossStyle.org

CONTENTS

Fulfillment of the Kingdom: The Application
Murder – Matthew 5:21-26

Matthew 5:21-48	Old and New	3
Matthew 5:21-26	New Teaching?	11
Matthew 5:21	What Did I Hear?	20
Matthew 5:21	"To" or "By"	28
Matthew 5:21	Liability of Murder	36
Matthew 5:22	I Say to You	44
Matthew 5:22	Anger is Murder	52
Matthew 5:22	Heavy Consequences	60
Matthew 5:23	Do I Want to Know?	68
Matthew 5:24	Utmost Importance	76
Matthew 5:25-26	Your Adversary	85
Matthew 5:26	The Final Word	93

Fulfillment of the Kingdom: The Application
Morality – Matthew 5:27-30

Matthew 5:27-30	Spiritual Adultery	103

Matthew 5:27-30	What a Link!	112
Matthew 5:28	Just a Look	122
Matthew 5:28	Looking at a Woman	130
Matthew 5:28	Sexuality and Priority	137
Matthew 5:28	In His Heart	145
Matthew 5:29-30	Essentiality: *Severity*	153
Matthew 5:29-30	Essentiality: *Stumbling*	161
Matthew 5:29-30	Essentiality: *Spiritual Priority*	169
Matthew 5:29-30	Proposition of Eternity	177
Matthew 5:29-30	Places of Eternity	185
Matthew 5:29-30	Physical Eternity	193
Matthew 5:29-30	Place of the Effects	201
Matthew 5:29-30	Punishment of the Effect	210
Matthew 5:29-30	Progression of the Effect	218

Fulfillment of the Kingdom: The Application
Marriage – Matthew 5:31-32

Matthew 5:31-32	The Divorce Issue	229
Matthew 5:31-32	Kingdom Marriage	237
Matthew 5:31-32	The Main Subject	245
Matthew 5:31-32	Spiritual Separation	253

Fulfillment of the Kingdom: The Application
Morals – Matthew 5:33-37

Matthew 5:33-37	Morals	263
Matthew 5:34	Never Swear	271
Matthew 5:34	Substitutes for God	279
Matthew 5:34-35	A Footstool	287
Matthew 5:35	Into Jerusalem	296
Matthew 5:36	My Own Head	304
Matthew 5:37	Logos	312
Matthew 5:37	A New Language	320

Fulfillment of the Kingdom: The Application
Malice – Matthew 5:38-42

Matthew 5:38-42	The Redemptive Idea	331
Matthew 5:38	Redemptive Principle	340
Matthew 5:39	Insults	349
Matthew 5:40	Insecurity	358
Matthew 5:40	Freedom From Insecurity	367
Matthew 5:40	Forgiveness in Security	377
Matthew 5:41	Inconvenience	386
Matthew 5:42	Inclusion	395
Matthew 5:42	Ownership	404

Fulfillment of the Kingdom: The Application
Motive – Matthew 5:43-48

Matthew 5:43-48	Kingdom Motive	415
Matthew 5:43	An Evil Appetite	424
Matthew 5:44	Love Your Enemies	433
Matthew 5:44	Love is Prayer	442
Matthew 5:45	Purpose of the Appetite	451
Matthew 5:45	I Am Caused	461
Matthew 5:46	Love Levels	470
Matthew 5:47	The Greet Sin	479
Matthew 5:46-47	Doing But Not Doing	488
Matthew 5:48	Perfect?	497
Matthew 5:48	Christian Perfection	505
Matthew 5:47-48	More!	514

About the Author   523

PART ONE
MATTHEW 5:21-26

Fulfillment of the Kingdom – The Application:

MURDER

Matthew 5:21-48

OLD AND NEW

We are on a progression through the Sermon on the Mount, and it is of utmost importance that we always return to the overall view. We can easily become so engaged in the immediate truth of one verse that we miss the essential truth of the paragraph, and the truth of the paragraph can block the reality of the complete view. We now enter the final section of this chapter, and it is long (Matthew 5:21-48). "The Fulfillment of the Kingdom, The Application" is the title. In this section Jesus proposes the elements that form the Kingdom of Heaven (Matthew 5:3-12), and we must apply them to our daily lives.

We want to start at the beginning, "The Formation of the Kingdom" (Matthew 5:3-12). The activities of the Kingdom do not define the Kingdom. Its application does not describe it. To comprehend the Kingdom, we must know its elements. In Jesus' description of the Kingdom, we understand our reality in the Kingdom. We are ***"poor in spirit"*** (Matthew 5:3). We are destitute in all resource, and we dwell in a state of helplessness, which causes our "mourning" (Matthew 5:4). We must have a consistent consciousness of our condition.

But we are not to be in a state of despair because in our helplessness Jesus unites with us. The Spirit of Jesus sources us! We are not destitute because of sin; we were created to be this way. All Jesus was in His humanity united with the Father, and this is what we are to be in unity with His Spirit. What sourced Jesus is now intertwined in our lives and sources us. God does not fill us as you fill a glass with water. He unites with us! The Kingdom is formed in this unity between God and man. The benefits of this unity are beyond comprehension. We are comforted, meek, filled, merciful, pure in heart, peacemakers, and victorious in persecution (Matthew 5:4-12). These are not qualities we accomplish to enter the Kingdom, but they are present because we are the Kingdom.

We can clearly see the imagery of salt and light in "The Function of the Kingdom" (Matthew 5:13-16). Salt and light are not doing activities. They are a state of being! This state is the Kingdom, my helplessness filled with God's presence. This oneness naturally demonstrates (functions) in the world. The world "sees" because we "are." The Father is glorified (Matthew 5:16). Because there are no rules or regulations there is no attempt to measure or judge. The intimate oneness between God and man forms the Kingdom and naturally displays itself.

This dream was presented in the Old Covenant and is now fulfilled in the New Covenant. Jesus proposes a beautiful picture, "The Fulfillment of the Kingdom, Acknowledged" (Matthew 5:17-20). The Trinity God has taken His heart and planted it in our world. He gave us the Scriptures, which is not typical literature or ancient writings. The Scriptures receive life from the nature of God. The Second Member of the Trinity leaped from His throne into our world. He submitted to the Scriptures. They became the fingers molding the shape of His life. Every law, proposal, and intent of the Scriptures is fulfilled in Jesus. They are so complete that Jesus is the Scriptures. The reverse is also true; the Scriptures are Jesus. The Living Word and the Written Word are united in one presentation.

Jesus is the first member of the Kingdom. He is the prototype of God's dream for us. Jesus, God, became a helpless man filled with God. The Scriptures proclaim it, and Jesus became it. We are called to it! This is the Kingdom. What does this look like

Old and New | **Matthew 5:21-48**

for us? This is the final section of this chapter, "The Fulfillment of the Kingdom, The Application" (Matthew 5:21-48).

As we step into this section, beware of the jolt. What Jesus proposed for the formation of the Kingdom was radical because it was a never-mentioned idea of religion, but it is conceptual. Something in your inner soul declares it must be true. But it is a religious proposal. Focusing on our weaknesses instead of our strengths is the opposite action from all other religions. To declare our helplessness is to admit we cannot "do it." All other religions encourage us to try harder, work more, and be stronger.

Now, in the application, Jesus steps into the arena of our daily lives. He talks about the best that our attempts, tries, and struggles can do. He compares this with what the unity of God and man in the Kingdom brings about. This relationship is not a new set of rules or a list of duties for us to perform. This is the Spirit of Jesus moving in us! He contrasts self-sourcing with Spirit-sourcing. Man's best effort is compared with the best effort of God and man united in the Kingdom. He declares that man's discipline cannot be compared with the wonder of Jesus' Spirit of discipline in the man. That declaration is the big jolt!

Six areas of comparison exist and are difficult for us. All six areas relate to our relationships. Jesus spoke directly to His Jewish culture. They had developed six hundred and thirteen oral traditions, which became more important to them than the Scriptures from which they supposedly were created. These oral traditions highlighted rules about "the Sabbath Day," "defilement," and "ceremonies," but there was little focus on "relationship." Jesus' application of the Scriptures fulfilled in the Kingdom is about relationship.

Jesus climaxed His application with a revelation of His Father's heart. He said, ***"Therefore you shall be perfect, just as your Father in heaven is perfect"*** (Matthew 5:48). This statement is the climax of the sixth application regarding "motive" (Matthew 5:43-48). He highlights His Father's activities

Part One: Fulfillment of the Kingdom – The Application: Murder

toward His enemies. *"For He makes His sun rise on the evil and on the good, and sends rain on the just and on the unjust"* (Matthew 5:45). God has one motive toward all mankind, and He does not determine that by what people do or do not do. He determines His motive by whom He is, the state of His being.

The Greek word "teleios," translated *perfect*, (Matthew 5:48) causes problems for many people. They equate the word with a state beyond mistakes. In our culture, human error and perfection do not go together. Doubly difficult for us is to grasp what Jesus means when He equates what we are to be *perfect* with the state in which the Father is *perfect*. God is omniscient, but we are not. He is omnipotent, but we are not. God is omnipresent, but we are not. In our passage, Jesus does not discuss any of these subjects. The single focus of His discussion is heart motive.

This verse (Matthew 5:48) is the climax of this section (Matthew 5:21-48). All these areas of application depend on God's motive uniting the heart of man with His. The Greek word "teleios," translated *perfect*, focuses on "finished, or reaching its end, term, or limit; it is therefore complete, or full, wanting nothing. This connects with the opening statements of the Sermon on the Mount, the Beatitudes. Jesus does not call us to a long journey, then after much struggle, we arrive at this point. We are helpless, *"poor in spirit."* He unites with us, and this union is called "the Kingdom of Heaven." In this union we are *perfect*. Completeness is in intimacy with His heart. The motive of His heart becomes the motive of our heart. His heart becomes our heart.

The six areas of application are remarkable. They are:
MURDER / hate and forgiveness (Matthew 5:21-25)
MORALITY / adultery and lust (Matthew 5:26-30)
MARRIAGE / divorce and concern (Matthew 5:31-32)
MORALS / swearing and honesty (Matthew 5:33-37)
MALICE / revenge and forgiveness (Matthew 5:38-42)
MOTIVE / hate and love (Matthew 5:43-48)

As we view these six areas of application, there are two things happening. One is INTENSIFICATION. Jesus became the visible expression of God's heart and nature. We must view the Scriptures as more than written literature. Without the flow of His life, it is nothing more than academic study. Because God spoke it, the Scriptures become the revelation of His heart. Jesus submitted Himself to the Scriptures. They shaped His life into an expression of God's heart, and Jesus wants us to experience this righteousness.

As Jesus closed the introductory statement to our study, He said, **"For I say to you, that unless your righteousness exceeds the righteousness of the scribes and Pharisees, you will by no means enter the kingdom of heaven"** (Matthew 5:20). The righteousness of the Old Covenant law does not end where the righteousness of the New Covenant begins. The Kingdom of Heaven is not a strengthened version of the Old Covenant. The Old Covenant is not the practice run of the real race to come. The Kingdom of Heaven is a different and new reality. This Kingdom is not humanity strengthening their already tired muscles, but is a new source enabling supernatural, divine activities.

Jesus illustrated this in each application area. In the Old Covenant, ceasing to murder was the standard (Matthew 5:21). The new intensified standard is ceasing to hate! How can anyone do this? According to the Beatitudes, the formation of the Kingdom, this is not a proper question. The individual who embraces *mourns* his state of helplessness *poor in spirit* experiences unity with God's heart. This unity expresses itself in peacemaking (Matthew 5:9). In fact, mercy is experienced in giving and receiving (Matthew 5:7). This is life lived on a level not conceivable in the oral traditions; it is ordinary in the Kingdom.

Morality can be understood only in doing one's best. After all, we are only human. What if an individual experienced the mind of God? What if in helplessness we could unite with God and become the Kingdom? The Old Covenant applauded a limitation of specific acts (Matthew 5:27). The Kingdom, the mind of Christ, gives an individual the perspective of God concerning the opposite sex (Matthew 5:28).

Would this not also affect marriage (Matthew 5:31-32)? When Jesus proposed the Kingdom thought about marriage, the disciples responded, *"If such is the case of the man with his wife, it is better not to marry"* (Matthew 19:10). This was the response of the human who lived the low level of the Old Covenant, and his righteousness was contained in the boundaries of self-benefit. The person entered marriage to get his needs met. How much greater is the righteousness that thinks only of others is the heart of God?

In the realm of morals, no one would be honest. Perhaps some level of honesty was accomplished through fear of being punished by the object on which you "swore" (Matthew 5:33-37). What if your honesty was not regulated by fear? What if you were always honest? Honesty is simply who you are, the Kingdom of Heaven!

Malice is a driving motive for endless revenge. The Old Covenant limited it to *"an eye for an eye and a tooth for a tooth"* (Matthew 5:38). The cry of God's heart is continuous forgiveness, but that is impossible for me in my helplessness. Jesus proposed a new level of living in unity with His divine heart. In fact, this radically changes the motive of the heart (Matthew 5:43-48). Living on this level makes us *"perfect, just as your Father in heaven is perfect."* For those who are helpless *poor in spirit*, it is unthinkable. What if there is a New Covenant? What if He joins you in your helplessness? What if He and you become the Kingdom?

Jesus does a second interesting thing in this application, the fulfillment of the Kingdom INTERNATIONALIZATION. Since the Babylonian Exile and the return of the Jews to Jerusalem, the Old Testament law was dominant. For four hundred years between the Old and New Testament, the Pharisees and scribes developed their application of this law. The six hundred and thirteen oral applications were all external, and the only way they viewed the Scriptures.

Jesus allowed the Scriptures to shape His life; thus, He fulfilled all the law's requirements and the prophecies. This fulfillment of God's heart in the Scriptures was not an external covering. It was at the core relationship between Jesus and the Father. An inward uniting exploded into a level of living beyond anything the external applications could imagine.

External murder was forbidden and could be prevented by proper discipline. However, the Kingdom is concerned about the inner heart's feelings. What is happening in relationship? How do you feel toward others? Outward adultery can be conquered by circumstances and fear, but inner purity can be found only in the mind of Christ. The Kingdom is the union of your mind and His. Marriage can be maintained because there are no other options; the uniting of two lives in intimacy is complete when Jesus sources each. Morals or integrity, determined by outward pressure of an oath, is false character. A helpless individual united with Jesus produces a state of being of honesty without pressure. Inward malice is curbed in its outward activities by such rules as **"an eye for an eye and a tooth for a tooth."** The Kingdom is the removal of all malice and is the flow of God's indwelling nature to all. Self-sourced motives perform many acceptable acts. However, the outward deeds are spoiled by improper motive. The Kingdom is the indwelling of Jesus' motives bringing us into the state of being designed for our lives.

No wonder Jesus cried out at the end of this chapter, **"Therefore you shall be perfect, just as your Father in heaven is perfect"** (Matthew 5:48). What else could we be? His nature indwells our poverty-stricken hearts and sources us with His being. We live an impossible life. We dwell in an impossible state. What we desperately try to achieve in the outward and fail is superseded by the inward reality through union with Him.

Part One: Fulfillment of the Kingdom - The Application: Murder

Effort is eliminated, and struggling is replaced with resting. The Kingdom of God becomes who we are. Our lives reveal His heart. Rejoice in this hour. Union with Him is the Kingdom.

Matthew 5:21-26

NEW TEACHING?

"You have heard that it was said to those of old, 'You shall not murder,' and whoever murders will be in danger of the judgment. But I say to you that whoever is angry with his brother without a cause shall be in danger of the judgment. And whoever says to his brother, 'Raca!' shall be in danger of the council. But whoever says 'You fool!' shall be in danger of hell fire. Therefore if you bring your gift to the altar, and there remember that your brother has something against you, leave your gift there before the altar, and go your way. First be reconciled to your brother, and then come and offer your gift. Agree with your adversary quickly, while you are on the way with him, lest your adversary deliver you to the judge, the judge hand you over to the officer, and you be thrown into prison. Assuredly, I say to you, you will by no means get out of there till you have paid the last penny" (Matthew 5:21-26).

Jesus spoke these resounding words at the end of the section we entitled "The Fulfillment of the Kingdom, Acknowledged." ***"For I say to you that unless your righteousness exceeds the righteousness of the scribes and Pharisees, you will by no means enter the kingdom of heaven"*** (Matthew 5:20). These words left the crowd confounded because it was a call to righteousness that exceeded the righteousness of those who were considered to be the most righteous. How could that be? Were they misunderstanding what Jesus said?

The Greek word "perisseuo," translated exceeds, means "to super abound in quantity or quality, to be in excess, or to be superfluous." In the New Testament the word refers to be or have more than enough. This word paints the imagery of a river overflowing its banks. However, this word is not adequate to propose the truth of Jesus' emphasis. Therefore, Jesus uses "pleion" as well! This word is not translated in any of our modern translations and could be translated *exceeds* as already stated by the word "perisseuo." In other words, *exceeds* is stated twice. "Pleion" focuses on "much, more, or abundant."

The Jews listening to Jesus that day could not fathom how anyone could be more righteous than the Pharisees. Can you go to church more times than every time the church doors are open? Can you tithe more than ten percent of everything, even your herb plants? The study of the law dominated every Pharisee's life. They developed six hundred and thirteen oral traditions as applications of the Scriptures. They refined each tradition to produce the maximum righteousness possible for mankind. The crowd might have understood Jesus encouraging them to be like the Pharisees, but His expectation that they could surpass, excel, or go beyond the righteousness of the Pharisees was ridiculous to them.

Jesus' conclusion of the six illustrations or elements paralleled this same expectation. He said, ***"Therefore you shall be perfect, just as your Father in heaven is perfect"*** (Matthew 5:48). He left no room for adjustment in either of these propositions. Perfection might be shaped by our common sense, thus making it achievable. But Jesus highlights God's perfection as the standard. The emphasis moves from the unattainable righteousness of the Pharisees to the unreachable perfection of the Father.

However, Jesus did not end with this statement. He gave illustrations for the key areas of our lives. His applications are divinely inspired! As we approach this first area, there is an obvious structure to His presentation. He repeats this structure for each preceding area. Jesus expressed His concern that we understand and experience the fullness of the New Covenant in our lives. To understand and experience His proposal, we must move beyond our initial shock. We have to push aside our feelings of resistance and rejection. We must squelch the thought that this expectation is impossible. We must be open.

As we move into the first of the six applications, Jesus presents a structure that appears in all the applications. He carefully designed each structure for clarification. He did not want any confusion. We must confront the truth directly and reject it or accept it. Each application begins with "what we have always known." He said, **"You have heard that it was said."** This knowledge is not limited to the Jewish culture addressed by Jesus, but it is a general knowledge present in the universe and consciousness of mankind. Note that although we have known, we have not obeyed. This makes the statements of Jesus even more radical. He shares with us a clarification of this knowledge, **"But I say to you."** This raises the level of expectation even higher. Then, Jesus applies the truth clearly to our daily lives.

Present Knowledge

"You have heard that it was said to those of old, 'You shall not murder,' and whoever murders will be in danger of the judgment" (Matthew 5:21).

Truth has a basic, core, and fundamental understanding. The proof of this statement is displayed in your life through guilt. Each time you go against "present knowledge" you experience guilt. Where there is no knowledge, there is no guilt. In the context of our passage, the reality of "prevenient grace" is present. God gives some of His grace and truth (Himself) to every individual. No person is void of truth.

Within the structure of God's plan for humanity, He planned distinct avenues for the communication of truth. One of those avenues is "Artistic Speaking." All true artistic works are a product of the individual; they constitute how the artist feels, thinks, and cares. Musicians write and play music according to their unique personalities. The music is an expression of the musician. God implanted this quality in each of us. All creation, flowing from His inner being, carries the touch of His Person. The truth of His nature determines the expression.

Paul echoed this through his epistles. He said, **"Because what may be known of God is manifest in them, for God has shown it to them"** (Romans 1:19). Did God not come from His throne to form you with His hands (Genesis 2:7)? Did He not mix the dust of the ground into clay and leave His fingerprints on you? Are you not made in His image (Genesis 1:26)? The pattern of His nature is implanted in us. Our spiritual and physical systems were designed to operate according to Him! This is the "present knowledge" of every individual. Our nature cries in us **"You shall not murder!"** God stamped this into the fiber of the universe as general knowledge of every human before He gave the law.

However, God is also speaking to us! This is the "present knowledge" of "Audio Speaking." Truth is coming to us from the audio speaking of God. He is not silent. The Book of Hebrews begins with this thundering statement. ***God, who at various times and in various ways spoke in time past to the fathers by the prophets, has in these last days spoken to us by His Son*** (Hebrews 1:1-2). God spoke in the Old Testament through a cloud by day, a pillar of fire by night, a burning bush, and a snake on a pole. God also gave us writings on tablets of stone. The list is endless! In our previous study (Matthew 5:17-20), Jesus declared God's proclamation through the Scriptures. He has not left us without instruction. We have had repeated encounters with Him. God spoke to us, **"You shall not murder"** (Exodus 20:13). Almighty

God wrote it in stone with His finger.

God also uses "Atmospheric Speaking." God consistently bombards the atmosphere of our living with His presence and speaking. Jesus did not say, "You have read." Many in the crowd Jesus spoke to could not read. Even if they could read, the Old Testament scrolls were not available to them. He referred to what they had been taught by their teachers. God permeated the atmosphere of their culture. However, humanity tends to adjust, make additions, and focus the fundamental teachings spoken by God. Although the core of what they heard was truth, the cultural atmosphere of the day adapted and adjusted this truth to their preference. This adaptation was the difficulty Jesus expressed.

We are consistent in manipulating what God says for our convenience. The teachers of Israel were guilty of this. Before the establishment of the law God said, **"Whoever sheds man's blood, by man his blood shall be shed; for in the image of God He made man"** (Genesis 9:6). The statement of our passage, **"and whoever murders will be in danger of the judgment** (court)**"** is not found anywhere in the Scriptures. They adapted the teaching for the convenience of their personal culture.

Proposed Knowledge

"But I say to you that whoever is angry with his brother without a cause shall be in danger of the judgment. And whoever says to his brother, 'Raca!' shall be in danger of the council. But whoever says, 'You fool!' shall be in danger of hell fire"
(Matthew 5:22).

God pours out His mercy on us. If God places His truth in us, He speaks to us, and He fills the atmosphere of our existence with truth. Is this not enough? Surely God is not obligated to allow one more statement of truth to come our way. A mission statement of the past generation was "You and I have no right to hear the Gospel message again until every man in the world has heard it at least once"! Our ears are bombarded weekly with the truth of the Gospel. We have heard it more than our share compared to those who have never heard it. But God is so gracious and merciful to us. To all spoken in the past, Jesus added, **"But I say to you!"**

Once "what they have heard" is established, Jesus moves to "what must I tell you." He has "Authoritative Speaking." The Greek word "lego," translated *"I say,"* is one word used as a verb with the first person singular pronoun indicated at the end of the word. This is the usual manner to write this statement. However, Jesus added the Greek word "ego," translated *"I,"* giving a double emphasis on the word *"I."*

Jesus now gives the proper explanation of the Scriptures. The "Fulfillment of the Kingdom, Acknowledged" (Matthew 5:17-20) provides the significance of this statement. Jesus does not discard the Scriptures. He fulfills and explains what God intended in the Scriptures. This explanation is true of the inner witness He placed in you. Jesus goes on to give content to the design of your being, His image. If there were any misunderstanding or wrong focus regarding what God intended, Jesus clarified it. No one has the right to do this equal to Jesus. He is the fulfillment of the Scriptures. Not one jot or tittle passed away until Jesus completed the Scriptures. In this fulfillment is the authority to speak to us.

In our passage, Jesus equates His words with the words of God, because they are the words of God. He said, **"You have heard that it was said to them of old"** (Matthew 5:21). The undercurrent of this statement is that God spoke to them in the past. The foundation of this truth is God Himself. The truth about *"murder"* was not first spoken in the law, but was spoken by God before the law (Genesis 9:6). God spoke this from the beginning. Now Jesus fulfilled this speaking with clarification!

Jesus used "Actuality Speaking." The section (Matthew 5:17-20) introduced our passage and declared the speaking of God. Jesus revealed His relationship with the Scriptures. He heard the voice of the Father through the Scriptures. God placed His nature on the table of our world in written form. Jesus, the Second Member of the Trinity, came to our world to submit His life to the formation of this nature. He fulfills everything God spoke in the Scriptures. Jesus is the speaking of God to us! No wonder the Scriptures call Him "the Word." All the Scriptures say about murder is clarified and made seeable in Jesus. If the Scriptures are the nature of God in written form, Jesus is the Scriptures in living form. The Living Word declares without confusion the reality of truth in the Scriptures. No more confusion.

You cannot understand the Scriptures without intimacy with Jesus. You cannot believe the Scriptures without believing in Jesus. The Living Word and the Written Word are linked; they are the same. Now Jesus speaks the Word to us! This is the foundation of His cry. ***"For I say to you, that unless your righteousness exceeds the righteousness of the scribes and Pharisees, you will by no means enter the kingdom of heaven"*** (Matthew 5:20). This is "Accusative Speaking." The standard of not committing the physical act of murder is considered a compromise to the truth of God's nature. What once was seen as a great accomplishment is now thought of as subnormal for even the beginner in the Kingdom of Heaven? This standard is a call for the intimacy Jesus has with the Father to become present in us.

Practiced Knowledge

"Therefore if you bring your gift to the altar, and there remember that your brother has something against you, leave your gift there before the altar, and go your way. First be reconciled to your brother, and then come and offer your gift.

Part One: Fulfillment of the Kingdom - The Application: Murder

Agree with your adversary quickly, while you are on the way with him, lest your adversary deliver you to the judge, the judge hand you over to the officer, and you be thrown into prison. Assuredly, I say to you, you will by no means get out of there till you have paid the last penny" (Matthew 5:23-26).

Jesus never participates in "Argument Speaking" of the Scriptures. In previous studies we discovered a fallacy that gripped the Jewish nation. They operated under the assumption that the study of the Scriptures was of more value than doing the Scriptures. This fallacy caused debates, arguments, and discussions of the law, but put little emphasis on practical living. The disobedience of the Scriptures had little consequence in their minds. Although the Pharisees were continually upset with Jesus because He and His disciples broke their laws, they were more upset about His teachings about the Scriptures. Jesus calling His disciples to live beyond the righteousness of the Pharisees irritated them.

Now Jesus gives His disciples His "Application Speaking." Everything Jesus lived and said about **"You shall not murder"** is now going to be applied to our lives. He equates anger with murder (Matthew 5:22). While the outside deed of murder is a product of anger, and the presence of anger is the same as murder. This revelation becomes even more disturbing as He applies it to our relationship with God (Matthew 5:23-24). The reality of our relationship with God is affected and conditioned on our relationship with others. This effect is shocking news!

I feel content and secure in my relationship with God. I am one of the "people of God," but this relationship with God is suddenly questioned. I could understand this if I had taken someone's life, but what does this have to do with my relationship with my fellowman? The focus is not on how my fellowman feels about me, but about how I feel about him. The two categories of relationship with God and relationship with man now overlap.

New Teaching? | Matthew 5:21-26

Jesus said, ***"You shall love the LORD your God with all your heart, with all your soul, and with all your mind. This is the first and great commandment. And the second is like it: 'You shall love your neighbor as yourself'"*** (Matthew 22:37-39).

Jesus continued to illustrate this truth in an "Adornment Speaking." He placed the truth in the middle of their daily hour of prayer and sacrificial offerings (Matthew 5:23-24). He planted this truth amid of an argument over practical matters, which might take them to court (Matthew 5:25-26). Live in inner peace and let this peace flow to your circumstances. All this connected to ***"You shall not murder."***

These would be impossible and frightening proposals except for the reality of the "Formation of the Kingdom" (Matthew 5:3-12). Our helplessness is filled with His resource. As the fullness of the Spirit produced this through Jesus, He will do this through us.

Matthew 5:21

WHAT DID I HEAR?

"You have heard that is was said to those of old, 'You shall not murder, and whoever murders shall be in danger of judgment'"
(Matthew 5:21).

The Sermon on the Mount describes a person who is the Kingdom of Heaven. In the opening statements of the sermon, Jesus proclaims "The Formation of the Kingdom" (Matthew 5:3-12). The Kingdom consists of a person ***"poor in spirit."*** In this state of "no inner resource," you can be filled with the nature of God! This combination of helpless man and God uniquely forms a new creature called the "Kingdom of Heaven." All God's resources begin to flow through this new creature, such as meekness, fullness, mercy, purity of heart, peace, and joy in persecution. The state of this new creature is one of "being"! Jesus used the imagery of ***salt*** and ***light*** (Matthew 5:13-16). This new creature is not defined by activity, although he or she is heavily involved in action. Activity is never the result of the person because he or she is poverty-stricken.

What is the connection of Jesus, this new creature, and the Scriptures? Is this an abolition of the Old Testament realities and the establishment of a New Testament reality? Jesus introduces this subject by saying "The Fulfillment of the Kingdom, Acknowledged" (Matthew 5:17-20). This statement contains the concept illustrated in "The Fulfillment of the Kingdom,

Application (Matthew 5:21-48). Jesus did not come to abolish the Scriptures but to fulfill them!

The imagery of fulfillment is strong. The Trinity God planted His nature amid our world in written form, the Scriptures. The Second Member of the Trinity sacrificially came to our world to submit Himself to the fullness of God's nature. He is the first man to be filled with this nature. The nature of God formed Jesus, and He became the visible image of God. Because the Scriptures are the nature of God in written form and Jesus is the revelation of this nature, Jesus and the Scriptures must be different forms of the same. Jesus did not come to destroy or alter the Scriptures. He came to submit Himself to the Scriptures so His life might fulfill everything contained therein!

The fulfillment of this nature expresses righteousness far beyond the righteousness of the scribes and Pharisees. This fulfillment is not a result of years of practice and discipline, but it is the combination of the essence of our helplessness and His nature forming the new creature, the Kingdom of Heaven. The scribes and Pharisees viewed the Scriptures from their self-centered perspective. They interpreted the Scriptures on a level they felt they could keep. A person without resource will never see the meaning of the Scriptures on a level ridiculously impossible to attain. We must trivialize the Scriptures to make it feasible. But what if the Scriptures are the image of God in written form? What if we can be intimate with God's living nature, and He can fulfill the Scriptures in and through us? This intimacy would elevate our righteousness from a compromise of doing our best to the wonder of His life in us!

Now Jesus launches into the proclamation of six illustrations giving explanation and validity to His proposition. Jesus spiritually weaves the illustrations to form one message, the message of the "perfect nature of the Father" (Matthew 5:48), addressing every area of life. Bible scholars have tried to link these illustrations in a variety of ways. They are not right or wrong but offer different perspectives on the truth.

I would like to offer you three sets containing two illustrations each. The first addresses the "Cardinal Truth" about life. It contains the illustrations of "Murder" (Matthew 5:21-26) and "Morality" (Matthew 5:27-30). Here we investigate our view of relationship within the context of life. If righteousness is not present in this realm, there is no possibility for purity in the remaining areas. The next two illustrations consider "Covenant Truth." "Marriage (Matthew 5:31-32) and "Morals" (Matthew 5:33-37) expand God's nature into our commitment to each other. Without His nature, we fail in all our covenant interactions with others. The last two illustrations address "Core Truth." "Malice" (Matthew 5:38-42) and "Motive" (Matthew 5:43-48) demand a heart filled with God's nature. We are called to be like Him!

The first illustration of this fulfillment is murder. Murder is the unlawful killing, with malice aforethought, of another human. Murder is the sixth commandment in the Ten Commandments (Exodus 20:13). Jesus gives new content to murder as He develops this illustration.

The Person of God
(His Image)

Why does Jesus begin with murder? Are the six illustrations a series of sins from the worst to the least? Is He going from the one that bears the most consequences to the one bearing the least? Perhaps as our study continues we will discover why each illustration is on the list. Murder is first on the list because it can be the physical act itself or an attitude. Murder is a violent act that tries to destroy the image of God.

God uses the Scriptures to convince us of our importance to Him. He spoke the world into existence. But the creation of man and woman involved His participation on a different level. ***"And the Lord God formed man of the dust of the ground and breathed into his nostrils the breath of life; and man became a living being"*** (Genesis 2:7). Our structure has the fingerprints of God on it. He shaped us with His creative hands, which is unique in all the creation. Genesis describes this involvement. ***"So God created man in His own image; in the image of God He created him; male and female He created them"*** (Genesis 1:27). The ***"image of God"*** is stated twice for emphasis.

All humanity was destroyed in the flood except Noah and his sons, and a new start for humanity began. God gave specific instructions to this family. The first biblical prohibition concerning murder was included in these instructions. God said, ***"Whoever sheds man's blood, by man his blood shall be shed; for in the image of God He made man"*** (Genesis 9:6). The evil of murder is connected with mankind being in the image of God. As Jesus expanded this in our passage, anger, ***"Raca"*** (treating your brother as worthless), and calling him a fool (a stupid one) expresses contempt for the image of God in which man was created (Matthew 5:22).

What is the image of God? This is obviously not the physical shape of our being. The biblical account highlights the essence of relationship. We are created beings capable of relationship with God's nature; the rest of creation does not have this. In fact, the indication is that all creation has connection with God through our relationship with Him. We are the key element that links all creation to God. The Kingdom of Heaven is the fulfillment of the image of God! We are helpless. He comes in His resource, His nature, and with God we become the Kingdom of Heaven. The capacity of this relationship is the heart of the image of God in our creation.

Murder is an attempt to abolish the physical expression of the relationship between God and man. For this reason Jesus quickly moves into the spiritual application of this physical act.

Anger has the same result as murder; therefore, anger equals murder. It abolishes relationships. This result is and has always been the demonic desire. Jesus said, **"You are of your father the devil, and the desires of your father you want to do. He was a murderer** (manslayer) **from the beginning, and does not stand in the truth"** (John 8:44). It seems the devil's single desire is to destroy the image of God that continually confronts him in every human being. In our fallen nature (carnal mind) we share the nature Satan personifies. Murder, anger, and hate flow from our heart's center attempting to abolish all evidence of the image of God around us.

The Plan of God
(His Impact)

Jesus proceeds to highlight division between your brother (created in the image of God) and you (created in the image of God). He offers the picture of the amazing daily sacrifice being offered on the altar (Matthew 5:23). This daily sacrifice illustrates all true about the relationship between God and man. This relationship is the image of God fulfilled in every person offering sacrifice. God has a distinct plan for my life! My fingerprints differ from all others who have ever been or will ever be. My DNA is distinctive to me! My personality is unique in all its expression of ideas and thoughts. Therefore, the image of God is not a focus on all humanity but on every person.

If my helplessness is filled with His Person, I do not become like you! God's image expresses itself through me uniquely and specifically planned and determined by God! Division between us murders the plan of God's image in each of us. How may I be in oneness with God's image in my life if I will not embrace the image of God in your life? How I feel about you affects how I feel about God!

God's plan involving the expression of His image through me differs from His plan expressed by His image through you. However, these two plans come together to express the larger plan God has for everyone, the plan of redemption. Murder, anger, treating you as worthless, and viewing you as stupid destroys the plan of God. Reconciliation restores the plan! A person cannot propose to embrace the plan of God for his or her life while destroying the plan of God for another. No wonder Jesus said that we must *"leave your gift there before the altar, and go your way. First be reconciled to your brother, and then come and offer your gift"* (Matthew 5:24).

In Matthew's Gospel account (Matthew 18), the disciples were arguing about positions in the Kingdom. Jesus questioned what such self-centeredness does to the immature person of the Kingdom. He pronounced punishment for destruction of the "little ones." Peter bragged about his generous desire to forgive his brother up to seven times. Jesus said that we must always forgive, and He backed that up with a parable. A servant forgiven an unbelievable amount by his master then refused to forgive a fellow servant a minuscule amount. When the master heard this news he nullified his forgiveness and punished the unforgiving servant. Jesus applied the truth of the parable when He said, *"So My heavenly Father also will do to you if each of you, from his heart, does not forgive his brother his trespasses"* (Matthew 18:35). Jesus equated murder with not forgiving.

The Portion of God
(Our Inheritance)

As you read our passage (Matthew 5:21-26), you will see that Jesus proceeds to go further with the subject of murder. In the last two verses, He discusses agreeing with your adversary so he does not take you to court. He does not say "your brother" as in the previous verses. Maybe this is your brother who refuses reconciliation and becomes your enemy. Does this not nullify the requirement to cater to his desires or demands? May I not shake the dust off my feet and depart? Have I not done my part trying to reconcile, therefore, need not going further?

In these last two verses (Matthew 5:25-26), Jesus is practical in His approach to the materialistic world, but He also is spiritual in His approach to our relationship with His Father. He insists that we must render to our brother, who becomes our adversary, everything necessary to keep our differences from coming to the public court. Jesus insists the result will be, **"you will by no means get out of there till you have paid the last penny"** (Matthew 5:26).

How does this relate to the beginning statements about murder? Jesus calls us to exceed the righteousness of the scribes and Pharisees by moving from not committing physical murder to not having an attitude of murder. Considering my brother stupid and viewing him as worthless is an attitude of anger. This high level of righteousness can be experienced only in the Kingdom of Heaven. The Kingdom of Heaven is your helplessness filled with His nature. If you are the Kingdom, there is no need to offer sacrifices at the altar of God unless you go to your brother with the attitude of God. Oneness with the Father cannot be known except in the flow of His nature through us to others. Whether your brother accepts reconciliation with you is not the issue. The issue is the flow of God's nature through you, and anything less than this flow is murder.

If you murder your brother, who becomes your adversary by not flowing God's nature to him, you will find the payment extremely high. It will move from the materialistic realm to the courts of the spiritual realm. The spiritual cost of losing your spiritual inheritance is profound. All through the Old Testament, God is our portion, our inheritance. **"O Lord, You are the portion of my inheritance and my cup; You maintain** *my lot"* (Psalm 16:5). Will I embrace His nature or maintain my self-dependency? Will I murder or love?

Matthew 5:21

"TO" OR "BY"

"You have heard that is was said to those of old, 'You shall not murder, and whoever murders shall be in danger of judgment'" (Matthew 5:21).

Bible scholars are divided about the introductory statement of this verse. Jesus said, **"You have heard that it was said *to those* **(tois) *of old*"** (Matthew 5:21). The Greek word "tois" is a definite article translated "the," "this," "that," or a variety of other ways. It relates in number to the plural "archaiois," translated ***"of old."*** Therefore, as far as the Greek grammar takes us, the translation is "them" or ***"those."*** Jesus said, **"You have heard that it was said,"** then He added the phrase, ***"those*** (tois) *of old."* The Bible translators are divided on using the words ***"to"*** or ***"by"*** to connect the two phrases. Either one is acceptable in the Greek grammar.

No, we must not rush past this as if it does not matter. If the proper translation is, **"You have heard that it was said *to those of old,*"** the focus is on what the fathers of Israel heard. In this light, Moses spoke in the law to the fathers, **"You shall not kill."** In our passage, Jesus assumes a superior position over Moses. He spoke an opinion besides the Scriptures. Some have claimed that Jesus established a new divine law when He opposed His view to the Word of the Scriptures.

If the proper translation is, **"You have heard that it was said *by those of old,*"** the focus is on what the fathers of Israel taught. The Scriptures teach, *"You shall not kill."* The rabbis and expounders of the law proposed a tradition that the scribes and Pharisees adopted. Jesus considered this tradition a violation of the intent and heart of God revealed in the Scriptures. He disagreed with their approach and considered it incomplete. In using *"by"* Jesus brings us back to the true meaning of the Scriptures. *"Those of old"* allowed their self-sourcing nature to adjust the truth of God to fit what they thought they could accomplish.

Which interpretation is right? The context of Jesus' message in the Sermon on the Mount is our guide. The immediate context is "The Fulfillment of the Kingdom, Acknowledged" (Matthew 5:17-20). This section focuses on Jesus' fulfillment of the Scriptures, not destroying or opposing them! He emphasized this twice (Matthew 5:17). Reversing His statement by setting the Scriptures aside would be strange.

"You have heard that it was said" is most likely associated with oral teachings and traditions. If Jesus referred to the Written Word of the Scriptures, He would have said, *"Moses commanded"* (Matthew 8:4) or, *"It is written"* (Matthew 4:4, 7, 10). His emphasis on hearing and speaking focuses us on the teachings of the rabbis. These teachers, such as Hillel and Shammai, were called "fathers of antiquity." The designation of *"those of old"* easily refers to them and their oral interpretation of the Scriptures.

Why is this an issue in our passage? Jesus continued without variance in regard to His relationship with the Scriptures, the nature and heart of God given to us in written form. Embracing the Scriptures is embracing the nature of God. Jesus became man and allowed the Scriptures to shape His life. The Scriptures express the nature of God, and Jesus reveals the nature of God. He wants to bring us back to the truth of the Scriptures. Nothing beyond or above this exists! What is the truth of the Scriptures?

The truth of the Scriptures is not about a physical ACTION but a spiritual ATTITUDE (Matthew 5:22). No one can approach this passage without making that admission! Perhaps we should begin with a disclaimer. We are not among those who advocate that physical actions do not matter. Neither do we propose that physical actions do not exist or are at random. The attitude of the heart will of necessity declare itself in a person's actions. Thus, the physical action becomes a symptom of the person's core. Jesus expressed this in His first statement about murder. Murder is a physical act that expresses the attitude of anger and the need to demean and belittle another person (Matthew 5:22).

Every generation battles with keeping this concept in proper perspective. When we do not hold this perspective, it is called antinomianism. You will never find this word in the Scriptures, but a variety of degrees of antinomianism is confronted and exposed in its fallacy. Antinomianism is the view that Christians are exempt from the demands of moral law because of the abundance of divine grace, the only source of salvation. Many accused the Apostle Paul of holding this false doctrine. He wrote, *"And why not say, 'Let us do evil that good may come'? – as we are slanderously reported and as some affirm that we say"* (Romans 3:8). Paul consistently and heartily denied the accusation that he considered right conduct irrelevant in the Christian experience. He also wrote, *"What shall we say then? Shall we continue in sin that grace may abound? Certainly not! How shall we who died to sin live any longer in it?"* (Romans 6:1-2). He continued, *"What then? Shall we sin because we are not under law but under grace? Certainly not! Do you not know that to whom you present yourselves slaves to obey, you are that one's slaves whom you obey, whether of sin leading to death, or of obedience leading to righteousness?"* (Romans 6:15-16).

John, in his first epistle, exposed the Gnostics of his hour.

They were antinomian in their teaching. This thought produced an unscriptural dualism that divorced matter from spirit. Irredeemably corrupted was the state of all matter or physical. In their belief only the inner spirit could be redeemed. The obvious conclusion of this thought is a dualistic world. It does not matter what you do in the physical because it is only the spirit of man that matters. The body passions should be indulged without inhibition so the soul might shine brighter in comparison. The Gnostics proposed, "Give to the flesh the things of the flesh, and to the spirit the things of the spirit."

Jesus brings us back to the Scriptural view! The physical and the spiritual of the human life must not be separated. The inner action of these two vital areas must be maintained. What goes on in one area deeply affects what happens in another area. Our spiritual attitude affects our physical action, as our physical action affects our spiritual attitude. However, do not be tricked into the perspective that the physical action is the only measure of the spiritual attitude. Murder must not be judged by its physical act. These physical actions are birthed from the attitude of the heart.

Because this effect is true, we must immediately change our approach to many things. For instance, we must change our approach to "correction." If I want a life change, where do I start? Do have to get off drugs, must I attend twelve-step meetings, do I stop drinking alcohol, and do I stop killing people? I will buy a punching bag, put a picture of the person I hate on it, and vent all my murderous thoughts on that picture and beat it to death. This type of therapy may eliminate the physical act of murder, but it only temporarily calms my murderous desire. This may be better than no correction at all, especially if I am the one you want to murder. However, this approach does not solve the problem. The problem is in the spiritual attitude. We need a nature change in the depth of our being. All other corrections are a bandage not a correction. We go to counseling, take anger management classes, and attend twelve-step programs. These only help us if they bring us to a nature change in our spiritual attitude.

The truth will also change our approach to "conviction," which is easy to justify my physical action. Yes, I did kill him, but after what he did to me, he deserved to die! I do not have any guilt about what I did. I was right! The scribes, Sadducees, and Pharisees were firmly in this category. They could justify their actions against Jesus and the disciples because of their law. The law told them they were right, so in their minds they were not guilty. But legalism measures only outward physical action. Are we guilty in our spiritual attitude? We may crucify Jesus according to the law and be wrong in the spiritual attitude. The measure of right and wrong is the spiritual attitude not the physical action.

This truth will change our approach to "communication." What causes ministry? What do we desire for our children? As a church ministering to our community, what do we want to achieve? Is it to get bad people to do good things? Is it to take homeless people and bring them back into society as productive people? Is it to take those in prison and establish their lives according to the laws of the land? Does not every person need a nature change in relationship with Jesus? How can I be satisfied until everyone knows Him? Everyone must be saved from his or her self-centered, sinful, physical actions. They must become right in their spiritual attitude!

Can we begin with who we are? Will you and I examine every physical act of our lives in light of the spiritual attitude that produces it? This examination will require no justification and no rationalization. Jesus will move in revelation to capture us with His truth. Oh, I want the mind of Christ! Please, I want His heart! Only as the Living Word communicates through the Written Word will this be a reality in my heart.

Furthermore, Jesus proposed that the truth of the Scriptures would move us from a physical ASSOCIATION to a spiritual

ATTACHMENT (Matthew 5:23-24). He became practical in His application of the Scriptures. Jesus addressed His disciples and many common Jews. They were all focused on the religious activities at the temple or synagogue. Two periods of prayer were for each day, nine in the morning and three in the afternoon, and the afternoon hour of prayer included the hour of sacrifice.

Although not all Jews would have participated daily in this sacrifice, all understood the importance of this activity. The significance of this sacrifice in the spiritual type or symbol it represented. Its value was found in the spiritual consciousness of its meaning as they accomplished the physical sacrifice. This truth is not difficult to understand. It is not the physical act of killing an animal that brings us into the presence of God. The slaughter companies who supplied the meat to the community do not bring people into the presence of God. The farmer's wife who kills a chicken for Sunday dinner does not bring her guests into the presence of God. The attitude of acceptance, belief, and the embrace of the spiritual value symbolized in the act is the heart of the matter!

This is why Jesus interrupted our physical association (whatever it may be) and pointed us to our attitude toward each other. God is not interested in a physical routine of worship. Is He thrilled with how high we raise our hands in praise? Is the issue how loud you sing or shout His name? If you and I do not embrace His heart as we sing His name on Sunday, we are the same as the one cursing His name on Monday. Moreover, if we have the right spiritual attitude in bringing our sacrifice to Him, we will be convicted of any wrong attitude toward our brother. In other words, there is no way to have a proper attitude toward God in worship and maintain a wrong attitude toward each other. We cannot overlook this conflict. God will continually remind us of how He feels about our brother.

The strength of this passage is verified by the consistent tone of the Scriptures. There are too many verses to list. We cannot live in forgiveness from God and not forgive each other (Matthew 6:14; 18:34-35). Even our expressions of love for God must be expressed to each other (Matthew 25:40, 45). If I want to embrace (receive) Jesus, I must receive you (Matthew 10:40). If I want to give God a cup of cold water, I must give you one (Matthew 10:42). My attitude toward those considered less than me is my attitude toward God (Matthew 18:5).

Now we want to add Jesus' instructions for us and move from a physical ADVERSARY to spiritual ACCOUNTING (Matthew 5:25-26). A progression is in the overall passage. Jesus moves from highlighting an attitude of murder (Matthew 5:22) to a conflict between brothers (Matthew 5:23) to an adversary (Matthew 5:25). If I do not have the nature or attitude of God, my relationship with others progresses downward. This downward progression is also true in the physical circumstances of that relationship. Jesus moves from an inner spiritual condition (Matthew 5:22) to an encounter with my brother (Matthew 5:23) to an officer, to the judge, to prison (Matthew 5:25).

In other words, do not allow anyone to become your adversary. Where do we begin? It starts with your attitude, the attitude of Jesus! The focus of this passage is on my spiritual attitude. I cannot control what others may do. How they feel or what they express is beyond my jurisdiction. However, this is not true of my state. I must know the mind of Christ! Those who might be my adversaries cannot because I will be reconciled with them. The adversarial attitude will be cleansed in my heart by the mind of Christ. In their mind I may be their adversary, but in my heart they are not.

This heart change is the plea of Jesus from the first words of the Sermon on the Mount. He describes Kingdom people. They are the helpless ones who embrace this poverty (Matthew 5:3-4). They are filled with the nature of God, forming the Kingdom of God. The union of our helplessness and His Person forms the new creature of the Kingdom. Flowing through and from this new creation is meekness, filling, mercy, and peace, and in the experience of persecution, these elements can be fully seen (Matthew 5:10).

In the darkness of the evil world, Kingdom people are **light** (Matthew 5:14). In a tasteless world they are **salt** (Matthew 5:13). The nature of God is poured into the world and has taken the form of the Scriptures. This nature is shaping our lives in this world. We do not act like our world; we do not think like our world; we do not respond like our world. We become an expression of the Living Word. His nature is displayed through us. It looks like the Scriptures, and appears to be Jesus. The display is Kingdom people!

We see this continuously in the life of Jesus. We can view the controversy between Jesus and the scribes and the Pharisees as adversarial. Did Jesus not follow His own admonition? He was not reconciled with them; they brought Him into the court and He ***"paid the last penny."*** It is clear from the Scriptures Jesus did not consider the leaders of Israel His adversaries. He wept over Jerusalem. ***"How often I wanted to gather your children together as a hen gathers her chicks under her wings, but you were not willing"*** (Matthew 23:37). The adversarial attitude was always in them not in Jesus! This is the call of God to Kingdom people. Our helplessness must be filled with His heart?

Matthew 5:21

LIABILITY OF MURDER

"You have heard that is was said to those of old, 'You shall not murder, and whoever murders shall be in danger of judgment'" (Matthew 5:21).

Our past few studies have been an attempt to understand the contrast of our passage with the insight of Jesus. **"You have heard that it was said to** (by) **those of old"** is contrasted with, **"But I say to you."** We are highlighting it again! Jesus is not adding to or at all discarding the Scriptures. He brings a correct understanding to the meaning of the Scriptures. If we are to comprehend the Scriptures, we must see it through the life of Jesus, and see Him through the Scriptures!

The difficulty with this language is our approach to the Scriptures. Because it is a book, we see it as literature. In this academic framework, we analyze its pages from our reasoning. Because your experience differs from mine, we each interpret it in a variety of ways. Who is to say which is right or wrong? The Pharisees' debates about the applications and requirements of the Scriptures were long and loud. They progressed from debating the Scriptures to debating the oral traditions of the Scriptures. They focused on the activities of the disciples, their conflict with Jesus. They asked Him, **"Why do Your disciples transgress the tradition of the elders?"** (Matthew 15:2). Jesus answered them with a question. **"Why do you also transgress the commandment** *of God because of your tradition?"* (Matthew 15:3). Their academic approach caused them to miss the true intent of the Scriptures.

Jesus explained the proper approach to the Scriptures in the "Fulfillment of the Kingdom, Acknowledged" (Matthew 5:17-20). He addressed the intent of the Scriptures about the six key areas of life, the "Fulfillment of the Kingdom, Application (Matthew 5:21-48). What was Jesus' approach to the Scriptures? He understood the Scriptures to be the written form of the nature of God. The Trinity God poured His nature into our world for man to see; it came in the written form of the Law and the Prophets. Jesus, the Second Member of the Trinity, became man. He submitted Himself to the nature of God, and the Scriptures shaped His life. Therefore, **"He is the image of the invisible God"** (Colossians 1:15). When you understand the Scriptures, you understand Jesus. When you understand Jesus, you understand the Scriptures.

The approach of, *"those of old"* was an academic approach. They said, **"You shall not murder, and whoever murders will be in danger of the judgment"** (Matthew 5:21). The Scriptures do indeed say, as the sixth commandment in the Decalogue (Exodus 20:13), **"You shall not murder."** In fact, **"You shall not murder"** is quoted five times in the Scriptures. The original account of God giving the Ten Commandments is in Exodus. Moses reminds the people of Israel of these Ten Commandments in his last message to them before God takes him away (Deuteronomy 5:17). Jesus quotes this commandment in our passage (Matthew 5:21). In His encounter with the Rich Young Ruler, Jesus reminded him of the commandments (Matthew 19:18). Paul proclaimed this commandment and others to expose them as fulfilled in love (Romans 13:9).

Murder, each time it is listed in the Scriptures, is in a list of commandments. This is significant. The commandment is quoted from the perspective of Old Testament law. Although the three New Testament quotations place it in the context of the Old Testament, in each case Jesus elevates it to a new level and expectation. Jesus called the Rich Young Ruler to go beyond the act of not murdering the poor to selling everything to give to them. Paul referred to this commandment and others to highlight the call to love. He proposed that all commandments are, **"summed up in this saying, namely, 'You shall love your neighbor as yourself'"** (Romans 13:9). In our passage, Jesus calls us to the true meaning of the commandment.

In each case the commandment contains the meaning of the higher level. The problem is in our perspective. A four-year-old is unwillingly brought to church. He cries, resists, and throws a childish fit as if he did not get a "happy meal" from the fast-food restaurant. What are his parents to do with him? He is put in the corner for timeout. He needs discipline and rules for his life. He is an immature four-year-old, and when he comes to church throwing a fit, we view him with understanding. He needs to grow up! The Old Covenant rule of, **"You shall not murder"** was needed - we were all four-year-olds. Then Jesus announced the arrival of the Kingdom. Our helpless, "four-year-old" state is filled with His sovereign being. Jesus gives us a mature Kingdom view of the Scriptures. As Paul preached to the people of Athens, **"Truly, these times of ignorance God overlooked, but now commands all men everywhere to repent"** (Acts 17:30). He continues to give us the reason for this reality, **"because He has appointed a day on which He will judge the world in righteousness by the Man whom He has ordained. He has given assurance of this to all by raising Him from the dead"** (Acts 17:31). When we are in Jesus, He brings the four-year-old approach to a mature, forty-year-old view.

Jesus challenged the scribes and the Pharisees to become mature! Let us take a careful look at how Jesus says this in our passage (Matthew 5:21).

Removal

The four-year-old views murder (or any wrongdoing) as a physical act, never seeing the spiritual aspect. Jesus again brings us to the interaction between the physical and the spiritual, a difficult subject to discuss. We can often describe the visual world with accuracy, but how do we describe the unseen world with certainty?

Many people refuse to acknowledge anything they cannot see. Perhaps we should start with embracing together the EXISTENCE of the spiritual realm. From a biblical perspective, the spiritual realm has greater presence than the physical realm. The dominating element is not the physical world but the spiritual. In other words, if you want to change the physical circumstances of your living, you must focus on the spiritual realm of your life. Paul exclaimed this with force! ***"For we do not wrestle against flesh and blood, but against principalities, against powers, against the rulers of the darkness of this age, against spiritual hosts of wickedness in the heavenly places"*** (Ephesians 6:12).

This spiritual battle was boldly displayed in the wilderness temptation of Jesus (Matthew 4:1-11). After forty days and nights of spiritual warfare, there were three last attempts by Satan to destroy Jesus. The first comes through the hunger drive of His physical body. The second regards His first physical act of ministry to win people to His new Kingdom, and the third attacks the potential to rule all the known physical kingdoms of the world. Each temptation is rooted in the physical world, but none are about the physical. If Jesus responded in physical obedience to Satan's request, the results would have been in the spiritual realm not the physical.

Jesus addressed this in our passage (Matthew 5:21). The scribes and Pharisees considered only the physical realm. What if murder in the spiritual realm is as destructive to human living as physical murder? If I physically murder someone, I destroy life. What if my hate in the spiritual realm also destroys life? If we allow hate, anger, demeaning, and belittling in our family relationships, daily exposing our children to its toxic rays, the heart of the child is destroyed. We kill the inner capacity for love in that child.

The EVIDENCE of the spiritual realm is in the debris of our physical world. The crucifixion of Jesus highlights this truth. The scribes and Pharisees saw the crucifixion of Jesus as the removal of a physical obstacle. They removed a physical barrier to maintain their physical organization and personal physical comfort. They did not realize they were staging war in the spiritual realm. *"There was darkness over all the land"* (Matthew 27:45). *"The veil of the temple was torn in two"* (Matthew 27:51) the protection for the most holy place in the temple. The physical Earth could not tolerate what was happening in the spiritual realm (Matthew 27:51). What happened in the spiritual realm was so powerful it gave evidence of its disturbance in the physical world.

Jesus exclaimed this in our passage (Matthew 5:21). The Kingdom of God calls us to a new understanding of the interaction of the spiritual and the physical. The scribes and Pharisees dismissed the spiritual aspect of life, limiting their view to physical activities. The physical expression of anger, demeaning, and belittling is equal to the physical activity of murder. The evidence of such is the destruction in our physical relationships, carrying in our lives the marks of spiritual death.

The physical world touches the spiritual world with EFFECTS, but the scribes and Pharisees did not consider this. They agreed the physical act of murder was wrong, but they accepted all other negative physical activities in relationships. They did not understand that the physical activities of anger, demeaning, and belittling had spiritual effects.

How quickly we dismiss the spiritual consequences of our physical acts. Drugs, drinking, and smoking are personal preferences of choice. Perhaps it is hurting my physical life, but I am willing to live with it. Could it be I do not understand the spiritual effects? I am not as patient as I ought to be, but it is just the way I am. Do I not understand the spiritual consequences of my impatience? I release death into the spiritual realm of my life! The ministry to the homeless is not about adjusting their physical condition. We must address the interaction between their physical condition and their spiritual lives.

Retribution

A four-year-old child's view sees punishment only in physical consequences. This immature level demands physical punishment for breaking the rules. Their obedience is motivated by fear of the consequences. A physical rule is in our passage, ***"You shall not murder."*** The motive for not acting in murder is, ***"whoever murders will be in danger of the judgment"*** (Matthew 5:21). The Greek word "krisis," translated *judgment*, is often a reference to a local court of the Jews. The local court was a seven-member court that sat in each city or town. This court was the lowest court among the Jews, and from it an appeal might be taken to the Sanhedrin. However, the same Greek word (krisis) refers to the judgment of God.

The scribes and Pharisees viewed the consequences of murder only in the physical world. If they were caught, they would be taken to the local court to be judged by their peers. In this immature view, if they did not get caught, they were freed from the consequences. Their approach to life became "how can I get by?" Even if I did get caught, I pay the physical consequences, and I am free. I fear we live with the same approach to life. I view my addictions through the lens of physical consequences.

Perhaps I will not get caught. If I do, I will pay the physical penalty and be free. Anger, demeaning, and belittling may cause broken relationships with people, but I do not care because I did not need them anyway.

The punishment for sin is not only in the physical realm. Being captured and brought before the local court is not the issue. Our physical responses produce spiritual consequences. "Not getting caught" has no chance. The seed of destruction abides in the act itself. No local court or even an eternal court will need to judge. Every attitude not expressing the nature of God leads to its own destruction. ***"For the wages of sin is death"*** (Romans 6:23). Death is not confined to the physical, but unfolds and grows in death to the total being, forever. Jesus introduced this in the Sermon on the Mount when He spoke of the reality of **hell** (Matthew 5:22, 29, and 30). The Greek word "geenna," translated "hell," was a valley outside Jerusalem that became a fiery human garbage pit. It was a physical picture of a spiritual reality. An individual earns these wages.

Redemption

A four-year-old child's understanding does not consider others, especially Jesus! An immature view sees only personal circumstance and consequences. The scribes and Pharisees focused on themselves. The six hundred and thirteen oral traditions were activities bringing self-satisfaction, comfort, and spiritual superiority. They developed an organized system creating personal gain. They focused on rules that catered to their desires. They did not grasp the plan of God or what they were doing to Jesus!

How easy it is to justify our actions and never see what we are doing to Jesus. The deterrent to anger, demeaning and belittling is not the physical local court. You can always find fellow human being who will join your justification. They will readily tell you that you had a right to be angry. Jesus calls us to a New Covenant, a higher standard. Jesus is the single element that moves us from the four-year-old status to being the Kingdom of God. He took the full penalty for my sins.

Paul said that, *"the love of Christ compels us"* (2 Corinthians 5:14). If so, then we must remove anger, demeaning, and belittling from our lives. We cannot participate in any activity or attitude outside the nature of God. The reason is, ***"we judge thus: that if One died for all, then all died; and He died for all, that those who live should live no longer for themselves, but for Him who died for them and rose again"*** (2 Corinthians 5:14-15). Everything outside the nature of God crucifies Jesus. In the spiritual world, I am still crucifying the Son of God by putting Him to open shame (Hebrews 6:6).

The Kingdom of God, my helplessness filled with His presence, is not about a rule against murder. The Kingdom is about the nature of God flowing through my life. Anything outside this nature violates the heart of God. To participate in the attitudes outside His nature, I must abuse the provision of His death and resurrection. I must join the soldiers in ridicule and scorn. I proclaim His death is not adequate for my victory, and His life is not enough for my living. I become the scribe or Pharisee who participated in His death. I must fall in love with Jesus.

Matthew 5:22

I SAY TO YOU

"But I say to you that whoever is angry with his brother without cause shall be in danger of the judgment. And whoever says to his brother, 'Raca!' shall be in danger of the council. But whoever says, 'You fool!' shall be in danger of hell fire"
(Matthew 5:22).

A contrast is in the six illustrations forming the "Fulfillment of the Kingdom, Application." In each illustration, the contrast is between what they heard from the ancient ones and what Jesus said. The first two illustrations begin with, **"You have heard that it was said to those of old"** (Matthew 5:21 and 27). The third illustration abbreviates this by saying, **"Furthermore it has been said"** (Matthew 5:31). Then Jesus returns to the original introduction but adds one word. **"Again you have heard that it was said to those of old"** (Matthew 5:33). The last two illustrations begin with, **"You have heard that it was said"** (Matthew 5:38 and 43). These slight variations do not change the basic meaning or interpretation of the statement.

"But I say to you" (Matthew 5:22, 28, 32, 34, 39 and 44) is the opening statement of the next verse of each illustration, creating the contrast. No variation is in these phrases! This non-variation produces a consistent rhythm of authority authenticating the illustrations. The statement is emphatic. There is no variance or adjustment. Jesus did not quote the source of, **"it was said**

to those of old." He did not derive authority from the ancient ones. He did not align His statements with any teachers of His day. He did not even quote the Old Testament Scriptures that He came to fulfill. These are a declaration of the person of Jesus.

This statement (**"But I say to you"**) is somewhat stronger than it appears! In the Greek text it reads as, *"I* (ego) **But** (de) *say* (lego) *to you* (humin)."* The pronoun "I" is found in the ending of the indicative verb, **"say"** (lego). However, Jesus was not satisfied with saying this once. He gave the pronoun, *"I"* (ego) alone! A literal translation is, "I Myself say to you" or "I, I say to you." In the Greek language this is strong. *"Say"* is a translation of the Greek word, "lego," used to focus on the content of a statement. The emphasis is not on the style of speech or the posture of the speaker. This flows the authority of the Speaker to the content of His speaking.

Jesus does not add or undermine the authority of the Scriptures. He does not complement the Scriptures as if they were not adequate. He brings us back to the truth of the Scriptures. He will not allow us to slip into the trap of discarding the Scriptures. He cried, **"Do not think that I came to destroy the Law or the Prophets, I did not come to destroy but to fulfill"** (Matthew 5:17). The introduction to these six illustrations (Fulfillment of the Kingdom, Acknowledgment) established the authority of the Scriptures. In fact, the last verse of this section introduced this resounding statement, **"For I say to you"** (Matthew 5:20), though He does not include the additional, *"I"* (ego).

What is His authority? What gives Jesus the right to speak on behalf of the Scriptures? Is His interpretation of the Scriptures the only correct view? Why should I trust His opinion? Dozens of well-known, highly respected scholars existed in His day. What is so special about a lowly Galilean from Nazareth without credentials?

Let us begin with what is not said in our passage or its context. These things are NOT the basis of Jesus' authority. First, consider His DIVINE DIVINITY. Many scholars propose the basis of Jesus' authority is His Divinity. After all, as God, Jesus wrote the Scriptures; therefore, He is the only One who can properly interpret them. But this violates the incarnation of Jesus. No denying or desire to negate His standing as the Second Member of the Trinity exists. Although He is divine, He set aside everything that distinguished Him from us. He limited Himself to the resource available to humanity. He was filled with the Holy Spirit as the first member of the Kingdom of God! He does not do what He does because He is God, but instead He does what He does because He is a man filled with God! In our six illustrations, He is not speaking to us as divine.

Second, consider His DOCTOR OF DIVINITY. No mention of any educational standing or degrees is throughout the Sermon on the Mount. This was one of the conflicts between Jesus and the educated scribes and Pharisees of His day. Where did Jesus get the credentials to teach as a rabbi? From what school did He graduate? From the beginning of His ministry it is said, *"Can anything good come out of Nazareth?"* (John 1:46). When speaking of Jesus the scholars of Israel said, *"Search and look, for no prophet has arisen out of Galilee"* (John 7:52). Jesus did not have the qualifications to be a prophet, and His authority was never based on His education.

Third, consider His DIVINATION OF DIVINITY. While Jesus gave the Sermon on the Mount in the early days of His ministry, the crowds were in abundance. His miracles were the attraction. Prior to the Sermon on the Mount, Matthew wrote, *"Then His fame went throughout all Syria, and they brought to Him all sick people who were afflicted with various diseases and torments, and those who were demon-possessed, epileptics, and paralytics, and He healed them. Great multitudes followed Him from Galilee, and from Decapolis, Jerusalem, Judea, and beyond the Jordan"* (Matthew 4:24-25). His position as a miracle-worker was well established prior to the preaching of this sermon. Matthew included foreign countries outside Palestine in this list. However, in our illustration miracles and the ability to do miracles are not indicated as a basis for the authority of Jesus.

According to our passage and its context, none of the above gives validity to the authority of Jesus' saying, ***"But I say to you."*** He did not speak out of His divine position as the Second Member of the Trinity. He did not speak out of a superior educational qualification. He did not speak from the authority of one who does miracles. What is the basis left for Him to give such irrefutable statements? Why should we trust Him?

Poor in Spirit

John the Baptist was publically announcing and forerunning the Kingdom of God. His message was quickly duplicated by Jesus, ***"Repent, for the kingdom of heaven is at hand!"*** (Matthew 3:2; 4:17). The Greek word "eggizo," translated ***"is at hand,"*** means "to be near" or "to approach." John and Jesus used it to announce the presence of the Kingdom. Jesus was the arrival of the New Covenant! He was the first man to experience all the prophets foretold concerning this covenant. Jesus did not come merely to establish the Kingdom; He was the Kingdom! The Kingdom of Heaven is the union of God and man in a new creature relationship.

In the Sermon on the Mount, Jesus began to describe the Kingdom, the New Covenant that was not a location in which to arrive. Heaven is a place to dwell but not the Kingdom. The opening statements of the Sermon on the Mount describe the Kingdom, the Beatitudes (Matthew 5:3-12). It is the combining, uniting, or merging of the Spirit of God and humanity is the Kingdom of God. Jesus is the first human to be filled with the Spirit of God in the New Covenant. He described it as, ***"Blessed*** *are the poor in Spirit."* This is a simple statement of who we are and an encouragement to embrace our condition, *"Blessed are those who mourn."* Embracing the helplessness of who we are enables us to be filled with His nature, His resource. Our helplessness and His Spirit form a new creation, the Kingdom of God. Jesus was the first living Kingdom on the scene.

Because this is true, Jesus must have been, *"poor in spirit."* Jesus did not appear to be helpless; He is seen in the Gospels as a Man of power and authority. However, He consistently reported that the resource of His life was not Himself. His resource came from His Father. He said, *"Do you not believe that I am in the Father, and the Father in Me? The words that I speak to you I do not speak on My own authority; but the Father who dwells in Me does the works"* (John 14:10). He continued in this discourse when He said, *"No longer do I call you servants, for a servant does not know what his master is doing; but I have called you friends, for all things that I heard from My Father I have made known to you"* (John 15:15).

As the first man to be the Kingdom of Heaven, Jesus was helpless and filled with the resource of the Spirit. When He said, *"But I say to you,"* He declared what He knew and heard from His Father. Jesus did not base His authority on the fact that He was God (although He was). He based His authority on the fact that He was a man sourced by God. We must listen to Him as the voice of God!

This sourcing is the call of the Scriptures for every Kingdom person. We are helpless individuals filled with the resource of God. Our lives reveal Jesus; we speak His word; we do not live out of ourselves. Anything less than this behavior is not acceptable. This behavior is not something Kingdom people do, strive to achieve, or try to model. This is the essence of who we are. We cease to exist without this!

Proved the Scriptures

If Jesus based His authority on the Spirit of God speaking through Him, how do I know it is the nature of God? After all, some accused Him of being filled with the devil (Matthew 9:34; 12:24). Jesus came to fulfill the Scriptures (Matthew 5:17-20). He did not come to destroy the Law or the Prophets, the Old Testament Scriptures. He boldly proclaimed this twice for emphasis (Matthew 5:17). This proclamation is contrasted with what He did come to do, to fulfill. This means everything in the Law's requirements and all prophesied will happen in the Kingdom person! The Scriptures are the written declaration of the nature of God. The Trinity God gave a revelation of God's heart, and that revelation is the Scriptures. Jesus submitted Himself to this nature revealed in the Scriptures. This nature shaped and determined His living. In seeing Jesus, we see the Scriptures. In seeing the Scriptures, we see the nature of God. Therefore, Jesus is the expression of the God's heart! What He says is a declaration of the mind of God.

What Jesus says to us (**"But I say to you"**) is authenticated by the action of His life. He did not *"fulfill"* the Scriptures because He studied them. He did not win the debates of truth because He was a skilled debater. Every detail of God's nature in the law was completed in Jesus. Every prophecy expressed the desire of God for the world He loves, and this love was completed in Jesus. He is the only man who completed the Scriptures.

No wonder the Father made Him King of this new Kingdom! You might say, "If this is true, He deserves it!" Jesus is not King because He earned or merited it. The Kingdom was given to Him! Jesus established an appointment with His disciples prior to His crucifixion. He wanted to meet with them at the base of the mountain in Galilee after His resurrection. He commissioned them to win the world. He told them, *"All authority has been given to Me in heaven and on earth. Go therefore and make disciples of all nations, baptizing them in the name of the Father and of the Son and of the Holy Spirit"* (Matthew 28:18-19).

Jesus is a helpless Man filled with the Spirit of God. This helpless Man submitted Himself to the nature of God, the Scriptures. This nature shaped His existence and formed His living. I can trust what He says. He speaks not as God but as a Man filled with God. His life and words are based on the Scriptures. He is a prototype of who we are to be, Kingdom people. If our surrender matches His, our lives will be like His! This likeness is the essence of the Kingdom of God.

Presented the Spirit

One other essential element exists. The basis of Jesus' authority is His submission to the Father. I can rely on His words because He is a helpless Man (***"poor in spirit"***) who is sourced by the Father. Everything He said was sourced from the mind of God. How do I know this is the case? The Scriptures validate it. The Trinity God reached into the depth of His heart encompassing His nature. He placed His nature into our world; it appeared in written form, the Scriptures. Jesus, the Second Member of the Trinity, leaped into our world and submitted Himself to the nature of God, the Scriptures. He was filled with this nature (Matthew 3:26). The nature of God shaped and determined His words and His life. He fulfilled all of the Law and all of the Prophets. This fulfillment is verified by His life. All contained in the nature of God is seen in the Scriptures of God, and everything in the nature and Scriptures is in the fullness of Jesus. Every aspect of His life displayed this nature of God, verified in the Scriptures. This is the authority of the word, **"But I say to you."**

This raises the issue of the authority of the scribes and Pharisees. Jesus admitted they studied the Scriptures because they believed eternal life was found there (John 5:39). What is the difference between Jesus and these scholars? The scribes and Pharisees love to sit in Moses' seat (Matthew 23:2). This was the primary chair facing the congregation in the front of the synagogue, and the person giving the authoritative interpretation of the Scriptures sat in that chair. But when these men spoke, they were sourced by their self-centeredness. They did not do what they said (Matthew 23:3). They loved to argue and debate the law, but they did not allow their lives to be shaped by it (Matthew 23:4). The works they did were motivated by the applause of men (Matthew 23:5). They fought over the seats at the head table (Matthew 23:6). They loved titles that announced their importance (Matthew 23:7).

The lives of the scribes and Pharisees demonstrated the opposite qualities of God's nature. The woes that Jesus gave to the scribes and Pharisees were based on their improper demonstration (Matthew 23). In fact, He called them *"hypocrites."* They were sourced by the demonic nature of self-centeredness. In all their religious fervor and dedication to their oral traditions, they missed the nature of God. What a contrast the new Kingdom Man was to them! He was sourced by the nature of God. When Jesus said, *"But I say to you,"* that was His authority base.

The new creature of the Kingdom was not self-sourced! You cannot live for self and be a Kingdom person. Think of the opportunity we have to live beyond self! The focus of the Kingdom is on Spirit-sourcing. The nature of God is in the Scriptures. Jesus is the prototype of being filled with the nature of God and living the Scriptures. Now we are given the same opportunity.

Matthew 5:22

ANGER IS MURDER

> *"But I say to you that whoever is angry with his brother without a cause shall be in danger of the judgment. And whoever says to his brother, 'Raca!' shall be in danger of the council. But whoever says, 'You fool!' shall be in danger of hell fire"*
> *(Matthew 5:22).*

Jesus struck a deathblow to anger! Wait! Didn't Jesus get angry? The Greek word "orgizo," translated ***anger*** in our passage, was never applied to Jesus. Jesus used it twice; of the eight times it is used in the New Testament, in parables as a metaphor for the wrath of God (Matthew 18:34; Luke 14:21). Paul and John refer to the wrath of God twice (Ephesians 4:26; Revelation 11:18) as used in the Old Testament Psalms. The four remaining times "orgizo" is used refers to the anger of people. In our passage this Greek word designates the sinful disposition of one person toward another, the opposite of the nature and heart of God, and is an expression of the self-centered demonic nature that perverts a person.

Without explanation, Jesus moved from the subject of ***murder*** to the subject of ***anger***. This is significant. Jesus was equating these two issues. He does not change subjects but gives content to what his congregation heard in the past. The Jews had a narrow view of murder, focusing on a physical activity. Jesus had a larger view of murder, seeing murder from a spiritual perspective. Murder is not a result of a spiritual condition, namely anger, but anger is the same as murder. In other words, Jesus did not say anger leads to murder, but Jesus did say anger is murder in the spiritual realm. Murder and anger are the same to Jesus!

The Greek word "phoneuo," translated *murder*, is defined by one lexicon as "to deprive a person of life by illegal, intentional killing" (Greek-English Lexicon Based on Semantic Domain). This Greek word occurs twelve times in the New Testament. It appears five times in Matthew; four times in James; and one time in Mark (10:19), Luke (18:20), and Romans (13:9). Eight of the twelve appearances of this Greek word are found in the quotation of the sixth of the Ten Commandments. Each appearance of the word is focused on the elimination of life!

In the spiritual world, the unseen heavenly realms, there is a disposition of murder. The spirit of murder permeates the inner spirit of the individual. We must view this as a domination of an individual's spiritual life. This is the emphasis of our passage. As stated above, the Jews had a narrow view of murder; it was isolated to the physical realm. Jesus could not and would not tolerate this as a correct biblical view. A man cannot murder his brother and say his heart is filled with God's love and a desire to see his brother prosper. Murder is never just a physical act that does not engage the core of an individual's spiritual life.

The anger an individual has for his brother does not exist merely in one small part of his spirit. You do not experience love and peace in most of your spirit while a little anger flows in a small area of your inner being. Anger permeates and dominates the entire spirit of a person. If you are consumed by anger, every area of your life is captured by its influence. This is the concept exposed in our passage.

Many commentaries attempt to interpret verse 22 as a scale of activities and punishments. Jesus begins with a person, *"angry with his brother."* This places the individual liable for, *"the judgment,"* with a focus on what is happening in the person. Some interpret the punishment as coming from the Jewish leaders who hold court at the city gates or square. Jesus progresses to calling a person **"Raca,"** expressing their inner anger by belittling and demeaning them. In this case the punishment is to be brought before the council or Sanhedrin. The final step is the inward anger that causes the person to call his brother **"You fool!"** This places him in danger of hell! To progress from a small city court to the Sanhedrin then to God's judgment is a severe progression.

Several problems are with this thought process. Anyone brought before a lesser court because he had inner anger is unlikely. If anger were present, how would it be determined or proved? Anger is acceptable so long as it is not expressed in demeaning ways. However, this is the thing Jesus highlights in this illustration. What happens in the spirit of a person is the issue not the physical symptoms or expressions.

What is Jesus saying in this verse? He is not building a scale of activities or punishments; He reveals what murder (anger) in the heart does to every area of life. Murder deprives a person of life by illegal, intentional killing. It happens in the physical and in the spiritual realms. When it is brought into our interaction with others, it destroys life. If it appears in our attitude, it destroys life. In the dream and plan of God, there is no place for murder. In the Parable of the Prodigal Son, Jesus described it. The prodigal son returned home, driven by the need for bread (Luke 15:17). He proposed the idea of coming back on the level of a hired servant because he thought he was not worthy to be a son. But the Father would not hear of it! The Father's love was not dependent on the actions of the son. Then the elder brother entered the story. He **"was angry and would not go in"** (Luke 15:28). But the Father pleaded with him. The anger of the elder brother revealed his lack of compassion and his hardheartedness. The anger of the elder brother is contrasted with the image of the Father's love. The anger of the elder bother destroyed him and all relationships in the home. Every area of the elder brother's life was affected by the inner murder.

In our verse, Jesus focuses on anger in our relationships with others.

Raging Silently

What Jesus said is startling! The form of the Greek grammar in this opening statement makes a clarification. In the New Testament, the Greek word "orgizo," translated *angry*, is always used in the middle and passive voice. This means the anger is not a result of the subject but is acting on the subject. In our verse, *angry* is not the main verb but a participle in the nominative case. Therefore, it is an adjective giving content to the main subject, **whoever**.

The main verb of this statement is the Greek word "esomai," translated **shall be**, the future active indicative of "eimi." It is a state of being. In other words, the angry person dwells in a state of being that acts on him. This state of being determines the person's attitudes, expressions, and interactions of relationships. These identify the problem! Our goal is to control our temper. We attempt to learn techniques to enable us not to explode into violent expressions of our feelings. We try to identify the triggers that bring about the explosions of anger in our lives. When these feelings arise, we walk away to calm. In this opening statement, Jesus addresses these violent expressions of anger. He points us to the inner state of being from which these expressions come!

What is this inner spiritual state of being? The opposite of the "Kingdom of Heaven" is the state of being. Jesus described the Kingdom of Heaven as the uniting of "a helpless individual" with "His resourceful Person" (Matthew 5:3-12). If I am not filled, merged, or sourced by Jesus' nature, I am sourced by my self-centered resource. I live in a state where I protect, guard, and acquire for myself. Anger is the response to everything that hinders this. When circumstances block my success, how do I respond? I get upset and become angry. When a person does not help me do what I need to do, it upsets me and I become angry. When those under my authority do not respond in obedience, I lose my patience and become angry. Anger is a response to this self-centered state of existence.

Anger management classes are an attempt to control the expression of these responses. We develop methods to curb the expression of our anger. However, we adjust only the symptom of the real issue. Jesus proposes a change in the core of our lives, allowing Him to alter the inner core that produces our anger. He calls us to embrace our helplessness (***"poor in spirit"***). In this embrace we mourn our condition, moment-by-moment admission. The nature of God, meekness, fullness, mercy, purity, peace, and joy even in persecution begins to flow through us. The flow is the result of the new creature we become, the Kingdom of Heaven.

Railing Speech

Jesus continued His revelation of the inner state of anger. He said, ***"And whoever says to his brother, 'Raca!' shall be in danger of the council. But whoever says, 'You fool!' shall be in danger of hell fire"*** (Matthew 5:22). The grammar of this sentence differs from the above. The main subject is, ***"whoever."*** This subject is formed by the main verb, ***"says"*** and the Greek word, "hos." ***"Says"*** is a translation of the Greek word "epo." This verb is in the active voice. This means that the speaking of this demeaning, belittling statement is the result of the main subject. This marks a difference between the first statement of Jesus in our verse and this second statement. The state of being, self-centeredness, produces the anger of the person.

Now the person responds to that anger to speak negatively to his brother. The person not only is responsible for the inner condition and state of his spiritual life, but he is responsible for responding to it.

The main verb, "epo," translated *says*, is in the subjunctive mood. This projects the tone of "maybe, uncertainty, or possibility." The Greek word "an" precedes the verb and is a primary participle used often with a subjunctive verb. This word is not translated in our passage, but is used in the Greek to present to the proposition or sentence a stamp of uncertainty and mere possibility that indicates a dependence on circumstances. It strengthens the idea of the subjunctive. In other words, the individual may never encounter the circumstances where he will call his brother, **"Raca,"** but the condition of his heart is still there. A person with the spirit of anger is always on the verge with the possibility of reacting to his brother. Jesus does not advocate controlling this state of self-centeredness with the potential of response, but He insists on the removal and replacement of that nature with His own! We must respond to our helplessness and allow His indwelling; we must become Kingdom people.

The Aramaic term, **"Raca"** expresses disparagement accompanied by anger and contempt. It means "blockhead" and is the most common term of abuse in Jesus' day. This word is used only here in the New Testament and is the beginning of Jesus' teaching about the tongue revealing the condition of the heart. He teaches us that our life is one big mouth. This "life expression" does not need to search for something to speak. ***"For out of the abundance of the heart the mouth speaks"*** (Matthew 12:34). The inner state of man's existence is extravagantly abundant. Our lives gather what is in excess from the heart and speak it.

Reproachful Slander

The third sentence in our passage is the climax. Jesus said, ***"But whoever says, 'You fool!' shall be in danger of hell fire"*** (Matthew 5:22). This sentence has the same grammar structure as the second statement. The Greek verb, "epo," translated ***says***, is in the active voice and subjunctive mood. This statement also has the primary participle "an" that strengthens the subjunctive mood. Again Jesus emphasized the action of the tongue as it speaks what is in the heart.

The Greek word, "moros" is translated ***"You fool!"*** It means "silly, stupid, or foolish." The English word "moron" is derived from this Greek word. Although there is similarity between ***"Raca"*** (rhaka) and ***"You fool"*** (moros), there is some distinction. ***"You fool"*** is a more serious reproach from ***"Raca."*** ***"Raca"*** scorns a person by calling him/her stupid. ***"You fool"*** (moros) scorns the person about his/her heart and character. One is a focus on the intellectual status of the person; the other is a focus on the moral and spiritual condition of the person.

Jesus used this root word (moros) as a verb (moraine) in the section entitled "Function of the Kingdom" (Matthew 5:13-16). He said, ***"You are the salt of the earth; but if the salt loses its flavor"*** (Matthew 5:13). In light of the imagery of salt, the Greek word "moraine" is translated ***"loses its flavor."*** However, it means to cause something to lose the purpose in its existence, becoming worthless or losing value. The same Greek word (moros) is used in the closing parable of the Sermon on the Mount (Matthew 7:24-27). Jesus said, ***"But everyone who hears these sayings of Mine, and does not do them, will be like a foolish man"*** (Matthew 7:26). He is a "moros," ***"foolish man."***

In our passage, Jesus speaks of a person whose heart is filled with spiritual murder. Out of his mouth he speaks judgments about the spiritual life and value of another. Again Jesus does not advocate control of what you say; He cries for the correction of the nature. Our self-centered nature that demeans and belittles must be replaced with Jesus' nature. This correction is not something the Kingdom person achieves, merits, or eventually masters through discipline. This is the essence of a Kingdom person. Our helplessness is joined with His powerful Person. In this new creature status of merging with Him we have His heart and nature. Jesus boldly said that our righteousness must exceed the righteousness of scribes and Pharisees, or we cannot begin in the Kingdom (Matthew 5:20). This requirement is the entrance level. We move from a righteousness we "accomplish" to a righteousness we "are" because of Him." This is the New Covenant.

Matthew 5:22

HEAVY CONSEQUENCES

"But I say to you that whoever is angry with his brother shall be in danger of the judgment. And whoever says to his brother, 'Raca!' shall be in danger of the council. But whoever says, 'You fool!' shall be in danger of hell fire" (Matthew 5:22).

We must continually realize Jesus never added to the Scriptures, and He did not compliment the instructions of Moses. He fulfilled the Scriptures, and in doing so He returned us to the reality of the nature of God as revealed in the Scriptures. If this is false, all He said in the previous section (Matthew 5:17-20) was a lie. Jesus fulfilled the Scriptures! The nature of God is present in the Scriptures. Jesus submitted Himself to the Scriptures, and the nature of God shaped His life. The Scriptures became a reality in His life, and He is the visible image of God's nature (Colossians 1:15).

The revelation of God's image is the righteousness that exceeded the righteousness of the scribes and Pharisees (Matthew 5:20). The scribes and Pharisees revealed a basic tendency of self-centeredness and self-sourcing. They were gripped with consciousness that it was impossible to achieve the nature of God. How could "self" live out the Law or the Prophets? Rather than live in constant guilt, they trivialized the Scriptures. The six hundred and thirteen oral traditions were an attempt to achieve a livable standard of the Scriptures, but they could not even do that. They then focused on the traditions they felt were most important, causing great debates. A lawyer came to Jesus asking, *"Teacher, which is the great commandment in the law?"* (Matthew 22:36).

In my study I found that many Bible scholars use the same approach to explain this verse (Matthew 5:22). They too seem to trivialize what Jesus said, arranging the penalties in a precise order to correspond to the anger and insults mentioned in our passage. They propose graduated penalties or punishments to match the crimes. In other words, anger will cause an offender to be brought before the local court consisting of several Jewish leaders in the city. Calling your brother *"Raca"* (a focus on his mental ability) would result in judgment from the Sanhedrin, the seventy Jewish leaders over the nation. If a person called his brother *"You fool!"* (a focus on his spiritual condition), he received God's judgment, *"hell fire."*

There are several difficulties with this interpretation. Jesus said, *"But I say to you that whoever is angry with his brother shall be in danger of the judgment."* The Greek word "krisis," translated *judgment*, is the same word used in the previous verse. *"You have heard that it was said to those of old, 'You shall not murder, and whoever murders will be in danger of the judgment* (krisis)'" (Matthew 5:21). This Greek word is used in a variety of ways. It refers to the local judicial authority, bringing a lawsuit, or the final judgment of Gehenna. Also it is used for human judging and deciding. To properly understand its use in our passage, we must interpret it in light of the context. The Greek Lexicons do not agree on the interpretation of "krisis" in our passage.

Whoever is angry at his brother is liable to the judgment; i.e., in view of the intensification in v. 22 b, he deserves to be handed over to the local judicial authority. Anger is equated with murder. This is the only passage in the NT in

Part One: Fulfillment of the Kingdom - The Application: Murder

which designates a judicial council.
(from Exegetical Dictionary of the New Testament © 1990 by William B. Eerdmans Publishing Company. All rights reserved.)

Linguistically it should be noted that like the Hb. the Aram. which lies behind the fourfold is not followed by a ref. to the specific court but to the penalty to which one is subject (or the obligation or guilt incurred). This is supported by a second linguistic observation, namely, that neither "krisis" nor the original Aram. means "court" or even "local court"; means "trial," "verdict," "penalty," so that (Matt 5:21 b) does not mean, as commonly thought, that "(the murderer) is subject to local justice" but that "(the murderer) comes under (capital) sentence," cf. Ex 21:12; Lev 24:17
(from Theological Dictionary of the New Testament. Copyright © 1972-1989 By Wm. B. Eerdmans Publishing Co. All rights reserved.)

In light of this, Jesus said, ***"You have heard that it was said to those of old, 'You shall not murder, and whoever murders will be in danger of the judgment*** (punished by death)*'"* (Matthew 5:21). This word has the same meaning in the following verse. ***"But I say to you that whoever is angry with his brother shall be in danger of the judgment*** (punished by death)*"* (Matthew 5:22). The warning for murder is being punished by death holds for anger. Therefore, the three phrases contained in our passage do not refer to three different courts: the local, the supreme, and the divine (hell). They are three expressions for the death penalty in a kind of crescendo.

This perspective proposes the following: "You have heard (in the reading of the Scriptures) that God said to the fathers; 'You shall do no murder; the murderer shall receive the consequences of death.' But I say to you: 'Any man who is angry with his brother deserves death. He who says to his brother, 'You blockhead!' deserves to be condemned (to death) by the Supreme Court. He who says, 'You idiot!' deserves to suffer (death) in hell'" (Matthew 5:21-22).

An amazing idea that must be discussed in light of the above information has three aspects.

Frivolousness of the Situation

"Raca" and *"You Fool!"* were the two most common terms of abuse in Jesus' day. The insult was regarded as harmless. This verbal abuse is like what we do consistently in our culture. We hear these insulting words daily: "You idiot," "You moron," "You imbecile," "You pile of rubbish," and more. If we confront the offender for using such language, their answer would be, "I didn't mean anything by it. I was just upset." Even in the church, we do not regard such statements as sin requiring the judgment of hell fire.

On the other hand, those words may not be the ones used, but the feelings behind those words are often present. They are feelings of viewing another person as worthless, insignificant, or "not worth my time." We treat people as if they do not exist. I ignore them because they cannot contribute anything to my accomplishments or to me. Often we have reduced people to a function, the sin of slavery. The strong young slave has greater value than the older weaker slave. Their value is determined by how well they function. The people of talent in the church have greater value over those who seem to contribute less. The wealthy person is held in higher esteem than those financially needy. James calls this partiality! *"For if there should come into your assembly a man with gold rings, in fine apparel, and there should also come in a poor man in filthy clothes, and you pay attention to the one wearing the fine clothes and say to him, 'You sit here in a good place,' and say to the poor man, 'You stand there,' or, 'Sit here at my footstool,' have you not shown partiality among yourselves, and become judges with evil thoughts?"* (James 2:2-4). Although we may not speak the demeaning words, the attitude is the same.

Jesus proposed that the commandment, **"You shall not murder, and whoever murders will be in danger of the judgment,"** must be seen from one perspective. We can only properly understand this commandment when we allow it to speak against every expression of human alienation and hostility toward another individual. We must see this demeaning and belittling attitude in light of the judgment of God (death), making this attitude serious!

Focus of the Situation

Without hesitation, Jesus moved from murder to the reality of anger. He gave no explanation or apology, and He did not attempt to justify His conclusion. Apparent in His statement is that our inner spirit understands the connection between murder and anger. The Greek word "phoneuo," translated **murder**, is specific in definition meaning unlawful killing with malice aforethought of another human being. The idea of "malice aforethought" is anger! You can conclude that no one has ever murdered without anger.

But let us be plain. Jesus does the same thing He consistently did throughout the Sermon on the Mount. The focus is not on "doing" but on the "being." The Kingdom of God is formed by the inner helplessness of the person being fused with the Spirit of our powerful God. The function of this Kingdom is in the imagery of salt and light. The focus is not on doing but on whom you are. Jesus naturally moves from the action of the person (doing) to the spiritual reality of the person (being).

The attitude of anger will not lie dormant. The assumption is this anger will find expression and will be manifested to those involved in the situation. You must be sure to understand this truth! Murder, emotional upset, calling someone **"Raca,"** and labeling a person **"You Fool!"** come from the same spiritual condition in the heart.

We must note this; anger always results in alienation from the hostility against another human being. Despite the degree of severity discovered in the expression of anger, its expression is always focused on the other person. This causes us to return to the idea of murder being connected to the "image of God." After the destruction of the world's population, for Noah and his sons, God gave instructions. Among those commandments, He said, **"Whoever sheds man's blood, by man his blood shall be shed; for in the image of God He made man"** (Genesis 9:6). Murder is an attempt to destroy the image of God. The image of God is our ability to be filled by and be one with God. This ability is what connects us with each other. Anger destroys both!

Although the focus of anger is the destruction of God's image, amazingly it is focused on the tongue's expression. Jesus mentioned murder and easily moved to anger. The moment he mentioned anger, He began to speak of the tongue. **"And whoever says to his brother, 'Raca!' shall be in danger of the council. But whoever says, 'You fool!' shall be in danger of hell fire"** (Matthew 5:22). Jesus highlighted the subject of the tongue repeatedly. It became dominant in His rebuttal of the scribes and Pharisees. When they accused Him of a link with Beelzebub, the ruler of demons, Jesus pointed them to this issue. He concluded our lives are one big mouth determined to give expression of what is produced by our hearts (Matthew 12:25-37). We do not search for what we speak, because the heart produces it in such abundance, it is readily available. Even in the final Day of Judgment, what we speak will justify or condemn us (Matthew 12:37).

Finality of the Situation

Again we must reiterate so you understand, Jesus did not give a progression from the superficial to the most severe either in the expression or the penalty of anger. He said that anger could operate within a variety of degrees of severity. Murder, emotional upset, calling someone ***"Raca,"*** labeling a person ***"You Fool!"*** are degrees of anger. In each case it is the same spiritual condition of the heart. Because this is true, the penalty described for each expression is the same. Therefore, the penalties arranged in our passage are in a precise order to correspond to the insults, and we must understand them as graduated penalties against crimes progressively more serious. They are a threefold restatement of one overwhelming truth. They form three equivalent statements of emphasis. The consequence of physical murder is the same as calling your brother ***"You Fool!"*** The three consequences, ***judgment***, ***council***, and ***hell fire***, are all intended to express spiritual death.

You might consider this the punishment for anger, but in each case Jesus said, ***"in danger"*** (enochos). That is an interesting word! It comes from the root word that means, "to be held in something." Thus it focuses on being subjected, exposed, or subject to something. The only passage in the New Testament where "enochos" appears without the context of judicial language is in the Book of Hebrews. The writer speaks of the deliverance Christ brings to our lives. He said that Jesus destroyed the devil that has the power over death, ***"and release those who through fear of death were all their lifetime subject*** (enochos) ***to bondage"*** (Hebrews 2:15).

Punishment for a crime does not seem included in the meaning of this term. It suggests that anger controls a person and ultimately brings him to the conclusion of judgment. God does not find a person filled with anger to punish him; rather, anger possesses a person and brings everything in his life to destruction and death. Anger carries its own judgment. It destroys the image of God not only in others but also in the one angry. It ultimately brings a person to a state of *"hell fire."*

This verse is the first time in the New Testament that the idea of *"hell fire"* is stated. *"Hell"* is the translation of the Greek word "geena" and it is of Hebrew origin that signifies the valley of Hinnom. At one time this valley was a pleasant valley near Jerusalem, on the south. A small brook ran through it and partly encompassed the city. This valley was used by idolatrous Israelites for the idol of Moloch (2 Kings 16:3; 2 Chronicles 28:3). Moloch was made of brass, adorned with a royal crown, and had the head of a calf. His arms extended as if to embrace someone. The Israelites offered their children to him as they heated the statue in a fire. When it burned hot they put the miserable child into his arms. So the cries of the child might not be heard, they made a loud noise with drums and other instruments. After the return of the Jews from captivity, this valley was held in abhorrence; it was made the place to throw the carcasses and filth of the city. The valley of Hinnom was the place of public executions. The fires that continually burned there polluted the air.

Jesus attached this imagery to the angry person. This place is the final destruction of the person held in anger. Not only is it the state in which he/she dwells, it is also his/her eternal resting place. Where else could he/she live, but in eternal fire of his/her own anger? He/she is consumed by his/her selfish, self-centered state! No wonder it is called *"hell fire."* In the Sermon on the Mount, Jesus described the Kingdom of God as the opposite. In my weakness, I am filled with God's presence and resource. I live in the "rest" of His presence. Anger is never a part of this relaxed living. God is my defense. This is the state of singing in a Philippi jail at midnight with a bleeding back. I am the Kingdom in my world!

Matthew 5:23

DO I WANT TO KNOW?

"Therefore if you bring your gift to the altar, and there remember that your brother has something against you" (Matthew 5:23).

Jesus proceeds from the subject of ***"murder"*** (what was ***"said to those of old"***) to anger (***"I say to you"***). There is no explanation for the transition except the reality of truth He has already presented. Murder in the physical realm and anger in the spiritual realm are two manifestations of the same condition. In fact, whether it is murder from the hand or demeaning in our speech, we express the heated passion of a self-centered demonic nature.

This self-centered nature is contrary to the Kingdom of God established by God in the New Covenant. Our immediate response is, "I cannot help it. I am learning to control my temper, but I feel the way I feel. When people hurt me, I can control my physical expressions, but my emotions can tolerate only so much. There comes a point of explosion where I need to express myself." But Jesus never advocated control, moderation, or anger management.

Jesus began the Sermon on the Mount by congratulating us on being weak and helpless. We are ***"poor in spirit"*** (Matthew 5:3). We are to embrace this condition with the same depth of grief that penetrates our hearts over the death of a loved one. In our state of mourning our helplessness, His Spirit is released in us. Our helplessness is united with His resource, and we become a new creature. The "new creature" is not "I" or "He," but it is "we." There is a merging, fusion, or welding of God and man into a new unit. In this oneness my weakness becomes the platform from which Jesus reveals His nature.

Trying, struggling, and attempting are no longer the focus of my life. I live relaxed in the flow of His nature, a state of "being" expressed in the imagery of salt and light (Matthew 5:13-16). This relaxed life is not a destruction of the Scriptures. In this relationship the Scriptures are the reality of God's nature. As Jesus submitted to the nature of God (the Scriptures), so we are to submit. The nature of God expressed and formed the life of Jesus. He became the demonstration of the new creation we become in Him.

Practically, how will this appear in our lives? It will not eliminate only physical murder, but anger will also cease. This Greek word "orgizo," translated **anger**, is used only eight times in the New Testament. "Orgizo" is used in our passage to designate a sinful disposition of one person toward another. This elimination seemed unbelievable to the congregation of the Sermon on the Mount. Today's evangelical congregations also think this is disconcerting. My nature cannot accomplish such an impossible level of living and expression. Will I embrace my helplessness? Will I submit and become a new creature?

Indication

Jesus immediately moves to another aspect of this truth by saying, ***"Therefore"*** (Matthew 5:23). He connects what He is going to say with the statements He has already given in this illustration. The tradition of the Jews taught them that murder would cause them to ***"be in danger of the judgment."*** In previous studies we found this *judgment* to be a translation of the Greek word "krisis." This word was used in what was taught in the oral traditions and in what Jesus proposed as the truth of the Scriptures. This Greek word is used in a variety of ways. It refers to the local judicial authority, bringing a lawsuit, and the final judgment of Gehenna. The word is also used for human judging and deciding. To properly understand its use in our passage, we must interpret it in light of the context.

The difficulty with the Greek word "krisis" is the difference in definition and application of the various Greek lexicons. Many Bible scholars equate this word with the lowest Jewish courts in the local towns. However, in the context of what Jesus said, this does not seem feasible. The focus of the word is not on any specific court but is on the penalty to which one is subject. The Old Testament consistently insisted the penalty for murder was death (Exodus 21:12; Leviticus 24:17). We must interpret Jesus' discourse on anger (Matthew 5:22) in light of spiritual death.

Thus we proposed the following translation. "You have heard (in the reading of the Scriptures) that God said to the fathers: 'You shall do no murder; the murderer shall receive the consequences of death' But I say to you: 'Any man who is angry with his brother deserves death. He who says to his brother 'You blockhead!' deserves to be condemned (to death) by the Supreme Court. He who says: 'You idiot!' deserves to suffer (death) in hell'" (Matthew 5:21-22).

In light of eternal spiritual death, any slight indication of self-centered division between you and your brother requires immediate attention. This immediate attention is an expression of intolerance for any division based on self-centered anger. The issue of the passage is **"that your brother has something against you."** This passage immediately indicates that you were involved in some measure in what he has against you. Unless you make some effort to reconcile with him by eliminating what he has against you, it will never be resolved. In our passage, the first thought might be that you have been angry with your brother. Perhaps you have expressed anger by demeaning or belittling him. You can always justify or rationalize what you said; however, the severity of death involved by participation in such anger requires immediate reconciliation. On the other hand, you were not the one who dwelt in anger. Your brother may be the one who responded in demeaning language. The severe consequences of death happening in his life must be addressed. Whether you are right or wrong, you cannot allow this to continue. Everything Jesus said in our passage is based on the severity of the consequences of the anger, *"Therefore."*

Intimacy

Jesus suggests the act of bringing your gift to the altar in each of these verses (Matthew 5:23-24). The procedure of bringing a gift to the altar focused on a particular aspect of religious worship, a solemn moment when a person casts himself on divine mercy. In making his offering, he seeks divine forgiveness. Jesus described the time when an Israelite brought his sacrifice to the court of the Israelites. He stood reverently waiting for the moment when the priest approached him to receive the sacrifice from his hands. A set of rails separated the court of the priests from the place the Israelite stood. The priest received the offering from the hands of the Israelite, took it into the court of the priests to be slain, and then presented it on the altar of sacrifice. The person casts himself on divine mercy, and in this solemn moment, Jesus speaks and we remember.

Jesus suggested this imagery to His culture. How does He apply it to our evangelical church? When we focus on worship, the following applies. We raise our hands in openness and surrender as our hearts and minds realize Jesus' worthiness. He catches our emotions as we become aware of His presence.

We surrender all the pressures of our week anew to His power and authority. Nothings matters but Jesus! In this moment Jesus speaks and we remember.

The body of Christ gathers to concentrate on hearing the voice of God. The Word of God captures us. Our worship fills the air and pushes back the demonic forces. As the believers focus on His Word, He removes all distractions. The pastor crawls from the surgical table, having been cut by the Word of God, sharper than a two-edged sword (Hebrews 4:12). This sword cuts and divides to bring healing and correctness. The pastor enters the pulpit to expose his cutting. In this sacred moment when the Word of God is exposed, Jesus speaks and we remember.

Our desperate need drives us to our knees, and we seek Jesus in a moment of prayer. We are alone with no distractions. We express our deepest heart's cry to Him. In this moment we are honest with no hypocrisy. Our complete openness exposes us to His divine presence. In such a moment, He elevates us from this world and its wisdom to the spiritual world of His presence. Here we clearly hear His voice. We will know His direction as our strength and ability melts. We are left with nothing but surrender and dependence to His divine resource. In this moment Jesus speaks and we remember.

You must select which imagery of your sacrifice brought to the altar applies best. Whatever you select is your moment of revelation and acceptance. If God is going to be real to you, it is in this moment. The true heart of God will tell you what He cares most about and how He feels. Whatever situation you have chosen, it is *"and there remember."* The Greek word "kakei," translated *and there*, specifically points to a place. Jesus highlighted this truth. When you come close to the heart of God, He reveals the conflict you have with your brother.

Jesus expressed this truth in another way. He said, *"And whenever you stand praying, if you have anything against anyone, forgive him, that your Father in heaven may also forgive you your trespasses. But if you do not forgive, neither will your Father in heaven forgive your trespasses"* (Mark 11:25-26). The moment we seek intimate communication and divine grace from God is the moment when He brings us face to face with our lack of forgiveness toward our brother. Jesus referred to our seeking or desire for personal forgiveness from God twice, *"and there"* in that place, we remember.

Information

The grammar is significant in Jesus' statement. He begins with *"if"* (ean). The normal conditional "if" is the Greek word "ei." The Greek word Jesus used is suppositional in intent. He did not establish a hypothetical situation that may happen. Rather He implied a condition that experience determines. In other words, you may bring an offering, and if you do, what will happen is what you will remember. Information about your brother will be given to you when you bring an offering to God.

Also notice, the Greek word "prosphero," translated *bring*, is a verb in the active voice. This means you are responsible for the act of bringing your offering. You must desire to receive divine grace and forgiveness from God and respond to His call to bring an offering. However, the Greek word "mimnesko," translated *remember*, is a verb in the passive voice. This means the subject is acted on. You may bring your offering to God with a desire for divine forgiveness and grace, and if you do God will cause you to remember your brother. He speaks to you about your brother. Your relationship with others will be central in the communication between you and God, and God's message to you will be about your brother. He will act on you in this manner.

Has Jesus gotten off the subject? You might look at this passage and decide Jesus is gripped by the rejection of the leadership of Israel. Although it is not full blown, it is noticeable.

Is He giving warning to those who reject Him? They are in direct violation of the worship they appear to offer to God. Jesus highlighted this repeatedly in the Sermon on the Mount. The fifth and sixth illustrations that He gave in this section of the Scriptures stress this principle. The individual who becomes your adversary must be genuinely loved. *"But I say to you, love your enemies, bless those who curse you, do good to those who hate you, and pray for those who spitefully use you and persecute you"* (Matthew 5:44).

Jesus continued to place the person who refused to be reconciled in the category of a tax collector (Matthew 5:46-47). The tax collector (an individual considered the worst of sinners in Judaism) loves those who love him. They greet only their brethren and shun their enemies. If Kingdom people act like this, how are they any different from tax collectors? The call of the Kingdom is to be filled with the heart of God. How does He think and feel? *"He makes His sun rise on the evil and on the good, and sends rain on the just and on the unjust"* (Matthew 5:45).

This command is also the conclusion of the opening statement of the Sermon on the Mount (Matthew 5:3-12). In the final beatitude Jesus highlighted persecution. This conclusion seems a bit strange. Jesus' approach is not casual and does not suggest persecution might not happen. He does not attempt to cover all the bases just in case a Kingdom person is persecuted. He is definite that there will be those who will not reconcile with the Kingdom person. They will be enemies. Jesus focused on the flow of God's nature through the Kingdom person to the one who will not be reconciled. *"Rejoice and be exceedingly glad, for great is your reward in heaven, for so they persecuted the prophets who were before you"* (Matthew 5:12).

How can I live like this? I must embrace my helplessness! I am *"poor in spirit"* (Matthew 5:3). This means I will consistently mourn in recognition of my condition (Matthew 5:4). In this state the Spirit of Jesus merges with me to form the Kingdom of heaven. This new creature consists of Jesus and me in oneness. We form the Kingdom. His nature flows through my helplessness. By His nature in me, we express meekness, fullness, mercy, purity, and peace. Although not everyone will be reconciled to me, this new creature, everyone will experience His nature and know His love!

True worship can be experienced only in the context of this state, the Kingdom of heaven. Any attempt to worship God apart from the flow of His nature is falsehood. We experience no embrace of divine grace and forgiveness unless it is expressed to others. This expression is the heart of God!

Matthew 5:24

UTMOST IMPORTANCE

"Leave your gift there before the altar, and go your way. First be reconciled to your brother, and then come and offer your gift"
(Matthew 5:24).

Throughout the Scriptures the sacred duty of man to offer sacrifice to God is highlighted. Even the casual student of the Scriptures concludes that God holds man's worship in priority. The Old Covenant focused on established ceremonies. Because God (the Trinity) set these ceremonies in order, you must conclude they are necessary. God founded these priorities from the beginning of sin. One of the first acts of God concerning sin was the slaughter of an animal to cover man's nakedness (Genesis 3:21). Adam and Eve had sewn leaves together to clothe themselves (Genesis 3:6). Their approach would never cover their shame and guilt: that covering required the life of another.

Children were born to Adam and Eve. They undoubtedly taught them the required ceremonies for worshipping God. Cain, a tiller of the ground, brought a beautiful arrangement of the fruit of the ground (Genesis 4:3). Abel, a keeper of sheep, brought the firstborn of his flock (Genesis 4:4). God would not accept Cain's offering; but Abel's offering fulfilled the requirements of worship. This produced envy in Cain, which progressed to anger and murder. Evidently, the content and method of sacrificial offering matters to God! At the close of the Book of Exodus, the law of God is given, and the tabernacle is established. The Book of Leviticus gives details about the various offerings and feast days. The daily requirements of sacrifice, as well as the annual observances, are given. If this much space is given to such matters in the Scriptures, it is clear they matter to God!

The statement in our passage focused on Jews in the setting of the Old Testament ceremonies of sacrifice. However, the idea can easily be applied to New Covenant Kingdom people. Although we do not bring sacrificial offerings to the temple as an act of worship, we have things important to our relationship with God. Times are set aside for us to worship and concentrate on His presence, and there are personal times of prayer and devotion. Any one, or all these, fit the context of bringing a sacrificial offering to God.

This raises a question about our passage. Does it not seem absurd to you that a disturbance in my relationship with my brother takes priority over my worship of God? You would think that on the priority scale "worship of God" outranks any differences I might have with my fellowman. But Jesus said when we are in the middle of these acts of worship, and we remember a division with our brother, our relationship with our brother takes priority. He said, **"Leave your gift there before the altar, and go your way. First be reconciled to your brother, and then come and offer your gift"** (Matthew 5:24). Does a mere disturbance in relationship with my brother take priority over my worship of God?

This idea was suggested in the controversy over the Sabbath day. This controversy lasted an entire day in a variety of settings; from the grain fields, to the synagogue, to the theological classroom, and ended with the Pharisees demanding a sign (Matthew 12). In the first scene, Jesus was walking with His disciples through the grain fields on the Sabbath. They were hungry, so they plucked heads of grain and ate them. The

Pharisees were following them to catch them in the act. The disciples broke the Sabbath day oral traditions on four accounts, and each count could result in their being stoned to death. The Pharisees immediately said to Jesus, **"Look, Your disciples are doing what is not lawful to do on the Sabbath!"** (Matthew 12:2). The focus of the Sabbath day was about worship to God.

Jesus gave three illustrations to highlight God's focus on the value of the human being over against His established rules of worship. David and thirty young men had been running from King Saul. They came to the tabernacle looking for food. No food was there except the twelve loaves of showbread. But God did not care about the rule He made in light of the human beings' need. The second example was the temple priests who broke all Sabbath day laws about their work in service to the temple. But God does not care; He views service to others as more valuable than the accomplishment of ceremonies. Then Jesus challenged the Pharisees to "saturate" on, **"I desire mercy and not sacrifice"** (Matthew 12:7; Hosea 6:6). The **sacrifice** involved God's established ceremonies and duties of worship. Mercy on your fellowman takes priority over duties of worship.

The Pharisees project another idea causing a controversy. A lawyer, skilled in debate, asked Jesus, **"Teacher, which is the great commandment in the law?"** (Matthew 22:36). A debate ensued, which was what the Pharisees wanted, and various opinions were given. Jesus responded with a quote from the Old Testament, which all Jews quoted daily. **"'You shall love the Lord your God with all your heart, with all your soul, and with all your mind.' This is the first and great commandment. And the second is like it: 'You shall love your neighbor as yourself.' On these two commandments hang all the Law and the Prophets"** (Matthew 22:37-40).

This statement seemed to place loving God as the priority and loving others in second position. However, the difficulty is in the Greek word "homoios," translated *like*. It means "one and the same." It denotes a correspondence in feature, property, or nature and a correspondence in measure, capacity, or position. In biblical Greek it means, "of the same kind." Jesus did not give one commandment first followed by the second, but He lists them one after the other because He cannot state them simultaneously. The commandments are the same kind. Loving God is so connected to loving others that they are considered the same!

Our passage proposes the same idea of an intimate connection between my love for God and my love for my fellowman. John, the disciple, speaks strongly about this. He proposed the question, "How do we know that we have passed from death to life?" The answer is, *"Because we love the brethren. He who does not love his brother abides in death"* (1 John 3:14). In fact, He says we are murderers if we hate our brother (1 John 3:15). Then John draws a parallel between our lives and Jesus' life. *"By this we know love, because He laid down His life for us. And we also ought to lay down our lives for the brethren"* (1 John 3:16).

Priority of Relationship
(With Jesus)

The call for reconciliation begins with our encounter with God. In the Old Testament setting, it was described as *"bring your gift to the altar."* In the New Covenant it is the continual awareness of God's indwelling presence and the source of such an indwelling. We are deeply aware of His sacrifice, and that is our inspiration for acts of worship. We can never forget! We did not initiate, contribute, or even comprehend the immensity of this sacrifice, but the message of prevenient grace. We did not come to Him; He came to us. We could not merit forgiveness, the right to be indwelt. *"For by grace you have been saved through*

faith, and that not of yourselves; it is the gift of God, not of works, lest anyone should boast" (Ephesians 2:8-9).

When you realize your gift of grace and salvation, and you know that your need has been provided for, it is then you remember the difference you have with your brother. Without the preceding paragraph, you can justify this division. After all, he offended you when you were within your rights. You are the one hurt. Because he is wrong, he should come to you humbly and ask forgiveness because there is no excuse for someone acting as he did. The things he has done to you, he has done to others. He thinks he can get by with his rudeness, and it is time someone holds him accountable. All these reasons are quite logical unless you are standing beside of the crucified One!

Again, the call for reconciliation begins with your encounter with God. As you bring your sacrifice to God, your heart pounds with anxiety about acceptance. Will the sacrifice be adequate? Did you meet all the qualifications necessary for this sacrificial act? Now we want to move from this Old Testament approach to the New Covenant view. My sacrifice for sin is adequate; it is Jesus. All the qualifications are met for me to dwell in intimacy with God, and they are met in Jesus! I am accepted and embraced, and in this context I now see my brother! If I do not see the offense between my brother and myself in this context, then I do not see the need for reconciliation. I am driven only in the context of Jesus' sacrifice for my offenses.

With Jesus' sacrifice for me in mind, the following statement is true. I have not truly experienced nor comprehended my guilt and forgiveness from Jesus if I am not driven to reconcile and forgive my brother. Jesus is strong and consistent in His presentation of this truth. As He continues in the Sermon on the Mount, He teaches us how to pray. He concludes this teaching with the need to forgive each other. The moment we move into communication with God, any disruption of fellowship we have with our fellowman appears. Jesus said,

"For if you forgive men their trespasses, your heavenly Father will also forgive you. But if you do not forgive men their trespasses, neither will your Father forgive your trespasses" (Matthew 6:14-15).

Jesus illustrated this brilliantly in the Parable of the Forgiven Servant (Matthew 18:23-35). While the master was gone, he left a servant in change of his finances. The servant stole **ten thousand talents** ($2,370,000.00). When the master returned, he demanded the full payment of that amount from his servant. The servant cried for mercy and the master forgave him the entire debt. As the servant rejoiced in his forgiveness, he found a fellow servant who owed him **a hundred denarii** ($16.69). He demanded his fellow servant pay him in full and cast him into jail. When the master heard this, He was angry, nullified his forgiveness, and demanded repayment of the **ten thousand talents**. We always find reconciliation with our brother within the framework of our relationship with the One who has forgiven us.

Priority of Relationship
(With Others)

Jesus' instructions are simple. When we are in the presence of God in worship and offering ourselves to Him, any disruption in fellowship with our brother will be revealed. Fellowship with God cannot be maintained with that disruption, and we must handle it carefully. Jesus gave us the procedure. He clearly said, *"Leave your gift there before the altar"* (Matthew 5:24).

The Greek word "ekei," translated *there*, is different from the previous verse. Jesus said, ***"Therefore if you bring your gift to the altar, and there remember that your brother has something against you"*** (Matthew 5:23). The Greek word **there** is "kakei." This projects the idea of two things happening in the same place. In other words, in the same location you bring your gift to God, you remember the difference between you and your brother. Remember that we have already said being in the location (or state) of worship automatically reveals any disruption in relationships. These two things happen in the same place, ***there***.

Once this occurs, you are to leave your sacrificial gift ***there*** (ekei). This Greek word pinpoints where you are to leave your gift. In the Old Testament framework you must leave your gift of sacrifice at the place of sacrifice. However, in the New Covenant framework, you are the temple of the Holy Spirit. The place of worship and sacrifice is in you. In the Old Testament pattern, reconciliation with your brother is a duty to perform for your sacrifice to be accepted. In the New Testament pattern, intimacy with Jesus is the inspiration and sourcing for the reconciliation to happen. You will become the expression of Jesus' redemptive heart to your brother. If you cannot have right relationship with God while you dwell in anger toward your brother, neither can your brother have right relationship with God. You are expressing the redemptive heart of God to your brother, to show him the way to have intimacy with Jesus.

This is expressed in the method of your going. Jesus said, **"Leave your gift there before the altar, and go your way"** (Matthew 5:24). The Greek word "hupago," translated ***go your way***, is from two Greek words, "hupo" denoting "secrecy," and "ago" meaning, "to go." Jesus presented a picture of the method, manner, and attitude of your going. You are not going to your brother to "straighten him out." You are not going in boldness and pride as if you are the bigger person. You are to slip away privately and share with your brother the love of your heart.

Priority of Relationship
(In Reconciliation)

After all this discussion, how important is reconciliation with your brother? On a scale of one to ten, where does Jesus place this? How concerned should I be about it? How necessary is it? Jesus answered these questions in the last phrase of our verse. ***"First be reconciled to your brother, and then come and offer your gift"*** (Matthew 5:24). The Greek word "proton," translated ***first***, refers to the order of ***things***, and is an emphatic statement. Jesus placed **be reconciled** with your brother as the priority.

This answers the question raised in the introduction of this study. Does it not seem absurd to you that a disturbance in my relationship with my brother takes priority over my worship of God? You would think that on the priority scale "worship of God" outranks any differences I might have with my fellowman. Do you not think reconciliation with my brother is minor in contrast to my worship and intimacy with God? Amazingly Jesus reverses the priority. One does not have priority over the other; they are so intimately linked that you cannot have one without the other.

The Greek word "dialisasso," translated **be reconciled**, is used only this time in the New Testament. It means seeing to it that the angry brother, who neither seeks nor envisages reconciliation, renounces his enmity. No way can you be responsible for your brother clinging to his bitterness and hatred. He may harbor his hurt, but you have to remove every obstacle for him to return to love, peace, and forgiveness. We are to go to him with the attitude of "whatever it takes." No expression or presence of pride, or indication of rights and self-protection can be in the encounter. You are to be the revelation of God's heart. Reconciliation to your brother is of priority, because it is intimately tied to your reconciliation with God.

Part One: Fulfillment of the Kingdom - The Application: Murder

What is present in your brother's heart cannot be controlled How he responds is not your responsibility. However, the focus of the passage is on what is present in you. Hindrance or blockage must not be in your attitude. You must be reconciled to your brother even if it is one sided. This reconciliation is the revelation of the Father through you and your brother. You are the hand of Christ nailed to a cross for him. Go to your brother!

Matthew 5:25-26

YOUR ADVERSARY

"Agree with your adversary quickly, while you are on the way with him, lest your adversary deliver you to the judge, the judge hand you over to the officer, and you be thrown into prison. Assuredly, I say to you, you will by no means get out of there till you have paid the last penny" (Matthew 5:25-26).

This generation of Christians is consistently looking for new language to express the heart of their Christian faith. Traditional language becomes lifeless because it loses its meaning with each new generation. In the Book of Psalms we are encouraged repeatedly to sing a new song. It seems our relationship and understanding of God expands and demands new expression for His greatness. "Cross Style language" is an attempt to give new expression to old truth.

God described Himself in the Scriptures as "holy" (Leviticus 11:44-45; 1 Peter 1:16). The crucifixion of Jesus Christ was a manifestation of the holiness in understandable vision. The nature of God was seen and declared in redemption. Redemption was not merely an event to celebrate once a year, but it was the setting of a style. The normal revelation of God's life is the cross style. This expression is an attempt to capture the attitude and heart of Christ's crucifixion and see it in the daily encounter of God with humanity. The incarnation illustrates the cross style. God emptied Himself of all the benefits of being God, and He sacrificially set Himself aside for others. This emptying is the cross style attitude. You cannot find any event or encounter in Jesus' life in all the Scriptures that does not expresses this style.

We understand God's holy nature in the style of the cross. Jesus' approach in the Sermon on the Mount was to flow this nature into the helpless nature of man. He described the human nature as "helpless." ***"Blessed are the poor in spirit"*** (Matthew 5:3). The divine nature of God will bring us comfort when we embrace our nature of helplessness (Matthew 5:4). These two natures are married; God creates a new creature called the "Kingdom of God." "Helplessness" bespeaks response, surrender, and dependence on the nature of God. "Doing" is not emphasized in this reality. Requirements of doing create only frustration and failure for the person who is helpless. Accomplishment is always attached to and found in the divine nature that flows through the helplessness of man.

Jesus was the first man to demonstrate this properly. He was filled with the Spirit (nature) of God. In helplessness He submitted Himself. The nature of God in the Scriptures and the nature of God in the Spirit shaped the life expression of Jesus. Every activity of His life gave visibility to the influence of the cross style nature of God. The influence is so forceful that He is the visible image of the invisible God (Colossians 1:15). Jesus set the standard for us. The cross style of God is to flow from God into the heart of our nature. He will shape us into the image of His nature.

The only element that can keep this transformation from occurring is the nature of self-centeredness, a pride that will not allow us to embrace our helplessness. Why would anyone hesitate to embrace the state of their inner being? There is no embarrassment in being made helpless and no need to feel superior to another. Something has happened to the human being, and a foreign nature of self-focus possesses us. We can only feel good about ourselves when we accomplish, produce, and acquire for ourselves. This feeling of accomplishment was to be ours in knowing intimacy with Jesus, being used by Jesus. Now Jesus proposes a New Covenant of the indwelling nature of God, the cross style nature, redirecting the human life.

Once the cross style nature shapes a person inwardly, you can see it in every circumstance. His approach to life becomes the approach of this nature. Jesus described it in the remaining beatitudes (Matthew 5:5-12). "Meekness" becomes the dominant trait of the Kingdom person. That person experiences "fullness," and finds completeness in his relationship with Jesus. "Mercy" flows through the Kingdom person, and "purity" and "peace" are his unmistakable traits. "Persecution" is the platform where God reveals His nature.

From the spirit of man as he is embraced by the cross style nature, flows this nature through all activities, relationships, and circumstances. He cannot turn it off and on, because it is his state of existence. He is a Kingdom person! This nature is the explanation for the verse (Matthew 5:20) that launches the six illustrations given by Jesus (Matthew 5:21-48). This cross style nature is a call to righteousness far beyond and exceeding that of the scribes and Pharisees. The scribe and Pharisees' nature of self (helplessness) is sourcing them. Every expression and circumstance of their lives gives evidence of their sourcing. They are the visible image of themselves, the best man can do.

But when the Spirit of Jesus indwells a person, that indwelling creates a new creature. This new creature gives constant evidence of righteousness far beyond his helplessness. The Spirit of God sources him. Every circumstance becomes a platform for the visibility of divine life, the cross style. The Kingdom person cannot be involved in a circumstance without feeling and knowing the cross style. The cross style is not a rule, a command, or a requirement, but it is God's nature joining man in his helplessness.

What if I decide to live out of my self-sourcing helplessness? The best I can accomplish is, **"You shall not murder"** (Matthew 5:21). The outward, physical activity of not taking a human life is the most I can expect. When your performance generates the applause of others for your accomplishment, there is nothing beyond. However, in the New Covenant, the Spirit of Jesus and a helpless man will launch the helpless man to a new level of living. Anger, demeaning, and belittling will be gone (Matthew 5:22). This new level of living is the cross style of bleeding, suffering, and dying for others, the expression of God's nature.

This way of life is such a core issue. If you live in the cross style, it will not allow any feelings, attitudes, or actions contrary to this bleeding, suffering, and dying style. Because you live in His presence and are sourced by His nature, you will be aware when you have division with your brother. You cannot tolerate any attitude that creates a division. This feeling of division will cause you to immediately take action, the action of the cross style. You bleed, suffer, and die for your brother. You must live in reconciliation with him. This reconciliation is not something you do, but it is an expression of the nature of God in which you dwell. Your helplessness integrated with God's nature cannot accept anything less.

How did your brother become your **adversary**? (Matthew 5:25). The Greek word "antidikos," translated **adversary**, is a combination of two Greek words, "anti" meaning "against," and "dike" meaning "a course or suit of law." It distinctly focuses on an adversary, enemy, or opponent in a lawsuit. This word is applied to the devil, the great **adversary** of man and the accuser of the brethren (1 Peter 5:8). How did your brother become your adversary?

There is only one explanation for such a condition! A Kingdom person cannot be an **adversary**. Being an **adversary** is contrary to the nature of God, the cross style. If a person embraces their helplessness and is filled with the cross style nature of God, he cannot be an *adversary*. The embrace of God's nature compels the helpless person to go to his brother immediately at the slightest sign of division. His heart is desperate for reconciliation because it is the nature of God. An adversary exists only because reconciliation is incomplete.

Let me remind you what Paul said on this matter. *"Now all things are of God, who has reconciled us to Himself through Jesus Christ, and has given us the ministry of reconciliation, that is, that God was in Christ reconciling the world to Himself, not imputing their trespasses to them, and has committed to us the word of reconciliation"* (2 Corinthians 5:18-19).

Does this mean if I have an *adversary* that I am not a Kingdom person, having God's nature? NO! NO! The Trinity God is one through the cross style attitude. Bleeding, suffering, and dying are expressions of the nature of the heart. Our God has an *adversary*. Jesus, the fulfillment of the nature of God in humanity, had adversaries who brought Him to court. He accomplished the warning He spoke to us regarding being brought to court by our adversaries. *"Assuredly, I say to you, you will by no means get out of there till you have paid the last penny"* (Matthew 5:26).

At the core of this illustration (Matthew 5:21-26) Jesus said that we must not be an *adversary*. We must be reconciled with him. I cannot determine the heart or mind of anyone else. I must be filled with the nature of God, and I must have a life flowing with the cross style. I must tear down every barrier between my brother and myself. I must make the way clear for reconciliation. I will be reconciled in my heart because of God's nature. Anger, demeaning, or a belittling attitude will not be in my heart. I may have adversaries, but I will not be one!

This is the contrast Jesus made between, *"You have heard that it was said to those of old"* and *"I say to you." "Those of old"* proposed RULES WITHOUT RELATIONSHIP. *"You shall not murder"* is the sixth commandment (Exodus 20:13). As *"those of old"* interpreted the meaning of this commandment, it is an activity from which you must abstain. I am committing my life to this standard. However, if I decide to meet this standard because it is the right, admirable, lawful, or for any other good reason, it is "I." I am living out of myself. No relationship is within keeping the rule.

Jesus proposed my helplessness filled with Him. This proposal is relationship with the heart of the Trinity. This relationship produces unintentional doing. The nature of God fills the human's helpless nature and produces a new creature. This new creature unintentionally flows with bleeding, suffering, and dying. Murder is not a goal set for the new creature. Actually, it is not pondered or even in the thinking of the new creature. Anger, demeaning, and belittling are not in the mind of those filled with God's nature. His nature flows through the new creature, creating the image of God. The focus is not on a rule to obey but is on embracing a relationship with Jesus.

Other relationships are fostered as well. This relationship with Jesus cannot be maintained without embracing others. If I am helpless and His nature produces me, I will care for whom He cares. His presence immediately brings awareness of any divisions (Matthew 5:23). I live in a state of reconciliation. I may have adversaries, but I will never be an adversary. His nature is mine!

"Those of old" proposed RELIGION WITHOUT RELATIONSHIP. *"You shall not murder"* was a part of the religious creed of the Pharisees' oral traditions. Few of their traditions, if any, focused on relationships. Their religious focus was on proper sacrifices such as, *"bring your gift to the altar"* (Matthew 5:23).

They were careful about tithing properly. Jesus said, *"For you pay tithe of mint and anise and cumin"* (Matthew 23:23). The mint, anise (dill), and cumin were herbs used as kitchen spices. They were considered farm produce. The Mosaic Law required a tithe be paid to the treasury of Israel (Leviticus 27:30). However, the scribes and Pharisees extended the provision to include the smallest potted plant grown in the kitchen window. Herbs were grown mostly for their leaves and seeds. When the scribes and Pharisees picked leaves from a mint plant or gathered seeds from the dill and cumin plants, they carefully counted out the leaves and seeds. They separated one for God from every ten leaves or seeds. They gloried in the self-righteousness of subscribing to details. Jesus continued, *"For you pay tithe of mint and anise and cummin, and have neglected the weightier matters of the law: justice and mercy and faith"* (Matthew 23:23). He lists these *"weightier matters"* as *"justice and mercy and faith."* The religious ceremonies became the measure of their religion instead of relationship.

Jesus exposed their priorities in a brief parable given regarding the Sabbath day laws. He healed a man with a withered hand on the Sabbath day. No one could perform a medical procedure on the Sabbath day unless it was a life-threatening situation. When they confronted Him, He asked them a simple question. *"What man is there among you who has one sheep, and if it falls into a pit on the Sabbath, will not lay hold of it and lift it out?"* (Matthew 12:11). No answer is recorded in the passage because every man knew the answer. Without exception they would rescue the sheep, ignoring the Sabbath requirement, because of a sheep's financial value. Jesus reminded them that a man is more valuable than a sheep! The priority of God is relationship not religious activities.

"Those of old" proposed REGULATION WITHOUT RELATIONSHIP. The determining influence regarding all outward activity was the law. *"You shall not murder"* was a law that regulated what you could do and not do, and it stipulated a penalty for the infraction of this law. A person who broke the law was in danger of and liable for the judgment. The deterrent for murder is the punishment of the judgment.

The New Covenant has a new focus. In each illustration Jesus highlighted relationship, which motivates action. We cannot have relationship with God and permit walls or barriers in relationship with others. John, the Apostle, strongly presented this message. *"If someone says, 'I love God,' and hates his brother, he is a liar; for he who does not love his brother whom he has seen, how can he love God whom he has not seen? And this commandment we have from Him: that he who loves God must love his brother also"* (1 John 4:20-21).

Even if your brother becomes an adversary, you should *"agree with your adversary quickly"* (Matthew 5:25). You must remove every obstacle from the path of reconciliation. If he remains an adversary, you will not be an adversary though he is an adversary. The focus of the passage is on your state of being. Is the nature of God manifested through our expression? Jesus tied eternal suffering (**hell fire**) with our internal state of expression. Therefore, His focus was not on the regulation of external activities such as murder, but on the internal state of anger, demeaning, and belittling.

Why did *"those of old"* ignore this? They had difficulty regulating their outward activities with the oral traditions. They had six hundred and thirteen oral traditions, which they were to obey. They argued about which one of these was the most important. This thought process would never include the possibility of a new motive from the heart. Yet, this was the cry of the prophets of old as they proclaimed the coming of the New Covenant. Jesus announced this new day!

Jesus' proposal can be experienced only when man embraces his helplessness and is then embraced by the presence of God. In this combination the Kingdom of God is formed, a new creature. This merger brings an expression to the human life that looks like the Father. We are a new species, sons of God. Jesus is the prototype, author, beginner, scout, and King of this new beginning. The same Spirit of God indwelling Jesus now indwells us. What a privilege!

Matthew 5:26

THE FINAL WORD

"Assuredly, I say to you, you will by no means get out of there till you have paid the last penny" (Matthew 5:25-26).

Jesus concludes in His discussion of the first of six illustrations. He visualized the call to living daily with an exceedingly greater righteousness. His cry was, ***"For I say to you, that unless your righteousness exceeds the righteousness of the scribes and Pharisees, you will by no means enter the kingdom of heaven"*** (Matthew 5:20). While He unfolds this first illustration, He reveals a natural division. It is a contrast between, ***"You have heard that it was said to those of old,"*** and ***"But I say to you."*** The root of this contrast is in the preceding challenge about Jesus and the Scriptures. ***"The righteousness of the scribes and Pharisees"*** was located in ***"You have heard that it was said to those of old."*** Based on this righteousness no one can adequately claim to be in the Kingdom of Heaven. The righteousness of the Kingdom of Heaven is in the proclamation from the first man who experienced the Kingdom. His insight into the condition of the righteousness is in, ***"But I say to you."***

As a man Jesus experienced helplessness but was filled with the resource and person of the Holy Spirit. In this intimate embrace, the nature of God was manifested through Him. Although His statements expressed His perspective, they also reflected the view of God's nature. This helpless man was filled with the mind of the Trinity. What drove the Father was driving Jesus. Jesus gave the perspective of God's heart.

Three natural steps are in this revelation. Jesus begins with the ATTITUDE. ***"But I say to you that whoever is angry with his brother shall be in danger of the judgment"*** (Matthew 5:22). The same consequence Jesus gave for, ***"You shall not murder,"*** He now gives for anger. If they are equal in consequence, they are equal in severity and importance. The Greek word "orgizo," translated ***angry***, means "a sinful disposition of one person toward another." A disposition is "a person's inherent quality of mind and character." In other words we live in a state of anger. Our anger focuses on a person but can shift from one to another. We seem to always be angry with someone or something. If we are angry about a circumstance, there is someone responsible for the circumstance. If we are angry with a person, it is normally because of a circumstance involving him or her.

The irony of this is the sinfulness of our anger. Although we speak of the terrible, sinful, and evil state of the other person, we do not recognize the terrible, sinful, and evil state of our heart's anger. Our condition was prior to the circumstance caused by our brother. Neither the circumstance nor our brother caused the anger. How easily we cry, "He made me do it!" We blame someone else to hide our guilt. In reality we should embrace our brother with gratitude. God used him to reveal the condition of our heart. Our brother is not the cause; he is the avenue of revelation. In the attitude of anger, we see what we are really like.

Jesus moves quickly from attitude to ACTIVITY. Automatically, the mouth speaks the attitude. ***"Raca"*** (you blockhead) escapes my heart into the airwaves of my world. ***"Fool"*** comes to the forefront and influences my life's tone. Everything Jesus proclaimed about, ***"For out of the abundance of the heart the mouth speaks"*** (Matthew 12:34) comes true. My life is a gigantic mouth that does not lack words to speak. My attitude of anger produces much material to permeate my world.

Actions are the invariable expression of what we are in the heart. We display our private convictions through our public actions. Someone said, "Actions are to the soul what streams are to the spring, what branches are to the root. Branches have no existence but what they derive from roots. Actions have no moral existence but that which they derive from the heart." Jesus anxiously pleads with us! Do not begin with the outward action, the symptom. Transformation must come from in the inner being. Please begin with the heart condition.

Jesus climaxed this illustration with the presentation of an ADVERSARY (Matthew 5:25-26). The picture of an adversary describes a person dominated by anger. He is the person who lives in a state of the attitude of murder. **Adversary** comes from the Greek word "antidikos," a compound word consisting of "anti" (against) and "dike" (a cause or suit of law). This word is the extreme picture Jesus gives for the person who lives in anger and will not reconcile. This dominating state of anger, a state beyond reconciliation cannot be satisfied until ***"you have paid the last penny."*** There is no compassion, understanding, or mercy.

This state is an expression of the demonic nature of self-centeredness. The adversary sees only his need and desires. He does not consider the need of anyone else except as it affects his desire. The adversary is blinded to the long-range consequences of the cancer of self-centeredness. This state is opposite of God's heart, the heart of reconciliation. We must be filled with God's nature! The call again comes clearly to embrace our helplessness. If Jesus does not fill us, the result will always be to become an adversary. This result is a fitting climax to this first illustration.

As we examine the condition of an adversary, several key ingredients give us clarity.

The Principle

Jesus expressed an obvious concept by injecting the position of the adversary in His first illustration. He presented two possibilities true for His generation and now for ours. We must see the adversary in light of the beginning contrast that shadows the illustration. The contrast is between, **"You have heard that it was said to those of old"** and **"I say to you." "Those of old"** adjusted the Scriptures to allow anger and hatred to dominate the human life. This adjustment paved the way for them to become adversaries. Jesus continually highlighted this throughout the other five illustrations in this chapter. Divorce for any reason was permitted by the oral traditions of the old (Matthew 5:31). Reconciliation was never encouraged. If you live in a state of anger in your home, will it not destroy your marriage and produce an adversary? Surely you do not expect me to be honest and withhold my words from those with whom I am angry? If I am an adversary, I will use every means possible to exact what I want from my brother (Matthew 5:33). Perhaps **"an eye for an eye and a tooth for a tooth"** would be fair (Matthew 5:38), but this does not express a heart that desires reconciliation. This expresses a heart filled with anger, malice, and revenge. Loving your neighbor and hating your enemy was a principle of those of old (Matthew 5:43). They embraced hate as acceptable, and it quickly consumed their lives. Neighbors becoming adversaries was easy.

The Kingdom person has the mind of Christ with an opposite view. Although the Kingdom person will never commit the physical act of murder, he will not be sourced by restraint or self-discipline. The Kingdom person is not angry with his brother. He does not make the Kingdom because of the absence of anger. He is made the Kingdom because of the flowing reality of God's love nature. The moment he experiences this flow, the Kingdom person is deeply conscious of all division and conflict with others. Any attempt he makes to be intimate with God involves an equal attempt to be reconciled to others. Even in Jesus' life, reconciliation did not always result in oneness. Reconciliation must happen in the Kingdom person, but my brother may not embrace it. The focus of our passage is not on my brother and his response, but it is on the Kingdom person's heart condition. My brother can quickly become an adversary if he will not reconcile. Jesus was never an adversary, but He did have adversaries.

Therefore, the decision rests in your heart. Murder, anger, demeaning, and belittling are produced by a heart condition. Each person's heart condition will source its own style and likeness, and the person has no choice in the matter. However, we do have a decision about our heart's condition. We can respond to Jesus and be Kingdom people. We do not need to choose to be dominated by self-sourcing. Once we make the choice, the results are determined by what we have chosen. A Kingdom person cannot be an adversary, nor live in a state of hatred and anger with his brother. His nature interlocked with the nature of God will not allow such a state. He has the mind of Christ, the redemptive heart of the Trinity.

The Progression

Jesus presented a distinct progression. We have already indicated it in "the principle." A Kingdom person cannot live in anger, demeaning, or belittling (Matthew 5:22). Living in the flow of God's nature requires reconciliation. We cannot dictate the response of another person. The Greek word for reconciliation is "diallassomai." It comes from two Greek words, "dia" meaning "to denote transition" and "allasso" meaning "to change." It refers to "changing one's feelings toward, to reconcile oneself, or to become reconciled." This Greek word is used only once in the New Testament (Matthew 5:24). The moment we live in the flow of God's nature, we will live a life of reconciliation. In other words, there will be no anger, demeaning, or belittling in me. My brother may continue in a state of anger, but I will not. I establish no walls of hatred. The moment he desires reconciliation with me, he will find I am already reconciled with him.

If my brother will not be reconciled, he progresses from the position of my brother to my adversary. This progression is not my choice, and I do not become an adversary to him. However, by not reconciling his anger, he takes the form of an adversary. If this happens, there is a price the reconciled one must pay to the adversary. We would do well to do everything possible to bring about reconciliation in his life. He must know the nature of God and be a Kingdom person. The brother who becomes an adversary lives in a progression. His anger, the state of his heart, must have revenge. He will influence people around him with his anger. Jesus said, **"You will by no means get out of there till you have paid the last penny"** (Matthew 5:26).

Jesus is the greatest example of this. He continually brought instruction to the scribes and Pharisees. His attitude was one of weeping over their condition. In the final week of His life, He reflected on His desire for them, which arose in His life repeatedly. He cried, **"How often I wanted to gather your children together, as a hen gathers her chicks under her wings, but you were not willing!"** (Matthew 23:37). A cry from His heart was to be reconciled to them, though they would not be reconciled to Him. The Gospel accounts often recorded, **"Then the Pharisees went out and plotted against Him, how they might destroy Him"** (Matthew 12:14). In refusing to reconcile, they became His adversaries. They took Jesus to court, and He did indeed pay the full amount!

The adversary lives in a progression of his own hate. It turns inward on him and devours him. His inward state of murder will not be satisfied until all is destroyed, including him. The person who refuses to forgive his brother destroys the bridge over which he must walk. The inability to grant mercy, love, and grace to your brother becomes the barrier keeping mercy, love, and grace from the state of your existence. No wonder Jesus said, *"For if you forgive men their trespasses, your heavenly Father will also forgive you. But if you do not forgive men their trespasses, neither will your Father forgive your trespasses"* (Matthew 6:14-15).

The Prognosis

You might tend to push aside Jesus' instruction and take the self-centered approach and say, "I'll try my best, but no one is perfect." Living with a reconciling spirit in yourself and enduring the difficulty of your adversaries without becoming one is a difficult issue. However, Jesus will not allow us to simply walk away. With every step we take, He attaches a description of what the attitude of murder does to us.

In a previous study, we discovered that Jesus did not present a picture of more destruction as He moved from anger to demeaning to belittling (Matthew 5:22). He focused on, *"in danger of the judgment."* The consequence of murder in your life has the same consequence as anger. The Greek word "enochos," translated *in danger*, comes from the Greek word "enecho" meaning "to hold in or to be snared." The word expresses the idea of bound by sin or guilt, and consequently obliged to the consequences of such. The Greek word "krisis," translated *judgment*, often expresses the final Day of Judgment.

Jesus gave content to this with a statement. He begins with, *"shall be in danger of the judgment"* and continues with, *"shall be in danger of hell fire."* The order of the words in the Greek language is "into" (eis) "the" (ten) "hell" (greennan) "the" (tou) "fire" (puros). This statement contains some of the most severe statements of Jesus in warning about the consequences of self-centeredness, the demonic nature. The issue of not reconciling with your brother is not about rules or not about failing in one of Jesus' commandments, but it is about keeping all the commandments. Therefore, Jesus will forgive me. The focus is not on a rule but a state of being that will not let us reconcile. If my brother becomes an adversary, I must not dwell in a state of being that will not agree with him. In other words, a state of being that fights back and becomes his adversary.

This state of being an adversary eventually becomes **"hell fire."** As discovered in a previous study, **"hell"** is a translation of the Greek word "geena." It was a valley outside Jerusalem that became the garbage dump. A constant fire was burning the waste of Jerusalem. Often there were dead bodies burned there. Interestingly, anger is often likened to a fire burning in a person. Could it be that the state of hell is a person being consumed by the hell fire and anger of his own self-centeredness? Jesus calls us to a nature change. This transpires because we mourn our helplessness, and Jesus fills us with Himself. This filling propels us into reconciliation with our brother. We may have adversaries, but we can never be one. Throughout our lives, meekness, fullness, mercy, purity, peace, and joy flow through us as Kingdom people. You are a Kingdom of God in your world!

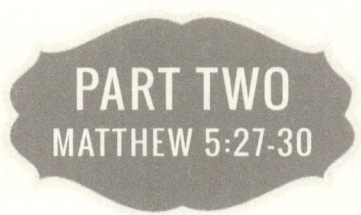

PART TWO
MATTHEW 5:27-30

Fulfillment of the Kingdom – The Application:

MORALITY

Matthew 5:27-30

SPIRITUAL ADULTERY

> "You have heard that it was said to those of old, 'You shall not commit adultery.' But I say to you that whoever looks at a woman to lust for her has already committed adultery with her in his heart. If your right eye causes you to sin, pluck it out and cast it from you; for it is more profitable for you that one of your members perish than for your whole body to be cast into hell. And if your right hand causes you to sin, cut it off and cast it from you; for it is more profitable for you that one of your members perish, than for your whole body to be cast into hell" (Matthew 5: 27-30).

I come to this passage with fear and trembling. My heart has no condemnation or judgment toward anyone joining me in the study. Jesus' grace is sufficient for all, despite our past or marital status. The depth of God's grace is astounding. We all stand guilty in the truth of this passage. All men and women have lusted and been unfaithful in their heart's response if not in their physical action. Often we say everyone is guilty; it is for self-justification. The teenager cries, "Everyone is doing it!" Guilt loves company. Although we admit that everyone is guilty of lust in the heart, we must never make light of it. The purpose of acknowledging our guilt is a simple reality; only by the power of Jesus are we able maintain sexual purity.

The results of sexual lust are devastating and can cause a negative view of sex. Sexual perversions are many in number and variety, thus creating a view of all sex as sin. The Bible does not take this position. Wanting to trap Jesus in a controversy of divorce, the Pharisees asked, *"Is it lawful for a man to divorce his wife for just any reason?"* Without hesitation Jesus examined them with their Scriptures, proposing the standard of God's heart for sex. *"Have you not read that He who made them at the beginning 'made them male and female,' and said, 'For this reason a man shall leave his father and mother and be joined to his wife, and the two shall become one flesh.' So then, they are no longer two but one flesh. Therefore what God has joined together, let not man separate"* (Matthew 19:4-6).

In quoting this Scripture, Jesus gives the origin of sexual intimacy, an expression of God's nature. Because we are created in God's image, and the sexual drive is a part of us, this drive expresses the passion for intimacy in God's heart. This intimate union of a husband and wife supersedes the relationship with father and mother. The power of this intimacy results in *"one flesh."* We find nothing negative or shameful in these statements. Jesus calls us His bride, expressing His relationship with us as Christians. This imagery contains all sexual involvements and ramifications; therefore, we embrace our sexuality in the beauty of God's nature.

The devil has never created anything. He has never brought something out of nothing. He is a created being who attached himself to God's creation, using it for his own ends. Every sin is a perversion of something wonderful that God created. At the heart of every sin is a virtue, something right and good. This is the issue Matthew presents in our passage. If adultery were the problem, those of old would be justified. The issue is the passion of God's heart expressed in relationships but especially in the first male to female relationship, sexuality.

There is a contrast between the approach of those of old and

Jesus' approach. Those of old were worried about the physical activity of adultery. Sexuality in their lives became an animal drive to control and limit. Marriage became glorified prostitution, justifying the satisfaction of selfish desires. Sexual expression, whether on the level of flirting, emotional involvement, or physical expression, must come from intimacy with Jesus. This is the life of a person merged with Jesus, expressing His nature and demonstrating His image.

Severity
Proclaimed in the Old Testament

Anyone studying the requirements of the law of God in the Old Testament is not surprised by the severity of Jesus' approach. In Leviticus God proclaimed the law for Israel, and more importantly the penalties for breaking the law. Concerning adultery, God told Moses, *"The man who commits adultery with another man's wife, he who commits adultery with his neighbor's wife, the adulterer and the adulteress, shall surely be put to death"* (Leviticus 20:10). God gave the same instructions in Deuteronomy. *"If a man is found lying with a woman married to a husband, then both of them shall die — the man that lay with the woman, and the woman; so you shall put away the evil from Israel"* (Deuteronomy 22:22).

These statements are severe. God is serious about sexual purity, the seventh commandment in the Ten Commandments. Through the progression of time into Jesus' day, the severity lessened. The scribes and Pharisees brought to Jesus a woman who had been caught in the act of adultery. They proclaimed Moses' instructions to stone anyone found in this woman's situation (John 8:1-11). The accusers applied this only to the woman, but where was the man? These men had so justified themselves that they were excused from the law concerning adultery.

Progressed into the New Testament

Jesus gave us the New Covenant understanding of sexual purity. The writers of the epistles said it repeatedly. Paul proposed, *"For this is the will of God, your sanctification: that you should abstain from sexual immorality; that each of you should know how to possess his own vessel in sanctification and honor, not in passion of lust, like the Gentiles who do not know God; that no one should take advantage of and defraud his brother in this matter, because the Lord is the avenger of all such, as we also forewarned you and testified. For God did not call us to uncleanness, but in holiness. Therefore he who rejects this does not reject man, but God, who has also given us His Holy Spirit"* (1 Thessalonians 4:3-9). This statement is so powerful that it deserves a study dedicated to its content. Do not allow the passion of lust to dominate your body. The dominance of your body is the right only of the Holy Spirit. He is the One merged with you. Live in His purity. If you do not allow the Holy Spirit dominance of your body, you are rejecting God not man! God must inhabit your sexual expressions.

We must hear the cry of the Scriptures. *"Do you not know that the unrighteous will not inherit the kingdom of God? Do not be deceived. Neither fornicators, nor idolaters, nor adulterers, nor homosexuals, nor sodomites, nor thieves, nor covetous, nor drunkards, nor revilers, nor extortioners will inherit the kingdom of God"* (1 Corinthians 6:9-10). Contained in this list of ten sins, four relate to sexuality. The writer of the Book of Hebrews said, *"Marriage is honorable among all, and the bed undefiled; but fornicators and adulterers God will judge"* (Hebrews 13:4). We can only conclude from this that your sexuality is important to God, and it is tied to His presence in you. Do not violate it!

Proposed in our Passage

As we view the various problems involved in oneness with Jesus, sexuality comes boldly to the front. Although all areas are important and may vary in importance to different people, sexuality leads the parade. The overall divisions of the material in our passage reveal the truth (Matthew 5:27-30). The opening verse reflects on the traditional view of **"those of old"** (Matthew 5:27), mentioned once and contained in one verse. Then Jesus gives His view, which is equated with the view of the Scriptures, and thus the view of God's heart. However, it is only one verse in length (Matthew 5:28). The next two verses give us the bulk of the material (Matthew 5:29-30). These bold statements call for radical action and leave an imprint on the reader. This is serious!

"Those of old" focused on the physical act of adultery, while Jesus focused on the lust of the heart. Whether a physical act or a fantasy of the heart does not make a difference in severity. There is never just a physical act of adultery. There may be a fantasy of the heart without the physical act, but there is never a physical act without the fantasy. The problem is the severity of the involvement. Jesus does not advocate the removal of the body parts involved in the sexual act. He speaks about the **"eye"** and the **"right hand."** We will discuss these body parts in additional studies. Jesus suggests these things as the avenue to the fantasy. Although the physical act was severe in the Old Testament, the lust of the heart is most important in the New Covenant. This condition matters!

Everything we have talked about thus far involves our eternal destiny. Our eternal destiny is not about good people compared to bad people, or moral compared to immoral. Family, raising children, and the proper role of the husband and wife are not highlighted here. Jesus ended this section of His discourse with the subject of *"hell."* Your sexuality controls your eternal destiny because it expresses "who you are" not "what you do." The call of God is not that you abstain from specific physical activities but that you embrace His nature through the framework of your masculinity or femininity.

Spirituality
Proclaimed by Paul

The Scriptures equate physical sexuality with spirituality in a realm unexplainable yet consistently highlighted. Paul applied oneness with Jesus as being filled with the Holy Spirit, calling everyone to submit to this union. Practically applied, submitting to God is submitting to one another. He started with, *"Wives, submit to your own husbands, as to the Lord"* (Ephesians 5:22). A wife's submission to her husband is not because she is submitted to God, but in her daily walk as she submits to her husband in the physical, she is submitting to God in the spiritual.

Husbands are not in a superior position because they are to submit to their wives as Christ submitted to the Church. Practically applied, this submission is to be, *"Just as Christ also loved the church and gave Himself for her, that He might sanctify and cleanse her with the washing of water by the word"* (Ephesians 5:25-26). In fact, *"Husbands ought to love their own wives as their own bodies; he who loves his wife loves himself"* (Ephesians 5:28). Think of the oneness and unity expressed in these statements! The sexualities of the husband and wife are merged until they are one. Paul then quotes God saying, *"For this reason a man shall leave his father and mother and be joined to his wife, and the two shall become one flesh"* (Ephesians 5:31).

What is the fabric of this oneness? Paul said, *"This is a great mystery, but I speak concerning Christ and the church"*

(Ephesians 5:32). The joining of the husband and wife in their sexuality is a mystery like the joining of Jesus and His Church, the believer. Paul does not give an example of oneness, or oneness in marriage as an example of the oneness of Jesus' Spirit merging with the believer. The sexuality of marriage engages the spiritual world in its oneness! This concept explains the belief that marriage is not complete unless God is involved. Marriage is not a simple union between two physical beings, but it is a spiritual union between God, the bride, and the bridegroom. Sexual intercourse is not a physical act but an encounter with the unseen spiritual world.

Those who have experienced spiritual warfare realize this reality. A study of the cities of pagan worship in the New Testament epistles reveals this truth. These pagan centers involved sexual activities because they believed the sexual ecstasy they had with temple prostitutes created a better union with their god. In the world of spiritual warfare, it is well known that the best way to pass demons from one person to another is through sexual intercourse. In the sexual union, the two people involved touch the spiritual reality of the other. Can you imagine what God intended in marriage? No wonder Paul called this intimate connection a mystery.

Now read carefully the words of Paul to the Church of Corinth. ***"Do you not know that your bodies are members of Christ? Shall I then take the members of Christ and make them members of a harlot? Certainly not! Or do you not know that he who is joined to a harlot is one body with her? For 'the two,' He says, 'shall become one flesh.' But he who is joined to the Lord is one spirit with Him"*** (1 Corinthians 6:15-17). The Greek word "kollao," translated ***"is joined,"*** means "to glue" or "to weld." The language Paul used for sexual oneness is the language used for oneness with Jesus. What a mystery!

Parallel in the Scriptures

God used the Old Testament prophets to accuse Israel of being a harlot. The prophecy of Hosea is based on this imagery. God selected Hosea. Over several years God trained Hosea in the school of practical ministry. Hosea married a prostitute, they began a family, and she led Hosea through years of heartache involving betrayal and unfaithfulness. Hosea experienced through his sexual union the same unfaithfulness that God was having with Israel. This experience enabled Hosea to stand before Israel and tearfully speak the words of God. *"My people ask counsel from their wooden idols, and their staff informs them. For the spirit of harlotry has caused them to stray, and they have played the harlot against their God"* (Hosea 4:12). This language is repeated often throughout the Old Testament.

John wrote, *"Then one of the seven angels who had the seven bowls filled with the seven last plagues came to me and talked with me, saying, 'Come, I will show you the bride, the Lamb's wife'"* (Revelation 21:9). Jesus used this imagery in parables (Matthew 22:1-14; 25:1-13). He did not give physical illustrations to express spiritual realities but to show the connection between the sexuality of husband and wife and the spiritual realm of oneness with Jesus.

Pattern of Jesus

Jesus brings us to this thought in our passage. He establishes a pattern in these illustrations. He did not come to destroy the Scriptures (Matthew 5:17). The opposite happened in Jesus' life. The Trinity God placed His nature in our world as a Book, the Scriptures, describing the core of God! Jesus, the Second Member of the Trinity, set aside all He had as God to become one of us.

Spiritual Adultery | **Matthew 5:27-30**

As a human being, Jesus was filled with the Holy Spirit, God's nature. Then Jesus stepped into the Scriptures, the nature of God, in submission to being shaped in His living. The nature of God in His being and in written form produced the life of Jesus. He fulfilled every jot and tittle of the Scriptures.

He was unusual for the Old Covenant hour but not for the New Covenant day. The righteousness of the New Covenant people will exceed the righteousness of the best of the Old Covenant, the scribes and the Pharisees (Matthew 5:20). If they did not live up to the potential of the Old, they could never match the righteousness of the New! To illustrate this Jesus said murder in the physical realm is now equated with hate in the spiritual realm (Matthew 5:21-26). Hate is spiritual murder, as real as physical death created by a physical man.

If this is true of murder, how much more it must be true with adultery (Matthew 5:27-30). Lust in the spiritual realm is spiritual adultery; it is as certain as the physical adultery created by lust. We are to be filled with the Spirit of Jesus, embrace His Word, and let His nature mold our inner and outward lives to show who He is. Our sexuality must be determined by His nature not by our body drives. This determination is not a call to sexual purity but to intimacy with Jesus. How often have we played the role of the harlot in the spiritual realm of our lives? We will know sexual purity only by our union with His nature!

Matthew 5:27-30

WHAT A LINK!

"You have heard that it was said to those of old, 'You shall not commit adultery.' But I say to you that whoever looks at a woman to lust for her has already committed adultery with her in his heart. If your right eye causes you to sin, pluck it out and cast it from you; for it is more profitable for you that one of your members perish than for your whole body to be cast into hell. And if your right hand causes you to sin, cut it off and cast it from you; for it is more profitable for you that one of your members perish, than for your whole body to be cast into hell" (Matthew 5: 27-30).

The Gospels of Luke and Mark give various parts of the Sermon on the Mount, leading some to conclude that the Sermon on the Mount is a variety of spiritual messages spoken by Jesus throughout His ministry. Matthew does not do this in his Gospel account. He shows a consistency in the message from the Beatitudes to the closing story with Jesus systematically declaring the content of the Kingdom of God.

The Beatitudes are the beginning and the foundation of Jesus' truth. In all otherworld religions there is a journey where you earn, merit, and discipline your life to progress to your goal. What these religions insist that you accomplish Jesus gives! In Christianity we are in a state of poverty, absolute helplessness in our spirit (Matthew 5:3). We are to embrace this helplessness with grief until it becomes the attitude of our lives (Matthew 5:4). In this state we are filled with His Spirit (Matthew 5:5), uniting His resource with our helplessness and forming a new creature called the Kingdom of Heaven. Meekness, fullness, mercy, purity, peace, and rejoicing flow through us in this intimacy. In this state of being, we become salt and light (Matthew 5:13-16), and it is not what we do, but who we are in Jesus.

This proposal is a radical idea, different from all other proposals. You might think it contrary to the Scriptures, the Law, or the Prophets. Jesus clarified His position regarding the Scriptures (Matthew 5:17-20). He did not come to destroy the Law or the Prophets but to fulfill. The Scriptures are the nature of the Trinity God in our world, not ancient creed or laws for living, and it is the desire of God's nature in written form. The Second Member of the Trinity became man filled with the Holy Spirit, God's nature. This Man filled with God's nature stepped into the Scriptures in submission. The Holy Spirit, the inner nature of God, and the Scriptures, the outward nature of God, shaped His life. He was the prototype of the New Covenant person, and He demonstrated God's nature. All Kingdom people are to be like Him, exhibiting a righteousness exceeding anything anyone has ever known, even the scribes and Pharisees (Matthew 5:20).

Jesus gave six illustrations of His proposition (Matthew 5:21-48). The first is "murder" (Matthew 5:21-26). Murder is in the physical realm while hate and anger are in the spiritual, which is spiritual murder. The contrast is between **"You have heard that it was said to those of old"** and **"But I say to you."** Those of old taught a self-centered adjustment of the Scriptures. The Holy Spirit, God's nature, speaks the truth of the Scriptures (the nature of God in written form). The Living Word and the Written Word communicate truth! Abstaining from a physical act is not the cry of God's heart; we must be indwelt with God's nature.

Jesus' second illustration is "morality;" however, there is a link between His first (Matthew 5:21-16) and second (Matthew 5:27-30) illustrations.

Partnership

These two illustrations have a "partnership." This partnership is between the inner being of man and the unseen spiritual world. Although this partnership is not the complete picture, it is the beginning of the idea we need to comprehend. According to the Old Testament, the creation of man's structure was a dichotomy. *"And the Lord God formed man of the dust of the ground, and breathed into his nostrils the breath of life; and man became a living being"* (Genesis 2:7). The *"dust of the ground"* constitutes the physical body of man. In other words, God formed the physical body of man from what was already created, but the inner being of man came from the inner being of God when He breathed into man His life. When God united with man in this way He created "a living being," uniting the inner being of man with his physical being.

The inner being of man is man's link with God's heart, the spiritual world. That link is why physical acts can never produce spiritual life. Mere physical existence is only death, and religious ceremonies carried out in the physical can never produce spiritual life. God made the inner being of man in His image, and only that inner being can link with God's nature. *"But the natural* (physical) *man does not receive the things of the Spirit of God, for they are foolishness to him; nor can he know them, because they are spiritually discerned. But he who is spiritual judges all things, yet he himself is rightly judged by no one"* (1 Corinthians 2:14-15). The *"natural man"* is a person without the link of his inner being with the Spirit of God. He is spiritually dead.

What a Link! | **Matthew 5:27-30**

We enter death through sin. The spiritual link that allows us to live in the resource of God's nature is broken. We live out of our flesh, satisfying the comfort and catering to the desires of the flesh. This life produces a religion sourced by the strength of the flesh, causing *"those of old"* to cry, *"You shall not murder"* (Matthew 5:21). They considered this a high standard, and although it was to be applauded and honored, it was difficult to carry out in the flesh. Man's control and discipline of his physical urges is the best he can accomplish in his flesh. From the physical view, these urges are acceptable but need limited expression.

What if man could again know the spiritual link in his physical life? Can he be born from above (John 3:3)? Can God breathe into my flesh the breath of His nature, reestablishing the link? If God's nature produces my life, will He not establish a new level of living? God's nature is love, and this love is the standard of the spiritual realm. All the feelings of anger, hurt, and jealously will be replaced with love, concern, and empathy. I will no longer need to control and manage my physical desires because God's nature in me changes those desires. My flesh cannot produce this change, and my discipline cannot source it. This change happens when the Spirit of God breathes in me!

Jesus was filled with God's nature, the Holy Spirit, making Him the prototype of this link. He submitted to God's nature in the Scriptures. The nature of God in Jesus and the nature of God in written form shaped His physical life. Thus, you can experience forgiveness from Jesus. He sources what is best for you with no agenda for Himself. He died on a cross, giving you the gift of salvation that you cannot earn, and establishing the spiritual link between you and Him.

Let me give you another illustration of this link between you and Jesus. If this link is reestablished, what will happen in your sexuality? *"Those of old"* could not conceive of victory in their sexuality beyond controlling their physical acts. *"You shall not commit adultery"* (Matthew 5:27) was a high standard for any person sourced by his flesh. The sexual body drive is natural, but they viewed it like their hunger drive or their need for sleep. Why should this sex drive, a natural part of man's physical life, not be satisfied? They saw it as a physical appetite with no significant ramifications.

"Those of old" thought Jesus' words, *"that whoever looks at a woman to lust for her has already committed adultery with her in his heart"* was an overbearing standard. How could this be? Abstaining from the physical expression of the sex drive was difficult to maintain, so how could Jesus expect anyone to control his or her thoughts as well? If He advocated purity in a person's thoughts, He would need to change the sex drive. The body craves what it craves! But Jesus spoke from the perspective of a Spirit filled New Covenant man! What if a link with the spiritual world could change the focus of our sexuality? Jesus did not want to remove the sex drive, but He proposed a refocusing of this drive in our lives!

If we are filled with God's nature, and our being is properly linked with the spiritual world, can Jesus' suggestion be a reality? Can a person's sexuality not be focused on selfish satisfaction? Can we view the opposite sex through the eyes of Jesus? If we are radically changed within, then there is no need for self-control of our sexual desires. Can the nature of God merge with me in every area of my life including my sexuality, producing His image in me? This merge between God's nature and me is the acceptable righteousness of the New Covenant!

Production

We now need to investigate the rest of this idea. When the inner being of man links with the spiritual, this link acts on the physical. Man's inner being produces the physical expressions, and we must not be confused on this issue. When the inner being of man links with God's heart (the spiritual), this link determines man's physical expression. When a person is not linked with God's heart, he or she suffers the consequence of spiritual death, but we must not see them as nonexistent. The inner being of man does not disappear, but he or she is separated from all that God intended and enters destruction.

When the inner being does not merge with God's nature, that man's surrender is to self-satisfaction, ultimately destroying his being. When man does not allow God to source his physical life, that man resorts to the demonic nature of self-centeredness. All thoughts and attitudes become selfish. Even when his actions appear to be generous, those actions are driven by selfish motives, and all relationships are fostered and maintained in selfishness. There is no righteousness in man; all our righteous acts are filthy rags (Isaiah 64:6). We become a product of self, taking God's place in our inner being.

Even the best of *"those of old"* could not imagine why Jesus would say, *"You shall not murder"* (Matthew 5:21). Are there no limits to the expression of one's self-centeredness? The prevenient grace of God does not leave us at the mercy of our own selfishness. Do we not have enough decency in the inner being to limit our evil expressions? The attitudes of hate, jealously, hurt, and revenge spring from the inner being left to "self." Without God's nature, "self" is the source of the physical activity.

Jesus said, *"But I say to you that whoever is angry with his brother shall be in danger of the judgment"* (Matthew 5:22). How can anyone who knows the state of humanity advocate such a proposal? A person might curb his or her physical action and resist murder, but the idea of not getting angry or hating is ludicrous. I cannot help the way I feel. No one understands me. I only hate people who deserve it because they are mean, vile, and hateful people who do terrible things to make me uncomfortable. I will not kill them, but I should at least be allowed to hate them!

Part Two: Fulfillment of the Kingdom - The Application: Morality

Can the inner being of man link with the Spirit of God, allowing that Spirit to control his physical life? Can I be filled with God's nature? Can God's nature saturate my life like a liquid fills a sponge? God's nature cannot be limited to the religious sections of my inner man, expressing that religion on occasion. God's nature must control and saturate all areas of my life. Jesus calls for a new production in my life, determined by our inner link.

"Those of old" advocated the standard that, *"You shall not commit adultery"* (Matthew 5:27) with pride. But can we expect any less from those possessed by their physical drive, controlled by a selfish inner being, living for pleasure, comfort, and self-gratification? Under this scenario the sex drive naturally becomes an instrument for self-pleasure, developing all manner of perversions. There must be some restraint, thus we do not commit adultery! To restrain from committing adultery is the best the self-centered man can ever think or dream of achieving.

Jesus said, *"But I say to you that whoever looks at a woman to lust for her has already committed adultery with her in his heart"* (Matthew 5:28). This sounds impossible! How can a person maintain such a standard in a body with a powerful sex drive? No one can master his sexuality to that extent. But what if this expectation is not about you controlling, mastering, or disciplining your sexuality? Jesus promotes a New Covenant, God's nature filling the heart of man. If man merges with the Divine Heart of God, his physical drives will be produced by God's motives. This merging means death to the self-centered motives that fill our lives and control our physical drives. We are to see the person of the opposite sex as Jesus sees them. Our weakness is filled with His nature (Matthew 5:3). In this merge we become the Kingdom of God, a new creature. God's attitude of meekness, hungering for righteousness, mercy, purity of heart, peace, and joy fill our lives (Matthew 5:3-11). God now produces our perspective, even our sexuality.

Presentation

We have one more fact that we want to highlight. The inner being of man linked with God's nature, acting on the physical world, reveals the content of the man's inner being. The linked man becomes an expression of his spiritual being. Our physical body was never intended to dictate or control our actions but is a platform to display the inner heart. The physical body is not useless or unimportant but is vital to mankind's eternal being.

Jesus is our example. In His flesh He is the visible image of the invisible Father. God's heart did not change because of Jesus. When we study the Old Testament, we are somewhat confused about the Trinity God's heart. What is He really like? Jesus clarifies this issue, and we must interpret the Old Testament revelation of God in light of Jesus, the complete revelation of God. As Jesus is this revelation He also shows us what we are to be, our destiny. Jesus was linked with God's nature in His inner being. This nature controlled and gave content to His physical life. Everything God's nature sourced through Jesus was purposed to bring us into the same relationship. Jesus was the prototype of who we are to be!

"Those of old" proposed the standard of, *"You shall not murder"* (Matthew 5:21). This standard was the best their inner hearts could produce, and it revealed the inward link they had with the spiritual, which left them filled with self. They were responsible for fulfilling the law of God and sourced their own righteousness. Their physical lives were filled with expressions of hatred, jealousy, and judgment. The Pharisees were more concerned about proper activity on specific days rather than the welfare of a man with a withered hand (Matthew 12:9-14). Their lives were filled with hypocrisy. They adjusted the Scriptures by their interpretation to foster their lifestyles (Matthew 15:3-9). Their physical actions displayed this hypocrisy, and they

acclaimed their relationship with God although they acted out this relationship with self.

Can a person merge with God's nature? Can our inner beings be filled with God's nature until we think as He thinks, see as He sees, and feel what He feels? Is that the purpose of Jesus' life? If we link with God's nature, that oneness produces Jesus' life in us, and we become the visible image of His nature. If Jesus possesses our inner being, we will express Him in our outward living. He cannot be hidden.

"Those of old" proposed, *"You shall not commit adultery"* (Matthew 5:23). `Flirtations, emotional involvements, and lust were acceptable to them. After all, "who we are" is demonstrated in the acts of our flesh. We cannot help ourselves! We must curb and attempt to control our urges. But Jesus said, **"But I say to you that whoever looks at a woman to lust for her has already committed adultery with her in his heart"** (Matthew 5:28).

This statement is ridiculous unless certain things are true. God created our sexuality, a natural element of our being. There is nothing wrong with sexual desire. The difficulty is in who is directing and determining the quality of this sexuality. The inner being of a person will determine the physical expression of their sexuality. When self controls my inner being, the motive of selfishness dominates and displays my sexuality. My pleasure and satisfaction are paramount to me. My physical expressions will be shaped by what is acceptable in my culture, but will always be expressions of self-centeredness. I will use others for self-gratification. Can I be filled with the Spirit of God? Jesus proposed a New Covenant where the inner being is filled with God's nature. Can the Spirit of God possess my sexuality in redemptive power? Can my sexuality become the expression of my inner being filled with God's nature?

How can we know who is linked with our inner being? Our physical lives demonstrate that link! This is not an appeal to change your physical activity. We do not suggest a program for retraining your physical response to the stimuli of your physical world. Jesus calls us to link our inner being with His. He is our only hope!

Matthew 5:28

JUST A LOOK

"But I say to you that whoever looks at a woman to lust for her has already committed adultery with her in his heart" (Matthew 5:28).

Our visual world is dominated and controlled by sexuality. Why use sexuality at the heart of our advertisements? Sexuality is what gets us to look, accept, and purchase. Sexuality influences and directs our fashion causing us to sacrifice comfort and convenience to appear sensual. Sexuality is about the visual; we must look! My wife watches the Food Channel on television. I walked in on a program where three pastry chefs were competing in a cake contest. The winning chef had created a beautiful, sleek display nearly five feet high where cake was formed into various objects resting on each other. The judges applauded the sensual appearance of the cake. Even our food is judged by sexuality.

Playboy published its first magazine in 1953, and today that publication is a 4.9 billion dollar business. The domain name (*sex.com*) is valued at 65 million dollars. 28,258 people view pornography every second. Every thirty-nine minutes, a new pornographic movie is produced. Christians are not exempt from these statistics. More than fifty-three percent of men attending Promise Keepers said they viewed pornography weekly. Forty-five percent of Christians admit pornography is a major problem in their home. "Looking" has taken over our lives!

The Scriptures place a significant focus on the "eye." In the Sermon on the Mount Jesus calls the eye, *"the lamp of the body."* He said, *"The Lamp of the body is the eye. If therefore your eye is good, your whole body will be full of light. But if your eye is bad, your whole body will be full of darkness. If therefore the light that is in you is darkness, how great is that darkness"* (Matthew 6:22-23). "Looking" becomes the entryway into our lives. When the perspective of looking has Jesus' nature, the being is filled with light, but when the perspective of looking is self-centered, darkness prevails.

The basis of the first temptation was the eye. The devil suggested to Eve that God did not tell the whole truth. *"So when the woman saw that the tree was good for food, that it was pleasant to the eyes, and a tree desirable to make one wise, she took of its fruit and ate"* (Genesis 3:6). But this was more than a temptation because the consequences of sin affected the "looking" of this couple. After Adam and Eve had eaten the fruit, *"then the eyes of both of them were opened, and they knew that they were naked; and they sewed fig leaves together and made themselves coverings"* (Genesis 3:7).

The miracles of healing the blind were highlighted signs of the Messiah. A person receiving their sight is never found in the Old Testament, and Jesus was the only one in the New Testament to heal blinded eyes. The opening of our eyes is a reality of the New Covenant. In the New Covenant, man's nature is transformed when Jesus removes blindness (false seeing) and gives sight (proper perspective).

The Greek language has only one word for hearing in the New Testament, which is "akouo," but there are five Greek words for "seeing." The Greek word "horao," translated "to look," conveys the idea to experience or perceive. The Greek word "optanomai" is rarely used and means "to be visible or to appear." "Theaomai" refers to a spectator or one who "beholds." "Theoreo" refers to a spectator at a religious festival. The Greek word in our passage is "blepo," translated "***looks***," means "to see" with an emphasis on the function of the eye. This word is as the opposite of blindness. "Blepo" is the absolute for insight and used for intellectual or spiritual perception, appearing one hundred and thirty-seven times. Most of those uses are in the present tense introducing a state of continual action.

Jesus presented the idea of a relationship between the inner being of a person and their physical life. This idea was a part of the theological battle that raged between Jesus and the Pharisees. The Pharisees, committed to the letter of the law, were outraged with Jesus because He was committed to the Spirit of the law. Jesus' view was different because He was the first Spirit-filled person, the prototype of the New Covenant person living in the fullness of God's nature. Jesus submitted Himself to the Scriptures; the written form of God's nature, and His physical life was an expression of His intimacy with that nature. Although physical activity was present, it was never the determining factor of His actions. Everything physical happened because of the inner spiritual nature. This was the conflict between Jesus and the Pharisees.

The Pharisees were concerned with only physical appearance. They gave money generously only because they wanted to be seen by those watching (Matthew 6:1-4), and they prayed to impress those listening (Matthew 6:5-7). They fasted so others would be in awe of their sacrifice (Matthew 6:16-18). In their opinion, ***"For they*** (the disciples) ***do not wash their hands when they eat bread"*** (Matthew 15:2) was a transgression of the tradition of the elders. Their concern was a focus on the physical activity.

Jesus called everyone to have a righteousness that exceeded the righteousness of the scribes and Pharisees. No one ***"will by no means enter the kingdom of heaven"*** without that exceeding righteousness (Matthew 5:20). Jesus had a central theme with six illustrations in "The Fulfillment of the Kingdom, Application" (Matthew 5:21-48). In these illustrations he contrasted the Pharisees' satisfaction with physical achievements with the state of the inner being. **"Those of old"** were concerned with only murder. They had anger management classes to teach the discipline not to kill. But the New Covenant went far beyond this physical standard. Why be angry? Why not eliminate murder in the spiritual realm as well as the physical (Matthew 5:21-26)? Jesus proposed this idea about sexuality. Let us look at this closely.

"Those of old" proposed **"You shall not commit adultery"** (Matthew 5:27). Jesus said, **"But I say to you that whoever looks"** (Matthew 5:28). But **"those of old"** DISREGARDED physical sight. The highest state of righteousness they could conceive was abstinence from sexual involvement with another man's wife. They considered refraining from the physical act of sex as the only guideline for righteousness. Why was that? They lived a self-sourced religion and that was the best they could produce. When a person controlled his sexual body drive enough to maintain this self-imposed physical boundary, he was applauded.

But the righteousness of the New Covenant, the fullness of the Spirit, is not content with this level. Then Jesus introduced the idea of **"looks"**! Seeing is not a negative in the Scriptures. The writers of the Scriptures emphasized God's looking. In the Old Testament, God rejected Saul as king and informed Samuel of His plan to find a king among the sons of Jesse. Samuel was to take a heifer to Bethlehem to offer a sacrifice and invite Jesse and his sons. Samuel chose Jesse's son, Eliab, as the most likely candidate to be the new king. **"But the Lord said to Samuel, 'Do not look at his appearance or at his physical stature, because I have refused him. For the Lord does not see as man sees; for man looks at the outward appearance, but the Lord looks at the heart'"** (1 Samuel 16:7).

Hundreds of years later Jesus reminds the Jews of how God sees! The Jews have rejected the way God sees by disregarding the *"looks"* in our passage. They want a god who *"looks,"* measures and judges them by their physical acts. That kind of judgment is more comfortable to them than God probing the depth of their heart motive. They want a physical religion where they can parade their achievements, but Jesus focused on *"looks."*

God requires from us only what is in His life. Could Jesus' challenge be to see as God sees? Our passage is not an intensified rule about sexuality. The old law was, **"You shall not commit adultery"** (Matthew 5:27). Is the new rule to not **"look at a woman to lust for her"** (Matthew 5:28)? Jesus' call to the Kingdom person is not that of maintaining a new level of physical activity, but He proposes a change in our nature where He controls our perspective!

Jesus' call is not focused only on sexuality but is at the heart of every life area. We are to see all situations as Jesus sees them, think as Jesus thinks, and have the mind of Christ (Philippians 2:5). If Jesus sources us with the same nature God sourced Him, we will see, feel, and consider all things as He does! Our passage is not a call to control what we see but to allow Jesus to fill our weakness with His strength (Matthew 5:3-12). Our view will be determined by which nature is sourcing self, Spirit or us.

We can expand this thought. Physical sight is a DOOR into our inner being's spiritual realm. In our verse, the link between *"looks"* and *"heart"* explodes with truth. The eye is the gateway into a person's heart. Some people think we can look into the eyes of a person and see his or her soul, and Jesus established this connection.

If the eyes are the gateway into a person's heart, then we can project the truth that what we see becomes food for the soul. Our eyes become the mouth of our soul, and we take in the supply of material that constructs our inner being. What the eye sees feeds the lust of the mind and produces adultery in the heart, which makes Jesus' statement in our verse obvious. The link between what the eye sees and what the heart produces is not minor. This link is the reason Jesus said, ***"If your right eye causes you to sin, pluck it out and cast it from you"*** (Matthew 5:29). This verse is Jesus' cry against the means that feeds the soul.

In biblical terms, the right eye is the strongest and gives visions into the distance. What if the right eye, designed to direct life toward the long range, the everlasting, becomes tricked? What if that eye becomes fixated on the present moment? Suddenly that person's life is thrust into immediate satisfaction, which is called pleasure. Instead of that soul being fed the building materials to construct a life worthy of eternity, that soul is fed the pleasures of destruction temporary and worthy only of damnation in hell.

If the problem of the inner soul were contained in what we see, it would be a simple matter. Blind people would be the most spiritual among us, but blindness does not guarantee righteousness. Two people looking at the same object may perceive two different things. Therefore, we must advance to this idea: physical sight is the DELIGHT of the inner beings' spiritual realm, and our spiritual life determines what we see!

Now we want to look carefully at our verse. ***"But I say to you that whoever looks at a woman to lust for her has already committed adultery with her in his heart"*** (Matthew 5:28). In this statement Jesus gives a purpose clause saying, ***"that whoever looks at a woman to lust for her has already committed adultery with her in his heart."*** This statement is based on the authority of the Person who fulfills every aspect of the Scriptures (Matthew 5:17). Jesus, filled with God's nature, submitted His life to the shaping of God's nature in the written Scriptures, which gave Him the proper insight. The main verb of the purpose clause is the Greek word "moicheuo," translated **has committed adultery**. The Greek word "blepo," translated ***looks***, is a participle (a verb acting as an adjective). The verb gives content to the subject, **whoever**. This English word is a translation of "pas ho," translated literally as "all the." Who is the "all the?" It is "the looking on a woman" ones. The problem Jesus presented is not contained in looking on a woman. The problem is for what purpose a person looks! If the purpose is to **"lust for her"** he **"has already committed adultery with her in his heart."** Jesus said the heart determines the motive, which controls the purpose for "looking." The problem is not in the "looking" but in the "heart."

Jesus again brings us back to the central issue of the Sermon on the Mount. Unless we embrace our spiritual poverty (Matthew 5:3-4) and are filled with His nature, we will continue to be sourced by our selfish, self-centered nature. The perspective of this nature sees everything for its own benefit and pleasure. This nature is the opposite of the cross style, the perspective of God. We were created in spiritual poverty, helplessness, to merge with God's nature. We were created to be dependent not independent.

Thus, our passage is not an intensified rule we are to obey. **"Those of old"** established their rule, **"You shall not commit adultery"** (Matthew 5:27). Jesus did not make a new set of rules in the New Covenant. The Kingdom person and those self-sourced look at a woman from different agendas. Jesus wants us merged with His divine heart to see with His perspective, revealing we are in the New Covenant.

You and I can now understand! In the New Testament, there is not a new discipline to control my physical appetite or correct an animal drive in me. I do not need to be motivated to protect my manhood. I now see myself as God sees me through His heart. "Turning the other cheek" becomes a possibility (Matthew 5:39). "Going the second mile" becomes a standard practice in my life (Matthew 5:41). Living without hate and anger becomes the state of my existence (Matthew 5:22). The nature of God fills my life and produces a new "look"!

The disciples questioned Jesus when He began preaching in parables. He said, ***"Because it has been given to you to know the mysteries of the kingdom of heaven, but to them it has not been given"*** (Matthew 13:11). Those sourced by self could not understand the parables Jesus told. For instance, who can understand leaving ninety-nine sheep in the fold to risk your life for a stray sheep lost in a storm at midnight (Matthew 18:10-13)? Who can understand the payment plan of God's heart? Jesus told of workers hired at various times throughout the day, some with only one hour of work while others toiled for the entire day. At the close of that day the owner paid everyone the same wage (Matthew 20:1-16)! Does that make any sense? That payment plan makes sense only to those sourced by God's nature and see with His eyes.

Being filled with God's nature and seeing with His eyes is the cry of Jesus! Will you allow God to source your sexuality by His nature?

Matthew 5:28

LOOKING AT A WOMAN

"But I say to you that whoever looks at a woman to lust for her has already committed adultery with her in his heart" (Matthew 5: 28).

Jesus is brief in His presentation of our passage. He gives the view of ***"those of old"*** in one verse (Matthew 5:27), and in the next verse He states His opinion (Matthew 5:28). The Greek word "ego," translated ***"I,"*** appears only as an emphatic emphasis. The subject ***"I"*** is included at the ending of the verb ***"say"***; therefore, ***"ego"*** is unnecessary except for forceful emphasis. Jesus proclaims His word above the authority of ***"those of old."*** He was the first to experience the Kingdom of Heaven, and He speaks from this platform. He does not add to or complement the Scriptures but points to what God intended in the Scriptures. ***"Those of old"*** missed the heart of God in the Scriptures.

Sexuality was a complicated problem in Jesus' day and remains so in our day. You would think we would have progressed further in our 2,000 years of learning. To correct this problem, Jesus could have exclusively focused on adultery, but He did not see that as the solution for His day or ours. He knew the root problem of sexuality was not adultery. If no one ever committed adultery again, it would not solve the problem of sexuality. The same was true with murder (Matthew 5:21-26). Murder is a symptom of anger. Jesus' Sermon on the Mount focused on our helplessness, which needs the resource of God's nature (Matthew 5:3). Our nature is perverted, and we need rebirthing. The perversion of our sexuality is only one expression of the problem, our nature.

Jesus clearly stated His intent when He said, ***"But I say to you that whoever looks at a woman to lust for her has already committed adultery with her in his heart"*** (Matthew 5: 28). A legalist approaches this problem by focusing on ***"looks."*** Is Jesus intensifying and increasing the rule for the New Covenant? The best the Old Covenant could conceive was, ***"You shall not commit adultery"*** (Matthew 5:27). In the New Covenant, the old rule is replaced with, "You shall not look on a woman." Jesus' proposal is not to solve the problem by raising our activity level; instead, He proposes we allow Him to make a radical change in our nature as He sources our activity.

A new rule would be a distraction from the New Covenant. The New Covenant problem is not sexual expression or the activity of "looking"! Jesus never condemned "looking." How can we exist a day in our world without looking at a person of another gender, knowing of their sexuality? When I look at another man I know his masculinity, and when I look at a woman I know her femininity, recognizing and honoring who each is. Jesus gives no condemnation for "looking" because it is right.

The problem is in the rest of the verse, ***"to lust for her,"*** focusing on intent and motive. Jesus highlights what drives the "looking." Previously we have studied the role of sexuality in the fall of the human race. The Scriptures say that the moment Adam and Eve sinned, ***"Then the eyes of both of them were opened"*** (Genesis 3:7). This does not mean that they were blind before their sin. They were "looking" from the moment of their creation to their sin. Their "looking" was not their sin! But when they sinned, ***"Then the eyes of both of them were opened, and they knew that they were naked; and they sewed fig leaves together and made themselves coverings"*** (Genesis 3:7). The first

Part Two: Fulfillment of the Kingdom - The Application: Morality

recorded effect of their sin was their new view of their sexuality. God came walking in the garden in the cool of the day. Adam and Eve hid themselves (Genesis 3:8). When God found them, Adam confessed, **"I heard Your voice in the garden, and I was afraid because I was naked; and I hid myself"** (Genesis 3:10). God asked, **"Who told you that you were naked?"** (Genesis 3:11). Their view of sexuality was different. "Looking" was not the problem but the motive for the "looking" had become one. Their nature was not the same!

We must never perceive sin as merely a deed that needs forgiveness. It is easy to say, "I sinned; God forgives me. I did it again; God forgives me again." Although sin does need forgiveness, we need to open the door that deals with the nature of the sin that possesses us! The Scriptures repeatedly tell us that Jesus came to destroy the works of the devil (Hebrews 2:14; 1 John 3:8). We must never be content to be saved "in" our sin; we must be saved "from" our sin. Jesus died not to only forgive but also to deliver us from the nature of sin! He wants to deal with our sexuality.

Let us examine the nature of man. What was altered in the perspective of man's nature when he sinned? It was a shift in PURPOSE! The picture of woman's creation is incredible, and the setting of woman's creation gives necessary information to the purpose. Who can know the mind of God? There are conclusions we can draw in the progression of the creation story. Adam was the crowning creation of God's endeavor. God created all living things with sexuality, weaving sexuality into the fiber of the nature both in plants and animals. He made all animals male and female. But this creation type was not true with Adam! There was no feminine complement to Adam as with all other creation.

"The Lord God planted a garden eastward in Eden, and there He put the man whom He had formed" (Genesis 2:8). Adam named all the animals. He enjoyed fellowship with God and all the goodness of the garden. God commanded Adam never to eat of the tree of the knowledge of good and evil (Genesis 2:17). It was his responsibility to tend and keep the garden (Genesis 2:15). We are never told how long he did this alone and without a counterpart. God had sexuality written into the creation of everything, but something was missing in Adam!

God recognized the problem and said, *"It is not good that man should be alone; I will make him a helper comparable to him"* (Genesis 2:18). She is a *"helper."* She is not the opposite but a complement, one who rushes to aid and fulfill. She is *"comparable to him,"* the same as he. She is not his subordinate, his servant, a tool for his pleasure, an instrument for use, or another of his objects among many. *"And the Lord God caused a deep sleep to fall on Adam, and he slept; and He took one of his ribs, and closed up the flesh in its place. Then the rib which the Lord God had taken from man He made into a woman, and He brought her to the man"* (Genesis 2:21-22). She completes man and is the final touch that makes up what is lacking in him.

Adam's response to God's gift was astounding. He said,
"This is now bone of my bones
And flesh of my flesh;
She shall be called Woman,
Because she was taken out of Man"
(Genesis 2:23).

The Hebrew word "etsem," translated *"bone,"* has the meaning of "substance or self." *"Bone of my bones"* can be translated "self of my self." Adam referred to this new aspect of his sexuality as *"Woman,"* and his reason for this title was, *"Because she was taken out of Man."* He was saying, "She is me!" This statement is a reference to God's intended relationship of sexuality, and the depth of this relationship is revealed in the following statement. *"Therefore a man shall leave his father and mother and be joined to his wife, and they shall become one flesh"* (Genesis 2:24). *"Therefore"* means that what has been spoken is the basis for what is going to be said. Based on the purpose and method of Eve's creation, a man and a woman will be joined (glued or welded) together as *"one flesh."* God's intent for creating woman was not to separate her from man! God never intended for male and female to be at odds, separated, or warring. His intent was that man and woman together are one! The purpose of her creation was a continuation of oneness.

There is a progression in the biblical statements. Woman was taken out of the body of man. Man breaks forth with a description of who she is. He proclaims, "She is me!" The biblical statement about marriage is, *"Therefore a man shall leave his father and mother and be joined to his wife, and they shall become one flesh"* (Genesis 2:24). God clearly defined this statement based on the method of woman's creation, the reaction of man to woman's creation, and the purpose of her creation. This is God's intent for marriage. Jesus reminded the Pharisees of God's purpose when they were arguing about divorce (Matthew 19:5). God made this statement in Genesis before there were *"father and mother"* to leave. He clearly stated His dream and purpose for the oneness to occur in sexuality.

Then Adam and Eve sinned, altering mankind's nature! How tragic! The sin was not a deed of sin that could be forgiven and forgotten. The nature affecting the "looking" of man was changed. They did not think in terms of unity, giving their lives to each other, but they became divided, using each other for personal benefit. Sexuality became self-serving, causing man and woman to be unglued, separated, and selfish, bringing the tragedy of divorce. Let us look again at our passage (Matthew 5:28). This passage is not Jesus' new commandment as the New Covenant approach to sexuality. He focused His attention on the problem in the nature of humanity. We do not "look" at each other correctly because our perspective comes from a changed nature. Jesus died to restore us to our previous condition, which is God's nature indwelling and filtering through our sexuality. He calls us to God's original plan of sexuality!

We not only have a shift in "purpose," but also a shift in PERFORMANCE. Sexuality is never just physical activity. The physical realm was designed by God to be a platform for the demonstration of the spiritual nature of man. Although the essence of man cannot be judged by his physical deed, his physical deeds are a demonstration of who he is. We see this in relation to God! Paul declared that the physical creation of the world gave clear evidence of the *"invisible attributes"* of God (Romans 1:20). We can see His eternal power and Godhead plainly manifested in Jesus. The eternal Word, God, **"became flesh and dwelt among us, and we beheld His glory, the glory as of the only begotten of the Father, full of grace and truth"** (John 1:14). *"He is the image of the invisible God"* (Colossians 1:15).

"Those of old" were concerned only with the physical activities of their sexuality. They saw their sexuality as an animal drive isolated from their spiritual life. They needed to control and limit it within the boundaries of the proper physical activity of marriage. Jesus expressed a view far beyond controlling performance. He asked, "What is the expression of the spirit interacting with your flesh?" The sexual act of marriage gives physical expression to the oneness (glued or welded) that exists between man and the one who is *"bone of my bones, flesh of my flesh."*

The physical expression of sexuality in biblical language (Greek) is "ginosko," translated "to know" (Matthew 1:25). This word is the strongest Greek word for intimacy, relationship, and oneness on the highest spiritual level. The expression of sexuality in the physical realm is the welding of two spiritual lives into one. All other expressions are a perverted demonstration of an inner soul focused on self. "Looking" is not the problem; Jesus did not propose a further physical regulation of restricted sight. His cry is for a heart change. Marriage has become a means to use our spouse for personal benefit and satisfaction instead of giving one's self to the other in oneness.

Our passage is also a shift in POSSESSION. The Greek word "epithymeo," translated "lust," is the same Greek word translated "covet." ***You shall not commit adultery"*** is the seventh of the Ten Commandments. The tenth commandment is, ***"You shall not covet your neighbor's house; you shall not covet your neighbor's wife, nor his male servant, nor his female servant, nor his ox, nor his donkey, nor anything that is your neighbor's"*** (Exodus 20:17). The heart of the word is the idea of possession. If I covet or lust after my neighbor's house, I desire to take it from him, claim it as mine, and possess it for myself. If this desire is achieved in the physical realm, I remove the possession from my neighbor and take it for myself.

In this act, I become a thief! In the spiritual world, I am stealing my neighbor's house. Now bring this truth to our passage. God intended for our sexuality to be intimate, share one flesh, and know another by giving one to the other. When my sexuality is driven by my sinful nature, I become a thief. In the spiritual, I carry out the action of King David of old (2 Samuel 11), stealing my neighbor's wife!

Additionally, in the spiritual I steal from the woman herself what is not rightfully mine. I rob from her what is not mine to possess. I do not give; I take. My self-centered nature becomes a cancer devouring others for my benefit. I am a spiritual thief.

Jesus did not give a new rule for the new Kingdom. He calls us to live His intention for our sexuality. God's plan is to fill our being with His nature. Our sexuality must be focused and purposed in Him. There is nothing wrong with "looking." The problem is in my heart. In my helplessness I am incapable of changing my heart. This is a call to be HIS!

Matthew 5:28

SEXUALITY AND PRIORITY

"But I say to you that whoever looks at a woman to lust for her has already committed adultery with her in his heart"
(Matthew 5:28).

Jesus extends a startling contrast in our passage so vivid that we cannot miss it! ***"Those of old"*** interpreted God's law according to their self-achievements. They viewed their sexuality as "an isolated body drive" to be controlled within the boundaries of decency. If they kept their sexuality in the boundaries of marriage, any pleasure or satisfaction was acceptable. The contrast here is with the Spirit-filled life, ***"But I say to you."*** The New Covenant restored us to God's intention from the beginning. Our sexuality envelops our creation and purpose for life. The presence of God must permeate every aspect of sexuality from the heart's intention to the practical physical expression. Jesus makes an amazing contrast!

The rule of old was, ***"You shall not commit adultery."*** The Jews loved this terminology because it was always about ***"you"*** and never about "them." We see this philosophy expressed when they drug a woman caught in the act of adultery to the feet of Jesus. They believed they were justified in their action; they leaned back ready to throw stones, their self-righteousness leading them to put this woman to death. Let us look carefully at what Jesus said in our passage. ***"But I say to you that whoever"***

(Matthew 5:28). ***"Whoever"*** is a translation of the Greek word "pas ho." "Pas" means "all," and "ho" means "the." The "looking ones" fall into the category of lusting and are included with no adjustment, no excuse, or no compromise! This does not allow us to drag anyone into the arena of scrutiny. We all stand in the spotlight of examination by the New Covenant standard!

We stand face to face with the truth that "looking at a woman" is not the problem. We live with a continual awareness of sexuality. Sexuality is in every facet of our lives, present in every relationship, and interwoven in all we are. As the passage unfolds, the problem is PRIORITY. The priority of life becomes our sexuality. Although sexuality may contribute to every area of living, it was not to dominate us. The male's expressions of masculinity are seen in his approach to circumstances, the way he walks, and in his relationships to the females around him. However, when masculinity dictates the man's life, he has violated the standard of the New Covenant. He may not have broken the commandment of ***"those of old,"*** but he has violated the intent of the New Covenant, which is intimacy with Jesus!

We see this in the Garden of Eden. Adam was the crowning creation of God, placed in the garden with a command. ***"Of every tree of the garden you may freely eat; but of the tree of the knowledge of good and evil you shall not eat, for in the day that you eat of it you shall surely die"*** (Genesis 2:16-17). Adam's only relationship was with God because Eve had not yet been created. After he had named all the animals and tended the garden for a while, God became aware that His man was not complete in his sexuality. He put Adam to sleep and created woman out of His man. One day the devil had a conversation with Eve. They discussed the commandment that Eve had heard from Adam. Adam must have been present for this conversation because Eve ate of the fruit and ***"gave to her husband with her"*** (Genesis 3:6). Regardless of what Eve's temptation might have been, sexuality was involved in Adam's temptation. He could not conceive of living without her, and Adam made a choice between God and Eve. He gave up the embrace and sacrificed the oneness he had with God for what he thought was oneness with Eve.

Adam's blindness was the tragedy. He did not realize that without oneness with God, he could not have oneness with Eve. When Adam separated from God there was a separation between male and female. You have to give this careful consideration! Man was created in the image of God, and the woman was created out of the man. When man separated from his oneness with God, his oneness with the female could not continue. It is only because Adam had oneness with God that he could have oneness with Eve, his flesh. Without oneness with God, their oneness with each other deteriorated to a self-satisfying use of each other, resulting in competition and jealousy. The masculine human, being the strongest, now dominates and abuses. The feminine human becomes a tool or instrument for the man's service and pleasure. God created sexuality to complete the man, but without God the destructive force of evil makes man incomplete. What has Adam done? He has chosen sexuality over God. The destruction of this priority entered his home, his life, his children, and his world. It was inevitable!

In our passage Jesus highlights PRIORITY. The problem is not "looking"; it is PRIORITY! There is still more for us to consider.

Focus

Sexuality is the focus of our day, capturing our children at much younger years than before. Ten percent of all thirteen-year-olds have had sex. Half of all teenagers have participated in sex by the time they enter the tenth grade. One out of every five teenage girls will become pregnant. Two-thirds of all young adults finishing high school are already sexually active. We are focused on our sexuality in advertisements, fashions, literature, movies, and even comedy. We are obsessed with our sexuality. Jesus declared this to be the problem in our passage. The problem is not about "looking"; it is about priority!

Listen to our passage again. ***"But I say to you that whoever looks at a woman to lust for her has already committed adultery with her in his heart"*** (Matthew 5:28). Included in this statement, Jesus speaks of looking ***"at her,"*** lusting ***"for her,"*** and committing adultery ***"with her,"*** as He highlights the priority of our sexuality. The Greek word "pros," translated ***"at,"*** is a preposition of direction. This word marks the direction toward or to which something moves or is directed. It carries the idea of "in order to," expressing purpose. Man looks at woman with a distinct perspective in mind. The priority of his life has now become the focus of his "looking." He is dominated by this focus in every aspect of his sexuality.

The Greek word "autos," translated ***"for her,"*** is a pronoun of "self" used as an intensive to emphasize, and sets the woman apart from everything else. "Autos" is used with a proper name as ***"Herod himself"*** (Mark 6:17). Jesus again uses "autos," translated ***"with her,"*** focusing everything on the woman. Each time he use "autos" He highlights "looking." Jesus points out that the intent and purpose of man's sexuality has changed in priority. Man no longer has the original nature God created him nature. His focus is altered!

Jesus is strong in His emphasis on priority. The problem is not in the "looking"; the problem is in the focus of the "looking" and is at the root of Christian experience. Our nature has radically changed from its intended focus. We focus on controlling our desires, relationships, and our physical acts have become depraved. Why do we think dirty jokes are humorous? What attracts us to pornography? We are never satisfied with a little, but our desires increase in degree and intensity. Why would ***"those of old"*** be satisfied with pushing their sexuality aside and look to a rule to control their physical acts? Our focus is wrong! Can Jesus become our focus?

Force

We might tend to think the "focus" of sexuality is proper because it is deeply ingrained in every aspect of our lives. What is wrong with that? No one ever suggested that our sexuality be removed or eliminated. The problem seems to be the "force" of our sexuality, and Jesus highlights this in our passage. The Greek word "blepo," translated *"looks,"* is a participle, a verb serving as an adjective modifying the subject of the main verb, *"has committed adultery." "Whoever"* is a translation of the Greek word "pas ho" meaning "all the," now modified by *"looks."* The subject becomes "all the looking ones." *"Looks"* is also in the present tense, and refers to the continuous process of looking. The problem of concern is not the incidental or involuntary glance but the intentional and repeated gazing, which is the "force" present in the "looking." The Greek word "epithumsai," translated *"lust,"* indicates a goal or an act that follows the "looking." *"Lust"* describes the force of the "looking" in terms of purpose. Sexuality becomes the dominating force in life dictating the purpose of "looking."

James uses strong language to describe the force of lust. He said that it was never God's purpose or in His nature to tempt man to sin (James 1:13). Temptation does not come from God but comes from deep in the nature of man. The force of man's sinful nature drives the desires and perspectives of man. James uses the Greek word "exelko," translated "to drag away." *"But each one is tempted when he is drawn away by his own desires and enticed"* (James 1:14). The sinful nature of man forcibly controls man's looking and drags him away in the act of lust. The sinful nature permeates the perspective that controls physical action.

James says this in the terms of sexuality when He writes, ***"Then, when desire has conceived, it gives birth to sin; and sin, when it is full-grown, brings forth death"*** (James 1:15).

Man can never break the force of sin in his life by a simple decision. ***"Those of old"*** could see no other way to maintain righteousness because they viewed sexuality as an animal drive they could not control. Therefore, they set their boundary to be that of refraining from sexual involvement with their neighbor's wife. All other sexual control was impossible because of the force of this sinful nature. But the force is not in the sexuality. If it were, then we must eliminate sexuality, not redeem it. The force is in the evil self-centered nature that fills man. God created man to be dependent on His nature, and sinful man decided to be independent, depending only on his self-focus and allowing this nature to dominate his sexuality.

Man's sinful nature not only dominates his sexuality, but it dominates his emotions also. Jesus gave six illustrations beginning with "anger" (Matthew 5:21-26). The best ***"those of old"*** could do was to control their anger within the boundaries of not committing murder. No one can love in every situation and forgive everyone because of the force of the sinful nature. The answer to this problem is not in the elimination of our emotions but in the redemption of our emotions through allowing God to remove the self-focus of our nature. So it is with our sexuality!

Jesus proposes a change in our nature. He wants to restore us to God's nature, making us the Kingdom filled with His presence. This proposal is not a call to anger management or a challenge to sexual discipline. This call is to a nature change. The self-centered nature must die. Listen to the cry of Paul. ***"I have been crucified with Christ; it is no longer I who live, but Christ lives in me; and the life which I now live in the flesh I live by faith in the Son of God, who loved me and gave Himself for me"*** (Galatians 2:20).

If the problem is "priority," what is the force of the priority? This is not a new message; it is "self." Self-centeredness focuses on self and is energized by self to satisfy its selfish desires. Sexuality dominated by self (the sinful nature) drives us to use sexuality for self-benefit and self-pleasure. This nature destroys God's purpose and intent of sexuality. I must die to my selfish, self-centered, self-focus.

Finality

There is another aspect of the "priority" in the "finality" of Jesus' statement. Any person who is possessed by his self-centered nature is dragged to a forced focus of self-possessed sexuality, and **"has already committed adultery with her in his heart."** The Greek word "ede," translated "already," means "even now." What happened in the physical "looking" is present in the heart of the person.

We must understand the proper progression of "looking." "Looking" at a woman lustfully does not cause a man to commit adultery in his thoughts. "Looking" does not control the thoughts; however, thoughts control the "looking" but not the heart. The condition of the heart dictates the thoughts, which dictates to the "looking." When lust reaches the "looking," it already exists in the heart, which is the dwelling place of man's nature.

The message was the same in Jesus' first illustration of anger and murder. ***"You shall not murder"*** was the priority of ***"those of old."*** The physical was the best their self-centered, self-sourced nature could conceive on its own. The emotions of anger, temper, and jealousy under self-sourcing must be curbed enough not to commit murder. Curbing emotions is the best self-centered man can do. But Jesus proposed a radical change in man's behavior. When the self-centeredness of man is changed, anger will not have to be controlled because it will cease to exist.

This progression is the same with adultery. Self-centeredness of the heart dominates the sexuality and focuses it on adultery. The thoughts of adultery control the "looking." The thoughts of adultery are controlled by sexuality under the dominance of self-centeredness. Jesus did not propose a removal of sexuality but a restoration of man's nature. This would change man's heart, changing his thoughts and his "looking"!

This restoration is the message of the Kingdom of Heaven. You and I are helpless (Matthew 5:3). We give the appearance of being strong and capable as we attempt to be sourced by our helplessness, yet our failures and brokenness testify to our weakness. Jesus calls us to embrace our helplessness (Matthew 5:4). We are not helpless because we have sinned; we are helpless because of the way God created us. The "Comforter" can invade us only when we embrace our helplessness (Matthew 5:4). This heart alteration changes our perspective; the change in our perspective changes our thoughts; the change in our thoughts changes our "looking." Jesus is our only chance!

Matthew 5:28

IN HIS HEART

"But I say to you that whoever looks at a woman to lust for her has already committed adultery with her in his heart" (Matthew 5:28).

The Scriptures express the focus of God on the heart! Samuel, the prophet, was instructed by God to go to Bethlehem and offer a sacrifice. He was to invite Jesse and his sons to accompany him, because God was going to select a member of this family to be the new king of Israel. Samuel was impressed by one of Jesse's sons, Eliab, because of his stature and his leadership among men. But God said to Samuel, **"Do not look at his appearance or at his physical stature, because I have refused him. For the Lord does not see as man sees; for man looks at the outward appearance, but the Lord looks at the heart"** (1 Samuel 16:7). This verse should give you insight into the importance of the heart in the mind of God as well as the content of the heart.

Have you had a moment when you became aware of how wrong you were about something, and this awareness swept over your life? Have you felt the heaviness of guilt crush in on you making it difficult to breathe? King David had such a moment. He had always been able to justify, excuse, and avoid all sense of responsibility, but when Nathan, the prophet, told a story that revealed truth to David's heart everything changed (2 Samuel 12).

David cried out to God, ***"Create in me a clean heart, O God, and renew a steadfast spirit within me"*** (Psalms 51:10). This was not a cry of David for God to remove a blemish on his face so he would look better, and it was not a cry for financial prosperity. David faced a deep-seated awareness of need in his life. This cry was nothing superficial; David was dealing with his inner heart.

The wisest man in the world of his day said, ***"For as he thinks in his heart, so is he"*** (Proverbs 23:7). There is something powerful about the heart as it reaches in to the essence of our lives and shapes us. Our inner being is not shaped by our physical existence; it is our inner being that sources our lives. What makes this heart so powerful? How can we ignore it for so long? How can our physical existence become so dominating that the heart diminishes in value and importance?

Paul could not have expressed it more clearly. ***"If you confess with your mouth the Lord Jesus and believe in your heart that God has raised Him from the dead, you will be saved. For with the heart one believes unto righteousness, and with the mouth confession is made unto salvation"*** (Romans 10:9-10). What is this heart that determines the salvation of our lives? Does this not tell us what must be our top priority? Should this not be the focus of our being? What about my heart?

Jesus gave six illustrations to secure the understanding of true Kingdom existence. His proposal was so radical that His listeners had to adjust it to fit their level of understanding. How can He move them from ***"those of old"*** to ***"I say to you?"*** These six illustrations are powerful and touch every area of life, clarifying what the Spirit of God produces in man's life.

The only illustration that mentions the heart is the one dealing with sexuality. Does that mean that sexuality is at the core of our existence? Is sexuality so intertwined in every area of life that we cannot dismiss it as a segment of life? Does sexuality have it roots in our heart? Sexuality gives expression to each area of life, dominating language, dress, physical expressions, emotional outbursts, affections, understanding, self, and mannerisms. Is it correct to say that *"looks"* and *"lust"* flow from the heart? The progression of "looking" is important in our passage (Matthew 5:28). A man does not look, lust, and then commit adultery in his heart. He has adultery in his heart, which causes the look of lust. Looking and lusting are expressions of the twisted, self-centered sexuality rooted in man's heart. To correct this condition a change at the heart of sexuality is demanded. Our sexuality is not evil, but the nature of the sexuality is perverted!

The Greek word "kardia," translated "heart," is familiar. ***"For the life of the flesh is in the blood, and I have given it to you upon the altar to make atonement for your souls"*** (Leviticus 17:11). Because blood comes from the heart and flows back to the heart, the heart is the core from which life comes, and it is the center of man's being. We need to investigate this heart idea as it applies to our passage.

Concentration

The heart always has a focus. We use phrases such as: "I love you with all my heart"; "Even though we are separated, you are in my heart"; "My heart's desire is . . ." The heart has become the symbol of Valentine's Day, cards shaped like a heart, candy hearts, and drawings of the heart. Love that focuses on an object is expressed as belonging to the heart.

Love's focus is one of the uses of the Greek word "kardia" in the Scriptures. We make statements that express the object of one's love as something held in the heart. Paul was open with the people of Corinth, crying to them, ***"Open your hearts to us. We have wronged no one, we have corrupted no one, and we have cheated no one. I do not say this to condemn; for I have said before that you are in our hearts, to die together and to*** *live together"* (2 Corinthians 7:2-3). He expressed love to these people because they were in his heart!

Paul had the same feelings for the people of Philippi, remembering their first contact as he shared the Gospel with them. He is grateful for their growth and progress in the faith, confident that God, who started this work in them, would complete it. He said, *"Just as it is right for me to think this of you all, because I have you in my heart, inasmuch as both in my chains and in the defense and confirmation of the gospel, you all are partakers with me of grace"* (Philippians 1:7).

The heart is the dwelling place of the most intimate and loved objects of our lives. My heart controls what I love and do not love. My heart determines the something or someone I will cherish in my life. Christianity is a "heart religion"! Jesus settled the Pharisees' argument about the greatest commandment by quoting the Old Testament. *"You shall love the Lord your God with all your heart, with all your soul, and with all your mind.' This is the first and great commandment. And the second is like it: 'You shall love your neighbor as yourself.' On these two commandments hang all the Law and the Prophets"* (Matthew 22:37-40).

We now have clear insight into our passage (Matthew 5:28). *"Those of old"* saw their sexuality as a body function they had to control, requiring a law, *"You shall not commit adultery."* This law was the acceptable boundary that allowed them to live in their sexuality. The New Covenant view of sexuality is an issue of the heart, because sexuality is a focus or object of the heart! Adultery happens when a man *"looks at a woman to lust for her."* To what *"woman"* does Jesus refer? It can be any woman. The woman is not the love object of the heart; rather, the "looking" man's sexuality is the love object. In other words, the focus or object of the heart is a person's sexuality.

Jesus said that God gave the essence of marriage in the Scriptures. *"Have you not read that He who made them at the beginning 'made them male and female,' and said, 'for this reason a man shall leave his father and mother and be joined to his wife, and the two shall become one flesh?'"* (Matthew 19:4-5). The object of man's heart is to be the "woman" (*wife*) not sexuality. Adultery lives in the heart where the pleasure of sexuality is the object. My illustration for this truth is a boy and girl alone in the moonlight. The boy whispers to the girl, "I love you, so come on!" What would happen if he told the truth? "I love me, so come on!" That line will not get him the desired results, so he lies. Perhaps we really do not know the truth of our hearts. If I really love you I will not risk, hurt, or use you for personal benefit. The object of the heart is not you, but I!

Regardless, the institution of marriage is not the solution to our passage. A husband's heart can worship his sexuality and legally use his wife as an instrument for his selfish pleasure. That is the reason Jesus' focus is not on the physical act of adultery but on the object of the heart's love. When my wife is the object of my heart, my sexuality becomes a beautiful expression of that love, and the intimacy of our "oneness" brings completeness. The heart cannot be satisfied when a person's sexuality is the object of his/her heart.

Our passage proposes a question. What is the object of your heart? Is it your sexuality? Or is your husband or your wife the object of your heart? And if you who are single think this does not apply to you, you are wrong! Jesus calls you His bride, and He is to be the object of your heart!

Contemplation

"Heart language" is a thing of the mind. When a person is moved by facts and truth, we say he is disturbed in his mind. When the mind comes to a new understanding of truth that truth upsets the thought pattern. When we file an event or activity in the back of our mind, we have "hidden it in our heart." We do not discuss it, but constantly think about it. What are the things you have hidden in your heart?

Mary and Joseph experienced many things with Jesus. The event of His birth saw an appearance of angels, shepherds gathering at the manger, and wise men coming from the East bearing expensive gifts. Their escape to Egypt must have been a frightening circumstance for this peasant couple. This escape was to protect Jesus from the hatred of King Herod. When Jesus was twelve years old, they unknowingly left him in Jerusalem as they traveled with friends toward home. When they discovered He was not with them, they frantically searched for three days in Jerusalem only to find Him in the temple. Luke wrote, **"Then He** (Jesus) **went down with them and came to Nazareth, and was subject to them, but His mother kept all these things in her heart"** (Luke 2:51). The Greek word "diatereo," translated "kept," comes from the root word meaning, "to guard or watch." Mary stored all these memories in her heart.

None of this knowledge is new to us. We consistently deal with events in the past that we have "stored up" in our hearts. Circumstances of our childhood, abuses experienced at the hands of others, ridicule by childhood friends, and personal failures haunt us in our hearts. These things are not light or superficial but lie at the core of our being.

Jesus relates our sexuality to our hearts. This relationship is not a surface issue that we can discard as minor. The color of your eyes is not hidden in your heart, never gives you life trauma, and is not tied to the core of your being because the color of your eyes is not a heart issue. Jesus says that our sexuality is extremely different because sexuality is a matter of the heart.

The approach used by **"those of old"** is not adequate. They considered sexuality a body drive to control. All they needed was an adequate rule to guide sexual activity. But Jesus insisted that it was a heart issue. The need of my sexuality cannot be legislated, because it is hidden in the heart. Jesus did not propose eradication or the elimination of sexuality. His cry was for proper understanding and pondering of your sexuality on the heart level. If our response is to ask about the right way to think about sexuality, we find ourselves with another set of rules. Jesus described our sexuality as the core of our "helplessness" (Matthew 5:3). Our helplessness must be filled with His resource. If His resource fills our helplessness, it will radically affect what we keep in our hearts. The proper approach to this problem is not about doing right but about being right.

Let us not forget to note the progression of sexuality in our passage (Matthew 5:28). We do not look, lust, and then commit adultery in our hearts. Adultery is already "hidden in the heart," which produces looking and lusting. Sexuality is in the heart. The question is, "What is the condition of my heart?"

Control

The Gospel accounts reveal the teaching of Jesus, which are filled with "heart language." The Pharisees became frustrated after an all-day controversy with Jesus over Sabbath day rules. They accuse Jesus of being sourced by the power of the devil (Matthew 12:24). Jesus answered their accusation by discussing the heart, the source of all actions. He used illustrations like trees bearing fruit (Matthew 12:33). ***"For out of the abundance of the heart the mouth speaks. A good man out of the good treasure of his heart brings forth good things, and an evil man out of the evil treasure brings forth evil things"*** (Matthew 12:34-35). The mouth speaks from the overflow of the heart. A person does not struggle to know what to speak, looking deep inside and finding nothing, because the heart produces responses, always full and overflowing. The mouth opens and outflows the content of the heart. The heart is in control!

Part Two: Fulfillment of the Kingdom - The Application: Morality

On another occasion, a controversy about defilement rules arose between Jesus and the Pharisees. At the end of the discussion the disciples were afraid that Jesus had offended the Pharisees (Matthew 5:12). *"So Jesus said, 'Are you also still without understanding? Do you not yet understand that whatever enters the mouth goes into the stomach and is eliminated? But those things which proceed out of the mouth come from the heart, and they defile a man. For out of the heart proceed evil thoughts, murders, adulteries, fornications, thefts, false witness, blasphemies'"* (Matthew 15:16-19).

The passages we have just quoted are all repeats of our present passage (Matthew 5:28). The main problem, according to Jesus, is the condition of the heart. *"Those of old"* approached their sexuality as a body appetite to be curbed, requiring discipline. The best they could accomplish was, *"You shall not commit adultery."* The New Covenant is a new way of living. The fullness of the Spirit of Jesus comes to fill the poverty stricken, the helpless heart. When man's helplessness merges with Jesus' nature, the heart takes on a new condition. We become the expression of God's nature. Our sexuality is now filled with the mind of Christ. "Looks" are not the problem! "Lust" is not the problem. What is in control gives expression through the heart. "Lust" is a sourcing issue!

Matthew 5:29-30

ESSENTIALITY: SEVERITY

"If your right eye causes you to sin, pluck it out and cast it from you; for it is more profitable for you that one of your members perish than for your whole body to be cast into hell. And if your right hand causes you to sin, cut it off and cast it from you; for it is more profitable for you that one of your members perish, than for your whole body to be cast into hell" (Matthew 5: 29-30).

Jesus' message is focused and deliberate. His opening verse is dedicated to the perspective of **"those of old"** (Matthew 5:27). Thinking they could never achieve the holiness of God and excusing their inability, **"those of old"** misinterpreted the seventh commandment, **"Thou shalt not commit adultery."** Then Jesus gives His perspective, which is a Spirit-filled man, sourced by God's nature (Matthew 5:28). Adultery is not an act of the physical body but the condition of the inner heart. Sexuality filled with self-sourcing pollutes the life, causing lust in what is seen.

Now Jesus moves on in His message (Matthew 5:29-30), intending to shock, disturb, and frighten the listener to a radical consideration of truth. He gives three concepts that underlie two identical statements. One is ESSENTIALITY of Spirit-sourced sexuality, forcefully highlighting the condition of the heart. Your

Part Two: Fulfillment of the Kingdom - The Application: Morality

spiritual life is more important than anything else! Second, Jesus proposes the ETERNALNESS of the physical body and the link of the spiritual with the physical going beyond the limits of time, an eternal experience. His third element is the EFFECTS of self-sourced sexuality in life. He leaves us without doubt about the severity of His statements as He boldly gives the consequences of self-sourcing. He has no judgment from His heart but reveals His dread and fear about self-sourcing in our lives!

The idea for our present study is the ESSENTIALITY of Spirit-sourced sexuality. Anything we say in this study will be far inferior to Jesus' intention! There is no way we can exaggerate what Jesus says, which may be the reason He uses such illustrations. His cry is, "Nothing is as essential as your spiritual heart condition." His desire is that we respond to His call to spiritual reality despite the cost. We must sacrifice everything; nothing is more valuable than your spiritual heart!

Let us begin with the *"severity"* of Jesus' presentation. At first these two verses seem out of place (Matthew 5:29-30). Is Jesus contradicting Himself? *"Those of old"* placed sexuality within the boundaries of a physical law regulating physical action. Jesus said the problem of spiritual adultery was a matter of the heart. He placed our sexuality in the core of our being and not in the physical eye or hand. Why does He now speak to us about fleshly things?

The TONE of these two verses is important. Jesus words are intense, and no one listening could miss the seriousness in His voice. He is not speaking casually or making a suggestion. I am certain His listeners felt the pressing penetration of His eye contact, and each person felt like they were the only one in the crowd. The Spirit of God surely took these words and drove them into the heart of each listener.

"If your right eye causes you to sin, pluck it out and cast it from you." Does this need an explanation? The Greek word "exaireo," translated *"pluck it out,"* is in the imperative mood,

followed by the Greek word "ballo," translated *"cast it."* Other versions of the Bible translate "exaireo" as "gouge it out" and "ballo" as "throw it out" or "throw it." This language expresses the tone and severity of the problem with sexuality.

"And if your right hand causes you to sin, cut it off and cast it from you." Do we not understand this statement? The Greek word "ekkopson," translated "cut it off," is in the imperative mood, followed by the Greek word "ballo," translated *"cast it."* Jesus' severe tone makes His message loud and clear. Whatever He intends by these statements, He is serious.

The severity of Jesus' intent is not only in His TONE, but also in the fact that His instructions were to *"cast it"* TWICE. Two of the four verses in this illustration go to this severity. You might think that Jesus should have given more explanation to the "looking," "lusting," and "committing" at the heart of the illustration. Matthew wrote this under the inspiration of the Holy Spirit, evidently believing the instructions about the heart condition were adequate. He did not belabor the point but knew his readers needed to understand the severity and importance of the heart's sourcing. The twist of self-centeredness in the heart determines the flow of sexuality in the life. Self-centered sexuality will destroy everything in its path including itself. The Spirit of Jesus must be the source of the life; therefore, sexuality must have the mind of Christ. We cannot overstate this reality!

Jesus states the severity twice in our passage and once later in the Book of Matthew. Jesus teaches His disciples the principles of the cross style (Matthew 16). The last six months of His earthly life and ministry were dedicated to this subject and His twelve disciples. They needed to understand His Messianic role. But the disciples were like the crowds, thinking only of the miracles, power, and position. Jesus is a bleeding, suffering, and dying Messiah. He gives them the first prediction of His death and resurrection (Matthew 16:21).

Part Two: Fulfillment of the Kingdom - The Application: Morality

Moses and Elijah visit with Jesus at the Mount of Transfiguration (Matthew 17:3). Their conversation is a verification of the cross style (Luke 9:31). The law and the prophets (Old Testament Scriptures) testify to this plan. The Father overshadowed the mountain to relay a message to everyone, gave His approval to His Son, and insisted that the disciples listen to Jesus (Matthew 17:5). As Jesus, Peter, James, and John made their way down the mountain, they discussed the coming of the forerunner to the Messiah. The three disciples were unaware that this one called Elijah had already come. They did not recognize John the Baptist as the forerunner of the Messiah. He did no miracles and his ministry ended abruptly with his tragic death! They did not identify John's ministry style with the style of Messiah, but Jesus told them this tragic death was exactly what would happen to Him (Matthew 16:21). John the Baptist verified the cross style by bleeding, suffering, and dying. The nine other disciples left at the base of the mountain failed to deliver a demon-possessed boy. When Jesus arrived He quickly delivered the demon from this young man's life. The disciples asked Jesus privately why they had failed. The answer was obvious; they had failed to embrace the new truth of the cross style (Matthew 17:20). There is no Kingdom ministry outside of the cross style!

Jesus' teaching sessions for the disciples were intended to bring them to the mind of Christ. Instead of heeding His words, the disciples disputed everything He told them. Each disciple was upset and filled with argument regarding their positions in the kingdom of heaven (Matthew 18:1). Each disciple saw himself better than the others, signifying they did not grasp the heart of the Kingdom. What would it take for them to see? Jesus began His instructions again, illustrating the heart of the New Covenant with a child. This child had no rights and could make no demands. He asked for nothing as He snuggled against Jesus' chest in intimate relationship. The surrender of personal rights and losing your life is the standard of the Kingdom (Matthew 18:3).

Then Jesus gives a strong warning to these self-focused disciples. He begins discussing the immature ones just beginning their Christian faith. He warns the disciples about offending one of these (Matthew 18:6). He describes a trap with the trigger set for destruction. Jesus uses the Greek word "skandalise," which is the stick in the trap that causes the destruction and death of its victim. Self-centeredness is like this stick in the trap. Self- centeredness produces handles that the devil can use to control us, causing our actions to destroy the little ones. Like the disciples, we can continue to follow Jesus arguing about our position but little ones will be ruined in the process.

At the moment Jesus gives his self-centered disciples a strong warning, He gives the same two verses in our passage (Matthew 5:29-30). The words are the same except He changes **"right hand"** to **"hand or foot"** and *"right eye"* to *"eye"* (Matthew 18:8-9). In our passage Jesus focuses on "sexuality" (Matthew 5:29-30). Now Jesus focuses on "destroying a little one" (Matthew 18:8-9). What is the connection between these two passages that gave Jesus the right to repeat these two verses of severity?

Maybe you think these are two different subjects. Is the real issue the self-centeredness governing the heart? Self-centeredness dominates the heart that produces sexuality. Sexuality expresses itself in every area of life. My sexuality determines how I walk, my approach to situations, my style of dress, my involvement in relationships, and even seeking positions. The disciples were asking like men, expressing their masculinity, but their sexuality was filled with self-centeredness. What governs the heart dominates sexuality and will cause the person to seek positions. These are not two different subjects at all!

Jesus emphasizes the severity of self-centered sexuality in

our passage. He sets the "TONE" of the passage, gives it "TWICE", and the "TIMING" of the passage verifies the statements of these two verses, conveying that the action of the severity should happen immediately. He does not suggest hesitation, and He does not advise six months of counseling, a forty-day fast, or spiritual discipline classes. He is bold and to the point. In other words, self-centeredness governing the heart creates action through our sexuality that cannot be tolerated. This message is urgent!

The obvious urgency is in the "damage" being done by the self-centered expression. The nature of sin, self-centeredness, permeates the heart. It does not abide there in idleness or neutrality. Self-centeredness overtakes the expression of the heart, which Jesus strongly tells us. If the heart is filled with self-focus, the expression of our sexuality will be self-centeredness. This self-centeredness is not limited to the view of **"those of old."** We cannot limit self-centered sexuality to lusting for a woman in a sexual encounter. Self-centered sexuality moves through every area of masculinity and femininity. Self-centeredness shows up in my cocky walk. I demand my preference not only with my wife but also with my children, my business associates, and in all other relationships. Self-centeredness affects the way I dress, style my hair, and present myself. My life thrives on the fulfillment of gratification, as I demand position and self-recognition. Although Jesus highlights specifically the damage done to the opposite sex (Matthew 5:27-30), it is just as true in my relationship with other disciples in decisions and positions (Matthew 18:1). Self-centeredness dominates my heart and sources the sexuality in my life!

The fallout of self-centered domination is inevitable and incredible. Its destruction is progressive, destroying my relationships repeatedly. Jesus quickly moves to a third illustration of higher righteousness exceeding that of the scribes and Pharisees. It is the illustration of marriage (Matthew 5:31-32). The expression of self-centered sexuality always destroys marriage. Self-centered sexuality never bleeds, suffers, or dies, which is the cross style. The self-centered argument over position and power always brings division in relationships. We do not divide when each of us wants the other to be fulfilled and experience the destiny of God for their life. We divide over what we think we want and need. The same self-centered sexuality destroys our homes, our careers, and our friendships.

Jesus wants all to know the ultimate destruction of self-centeredness. It is *"hell."* Any idea that "hell" will be a fulfillment of our self-centered dreams and a fun party is not in these verses. The severity is in the idea that self-centeredness must be eliminated from our hearts. There is no sacrifice great enough to escape this damage. In each picture, Jesus expresses *"cast it from you."* In other words, whatever self-centeredness uses to bring destruction to your life, you must cut it off and get rid of it. Nothing is worth the present and future destruction of self-centeredness.

The urgency here is that we understand the "designs" of self-centeredness that establishes a permanency in our lives. The severity of self-centered sexuality is in long-range patterns entrenched in the heart of a person. *"Those of old"* had the opposite idea, thinking if they controlled the expression of their body's appetite, "not committing adultery," they could maintain their righteousness. Jesus was concerned with the self-centeredness in the heart, establishing patterns of self-centeredness in the thought process. The self-centered heart dominates the thought process with the desire to use another for personal satisfaction. The cross style pattern is the opposite of self-centeredness. "Lust" cannot thrive on "How can I meet your need?" "Lust" establishes a pattern of abuse as it expresses self-centeredness. "Lust" sees abuse residing in the person who does not meet my needs; they made me do it. Sometimes to even tolerate or receive abuse is self-centeredness. Such a person is not thinking of getting help for their abuser; they are thinking of their need for self and security.

Self-centeredness dominates the heart, and the heart produces sexuality. The designs of self-centeredness become dominate and ingrained in the expressions of the person. Every expression of my masculinity or femininity becomes self-centered. The self-centeredness that produces lust for my neighbor's wife is the same self-centeredness that produced the disciples' desires to dominate their brothers. The argument they had over which of them would be number one was a product of the same design.

Jesus wants us to know that the ultimate deepening and penetration of self-centeredness in our lives will destroy us. He sees the long-range establishment of *"hell."* His view is not one of punishment because we are self-centered but that self-centeredness can overcome our lives. If self-centeredness dominates your sexuality, it expresses itself in every thought and act of your life. Self-centeredness in its final state of growth and fulfillment is *"hell."* When this nature grows through your system and takes over, that is *"hell."* There will never be a better time than now to break the binding control of self-centeredness. It is the plea of Jesus as He calls us to the righteousness of the New Covenant, the indwelling of God's nature.

Matthew 5:29-30

ESSENTIALITY: STUMBLING

> *"If your right eye causes you to sin, pluck it out and cast it from you; for it is more profitable for you that one of your members perish than for your whole body to be cast into hell. And if your right hand causes you to sin, cut it off and cast it from you; for it is more profitable for you that one of your members perish, than for your whole body to be cast into hell" (Matthew 5: 29-30).*

How do you awaken a person sleeping soundly in a burning house? How do you warn someone about to walk over a precipice? How do you get the attention of a fisherman in a boat headed for the falls? What voice do you use when speaking to an addict destroying himself with drugs or alcohol? How do you stop the person flirting with sin? Is the gentle approach adequate in each of these cases? Is it okay to yell in desperation? In our passage Jesus' method is the use of extreme illustrations. He uses violent speech!

Jesus uses instructive verbs, all imperative, in each of His statements, giving the instruction a sense of command, order, and urgency. The logic of His statements has an explanation of urgency. The foundation of His logic is eternal life, taking on a tone of loving compassion. He is not judgmental or condemning in His approach, but He pleads with us to follow His instruction so we will not end in hell, highlighting the emotional involvement coming from His heart of love.

He gives three elements underlying these two identical statements. The first is ESSENTIALITY of Spirit-sourced sexuality, giving the condition of the heart importance. The value of your spiritual life is greater than anything else! He brings into focus the ETERNALNESS of our physical bodies. He links the spiritual intimately with the physical, going beyond the limits of time in an eternal experience. In His third consideration, He warns that the EFFECTS of self-sourced sexuality are a danger to our lives. He so boldly tells of the consequences of self-sourcing that we can feel the severity of His instructions. He has no judgment or condemnation coming from His heart, but we can sense His dread and fear that such will happen in our lives!

The concept for our present study is the ESSENTIALITY of Spirit-sourced sexuality. We will not be able to match the level of these statements. Nothing we can say will equal the forceful yet simple, concise statements of Jesus. My fear is that what we say about them will only degrade the intensity and emphasis Jesus intended. He cries out to us, "Nothing is as essential as the spiritual condition of your heart." He calls us to spiritual success regardless of the cost. Nothing has more value, which means we can sacrifice everything for the sake of our spiritual victory.

Our concentration in our previous study was on the **severity** of these statements, found in the "tone" of Jesus' words. The grammar and general focus of His statements present urgency. The statements are given "twice," which highlights the severity. Jesus presents these statements twice in our passage, but these statements appear one other time in Matthew's Gospel (Matthew 18:8-9). The "timing" of the statements presses us to the urgency of what we must do immediately. There is no room for neglect.

Now we come to the second aspect of the ESSENTIALITY of Spirit-sourced sexuality; it is the **"stumbling block."** You must not be naïve! Never let yourself think there is no enemy. The evil one fights to destroy you because he knows how valuable and important the Spirit-sourced life is! The two statements in our passage are tied to *"looks"* (Matthew 5:28). The Spirit of Jesus determines the view of what we see. We do not always have control over what we see, but the condition of our hearts determines how we think about what we see. The spiritual battle rages on the level of our viewpoint. Will we embrace the mind of Christ?

Jesus speaks with a definite "TONE" in regard to the enemy and the possibility of **stumbling**. He uses the Greek word "skandalizo," translated *"causes you to sin."* In the Greek text, the word **"sin"** is not present; but was placed there in the English to give the idea of the Greek word. This verb is in the active voice and must be treated in the causative sense. It means, "to offend, lead astray, or lead into sin." The act of offending is not to upset, annoy, vex, or irritate; rather, the context of the word is one of violence, destruction, or ruin.

We must not think the English word *"causes"* should be interpreted as "makes" or "forces" someone to sin. "Skandalizo" is the picture of the trigger in a death trap not the wire that forms the cage of the trap, or the bait that lures the animal into the trap, but the stick that holds the door in place. Once the animal enters the cage and disturbs the stick, the door swings shut and kills the animal. In a mousetrap this word refers not to the wood forming the base, or the cheese attracting the mouse, but is the strong wire that holds the spring in place. Once that spring is disturbed, the trap is sprung and the mouse dies.

In our passage Jesus refers to the *"right eye"* and the *"right hand"* as the stick in the death trap. Your eye or your hand cannot destroy your life. These body parts are not sinful and should not be discarded. In this illustration the eye and the hand are symbolic of anything that is used to trap you in a sinful state. Jesus ties these body parts to the sexuality, because "looking" is a function of the eye, Jesus begins with the *"right eye."* The eye is not sinful, because there is nothing sinful about looking, but adultery occurs in the motive of the looking. If the motive of the looking is a product of the heart, should we cut out our heart and cast it from us? No, because the physical heart is not sinful. It is the sinful nature that controls the core of a person.

When we are mastered by our self-centeredness, it infiltrates and dominates our sexuality, which expresses itself in our lives. How can you *"pluck it out and cast it from you?"* We have to take another look at the premise of the Sermon on the Mount. We are helpless, without resource (Matthew 5:3). Will we embrace this helplessness as a mother embraces her grief over losing her child (Matthew 5:4)? When we surrender, we will spiritually experience the equivalent to *"cut it off and cast it from you."* Jesus can then deliver us from ourselves and fill us with His nature! We have to lose ourselves to save ourselves, not just the eye or the hand. It is a desperate measure.

How can I be sure this surrender is true? Jesus repeated it "TWICE," once for the right eye and again for the right hand. Matthew also records Jesus making these references later in another crucial scene (Matthew 18:9-10). In the context of these two statements and after six months of Jesus' ministry with the disciples, He works to prepare them for the coming crucifixion, predicting His death and resurrection three times (Matthew 16:21; 17:22; 20:18). He describes to them the Kingdom of God, but they argue with Him about this for six days. Their self-centeredness keeps them from accepting the bleeding, suffering, and dying of the cross. Even after Moses and Elijah confirm this truth at the Mount of Transfiguration (Matthew 17:3), God, the Father, assures them of this truth (Matthew 17:5). John the Baptist foreran this reality (Matthew 17:11), and the disciples experienced failure in ministry because of their arguing (Matthew 17:20), they still do not understand.

Essentiality: Stumbling | **Matthew 5:29-30**

The disciples reveal their self-centeredness when they come to Jesus, arguing among themselves and demanding He choose one of them for the number one position in the Kingdom (Matthew 18:1). Jesus tells them that they must become like the child sitting on His lap (Matthew 18:2-5). This child is a symbol of helplessness, especially in the culture of Jesus where children had no status. The child is in love with Jesus, and he makes no attempt to do anything on his own. Can we do the same?

Jesus begins to warn the disciples of the consequences of continuing in their self-centeredness. He said, **"Whoever causes one of these little ones who believe in Me to sin, it would be better for him if a millstone were hung around his neck, and he were drowned in the depth of the sea"** (Matthew 18:6). He uses the Greek word "skandalizo," translated **"causes ... to sin."** Self-centeredness gives Satan a foothold in our lives, which he can then use as "a stick in a death trap" for someone who embraces Jesus in helplessness.

Jesus goes on to make an even stronger statement, saying, **"Woe to the world because of offenses! For offenses must come, but woe to that man by whom the offense comes!"** (Matthew 18:7). The Greek word "skandalizo," translated **"offenses,"** is the same word He uses in the previous verse. Jesus warns of many "sticks in death traps" in our world, but we must never be one of them. We cannot tolerate self-centeredness in our lives. Then Jesus repeats to the disciples the two verses from our passage (Matthew 18:8-9).

The same self-centeredness that controls our sexuality expresses itself by demanding position and lording itself over others. Self-centered sexuality will always express itself through self-centered masculinity. The disciples demanded power and control over others. This self-centeredness is a "stick in a death trap," and it will always cause us to sin. In other words, our self-centeredness becomes a trap for others as well as for ourselves. We must allow Jesus to eliminate it; we can never tolerate or control it. We must surrender to Jesus as our only source and embrace our helplessness, whatever the cost.

Jesus gives us a prime example of this in the first prediction of His death and resurrection (Matthew 16:21). He opens His heart to His disciples with the expectation that they will have open and teachable spirits. **"Then Peter took Him aside and began to rebuke Him, saying, 'Far be it from You, Lord; this shall not happen to You!'"** (Matthew 16:22). Peter did not say that He did not believe Jesus was the Messiah, but he rebuked Jesus because he did not see Jesus as the kind of Messiah He was describing. In Peter's mind the Messiah who would deliver Israel could never bleed, suffer, or die. That was not the style of the Messiah. **"But He turned and said to Peter, 'Get behind Me, Satan! You are an offense to Me, for you are not mindful of the things of God, but the things of men'"** (Matthew 16:23). Satan was using Peter to set a trap for Jesus, and Peter had become a "stick in a death trap" for Jesus. Peter became an instrument of the devil.

Returning to our passage, how could Jesus have been more serious with His warning? What other words could He have used to impact us? Self-centeredness controls the heart and will use sexuality to set "a stick in a death trap" for those around us, trapping them and us. Would it be easier to pluck out our right eye or cut off our right hand than to surrender our lives? We must embrace our helplessness as if overcome with grief. There are no traps in surrender. When we are filled with God's nature we know only His freedom and victory!

"TIMING" is another element to consider in **stumbling**. The Greek word "skandalizo," translated *"causes . . . to sin,"* is in the present tense. In the Greek language, the present tense is used when the writer portrays an action in process or a state of being with no assessment of the action's completion. In other words, the action of the verb happens at the present moment and continues into the future, an ongoing experience. The

Essentiality: Stumbling | **Matthew 5:29-30**

action of the verb happens in this present moment, but when this moment becomes a past moment, the action moves into the new present moment. The reality of being "a stick in a death trap" is not something that happened and is now behind us; it is not contained in the boundaries of one evening, a single event, or a moment of weakness. "A stick in a death trap" is an ongoing, always present, occurrence in life.

Our self-centeredness grips and controls the heart flow into our sexuality. Self-centered sexuality continually moves in the activity of being "a stick in a death trap." Self-centeredness is always baiting, alluring, and trapping. This self-centered sexuality is easy to understand in the life of a prostitute because dress, mannerisms, speech, walking and tone of life are to allure and trap. The self-centered prostitute uses sexuality as "a stick in a death trap." We are quick to say, "I am not that way!" Although this may be true in our intent, is it true of our nature? Could it be true that self-centeredness expresses itself throughout your sexuality by dominating your spouse, demanding your own way, becoming angry with your boss, or a thousand other expressions? Perhaps it is not a single expression that you can eliminate, but a tone of your life that is present tense with continual action throughout your life.

If there is any possibility of this being true, can I eliminate it? If every expression of my life is under the control of self-centered sexuality, am I capable of recognizing my condition? How can I take my thousands of self-centered expressions and surrender my heart condition? I can only adjust, compromise, and excuse my actions. My only victory comes in embracing my helplessness and allowing Jesus to conquer my heart!

Self-centered sexuality seems to be a key issue! We often substitute religious reform for crucifixion. We tackle the obvious expressions of self-centered sexuality and admire ourselves for our achievement. We become examples of discipline and religious success. However, these may only be another form of the same self-centered sexuality of the prostitute. These forms being the same is why Jesus was so radical in His imperatives insisting that all expressions of self-centered sexuality have to come to an end. When we approach sexuality as a body drive that can be expressed only within the boundary of not committing adultery, our self-centered sexuality will dominate our lives in all our expressions, and we never confront our heart problem.

Jesus calls us to righteousness beyond the righteousness of the scribes and Pharisees (Matthew 5:20). Religious reform is not His challenge. His premise is that we must embrace our helplessness, and to do this we must abandon the self-centeredness determined to seek only for self. The problem is that we are not capable of this. We are so dominated by self-centeredness that we cannot adequately surrender. Will you join me in posturing ourselves in humility and admit our helplessness? Will we allow the Spirit of Jesus to crucify our self-centeredness and fill us with His nature? This is our only salvation!

Matthew 5:29-30

ESSENTIALITY: SPIRITUAL PRIORITY

> *"If your right eye causes you to sin, pluck it out and cast it from you; for it is more profitable for you that one of your members perish than for your whole body to be cast into hell. And if your right hand causes you to sin, cut it off and cast it from you; for it is more profitable for you that one of your members perish, than for your whole body to be cast into hell" (Matthew 5: 29-30).*

Some things are a mystery, "something that cannot be understood unless someone reveals it to you." Paul used the word often to describe things in the spiritual realm of life (Romans 11:25; 16:25; 1 Corinthians 2:7; 15:51; Ephesians 1:9; 3:3; 5:32; 6:19; Colossians 1:26-27). Jesus used the word "mystery" regarding the Kingdom of Heaven, using parables to reveal **"the mysteries of the kingdom of heaven"** (Matthew 13:11). In the New Testament, the idea of "mysteries" relates to aspects of the spiritual. Although we may not know everything, we can know something!

Our physical sexuality definitely exposes a spiritual mystery. Although other areas of our physical may not reveal the spiritual, that is not true of our sexuality. In this section of the Sermon on the Mount, Jesus gives six illustrations (Matthew 5:21-48), but the illustration of sexuality is the only one where He highlights the heart. The sexuality in my life is distinctly connected to the spiritual.

"Those of old" isolated their sexuality to a simple body appetite they maintained with a law, **"You shall not commit adultery"** (Matthew 5:27). But the New Covenant Man, filled with the Spirit, sees sexuality from a spiritual perspective (Matthew 5:28). That which controls the "heart" controls the "looking." If the heart is self-centered, then every aspect of sexuality is self-centered; the way we walk, talk, flirt, think, see, and act. Adultery happens in the spiritual realm of the heart long before it expresses itself in the physical. We must be filled with the Spirit of Jesus to refrain from adultery.

How serious is this issue? Jesus is serious when He launches into the two verses of our passage (Matthew 5:29-30). The tone of His words is equivalent to "yelling," "pressing," or "demanding," and is filled with urgency, indicating priority. There are three major ideas underlying these two statements. One is the ESSENTIALITY of Spirit-sourced sexuality. Jesus was forceful about the importance of the inner heart's condition. Your spiritual life is above all else in importance! Secondly, He proposed bringing into focus the ETERNALNESS of the physical body. The intimate link of the spiritual with the physical goes far beyond the limits of time; it is eternal. His third consideration regards the EFFECTS of self-sourced sexuality in life. He boldly says the consequences of self-sourcing are severe. There is no judgment or condemnation from His heart. He fears these effects will happen in our lives!

The idea for our present study is the ESSENTIALITY of Spirit-sourced sexuality. We must set aside everything to experience victory in our sexuality. In a previous study, we concentrated on the **severity** of Jesus' statements, His "tone." The grammar and focus of the statements present His urgency. He gives each statement "twice," which highlights the severity. He repeats these statements in a later encounter with His disciples

(Matthew 18:8-9). The "timing" of the statements presses us to the urgency of what we must do immediately. There is no room for neglect.

We also considered the **stumbling block**. Do not be naïve! Never forget there is an enemy! He is fighting to destroy you! Only the Spirit-sourced life can keep you in victory. The "tone" of the blockage is in the Greek word "skandalizo," translated *"causes . . . sin."* "Skandalizo" is the stick in a death trap. Jesus emphasizes this "twice" in our passage and "twice" again in a dispute among the disciples (Matthew 18:8-9). The "timing" of the verb is present tense with continual action. This offense is not an event but a continual alluring or entrapment. The **severity** is connected to the **stumbling block**. The only safe place is in Jesus!

The third aspect of ESSENTIALITY of the Spirit-sourced sexuality is **spiritual priority**. This aspect introduces us to the "mystery" of the Kingdom of God. In the Scriptures an explanation of a spiritual mystery is most often given in the physical. We see this in the parables of Jesus. He explained the Kingdom of God and its spiritual involvement through farming (Matthew 13). The mystery of Jesus' relationship with His bride, the Church, is seen through the physical relationship of marriage (Ephesians 5:32). In our passage, Jesus declared the value of our spiritual lives by comparing it to valuable body parts.

Jesus highlighted the priority of our spiritual lives through the "tone" of the passage. The suggestion of plucking out the right eye or cutting off the right hand suggests a violent act of desperation. The Greek word "exaireo," translated *"pluck out,"* is a compound word, "ek" meaning "from," a movement term, and "haireo" meaning "to take." You would think the suggestion of the violent act of gouging out your eye would be enough to establish the priority of the spiritual parallel. But Jesus added the phrase, *"and cast it from you"* (Matthew 5:29). This adds another dimension to the violent desperation of the act. Jesus

Part Two: Fulfillment of the Kingdom - The Application: Morality

demanded that the instrument of the body that becomes "a stick in a death trap" should not only be gouged out but also thrown far from you. You are to despise this as despicable, contemptible, and loathsome. You are not to treasure it, save it, or have longings for it.

Gouging out your eye should be enough to convince you of His intent, but Jesus continued with another example of the right hand. If your right hand becomes "a stick in a death trap," you must **"cut it off,"** another violent picture. This command is the compound Greek word "ekkopto," which combines "ek" meaning "from or out," a movement term, and "kopto" meaning "to cut." The picture Jesus offers again is unthinkable, the violent act of chopping off your hand. This should convince us that the spiritual realm is far superior in importance to the physical realm. But as before, Jesus adds the statement, **"and cast it from you"** (Matthew 5:30). You must not compromise or hesitate. Any thought of saving or cherishing the hand after cutting it off must be renounced. You are to view it as an instrument of evil to be eliminated.

The Greek word "ballo," translated **"cast,"** is specific. It is used twenty-five times in the New Testament and most often has the tone of violence. However, there is a definite tone each time it is used, the tone of "impulsiveness." We see this in the temptations of Jesus that occurred immediately after He was filled with the Holy Spirit. The devil conveyed Him to the pinnacle of the temple in the holy city (Matthew 4:5). Jesus was ready to launch His earthly ministry and fulfill the call of the Father. What would be His first official act of ministry? The devil suggested a method of sure success, **"If you are the Son of God, throw Yourself down"** (Matthew 4:6). The devil based this suggestion on two Scriptures. The Greek word "ballo," translated **"thrown down,"** carries the suggestion of "impulsiveness." Do not hesitate, do not think about it, and do not consult the Father. Just "do it."

This impulsiveness is the indication in our passage as well! In regard to our spiritual lives, we must not hesitate. We must do whatever is necessary to secure and maintain spiritual victory! We do not need to counsel, discuss, or contemplate the need. The value of your spiritual life is so far superior to the physical realm that it presents no contest. Everything must be treated as insignificant compared to the spiritual. Jesus is the only One to have our focus. Do not allow anything to hinder your seeking Him. He is not a means to an end; He is *the* means and *the* end. He must capture you and me!

Listen to Paul's heart: *"But what things were gain to me, these I have counted loss for Christ. Yet indeed I also count all things loss for the excellence of the knowledge of Christ Jesus my Lord, for whom I have suffered the loss of all things, and count them as rubbish, that I may gain Christ and be found in Him"* (Philippians 3:7-9). The Greek word "skubalon," translated *"rubbish,"* is a compound word, "kusi" that is plural for dogs and "ballo" meaning "to cast." "Skubalon" is the refuse cast off to the packs of wild dogs that feed on the garbage of the city. This is the call of our verse. Everything must be considered unimportant in comparison to your spiritual life. No pride, no relationship, no material thing, no emotional feeling, no tradition, or any other thing will keep me from Him!

We must understand these statements in light of this reality. *"Who shall separate us from the love of Christ? Shall tribulation, or distress, or persecution, or famine, or nakedness, or peril, or sword? As it is written: 'For Your sake we are killed all day long; we are accounted as sheep for the slaughter.' Yet is all these things we are more than conquerors through Him who loved us. For I am persuaded that neither death nor life, nor angels nor principalities nor powers, nor things present nor thing to come, nor height nor depth, nor any other created thing, shall be able to separate us from the love of God which is in Christ Jesus our Lord"* (Romans 8:35-39). Jesus is our priority.

We will pluck out, cut off, and cast from us everything to be His!

Jesus used **spiritual priority** "twice" in our passage sharing the two examples of the *"right eye"* and *"right hand."* The significance is not in the body part; it is in the emphasis on *"right,"* signifying the "instrument of performance!" For instance, in important transactions when action must be determined, resolute, and involve the full participation of the doer, the right hand is used. Also when the full energy and emphasis of a person are intended, the right hand is used (Revelation 1:16, 17, 20; 2:1; 5:1, 7). The right eye or right hand becomes the symbol of focus for the total person.

In this illustration, Jesus' message is that my sexuality has spiritual priority. Sexuality is not one among many body drives I can control with a rule. Sexuality is integrated into every aspect of my life, rooted in the heart, the core of my being. Sexuality flows into every expression of my being and has high priority because it controls the action of my life in the spiritual realm, expressing itself in the physical realm. Jesus spoke about the right eye and right hand, confronting the expression of my being. Sexuality has spiritual priority. Whatever it takes for my life to be filled with the Spirit of Jesus, I must do it. Jesus not only expressed this in words but also physically gave Himself. I must do the same!

Jesus' emphasis on *"right"* also signifies the "instrument of power!" The whole person is claimed by the right hand, whether in action or in suffering (Psalms 109:6, 31; Acts 2:25). The significance is not on the body part but on the person's power of expression. Sexuality is the power basis of our manipulation of each other and the basis of advertisement and selling. Sexuality is an instrument of manipulation in marriage. We use sexuality as a bargaining tool to dominate and secure our own way. No wonder Jesus cried out about this flow of power in our lives. The problem is not in the power of our sexuality because our sexuality is a result of our creation. The problem is in what nature controls this power. Are we filled with self-centeredness or the Spirit of Jesus? This filling is the heart of our spiritual priority.

The biblical "instrument of position" is the **"right."** A person of high rank who puts someone on his right hand gives him equal honor with himself and recognizes him with equal dignity (Matthew 20:21, 23; 22:44; 26:64; 27:38). Jesus sees our sexuality as an expression of this honor. In marriage extreme honor is placed on the woman. As the husband honors his own flesh, so he honors his wife. Paul uses the imagery of Jesus' relationship and involvement with the church. The husband is to love his wife as his own body; he loves his wife as he loves himself (Ephesians 5:28-31). Jesus again highlights spiritual priority. Our spiritual nature, which controls our sexuality, determines the honor and value of our sexuality.

Jesus climaxed each of these statements with the issue of "timing." Spiritual priority is determined by "timing." Sexuality dominated by self-centeredness is temporary; it will destroy itself. Self-sourced sexuality soon finds the years have passed, and the beauty and sexual attractiveness a person dedicated themselves to have slipped away. The spiritual life that matters forever was neglected. It does not take long until we say, "I used to." I used to be a star; I used to hold the high position; I used to impress people with my looks. Life quickly becomes a memory of what we used to do and be, and it is an expression of sexuality filled with self.

Although the illustration Jesus uses is physical (eye or hand), the issue is the spiritual. We must apply the logic of the physical world to the spiritual world. It is better to be without an eye or hand in this physical life than for your whole body to perish in spiritual hell. The priority is not in the physical but in the spiritual. These two verses bring into perspective the contrast between **"those of old"** (Matthew 5:27) and **"But I say to you"** (Matthew 5:28). This contrast is not a discussion about controlling a body appetite with a rule. Sexuality is an issue of the heart that flows from the core of mankind into every expression of life. Our thinking, perspective, approach, walk, talk, dress, attitude, how we respond, what we eat, and what we desire are all influenced by our sexuality. This influence comes from the helpless heart, and this heart will be controlled either by the nature of Jesus or by our self-centeredness. This control is a spiritual issue.

These two verses cry out the *severity* of our situation. We cannot control our sexuality by a rule about physical activity. We must approach our sexuality with a spirit of desperation. Sexuality is not one problem among many, but it is many problems brought down to the single problem of our nature. We must overcome or eliminate every **stumbling block**. The Spirit of Jesus will enable us. Nothing can stop us from being His. A new nature is ours for the asking; we can be reborn! Do not be fooled by the emphasis of old on a rule about a physical appetite. This new nature is a **spiritual priority.** This is not about a moment or moments of pleasure, but it is the fulfillment of our lives forever. Jesus is our new nature!

Matthew 5:29-30

PROPOSITION OF ETERNITY

"If your right eye causes you to sin, pluck it out and cast it from you; for it is more profitable for you that one of your members perish than for your whole body to be cast into hell. And if your right hand causes you to sin, cut it off and cast it from you; for it is more profitable for you that one of your members perish, than for your whole body to be cast into hell" (Matthew 5: 29-30).

Eternal life is a marvel! Eternity is "the merciful Trinity God giving us a state of blessedness in His presence that endures without end." This state of blessedness is the quality of life in this age and the quality and duration of life in the age to come. Paul highlighted this when he said, **"Blessed be the God and Father of our Lord Jesus Christ, who has blessed us with every spiritual blessing in the heavenly places in Christ"** (Ephesians 1:3).

Bible scholars contradict each other concerning eternal life in the Old Testament. Some propose the absence of awareness of the eternal state. However, the Old Testament clearly declares, "God is eternal" (Deuteronomy 33:27; Psalms 10:16; 48:14). Our Lord is the Rock Eternal (Isaiah 26:4) and the eternal King (Jeremiah 10:10). God's word, rooted in His being and will, is likewise eternal (Psalms 119:89), as are His righteous laws (Psalms 119:60), His ways (Habakkuk 3:6), and His kingdom or dominion (Daniel 4:3, 34). God is eternal; therefore, His love (1 Kings 10:9), His blessings (Psalms 21:6), and all His attributes and blessings are eternal. As long as God exists, so do they! "His mercy endures forever" is repeated twenty-six times in Psalms (136). "Forever" describes His reign (Psalms 9:7), His protection, (Psalms 12:7), His plan (Psalms 33:11), the inheritance of His people (Psalms 37:18), His throne (Psalms 45:19), His rule (Psalms 66:7), His covenant (Psalms 105:8), His righteousness (Psalms 111:3), His faithfulness (Psalms 117:2), His statutes (Psalms 119:111, 152), and His name (Psalms 135:13).

If God is eternal, what are His children's possibilities? The progressive revelation of the Scriptures brings us into the New Testament view of eternity where eternal life is the dominant theme. Eternity describes the time that God's favor extends to His people, and the quality of existence they are to experience in His fullness. We must not confuse eternal life with endless existence, which all have, saved and unsaved. Natural life is subject to death, and we derive it through human existence. Eternal life comes through the indwelling nature of God's Spirit. Therefore, separation from God is eternal death, and union with Jesus' Spirit is eternal life. Augustine said, "Join thyself to the eternal God, and thou wilt be eternal."

Nicodemus came to Jesus in the night hour for a conversation on eternal life. The heart of their discussion produced the most memorized verse in the Scriptures. *"And as Moses lifted up the serpent in the wilderness, even so must the Son of Man be lifted up, that whoever believes in Him should not perish but have eternal life. For God so loved the world that He gave His only begotten Son, that whoever believes in Him should not perish but have everlasting life"* (John 3:14-16).

On a journey through Samaria, Jesus talked with a Samaritan woman. He assured her that trust in Him would relieve the thirst of her soul; she would receive, *"a fountain of water springing up into everlasting life"* (John 4:14). Jesus defined eternal life in His high priestly prayer. *"And this is eternal life, that they may know You, the only true God, and Jesus Christ whom You have sent"* (John 17:3). Eternal life results from an intimate relationship with the eternal God!

The Greek word "monai," translated "eternal" or "everlasting," appears six times in the Gospel of Matthew. It is the heart's cry of a Rich Young Ruler who came running to Jesus with a question about his life. ***"Good Teacher, what good thing shall I do that I may have eternal life?"*** (Matthew 19:16). This encounter between Jesus and the Rich Young Ruler concerned the disciples. They wondered what they should consider since they had left everything to follow Jesus. Jesus said, ***"And everyone who has left houses or brothers or sisters or father or mother or wife or children or lands, for My name's sake, shall receive a hundredfold, and inherit eternal life"*** (Matthew 19:29).

Jesus emphasized the word eternal in the parable of the judgment, saying the sheep will be separated from the goats. ***"Then He will also say to those on the left hand, 'Depart from Me, you cursed, into the everlasting fire prepared for the devil and his angels"*** (Matthew 25:41). The goats will depart because they did not recognize Jesus in the hungry and thirsty around them. The Jesus said, ***"And these will go away into everlasting punishment, but the righteous into eternal life"*** (Matthew 25:46). In this parable Jesus distinguished the forever life of the unsaved with the eternal life of the saved.

The words "eternal" or "everlasting" are not used in our passage (Matthew 5:29-30). When Jesus quotes this passage a second time, He inserts this word. The disciples were arguing over position, demanding that Jesus choose one of them to be the leader. He urged them to become as little children without rights. If they did not die to their self-centered nature, they would be an offense to the little ones. The results of this were severe and unthinkable. He cried, ***"If your hand or foot causes you to sin, cut it off and cast it from you. It is better for you to enter into life lame or maimed, rather than having two hands or two feet, to be cast into the everlasting fire"*** (Matthew 18:8).

Here Jesus interprets the word *"hell,"* referring to the eternal state of a person.

There is a TONE to our proposition of eternity. In our passage Jesus definitely relies on the logic of the reality of eternity. If you and I are not going to live forever, then Jesus' statement has no impact on us. The logic is that we would be better to spend a few years in this present life without an eye or a hand, than to live eternally in a place of torment with all our body parts intact. However, this makes sense only if we are going to live forever.

Jesus surrounds our sexuality with eternity! His approach revolves around the idea of *"it is more profitable,"* a translation of the Greek word "sumpherei." This word is used in various ways fifteen times in the New Testament. "Sumpherei" is a compound word, "sun" means "to gather," and "phero" means "to bring." However, it is used in this sense only one place in the New Testament (Acts 19:19). The other uses highlight the ideas of "profitable, advantageous, to contribute, to bring together for the benefit of another."

The strength of the Greek word "sumpherei" is found in the context of the passage. Jesus uses this word in exaggerated or outlandish figures of speech. *"Whoever causes one of these little ones who believe in Me to sin, it would be better for him if a millstone were hung around his neck, and he were drowned in the depth of the sea"* (Matthew 18:6). Jesus is not declaring the punishment for offending a little one, rather He suggests that before we offend a little one, we should get a millstone around our neck and drown ourselves. This severe suggestion would be an advantage to us! It is exaggerated language illustrating how profitable it is not to offend a little one.

Jesus gives the disciples and the crowds the binding qualities of oneness in marriage. I must lose my life to enter marriage. The only reason Moses commanded to give a certificate of divorce was because, *"of the hardness of your hearts"* (Matthew 19:8). The disciples' response was revealing. *"If such is the case of*

the man with his wife, it is better (sumphero) ***not to marry"*** (Matthew 19:10). They were saying that there was no profit for them in marriage if they could not use their wives to their advantage. Jesus then uses exaggerated language about the eunuchs (Matthew 19:11-12). Jesus took an unequivocal stance on divorce (no more divorce); this is contrasted with the human excuses (then better for no marriage at all). The difference is that in the first instance there is a genuine "spiritual" advantage or benefit, whereas in the second there is merely an "earthly-human" one.

Jesus uses the same exaggerated and outlandish language in our passage. The suggestion of plucking out your eye and casting it away or cutting off your hand and throwing it is unthinkable. But it is reasonable in light of eternity. If you adequately understand the present in contrast with forever, you would not hesitate. You and I must not be shortsighted by the present. We must see everything in view of eternity!

The advantage is in eternity. Jesus clearly says this in His purpose clause. He introduces eternity with the Greek word "iva," translated "that." The severity of removing everything that blocks my embrace of His resource is for one purpose, for my profit and advantage. The purpose is, ***"that one of your members perish, than for your whole body to be cast into hell"*** (Matthew 5:29-30). This issue is eternity! You are going to live forever; what will be the quality of your life? The state of your eternalness is worth every sacrifice in the present. Nothing must hold a higher priority in your life now than your spiritual destiny then!

In greeting another person, we often ask, "How are your doing?" "One day at a time," is a common answer. We are living in the "now" generation because we want everything "now." We determine our priorities by what is pleasurable in the present, what seems acceptable and good for the moment. But this has been a problem for every generation. Jesus struck a blow at the heart of this concept when He declared there is an eternity!

We must understand the proposition of eternity in view of TWICE. In previous studies we discovered that Jesus proposed this idea twice (Matthew 5:29-30). In the first statement the focus regarded *"your right eye"* (Matthew 5:29). In the second statement the focus regarded *"your right hand."* It seems Jesus carefully selected each of these statements concerning sexuality.

There is significance to the *"right eye"* and the *"right hand."* Each *"right"* presents a powerful and important instrument of life, the frontline, and the first body part engaging our sexuality. The *"right eye"* is the power eye and is the eye used for long distance and gives the body a complete view of life. Therefore, the eye conveys the viewpoint affecting the response of the rest of the body, and Jesus suggested it in relation to our sexuality. It is about *"looks," "lust,"* and *"committed."* The eye, under the domination of the heart, controls all this. What if the eye supplies wrong information to the body? Instead of the eye grasping the long-range view for the body, it is shortsighted, seeing only the immediate and inappropriate response.

Jesus pleads with us to have the long-range view. We must see and understand the immediate in light of the eternal. If we sacrifice the eternal future for immediate satisfaction, we are of all people the most miserable. This emphasis was not a single focus for Jesus, but He continually highlighted it in His ministry. Jesus told a parable of a rich man whose crops were in abundance, and he did not have enough room to store them all. His right eye was shortsighted causing him to conclude only one solution; he must pull down his barns and build bigger ones. His larger, well-stocked barns gave him a false sense of security. Thinking he had many goods laid up for years to come, he lounged in his false security. He decided to take his ease, *"eat, drink, and be merry"* (Luke 12:16-21). That night his soul was required of him. What then happened to all the treasure he had stored? His right eye had failed him!

The ***"right hand"*** is considered to be the hand of power. The "right hand" is used nine times in the Gospel of Matthew; seven of those refer to its power. The mother of two of Jesus' disciples sought the right-hand position for one of her sons (Matthew 20:21). Jesus quoted the Psalms to the Pharisees, ***"The Lord said to my Lord, 'sit at My right hand, till I make Your enemies Your footstool'"?*** (Matthew 22:44). In the parables of judgment, Jesus spoke of separating the sheep from the goats by placing them on the right hand (Matthew 25:33-34). In the final trials of His life, Jesus said to the Sanhedrin, ***"Nevertheless, I say to you, hereafter you will see the Son of Man sitting at the right hand of the Power, and coming on the clouds of heaven"*** (Matthew 26:64). The soldiers in the Praetorium mocked Jesus as a King. They put a scarlet robe around His shoulders, a crown of thorns on His head, and a reed in His right hand (Matthew 27:27-31).

The right hand and the right eye are to protect us from the swift approach of eternal hell. But when the right eye fails to see the long-range view and cares only for the moment, you are led astray. When the power of our life (right hand) focuses its strength on the moment and misses the eternal values, you are damned. We are stripped of all caution and cascade through the days of our lives unaware of eternal values. Stop this process; whatever you have to do to gain proper perspective, do it!

We must see the proposition of eternity in light of TIMING. Your sexuality and its expression must never be considered private or without consequence. Is there any doubt that Jesus warns us about present moments affecting eternal moments? As the condition of the heart determines the expressions of our sexuality, so the combined expression of our lives determines the destiny of our eternity. It is as if this present life is a period of probation, which has long-range eternal consequences. This life with all of its involvements sets the stage for the eternity of your life!

Part Two: Fulfillment of the Kingdom - The Application: Morality

These forceful thoughts should produce concern and fear in the hearts of men. The Rich Young Ruler runs to Jesus crying, **"Good Teacher, what good thing shall I do that I may have eternal life?"** (Matthew 19:16). This young man had everything life could offer. He was wealthy and lacked nothing in the materialistic realm. He had position and authority; therefore, he experienced self-esteem and self-worth. Yet, there was a deep-seated awareness that something was missing; there was more involved than just this life. This life with all its involvements is preparatory for the "forever" to come.

"Those of old" viewed their sexuality as an appetite to be regulated and controlled. They placed a boundary around its expression, **"You shall not commit adultery."** Jesus did not give another rule not even an intensified rule, "You shall not look **at a woman to lust for her."** He applied the basic premise of the Sermon on the Mount to the sexuality affecting life. We are **"poor in spirit"** (Matthew 5:3). We must embrace our helplessness with mourning (Matthew 5:4). When we live in our helplessness, we open the doors of our heart for the Spirit of Jesus to invade our lives, and we become the new creature called **"the kingdom of heaven."** Our helplessness filled with His presence produces a new view of sexuality. We change our dress, our manner of walking, our approach to life, our attitudes, our view of marriage, and the way we treat those of a different gender. Entering this Kingdom of Heaven is the essence of eternal life. We have entered into the spiritual realm of the eternities.

Matthew 5:29-30

PLACES OF ETERNITY

> *"If your right eye causes you to sin, pluck it out and cast it from you; for it is more profitable for you that one of your members perish than for your whole body to be cast into hell. And if your right hand causes you to sin, cut it off and cast it from you; for it is more profitable for you that one of your members perish, than for your whole body to be cast into hell" (Matthew 5: 29-30).*

To understand any part of the Sermon on the Mount, we must yield to the basic premise of the sermon. Jesus did not give a series of random thoughts. He began with a premise, and every thought that followed complemented the premise. He proposed the helplessness of humanity (Matthew 5:3). We are poor with no resource. He never speaks of our talents, finances, or thoughts; we are poverty stricken in our "spirit." This helplessness is not a result of our sin, but it is the purpose of God's plan for us. We are to embrace this as we embrace the grief of losing a loved one (Matthew 5:4). In this embrace Jesus merges in oneness with us, and together we become the Kingdom of Heaven.

    The opposite of this embrace becomes a place called **"hell."** Jesus is implicit about our lack of embrace, and the severity of the passage is contained in this problem. Our sexuality must embrace Jesus in oneness, sacrificing anything that hinders this oneness. Refusing this embrace will bring us to **"hell."** Jesus does not use *"hell"* as a fear technique, but that does not mean it should not frighten us.

It will help us to understand some fundamental biblical definitions. The word "eternity" is a basic idea in the Scriptures, but we may not understand it properly. This English word does not appear anywhere in the New International Version. In the New King James Version (Acts 15:8), it is used once and twice in the New American Standard Version (2 Timothy 1:9; 2 Peter 3:18). "Eternity" is a translation of the Greek word "aion." "Aion," translated "age," "world," "ever," and "forever," appears 126 times in the New Testament. It refers to a definite period called an "age" or "time," and it is in contrast with "kosmos" that refers to "people" or "space." Therefore, eternity is duration of time whether endless or limited. We are living in a period, an age. This age will end, and we will enter into an endless age.

We must properly understand the word "eternal." "Eternal" is most often translated from the Greek word "aionios," a form of the word "aion," speaking of the entirety of an age. This definition is true whether the new age ends or is endless in time. Paul said, *"While we do not look at the things which are seen, but at the things which are not seen. For the things which are seen are temporary* (proskairos*), but the things which are not seen are eternal* (aionios*)"* (2 Corinthians 4:18). The things that we see do not last the duration of this age (aion), but the unseen things last the duration of the eternal age (aionios).

When the Greek words "aionios" and "zoe" are combined, the translation is *"eternal life"* (John 3:16). The merging of Jesus and the believer generates eternal life, a focus more on the quality of life in the believer than the duration. This life is more than its duration, and is vastly different from the natural life of man because God's life generates the believer. John declared that life is present in the believer during the present age (aion). Jesus said, *"Most assuredly, I say to you, he who hears My word and believes in Him who sent Me has everlasting life, and shall not come into judgment, but has passed from death into life"* (John 5:24). In Jesus' high priestly prayer, He cried, *"And this is eternal life, that they may know You, the only true God, and Jesus Christ whom You have sent"* (John 17:3).

With this understanding of eternity, let us look at our passage. In the TONE of Jesus' severity, He makes a primary assumption. He did not need to explain it to those listening because they all understood. Jesus assumes everyone lives forever! All six illustrations (Matthew 5:21-48) prompted the truth of one statement, *"For I say to you, that unless your righteousness exceeds the righteousness of the scribes and Pharisees, you will by no means enter the kingdom of heaven"* (Matthew 5:20). According to the understanding and teachings of *"those of old,"* this would be impossible. From the legalistic approach of relationship with God, no one could dedicate themselves more than the scribes and Pharisees. But in the New Covenant the law is fulfilled in relationship. Our helplessness is filled with His presence; the empowerment for living happens on a new level.

How does this relate to our sexuality? *"Those of old"* viewed their sexuality as a body drive. Sin was involved only when the boundary placed on that drive was violated. A person must not go beyond the limit of satisfying that drive, *"You shall not commit adultery."* A passionate Jesus tried to explain that this problem is greater than breaking a rule. Sexuality is an issue of the heart. This means the heart, which you are, is expressed through your sexuality. If lust is involved in your looking, it is because you have self-centered sexuality in your heart, and adultery is present in the nature of your sexuality rather than the activity. What adultery is in the physical, self-centered sexuality is in the spiritual. Because the problem is the self-sourcing nature of the heart, the adultery of the heart may be expressed in the way you walk, talk, dress, approach life, or look at those of the opposite gender. Because you are an eternal being, this expression of who you are will exist forever.

Jesus' logic was simple and indisputable. Because you will live forever beyond this age and in the age that never ends, you would be better to be without a right eye or a right hand in this short age than to be constantly destroyed by self-centered sexuality in the age to come. The logic of His statement depends on the fact that everyone is going to live forever! To the Jews who were plotting to kill Him, Jesus said, ***"Do not marvel at this; for the hour is coming in which all who are in the graves will hear His voice and come forth — those who have done good, to the resurrection of life, and those who have done evil, to the resurrection of condemnation"*** (John 5:28-29). The righteous and the unrighteous live forever. Endless life is never the issue of the Scriptures. Everyone lives forever. The eternal age is not the continuation of life but the quality of life.

The continuation of life forever is a major issue! If a person makes careful plans for retirement, will he or she not more carefully plan for the eternal days of the age to come? Thoughts of how will I live, what if I am sick, or what resources will I need compel me to prepare for when we become senior adults. How much more does the eternal age demand our preparation? You and I are going to live forever!

Jesus taught the endless age, but He also proved the endless age by His resurrection. Some in the early Church who were concerned about their loved ones who died before them. They were expecting Jesus to return immediately the second time. However, when He did not, some of them died. Paul declared the continual message of the early Church as, ***"Christ is preached that He has been raised from the dead"*** (1 Corinthians 15:12). If so, why would anyone among us propose there is no resurrection of the dead? The logic is that if there is no resurrection of the dead then Jesus is not raised from the dead. If He is not raised from the dead, we are liars, and our preaching and our faith are empty (1 Corinthians 15:14-15).

The Pharisees were the force behind the crucifixion of

Jesus. But the Book of Acts records that the Sadducees were the force of the persecution of the early Church. The message of the early Church was the resurrection of Jesus from the dead. If you embraced this resurrection that meant there is a resurrection from the dead and life beyond this short age. When being judged by the council, Paul proclaimed, ***"Men and brethren, I am a Pharisee, the son of a Pharisee; concerning the hope and resurrection of the dead I am being judged!"*** (Acts 23:6). This split the council because the Pharisees embraced the resurrection of the dead but the Sadducees did not. If you acknowledge the resurrection of Jesus, you must acknowledge the resurrection of every person. Everyone will live forever in the endless age to come.

This brings us to another conclusion of Jesus in our passage, the reality of TWICE. According to Jesus, there are only two destinations in which one may dwell in the coming endless age. We must continually remember that Jesus does not condemn or threaten. In our passage Jesus' approach is one of compassion and concern. Immediately after the Sermon on the Mount, Jesus went with His disciples to the cities and villages. ***"But when He saw the multitudes, He was moved with compassion for them, because they were weary and scattered, like sheep having no shepherd"*** (Matthew 9:36-37). He saw them under the weight of the leadership of ***"those of old."*** The burden of legalism was crushing them. He viewed them as they made their way to destruction with no shepherd, and He pleaded with them in the Sermon on the Mount.

In the first two illustrations, Jesus highlighted hell. In discussing the incarnation of Jesus, the Hebrew writer declared Jesus' victory over death. Through death He destroyed the one who had the power over death. In this context the writer declared, ***"For indeed He does not give aid to angels, but He does give aid to the seed of Abraham"*** (Hebrews 2:16-17). When the angels rebelled against God, their destruction was determined. God made no attempt to redeem or forgive them.

However, when mankind sinned, God spared not His Son! The resource of the Trinity God focused on restoring us! This is why Jesus said in the parables of judgment, *"Then He will also say to those on the left hand, 'Depart from Me, you cursed, into the everlasting fire prepared for the devil and his angels'"* (Matthew 25:41-42). Hell was not prepared for man! Redemption was intended for man!

Jesus gave a further description of hell in the parables of judgment. *"And these will go away into everlasting punishment, but the righteous into eternal life"* (Matthew 25:46). The Greek word for *"everlasting"* is "aionios," describing the time of the endless age to come. We must properly understand the word *"punishment."* Two Greek words are translated "punishment," "timoria" and "kolasis." They may not differ in what the person being punished experiences, but they vastly differ in motive or intent of the one responsible for the punishment.

"Timoria" comes from classical Greek; it carries the predominant thought of the vindictive character of the punishment. This kind of punishment satisfies the inflictor's sense of outraged justice in defending his honor or that of the violated law. "Kolasis" is the Greek word used here (Matthew 25:46). It conveys the notion of punishment for the correction and bettering of the offender, but when "aionios" (everlasting) is included, it equals *"hell."* This is a final punishment from which we cannot return. However, there remains an important distinction between these two Greek words. In "kolasis" the relationship of the punishment is to the one being punished, and in "timoria" the relationship is to the punisher. In other words, the punishment of *"hell"* is not something forced on an individual because God is offended. The punishment is a direct result of the individual's choice; they embrace the punishment as a part of their lifestyle and choice.

The place of man's eternity was the intent of Jesus throughout the Sermon on the Mount. He highlighted the two possibilities of the endless age to come. As He closed the Sermon on the Mount, He spoke of those who proclaimed what they did in His name. He *"will declare to them, 'I never knew you; depart from Me, you who practice lawlessness!'"* (Matthew 7:23). These individuals had no relationship with Jesus, but they did have relationship with their lawlessness; thus, they will experience the consequences of this relationship. This relationship is the *"hell"* of our passage (Matthew 5:29-30).

We must not miss the TIMING of Jesus' conclusion. Jesus proposed that everyone lives forever in the endless age to come with the option of dwelling in one of two places. The one being emphasized in our passage is *"hell."* This place is not the result of the vindictive desire of Jesus but is the result of a person's choice. The choice we make in this age of time will determine our destination in the endless age to follow. The subject we are discussing is sexuality. Achievement of the standard of *"those of old"* will not suffice for the New Covenant, the Kingdom of Heaven. Jesus makes this plain with His challenge of a righteousness exceeding the righteousness of the scribes and Pharisees (Matthew 5:20). The choice is about embracing (mourning) our helplessness (poor in spirit). If this does not happen, we will remain self-sourced in our hearts, which will permeate our expression of sexuality including our viewpoint (looks).

If self-sourcing is maintained in this "time age," you will cross into the endless age with the focus of the condition you have maintained. Whether the crossing is death or Jesus' second coming, you will maintain the self-centered focus of your sexuality. Death does not save you; it is the blood of Jesus that transforms your inner heart. The focus of your life going into death is the focus of your life coming out of death into the endless age. Death does not afford you the option of change!

Involved in self-centeredness is the continual expansion of the focus. Even in this life, the self-centered focus in our sexuality cannot be limited or even maintained at a minimum because it is continually expanding. What satisfied the lust of your inner heart yesterday does not satisfy it today. The need is like a growing cancer that devours your life. When you view this from the perspective of the endless age, the raging lust of the inner heart filled with self-centeredness expands for unlimited ages to destroy all decency, morality, and relationship. You are warped, twisted, and completely dominated by your self-centered lust that cannot be satisfied. You have embraced your *"hell."*

Jesus cried, "Whatever is necessary to experience the Kingdom of Heaven, do it!" No self-centeredness can be tolerated! The inner self-centered heart must not be protected or pampered; pride must be radically exposed, and helplessness must be embraced. In this short age, there is no self-centered satisfaction worth the destruction of your self-centeredness in the endless age to come. This is a call to embrace Jesus!

Matthew 5:29-30

PHYSICAL ETERNITY

"If your right eye causes you to sin, pluck it out and cast it from you; for it is more profitable for you that one of your members perish than for your whole body to be cast into hell. And if your right hand causes you to sin, cut it off and cast it from you; for it is more profitable for you that one of your members perish, than for your whole body to be cast into hell" (Matthew 5: 29-30).

Many subjects were ignored in my religious training. I am not sure that the choice to ignore certain subjects was purposeful or the focus was on other important issues, but the result of this ignorance was assumptions. The knowledge of the things we talked about filtered into those areas we did not discuss. This caused me to assume many things that contradicted each other but were still accepted. Because we never spoke of these assumptions, there was never any correction.

One of these subjects was the extension of time into eternity. I understood from my training that Christians would live forever. Non-Christians would dwell in hell, but I was never told that they would live forever. We never discussed the reality of everyone living forever and being resurrected from the dead (John 5:29). Although living forever is a benefit for the Christian, the quality of that forever life is the ultimate experience. As we have discovered in these studies, everyone lives forever; everyone will be raised from the dead.

Part Two: Fulfillment of the Kingdom - The Application: Morality

In what state will I dwell in my eternal life? I fear in our assumptions we have viewed the physical body as negative and an instrument of temptation because it is under the curse of sin. The deeds of sin that require physical action are directly connected to the physical. Even the sins of the spirit demonstrate themselves in the physical body. The limitation of the physical body such as sickness, tiredness, weakness, and pain contribute to the negative view. It becomes easy to assume that my eternal state will not have limitations of a body, but this assumption is wrong! In the context of a human body, Adam lived in intimacy with God before he sinned. God viewed His creation of Adam's physical being as good (Genesis 1:31).

Listen to the TONE of our passage. The presence of the physical body is unmistakable. Jesus referred to various parts of the body in the present and the *"whole body"* in the eternal. He did not reference our soul, spirit, or mind dwelling in hell. The issue is the *"whole body"* (holos soma). To understand the significance of Jesus' statement, we must investigate the Greek word "soma," translated *"body."* Its use in the New Testament is covered in four basic ideas.

One thought is "the complete person." "Soma" expresses the identity of the whole person as an entity before God, the inner person and the physical form. Paul challenged us, *"I beseech you therefore, brethren, by the mercies of God, that you present your bodies* (soma) *a living sacrifice, holy, acceptable to God, which is your reasonable service"* (Romans 12:1). In regard to Paul's personal dedication to Jesus, he said, *"But I discipline my body* (soma) *and bring it into subjection, lest, when I have preached to others, I myself should become disqualified"* (1 Corinthians 9:27).

We must align our perspective of "body" (soma) with the incarnation. The writers of the New Testament accepted the humanity of Jesus (Romans 7:4). There are many references to His physical body at the time of His death (Matthew 27:58;

Luke 24:3, 23; John 19:38, 40; 20:12). The incarnation is God's ultimate endorsement of the physical body (Matthew 1:20-25; Luke 1:26-35; Romans 1:3; Galatians 4:4; 1 Timothy 3:16; 1 John 4:2-3). Jesus' body was the location of humanity's redemption. This redemption demanded that the Word become flesh and dwell among us (John 1:14). Jesus' body was the temple of God's glory and the sacrificial offering for the sins of a world! Even His resurrection demanded a physical body (to be discussed later).

In light of the integration of body and spirit, "soma" does not mean something external to man himself. The body is not something man has but something he is! Although we recognize the distinction between the spiritual and physical existence of man, he cannot be without the unity of the two. Even in our passage Jesus points to this interworking. Adultery, a physical act, happens in the spiritual realm of the heart that controls the viewpoint of the *"looks"* of the physical eye. If it is the right eye or the right hand that causes you to sin, it should be cut off and thrown away. However, the right eye or the right hand is not the cause the sin. Sin comes from the spiritual heart. The merging of the spiritual and physical is the core consideration of redemption.

Another consideration of "soma" is "the context of the person." The body is the location or dwelling place of the spiritual man, where the sourcing of the Spirit of Jesus can be seen. The spiritual man expresses the sourcing of the Spirit of Jesus through his body. The body is the arena in which he practices his faith (invoking the activity of the Second Party). Paul cried, **"Or do you not know that your body is the temple of the Holy Spirit who is in you"** (1 Corinthians 6:19). Through the sourcing of the indwelt Spirit, the body becomes the expression of the Kingdom relationship in the present.

Man cannot be himself unless the body and spirit coordinate and function as a whole through the sourcing of the Spirit of Jesus. The body merges with the spirit providing the agency for expression. Neither the body nor the spirit takes precedence over the other because each benefits the other. Thus, the body is the platform for the expression of the whole person. What value is the brain without the hands to act out its thoughts? What value is the love filled heart without arms to embrace? What value is a song in the inner soul without the voice to declare it? The body is the context through which a person gives expression.

Our passage declares this truth. While *"those of old"* considered their sexuality an animal body drive to be controlled, Jesus understood that the sexuality expressed through the body is a product of the heart. Paul said, ***"Flee sexual immorality. Every sin that a man does is outside the body, but he who commits sexual immorality sins against his own body"*** (1 Corinthians 6:18). When a man murders, he sins against his brother, but sexual sins are the destruction of self! In sexual sin we war against our being! That is why Paul admonished, ***"So husbands ought to love their own wives as their own bodies; he who loves his wife loves himself"*** (Ephesians 5:28).

"Soma" is also the "combination of the person." This is the reality of the resurrection because "soma" was the vehicle of the resurrection. The New Testament does not speak of the soul or the nonmaterial aspect of man's existence being resurrected. The consistent focus is on the resurrection of the physical body. ***"But if the Spirit of Him who raised Jesus from the dead dwells in you, He who raised Christ from the dead will also give life to your mortal bodies through His Spirit who dwells in you"*** (Romans 8:11). The total man is both spirit and physical body!

Jesus linked sexuality with the inner spirit of man, *"his heart"* (Matthew 5:28), but when considering eternity, the concern is the physical body (Matthew 5:29-30). Lust in the spirit of man bears consequences in the physical body. The spirit of man and the physical body merge until either one can represent both. They are so intimately combined that each participates in the function of the other. The damnable doctrine of separating the spiritual from the physical is never suggested. Jesus said that sexuality is not exclusively a matter of the inner spirit, but it determines what the physical eye sees.

The fourth use of "soma" is the "commitment of the person." The physical body becomes the platform for spiritual testing and the demonstration of the inner spirit's commitment. Jesus called our inner spiritual condition, *"poor in spirit"* (Matthew 5:3). The inner spirit is helpless, and when it tries to control the body, the physical dominates and dictates the expression of the inner being through the flesh. Therefore, Paul said, *"For those who live according to the flesh set their minds on the things of the flesh, but those who live according to the Spirit, the things of the Spirit"* (Romans 8:5). Therefore, Jesus taught that sexuality gives expression to the spirit that controls it. If we are filled with self-centeredness, the physical body will serve the self-sourced flesh. If the Spirit of Jesus controls us, the body will respond to the discipline of the Spirit. Everyone is surrendered either to self-sourcing or to the sourcing of Jesus. The physical body reveals the surrender! Thus, the physical body and its demonstration becomes a key factor in our eternal state!

Jesus used this emphasis TWICE in our passage. The dual statement concerning the body being cast into hell is significant, but we could logically question it. Throughout the Sermon on the Mount, He moved us from an external view to an internal view. Regarding physical murder, He said anger is spiritual murder and is the real issue! In sexuality the issue is the inner heart. The inner spirit controls what we see when looking. We would expect the inner heart or spirit of man to be cast into hell, but in this passage Jesus highlights the *"whole body."*

Jesus did not want us to miss the truth of His statement. It would be easy to develop a religion that separates the outward activity of the body from the spirit of the heart. Many New Testament epistles deal with this kind of "Gnosticism," a separation between the spirit of man and the physical body.

Gnosticism believes the flesh of man is evil and will never be redeemed. The Gnostics taught that the flesh of man could continue in lust and sinful sexuality while the spirit of man could be pure and holy and could not be defiled regardless of the gross evil of the flesh. Their teaching said the spirit of man could go its way in waves of holiness and purity but the body was free to indulge its fleshly desires. This teaching is never the message of the Bible!

Jesus supported the Old Testament concept of man's creation, a dichotomy in structure. ***"And the Lord God formed man of the dust of the ground, and breathed into his nostrils the breath of life; and man became a living being"*** (Genesis 2:7). The Hebrew word "yatsar," translated ***"formed,"*** describes how the hands of God fashioned man. "Yatsar" is the image of the potter skillfully working with clay to form his mind's design. God creatively formed man's physical body, but that did not end His involvement. He ***"breathed"*** into man the ***"breath of life."*** God shared or imparted His spirit and life into man, and in this union of body and spirit, man became a ***"living being."*** Man was not a living being until God gave him a body and added His spirit. Man is a union of body and spirit.

You are unique in personality and physical structure. Your fingerprints are different from all others; your DNA is yours alone. God created your physical structure to match your spirit. You are a matched set! Jesus died to redeem not only your spirit but also your body (Romans 8:23). In our passage Jesus interlocks the relationship of man's heart with his physical body. When adultery reigns in the self-centered heart, it expresses itself through the lustful looking of the physical eye. The entire body participates in the desires of the self-centered heart; therefore, hell is for the whole being, which includes the physical.

Currently we understand that the spiritual heart and the physical body are interlocked. We live this experience daily, the truth of TIMING. We display through physical interaction what is happening in our spiritual hearts. Our physical circumstances can cause anxiety in our hearts, which pressurizes our bodies with emotional stress and sometimes creates physical illnesses.

When man's heart is filled with self-centered sexuality the body drives respond to fulfill that desire. Jesus said that lust is not a product of our body's sexual drive but is a product of the self-centered heart dictating its desires. That self-centered heart seeks to intensify, focuses, and control the natural sexual desire of the body. **"Those of old"** wanted to attack the problem with a commandment, an effort to control the body drive. Jesus warned that the issue is not the sexual body drive but the self-centeredness of the heart. This issue is the predicament of our present age.

We must not think that the connection between the inner heart and the physical body is true only for our days on Earth. This problem extends into eternity! There is the mistaken idea is that death will cure the sinful desires that flow from the heart to the body and at death our sinful desire will magically disappear, freeing us. But death is not our savior; Jesus is our Savior. We must embrace our helplessness, **"poor in spirit."** When we embrace our helplessness in mourning grief, Jesus can enter our hearts and save us from ourselves. This entrance has to happen in the present age.

Can you imagine passing from this life into the next with the self-centered heart continuing to demand satisfaction from the physical body? The dominant characteristic of self-centeredness is lack of satisfaction. That which satisfies you today will need to increase tomorrow. If two pills satisfy the addict today, he will need four pills tomorrow for the same effect, and in a month he will need thirty. It should terrify us to think about what self-centeredness will demand of us in the millions of years to come. That demand of the growing and increasing rage is the state of hell. The body will not be able to keep up with the demanded level of satisfaction from the

Part Two: Fulfillment of the Kingdom - The Application: Morality

self-centered heart. Self-centeredness destroys the life of the living being, body and spirit.

The cry of Jesus warns us to deal with whatever "causes us to sin" in light of eternity. Eternity's consequences are extreme! Self-centeredness is the core issue of the heart, and we must confront it with severity because it is the most difficult issue of my life! ***"Pluck it out and cast it from you." "Cut it off and cast it from you."*** We must take sides with Jesus against our self-centeredness. He has already won the victory for us!

Matthew 5:29-30

PLACE OF THE EFFECTS

"If your right eye causes you to sin, pluck it out and cast it from you; for it is more profitable for you that one of your members perish than for your whole body to be cast into hell. And if your right hand causes you to sin, cut it off and cast it from you; for it is more profitable for you that one of your members perish, than for your whole body to be cast into hell" (Matthew 5: 29-30).

Maintaining the perspective or idea of our passage is important (Matthew 5:27-30). We are thrust into a new level of living when our helpless being merges with Jesus' empowering Person in the new Kingdom relationship. As a Kingdom person, we experience a righteousness that exceeds that of the scribes and Pharisees (Matthew 5:20). In the Sermon on the Mount, Jesus gives six illustrations of this righteousness, of which our passage is the second.

"Those of old" saw their sexuality as a body appetite they needed to control. The best they could do was to follow the standard, ***"You shall not commit adultery"*** (Matthew 5:27). In the Kingdom relationship, the "heart" is the issue. The "heart" determines the view of the eye, the stride of the walk, the style of the dress, and the approach to life. In other words, sexuality permeates the expression of the life; this expression is determined by the nature of the heart. When self-centeredness controls the heart, the expression of masculinity or femininity is selfish. At the conclusion of Jesus' illustration He becomes serious and forceful, using extreme language (Matthew 5:29-30).

Jesus uses two identical statements to express three ideas. One is the ESSENTIALITY of Spirit-sourced sexuality. A person's spiritual life has value above all else! We must eliminate from our sexuality anything self-centered that causes stumbling. This elimination does not come through forgiveness but through crucifixion. We must cut it off and cast it from us. Jesus' second proposal brings into focus the ETERNALNESS of our physical body. The intimate link of my spiritual with my physical goes far beyond the limits of time. This link is an eternal experience. The physical body is an intricate element of the eternal being of every individual. Jesus' third consideration is the EFFECTS of the self-sourced sexuality in life. To understand the seriousness of self-sourced sexuality, we must consider the consequences. In our present study, the place of the effects is the first of three in an investigation of the effects of self-sourcing.

We will begin with the TONE of the place. If you are seeking truth, it is unwise to be dogmatic about the Old Testament view of eternity. That view was so vague that the Sadducees dismissed it entirely. We are left to surmise only a surface understanding of the progression that brings us to our present state. The Old Testament presented to us a place called "Sheol." This Hebrew word appears in the Old Testament sixty-five times. "Sheol" is translated "grave" thirty-one times (Genesis 37:35; 42:38; 44:29, 31; 1 Samuel 2:6, etc.). The inhabitants of "Sheol" were "the congregation of the dead" (Proverbs 21:16), the abode of the wicked (Numbers 16:33; Job 24:19, Psalms 9:17; 31:17, etc.), and of the good (Psalms 16:10; 30:3; 49:15, 86:13, etc.). "Sheol" is described as deep (Job 11:8), dark (Job 10:21-22), and with bars (Job 17:16) where the dead "go down" to it (Numbers 16:30-33; Ezekiel 31:15-17). "Sheol" was an intermediate and shadowy place where souls went after earthly death.

"Sheol" contained two compartments. The upper chamber

was called "paradise." Jesus assured the thief on the cross that he would be with Him in "Paradise" (Luke 23:43). *"Paradise"* was not a promise for a future, but a promise fulfilled at his death, a place for the abode of the dead who were righteous. The lower compartment was called "Hades," not to be confused with "hell," and it was an intermediate dwelling place for the wicked. Neither the righteous nor unrighteous reached their final dwelling place in "Sheol."

Again we must emphasize the vast opinions on the dwelling places after earthly death. The Old Testament view is vague about eternity and equally vague on what the death of Jesus accomplished in regard to "Sheol." Surely Jesus' entrance into the abode of the dead, burdened with our sin, and His experience of the resurrection power of the Father altered "Sheol" forever. From that point forward we are told of the New Testament concept of heaven and hell. Paul assured us that *"to be absent from the body and to be present with the Lord"* (2 Corinthians 5:8). We might conclude that Jesus entered into "Sheol" and in the power of His resurrection disassembled it. Heaven and hell were established through the judgment of His death on the cross. Jesus referred to His crucifixion as, *"the judgment of this world; now the ruler of this world will be cast out"* (John 12:31). We no longer need to abide in an intermediate place waiting for judgment because judgment took place at the cross. Our response to His death is the judgment of our lives, and we dwell in that judgment now. Eternal life or eternal death is already happening in us. Death does not bring us to judgment; death is a transition into a permanent dwelling place called "heaven" or "hell." The state of judgment in which we dwell now and will dwell at the time of death will continue forever.

In our passage Jesus expressed deep concern about sin in our hearts. When our sexuality is controlled by a heart ruled by self-sourcing, our lives give continual expression to sin. He presents His concern within the framework of a place called *"hell."*

"Hell" is a translation of the Greek word "geenna," used twelve times in the New Testament. Outside of the Epistle of James (3:6), Jesus was the only one who used this word! In the New Testament Jesus said more about *"hell"* than any other biblical person.

When and where was Jesus compelled to address the issue of *"hell"*? He used *"hell"* nine times in speaking to His disciples, calling attention to their self-centeredness. In His final public message, Jesus used this word twice in reference to the self-centered scribes and Pharisees (Matthew 23:15, 33). All of these discussions were focused on self-sourcing religious people working within the context of religion.

Now with this understanding of Jesus' references to *"hell,"* let us consider our passage (Matthew 5:29-30). The Sermon on the Mount was the message Jesus designed for His disciples (Matthew 5:1-2). However, in the immediate context of our passage, He addressed the self-sourced approach of the religious leaders of Israel. The righteousness of the Kingdom person must exceed the righteousness of the scribes and Pharisees (Matthew 5:20). Concerning sexuality, the scribes' and Pharisees' hearts were sourced by their self-centeredness, which determined the expression of their sexuality. Their self-centered sexuality shaped their culture, religious rules, and the treatment of the opposite gender. Jesus discussed *"hell"* in connection only with this self-centeredness. If the demonic nature of self-centeredness creates a spiritual death, it can be described only in terms of *"hell."*

Knowing that Jesus spoke to His disciples and the self-sourced religious leaders of Israel about *"hell,"* let us contrast that with all the times He spoke to other sinners but did not speak about *"hell."* **"Then the scribes and Pharisees brought to Him a woman caught in adultery"** (John 8:3). The law demanded that she should be stoned, and they confronted Jesus to test Him. Jesus addressed the woman caught in the act and her accusers, but He never spoke of *"hell."* In the biblical encounters between Jesus and the wicked tax collectors, *"hell"* was never mentioned (Luke 19:1-10; Luke 5:27-32). Therefore, if we were to preach as Jesus did, we would preach only on *"hell"* to self-centered religious people. Jesus never used *"hell"* to frighten the sinful majority into responding to His message. He spoke of *"hell"* only to awaken those who received so much knowledge and light from God but used such revelation for their self-centeredness.

Now let us consider the TWICE of the place to discover the content of *"hell."* We have learned that the Greek word "geenna," translated *"hell"* (Matthew 5:22), is derived from the Hebrew expression, "Valley of Hinnom" (Joshua 15:8; Nehemiah 11:30). This valley lay to the south and southwest of Jerusalem. Topographically it provided the border between Judah and Benjamin (Joshua 15:8; 18:16) and the northern limit of the district occupied by the tribe of Judah after the captivity (Nehemiah 11:30), and it lay in front of the gate Harsith in Jerusalem (Jeremiah 19:2).

The "Valley of Hinnom" became a place of idolatrous and human sacrifices. These sacrifices were first offered by Ahaz and Manasseh who made their children to *"pass through the fire"* to Molech in this valley (2 Kings 16:3; 2 Kings 21:6; 2 Chronicles 28:3; 33:6). These sacrifices were probably made on the **"high places of Tophet which is in the Valley of the Son of Hinnom"** (Jeremiah 7:31). In order to put an end to these abominations, Josiah polluted it with human bones and other corruptions (2 Kings 23:10, 13, 14). But this worship to Molech was revived under Jehoiakim (Jeremiah 11:10-13; Ezekiel 20:30). Because of these idolatrous practices in the Valley of Hinnom, Jeremiah prophesied that one day it would be called the *"Valley of Slaughter"* (Jeremiah 7:32), and that they should, **"bury them in Tophet, till there be no place to bury"** (Jeremiah 19:11).

In New Testament days, the *"Valley of Slaughter"* became the garbage dump of Jerusalem. No other use was possible because of its defilement. A constant fire was burning the refuse. The stench of burning human flesh hovered over Jerusalem because the dead were often thrown into this valley. As Jesus spoke to the disciples or the leaders of Israel about "Geenna," they had a vivid picture of this place called *"hell."*

Many descriptive statements in the New Testament strengthen the physical imagery of the valley constantly burning refuse. Even the ungodly will be raised from the dead and will be given an eternal body that can endure the pain and agony of *"hell"* forever. Jesus cried, *"And do not fear those who kill the body but cannot kill the soul. But rather fear Him who is able to destroy both soul and body in hell"* (Matthew 10:28). The destruction includes the spiritual part of man and the physical body of man; it is not destruction in the absolute sense of annihilation but an eternal state of progressive pain and ruination.

Gehenna is as a fire. Jesus said, *"But whoever says, 'You fool!' shall be in danger of hell fire"* (Matthew 5:22). The words of Jesus in our passage (Matthew 5:29-30) are repeated in chapter eighteen (Matthew 18:8-9), with additional statements, *"to be cast into everlasting fire"* (Matthew 18:8), and *"to be cast into hell fire"* (Matthew 18:9). Mark also records this same statement. *"If your hand causes you to sin, cut it off. It is better for you to enter into life maimed, rather than having two hands, to go to hell, into the fire that shall never be quenched — where 'Their worm does not die And the fire is not quenched.'"* (Mark 9:43-44).

Mark also quotes Jesus saying this about the foot as well as the hand and eye (Mark 9:43-48). The same description is given three times, twice by Matthew and once by Mark.

Jesus explains the Parable of the Tares in the Parables of the Kingdom. He said, *"The Son of Man will send out His angels, and they will gather out of His kingdom all things that offend, and those who practice lawlessness, and will cast them into the furnace of fire. There will be wailing and gnashing of teeth"*

(Matthew 13:41-42). Jesus makes the same statement in the Parable of the Dragnet (Matthew 13:50). He used the imagery of, *"outer darkness; there will be weeping and gnashing of teeth"* in the Parable of the Wedding Feast (Matthew 22:13) and the Parable of the Talents (Matthew 25:30). The Book of Revelation often uses the imagery of *"cast alive into the lake of fire burning with brimstone"* (Revelation 19:20; 20:10, 14, 15; 21:8).

The Bible exhausts human language in its description of the horrible suffering and state of existence in hell. However, the same occurs in its description of the abundance of life found in heaven. How much of the language is literal or symbolic? For instance, is there physical fire experienced in hell? The contradictions in the descriptions point toward symbolic language. *"Outer darkness"* and the idea of burning *"fire"* seem opposite. Despite your conclusion on the matter, heaven is more glorious and hell is more terrible than human language can express! We must be careful not to let the materialistic mindset of our culture dominate our viewpoint of heaven or hell.

The results of this study must bring us to the important conclusion of the TIMING of the place. Finality is the emphasis of Jesus! The logic of His statements vibrates with the temporary of the present and the forever quality of eternity, *"hell."* In fact, as Jesus makes these two statements to the disciples seeking position, He emphasizes this fact. Again, He expresses the seriousness of the self-centered focus of their masculinity. He changed the word *"hell"* to *"everlasting fire"* (Matthew 18:8). *"Hell"* is forever, consisting of an endless time. There may be a beginning but there is no end.

If we conclude that "hell" is not to be the final dwelling place for our lives, then the consideration immediately becomes how to avoid this dwelling place. The answer is not found in the moment of physical death, which is not the solution. Many people have accepted the deception that physical death will change their attitude, spiritual condition, and character. All their bad habits will suddenly disappear; hatred and bitterness will vanish; inner stress and anxiety will no longer plague them. This conclusion may be a result of the belief that this world creates these problems for them, and they are not responsible. These ideas are a part of the deception of the enemy; do not be fooled!

In our passage Jesus addressed our sexuality. Adultery and lust are natural in this life that causes us to conclude that these things are a result of living in this world, and the next world will be different. Jesus boldly said this conclusion is false! Adultery and lust are a direct result of the heart's condition. If you die with this heart, you will dwell in another world with the same condition. Death is not the savior; Jesus is the only One who can change our hearts!

This brings us to the awareness of the importance of immediate inner change. If we do not want to go to the place of eternal death, we must not possess the condition of eternal death now! Hell is not a future experience but the beginning stage of this place that exists within the individual. Physical death is a door closing behind us, and it removes us from the possibility of any change of our inner condition. Whatever you and I are in our hearts when we physically die will be what we will be forever. Physical death is not the cure.

Is this not why Jesus desperately hounds us? John, the Apostle, consistently referred to Jesus as "the Light." John the Baptist was not the light, but he gave testimony to **"the Light."** He said that Jesus **"gives light to every man coming into the world"** (John 1:9). By every circumstance of your life, by every word spoken to you, and by the determined plan of God for your intervention, God is drawing you into His eternal life. If you remain in eternal death and dwell forever-in eternal hell, you will have to fight against the consistent revelation of truth from Jesus! Those dwelling in eternal hell will admit forever of their personal choice to do so. Today is the time of choice!

*"Today, if you will hear His voice,
Do not harden your hearts as in the rebellion"*
(Hebrews 3:15).

*"Today, if you will hear His voice,
Do not harden your hearts"*
(Hebrews 4:7).

Matthew 5:29-30

PUNISHMENT OF THE EFFECT

"If your right eye causes you to sin, pluck it out and cast it from you; for it is more profitable for you that one of your members perish than for your whole body to be cast into hell. And if your right hand causes you to sin, cut it off and cast it from you; for it is more profitable for you that one of your members perish, than for your whole body to be cast into hell" (Matthew 5: 29-30).

The Sermon on the Mount flows from a Divine attitude. Matthew was specific when he gave us the sequence of events to bring us to this presentation. ***"In those days John the Baptist came preaching in the wilderness of Judea, and saying, 'Repent, for the kingdom of heaven is at hand!'"*** (Matthew 3:1-2). John's call was to "give up a former thought to embrace a new thought." Although this involves confession of sins and turning from them, the impact of our response is that we give up the Old Covenant (law-sourcing) to embrace the New Covenant (Spirit-sourcing). The Greek word "gar," translated ***"for,"*** is the reason for repentance. The Kingdom of Heaven is now present. We are not to repent so the Kingdom will come, but we repent because the Kingdom has come. Repentance is a response to an act of God on our behalf. The message contains no threat, warning, or ultimatum, only an urgent invitation. Any hint of warning is given to the self-centered leaders of Israel (Matthew 3:7-12).

Jesus was the first man to be filled with the Spirit

(Matthew 3:16). The Spirit led Jesus into the wilderness temptation (Matthew 4:1-11) and gave Him victory over that temptation. The leaders of Israel put John the Baptist in prison at the same time Jesus began His Galilean ministry, attracting multitudes from every region (Matthew 4:25). Jesus, a Spirit-sourced Man, met the needs of thousands of hurting people, revealing His attitude of mercy, love, and concern!

The Sermon on the Mount is Jesus' manifesto on the Kingdom of God. His message begins with a blessing. The Beatitudes flow with Jesus' excited congratulation not condemnation (Matthew 5:3-12). The final Beatitude encourages this attitude amid persecution. Jesus does not consider hating those who persecute you a part of the Kingdom person. In fact, the function of the Kingdom person is one of *"salt"* and *"light"* (Matthew 5:13-16) with the absence of punishment or judgment. *"Let your light so shine before men, that they may see your good works and glorify your Father in heaven"* (Matthew 5:16). Letting your light shine demonstrates nothing negative, partial, or prejudiced.

Jesus presents Himself in a clear revelation of "fulfillment." The negative of destruction, elimination, or brokenness is not in His destiny. This "fulfillment" produces righteousness beyond the limited love, judgment, and condemnation of the scribes and Pharisees (Matthew 5:17-20). Jesus provides six illustrations to prove this righteousness. *"You shall not murder"* is the focus of the first illustration. Not committing murder was a boundary for living of *"those of old."* They allowed judgment, ridicule, and hatred in contrast to the love, reconciliation, and respect of the Kingdom person. Jesus' second illustration concerns sexuality. *"Those of old"* established a boundary permitting everything except adultery, but the Kingdom person rejects this thought process! The sexuality of the Kingdom person does not use, abuse, or manipulate another for their satisfaction (Matthew 5:27-30). In Jesus third illustration, He says we should demonstrate this attitude of honor in marriage (Matthew 5:31-32) because a Kingdom person has integrity. This integrity eliminates the need of swearing by an oath because your word is your bond as Jesus presented in His fourth illustration (Matthew 5:33-37).

In His last two illustrations, Jesus said the intention of a Kingdom person is to never *"resist an evil person."* The Kingdom person's heart motive is one of giving, turning the other cheek, and going the extra mile (Matthew 5:38-42). The Kingdom person loves his enemies, blesses those who curse him, does well to those who hate him, and prays for those who spitefully use him. The Father's heart is the heart of the Kingdom person because they feel as the Father feels (Matthew 5:43-48).

The Kingdom has a TONE echoed by every statement of Jesus in the Sermon on the Mount! *"Those of old"* had their limits, but Jesus broke through and beyond these boundaries because there are no limits to love and its expression. By their attitude, *"those of old"* asked, "When have I loved enough?" "When have I turned the other cheek enough?" "When have I gone the second mile enough?" "When have I done enough good to those who hate me?" Jesus presented a limitless love and grace. He advocated continuous redemption without boundaries. He proposed that we are to have redemption without boundaries because in our helplessness we are filled with the nature of God. Was He telling us that God is like this?

Wait! If redemption without boundaries is true, what about our passage (Matthew 5:29-30)? Here Jesus proposed the punishment of *"hell."* Have we been wrong? Maybe *"hell"* is a reality but "punishment" is a misconception! Can there be an eternal death that dwells in an eternal hell, but it is not a punishment? Every parent should understand this! A child screams from the burning pain of touching a hot stove. He did not listen to his father's instruction to not touch the stove. Is the pain the punishment of the father or a natural consequence of the child's disobedience? Does the father delight in his child's suffering, or does he desire to bear his child's pain?

We must listen to the TONE of the Sermon on the Mount! If the "poor in Spirit" (helpless) are filled with the Father's nature, they will exhibit meekness, fullness, mercy, purity, peace, and rejoice in persecution. Where in the Sermon on the Mount does Jesus tell us to punish, hate, and seek the destruction of those who hurt us? We are the expression of the Father's nature! Does the Father not see us in the pain of our sin's consequences and want to take these consequences for us? Did He not do this in Christ on the cross? Has He not embraced all sin's results in its destruction? Did Jesus not go to hell for you? He has no desire to punish you! He wants only to save you!

Does this mean no one goes to hell? Obviously not! But it does mean that Jesus does not send you to hell. If anyone goes to hell, it is a consequence of his or her choice! I want to restate briefly from a previous study the biblical concept of "punishment." The two Greek words "timoria" and "kolasis," translated "punishment," do not differ in the experience of the person being punished, but they are vastly different in the motive or intent of the one responsible for the punishment.

"Timoria" comes from classical Greek, and it carries the predominant thought of the vindictive character of punishment. This kind of punishment satisfies the inflictor's sense of outraged justice in defending his honor or that of the violated law. "Kolasis" is the Greek word used in the parables of judgment. **"And these will go away into everlasting punishment, but the righteous into eternal life"** (Matthew 25:48), conveying the notion that punishment is for the correction or betterment of the offender. But when "aionios," translated **"everlasting,"** is included, it equals **"hell."** This is a final punishment from which you cannot return. However, there remains an important distinction between these two Greek words. In "kolasis" the relationship of the punishment is to the one being punished while in "timoria" the relationship is to the punisher. In other words, the punishment of *"hell"* is not something God forces on a person because He is offended. *"Hell"* is a direct result of the person's choice; they embrace the punishment as a part of their lifestyle and choice.

In the Sermon on the Mount, it was Jesus' intent to highlight the possibilities of heaven and hell for the endless age to come. As he closed the Sermon on the Mount, He spoke of those who proclaimed to prophesy, cast out demons, and do many wonders in His name. *"And then I will declare to them, 'I never knew you; depart from Me, you who practice lawlessness!'"* (Matthew 7:23). These people had no relationship with Jesus, but they did have relationship with their lawlessness. Therefore they will suffer the consequences of their choices. One consequence is the *"hell"* of our passage (Matthew 5:29-30). Listen to the tone of the Sermon on the Mount. If the Father's nature will not allow us to condemn, destroy, and hate, how can the Father have these vices? If the Father's nature causes us to love, forgive, and express mercy, can the Father damn, condemn, and destroy? Does He require more from us that He does from Himself? Are we not the expression of His heart?

It amazes me how often this tone appears in the biblical references to eternal death giving contrast between eternal life and eternal death. Paul said, *"For the wages of sin is death, but the gift of God is eternal life in Christ Jesus our Lord"* (Romans 6:23). The contrast is not between eternal life and eternal death but between *"wages"* and *"gift."* Eternal death does not come from God; eternal death is man's choice. We understand and participate in the economy of *"wages,"* because we deserve, earn and merit wages for our work. Our wages are not a result of revenge, anger, or punishment. Although our wages may come from an employer, we do not posture ourselves in the position of deserving them. We do not receive our paycheck then proclaim, "The boss is punishing me!" How is God pictured in this passage? He is the gracious, loving, and merciful one giving gifts! He did not select some to receive gifts and not others. He presents the gift to every person, but some stubbornly collect the wages they have earned while God offers His gift.

In the Parables of the Kingdom (Matthew 13), Jesus uses the imagery of farming. In the Parables of the Wheat and the Tares (Matthew 13:24-30), the climax of the story is the harvest. The good seed and the evil seed grow together in the world. The servants are upset over the conditions and desire to uproot the tares, but the owner is not, wisely instructing the servants to wait for the harvest. Tares will be gathered and burned at the harvest. This outcome is not a matter of anger, revenge, or punishment. Poisonous tares are worthless, making the proper action their destruction. This destruction is not a punishment but a natural conclusion of the harvest.

Jesus proposes the same idea TWICE in our passage (Matthew 5:29-30). It is important to know that the word *"cast"* appears twice in each statement and four times in the passage. The Greek word "ballo," translated *"cast,"* means "to drive out, expel, or throw away." This casting relates directly to sin. Jesus encourages us to find what causes us to sin and deal severely with it. We are not to pamper, save or coddle the instrument of sin. Sin must be so hideous in our sight that we "ballo" it from our lives. The word *"cast"* is in the active voice, meaning the subject of the imperative is responsible for the action of casting. The subject is you and I; we are responsible for throwing away the instrument that causes us to stumble.

Jesus uses the word *"cast"* again in the same sentence. He relates it to sin and the consequences of going to *"hell."* However, it is in the passive voice, meaning the subject (body) receives the action of the verb. In other words, you and I are not responsible for throwing ourselves into *"hell,"* but we receive *"hell"* as a consequence of our sin.

Jesus is logical in His approach to the subject of God's slightest involvement. He never said that God would punish us, or *"cast* (us) *into hell."* This act is a result of the destructive sin in our lives because of what we tolerate. If we do not severely confront whatever causes us to sin, sin will dominate our lives, and the end result of sin is *"hell."*

"Hell" is a reality. We never want to undermine its severity. We are not tying to lessen the destruction, lighten the suffering, or devalue the terrible fate of hell. But we do want to carefully examine the heart motive of God, who either causes or allows everything. His motive is one of love and deep concern. There is no hatred, bitterness, or anger in the heart of God for the sinner. However, there are consequences for choices we make. Although many may go to *"hell,"* it is not God's desire that any perish (2 Peter 3:9). *"Hell"* is a consequence and not a punishment!

In light of this truth about *"hell,"* we need to consider the TIMING. Jesus indicates a progression although it is not dominate. He contrasts this progression with the approach of *"those of old."* Their legalistic approach to *"You shall not commit adultery"* is a stagnant matter; you either do or you do not. However, Jesus spoke of an attitude of the heart (self-centeredness) controlling your sexuality, with the possibility of various degrees and intensity. What controls your heart begins to control your perspective. Your perspective begins to control the mannerisms, jokes, your approach to the opposite gender, and your attitude. Life becomes more controlled by your self-centered sexuality. *"Hell"* is the end of this progression? Sin will not rest until it brings destruction.

Jesus was persistent in presenting this progression though out His parables. The imagery of farming, seeds, and harvest offer this concept. This progression is not isolated to sin in the life of those who are evil, but is also present in the righteousness of the good seeds. In the Parable of the Wheat and the Tares, the owner discovers the tares and will not allow the servants to gather them. As the tares begin to show their presence among the wheat, any attempt to gather the tares will uproot the wheat as well. The owner's instructions are to, *"Let both grow together until the harvest"* (Matthew 13:30). Through the growth progression, the tares can be easily distinguished from the wheat.

Eternal death is not a condition to be experienced only in *"hell."* We experience eternal death when we are separated from God. Self-centeredness fills us because we lack His presence. Self-centeredness seems to be beneficial but consistently destroys everything it touches. Relationships are destroyed; peace and security change to anxiety and frustration when self does not achieve its goal. This spiritual death devours the person daily until death. Death is a moment of transition into a permanent state of separation from God. The person is released to a consistent and everlasting destruction of the self-centeredness he or she so desperately clung to in life. This state is called *"hell,"* and it is a continuation of what is experienced from the beginning and has come to full harvest.

No wonder Jesus used severe language. He urges us to do whatever it takes to break this cycle of self-centeredness. We must step out of eternal death and into eternal life in this moment. There is no better time than now. Jesus is life!

Matthew 5:29-30

PROGRESSION OF THE EFFECT

> *"If your right eye causes you to sin, pluck it out and cast it from you; for it is more profitable for you that one of your members perish than for your whole body to be cast into hell. And if your right hand causes you to sin, cut it off and cast it from you; for it is more profitable for you that one of your members perish, than for your whole body to be cast into hell" (Matthew 5: 29-30).*

This chapter concludes our study of these two verses. This compels me to summarize the concepts we have discovered. We will repeat many things we previously said, cementing deep in our hearts our search for the truth as Jesus reveals who He is in us! Jesus gave us three basic ideas in these verses. ESSENTIALITY is an emphasis on the necessity of dealing with self-centered sexuality. He speaks to us in severe language. If you have any regard for your life, you will not hesitate to encounter this issue. The second idea is the ETERNALNESS of your destiny. Eternity for each of us involves endless years, but our greatest concern should be the quality of those years with respect to our physical bodies. The concluding idea centers on the EFFECTS of self-sourced sexuality.

Although we may understand the principle of "cause and effect," we do not seem to apply that understanding to the circumstances of our lives. Even when we have irrefutable evidence that links cancer and smoking, many have asked,

"Why do I have cancer?" The Greek word "dia" is often used in the Scriptures to highlight the "cause and effect." Many members of the Church of Corinth unworthily participated in the Lord's Supper. Paul said, ***"For this reason many are weak and sick among you, and many sleep"*** (1 Corinthians 11:30). Their sickness was the effect and a cause. In another place Paul described ungodly people, ***"who exchanged the truth of God for the lie, and worshiped and served the creature rather than the Creator, who is blessed forever"*** (Romans 1:25). Their actions caused a direct effect. ***"For this reason God gave them up to vile passions"*** (Romans 1:26).

The philosophical world debates the various theories of cause and effect, but none of that is necessary to our investigation. However, we can be certain of a link between cause and effect. They are so joined that the one is involved in the other with no way to divide them. When there is a definite relation between two events or state of affairs, the first is necessary for the second to occur.

The philosophers of old said there were four aspects of "cause." These are not four different "causes," but four elements that are necessary for forming "the cause." The first one is "The Formal Cause" and is the structure of the shape a thing takes. A blueprint is the cause of an airplane. The architectural drawings are the cause for the structure of a building. Jesus is the ***"Word"*** (John 1:1). The Greek word is "logos," an idea or thought. Jesus was the idea in the mind of God about mankind; He was the blueprint. In our passage (Matthew 5:29-30) sexuality is the blueprint in the creation of God. Every aspect of my life is shaped or determined by this blueprint. This blueprint determines the way I walk, think, react, approach life, and look at the opposite gender. ***"Those of old"*** missed this view. They thought their sexuality was a body appetite they had to control with a boundary rule, ***"You shall not commit adultery."*** The truth is that sexuality is a blueprint of the cause of your life, the important element of who you are!

Second, we have "The Material Cause." This element is the stuff of which a thing is made, determined by the blueprint. Sexuality is the internal nature acting itself out on the physical stage of my life. Sexuality is not a physical body drive that needs to be curbed or controlled, shifting the issue from my discipline of the physical drive to all expressions of my sexuality. My response when people hurt me is an expression of my internal nature. This "material" causes how I dress, walk, and my general attitude of life. Aristotle, the philosopher, treated this material cause as a relative term, relative to the structure that holds it together. For instance, the elements are the material cause of tissue while tissues are the material cause of the body organ. Body organs are the material cause of the living body. This thought means that the controlling nature of my life is the material cause of my sexuality. My sexuality is the material cause of my physical desire, and my desires become the expression of my life.

Sexuality is the blueprint for my life's formation. Through the nature of my sexuality, the material formed gives physical expression for my life. The third one is "The Efficient Cause." Although there may be a blueprint with the material fulfilling it, a builder created the blueprint. Jesus is our Creator. However, at this point is where the tragedy of sin enters the story. The demonic self-centered nature wooed man into independence from God. The blueprint of sexuality became tainted with self-satisfaction and focus. The self-centered nature shapes the material of sexuality for the fulfillment of pride. The self-centered nature dominates the expression of my sexuality for its fulfillment. The desires of the flesh become my passion under the domination of this builder.

"The Final Cause" is our fourth. Let us review! "The Formal Cause" is the blueprints of the airplane, and "The Material Cause" is the material that fulfills the blueprint. "The Efficient Cause" is the creator of the blueprints, but these three lead to purpose, "The Final Cause," the airplane is to transport people and cargo. We must now apply this to our passage (Matthew 5:29-30). Sexuality is God's blueprint for my life. The material fulfilling the blueprint and forming me is His nature! He is the Prime Mover of my life's expression, my sexuality. The purpose is the visualization of who He is! My world sees Jesus through my sexuality! But sin invaded my sexuality. It refocused my blueprint, reshaped the material of my sexuality, became the new creator of my sexuality's expression, and this self-centered nature came with a new purpose experienced in the effect of the cause!

In this section (Matthew 5:27-30) the TONE of the effect is destruction. Jesus is consistent in His Kingdom message. He crystallized this destruction in bold statements. ***"If anyone desires to come after Me, let him deny himself, and take up his cross, and follow Me. For whoever desires to save his life will lose it, but whoever loses his life for My sake will find it"*** (Matthew 16:24-25). When people focus on themselves for self-gain, they produce an effect of destruction, and the nature of self-centeredness becomes the cause ending in the effect of destruction. Every area of life operates under this principle. The opposite is also true. When people focus on self-giving and self-sacrifice, they find the effect of growth and strengthening in their lives.

Who are the people you consider your best friends? They are the people you can depend on. They have your back, go out of their way to help, and support you with encouragement. Who are the people with whom no relationship is possible? They consistently use you for their benefit and enjoy your defeat. You are only an instrument to acquire their desire. Their self-centeredness destroys any chance of relationship.

Jesus applies this principle to our sexuality. If self-centeredness is at the ***"heart"*** of our lives, it will manifest itself through our sexuality. Because our sexuality encompasses every area of our living, self-centeredness will be the dominant expression of our lives. The effect of this expression is destruction in every area. For instance, my self-centered sexuality will determine the perspective of my "looking." The effect of this in my life is **"lust."** The Greek word "epithymeo," translated **"lust,"** is the same Greek word translated "covet." **"You shall not commit adultery"** is the seventh commandment of the Ten Commandments. **"You shall not covet your neighbor's house; you shall not covet your neighbor's wife, nor his male servant, nor his female servant, nor his ox, nor his donkey, nor anything that is your neighbor's"** (Exodus 20:17). The heart of the word is the idea of having. In other words, if I covet, lust after my neighbor's house, I desire to take it from him, claim it as mine, and have it for myself. If I were to achieve this desire in the physical realm, I would remove the possession from my neighbor and take it for myself, becoming a thief! In the spiritual world, I am stealing my neighbor's house.

Our sexuality is intended to be intimate, sharing in one flesh and knowing each other by giving to each other. Now my sexuality, driven by my self-centered nature, becomes stealing. By self-centered lusting in the spiritual world, I not only steal my neighbor's wife, but I also steal from the woman what is not rightfully mine, robbing from her what is not mine. I am not giving; I am taking. My nature becomes so self-centered that I have become a cancer devouring others for my benefit. I am a spiritual thief, which is destruction.

When self-centeredness rules in the marriage relationship, it cannot produce "one flesh." Intimacy and love are absent. Marriage is destroyed, and we become instruments used by each other for self-satisfaction. No wonder Jesus uses such strong language, calling us to the elimination of all self-centeredness because the effect is far too costly.

To give a clear picture of the destruction, Jesus gives His answer to it TWICE. He presents the two realms of existence in each statement. The present state in which we dwell is a period of choice. The prevenient grace of God is aggressively manifesting itself in and around us. The Spirit of Jesus' nature and the self-centered demonic nature are contrasted and visualized before us.

Jesus begins with, *"If your right eye causes you to sin, pluck it out and cast it from you"* (Matthew 5:29). Jesus' appeal is that we embrace the opportunity we have in the present. We live in the present moment of decision, the most convenient, painless, manageable, uncomplicated, and simple time to deal with our self-centeredness. However, your pride will proclaim the opposite. Your circumstances will propose that leaving your self-centeredness is impossible. But the truth is clear; there will never be an easier time to surrender self to Jesus' nature. Your life is in an hourly progression. You establish patterns in each moment, and your heart is governed by your self-centered principles, collecting around you the things that cater to your self-centeredness. Now is the time to break free in Jesus!

But Jesus emphasis is not just on the present moments. He says, *"for it is more profitable for you that one of your members perish, than for your whole body to be cast into hell"* (Matthew 5:29). Our present moment of decision will not last. The effect of our self-centered sexuality casts its influence on all our relationships, mannerisms, and involvements, and that effect is long range! We cannot make decisions or corrections to our lifestyle in our final dwelling place because truth will not be heard. Darkness will be total. The self-centered cause of this hour not only affects the circumstances of your present life, but it also determines your eternal dwelling place.

Jesus told the story about a certain rich man. He described the man's fine apparel and how he, *"fared sumptuously every day"* (Luke 16:19). He compared this rich man with the beggar named Lazarus who was covered in sores, laid at the gate daily, and ate the crumbs from the rich man's table. Each man lived in the present moments of decision and then died. The eternal state of each man's dwelling place was fixed. The rich man cried for change and relief but found none. The story is not about riches compared to poverty, but about self-centeredness versus self-giving. The selfishness of the rich man consumed him in this life and in eternal life. Self-centeredness is destructive in the present, and it will continue to be in the eternal state!

The proposition of Jesus is that what is going on in your life now will continue to grow in the eternal realm, which brings us to the consideration of the TIMING. We cannot say this too often. The effects of self-centeredness are not temporary. These effects will not pass away, and you cannot shake them from your life in death. The cause of a self-centered heart will bring effects that span the course of time into eternity. What you are becoming now is what you will be forever.

What you are in your inner heart, your nature, is in constant progression. The effects in your state of existence will not level or plateau but will become permanent, growing in greater control and expanding in desire. We do not begin with a life of deceit, but as one lie builds up another deception takes over. Whatever your addiction it grows and increases the desire in you. What once satisfied you does not satisfy you now but increases daily to a greater degree in you.

The ancient philosophers held three beliefs about causality to be indisputable: nothing comes from nothing; nothing can give what it does not itself possess; and a cause must have as much perfection or being as it effects. The *"looks"* that produce *"lust"* and results in *"adultery with her in his heart"* does not happen accidentally. Nothing comes from nothing. There is a cause and effect. Jesus calls us to confront the cause and not the effect. This is not an hour for reform or newly applied disciplines. Now is a moment for the transformation of the self-centered heart!

The self-centeredness we demonstrate in our daily expressions of sexuality does not come from a heart filled with the Spirit of Jesus. We cannot give what we do not possess. A self-centered heart does not evolve into expressing kindness, love, and holiness. Hate does not evolve into love, anger does not evolve into patience, and sinfulness does not evolve into purity. Jesus calls us to deal with who we are in our hearts.

There is a parallel between the status of the heart and the status of the life we express. Do not be abhorred by the selfish condition of your action without realizing that your heart is filled with the same condition. A cause must have as much perfection or being as it effects. Look carefully at your expressions, and realize you are seeing the condition of your heart. Do not view the best of your deeds, the one you parade for the applause of others as your best. You must take a close look at your worst secret moments, the ones you do not want anyone else to know about. Realize in repentance that these secret moments are what you really are in your heart.

Think of the terribleness of a self-centered hell forever. That hell is the revelation of the self-centered heart reaping total destruction of the human life. Whatever you may think hell will be like in the physical, realize with clarity that this will be the state of your inner heart, the cause!

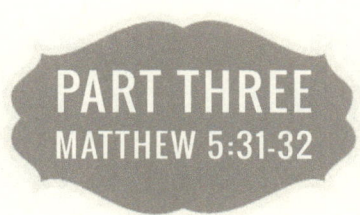

PART THREE
MATTHEW 5:31-32

Fulfillment of the Kingdom –
The Application:

MARRIAGE

Matthew 5:31-32

THE DIVORCE ISSUE

"Furthermore it has been said, 'Whoever divorces his wife, let him give her a certificate of divorce.' But I say to you that whoever divorces his wife for any reason except sexual immorality causes her to commit adultery; and whoever marries a woman who is divorced commits adultery"
(Matthew 5:31-32).

Jesus is far too brief in His instructions about marriage and divorce. What is the subject of these two verses? Is it "marriage" or "divorce?" Perhaps it is not about either! We reserve that discussion for another study. "Divorce" was a major cultural problem in Jesus' day, but I am not sure that is comforting to anyone. The Pharisees used this controversy in their attempt to discredit Jesus (Matthew 19:1-10). Two thousand years later we are still in that controversy with various problems of sexuality related to marriage increasing in their complexity. How you feel about these problems is for you to decide, and we encourage you to allow your conclusions to flow from your saturation in His Word and His presence!

The biblical background for marriage and divorce comes from the Old Testament culture where God made provision through Moses for divorce. Jesus was clear in his statement about God's motivation to provide for divorce. **"Moses, because of the hardness of your hearts, permitted you to divorce your**

Part Three: Fulfillment of the Kingdom - The Application: Marriage

wives, but from the beginning it was not so" (Matthew 19:8). That is very plain! God never intended the option of divorce from the beginning or in the present day, but because of the evil in the heart of man, God made the provision in the laws of Deuteronomy. *"When a man takes a wife and marries her, and it happens that she finds no favor in his eyes because he has found some uncleanness in her, and he writes her a certificate of divorce, puts it in her hand, and sends her out of his house"* (Deuteronomy 24:1).

The "certificate of divorce" was a legal document to dismiss the marriage. Such a document would appear as follows:

On the day of the week A. in the month B. in the year C. from the beginning of the world, according to the common computation in the province of D., I, N. the son of N. by whatever name I am called, of the city E. with entire consent of mind, and without any compulsion, have divorced, dismissed, and expelled thee-thee, I say, M. the daughter of M. by whatever name thou art called, of the city E. who wast heretofore my wife: but now I have dismissed thee-thee, I say, M. the daughter of M. by whatever name thou art called, of the city E. so as to be free, and at thine own disposal, to marry whomsoever thou pleasest, without hinderance from anyone, from this day forever. Thou art therefore free for any man. Let this be thy bill of divorce from me, a writing of separation and expulsion, according to the law of Moses and Israel.
REUBEN, son of Jacob, Witness.
ELIEZAR, son of Gilead, Witness.
(from Adam Clarke's Commentary, Electronic Database. Copyright © 1996, 2003, 2005, 2006 by Biblesoft, Inc. All rights reserved.)

We must understand this information through the Jewish culture of the New Testament. The husband paid a dowry to secure the right of marriage to his wife. Wives were considered the property of their husbands, and by Mosaic statutes women did not possess the right to dissolve the marriage. Only the husband had the privilege of giving a bill of divorce. Josephus (Jewish historian during New Testament days, a non-Christian) was of the opinion that the law did not permit women to divorce their husbands. He thought that Salome, sister of Herod the Great, was the first woman to put away her husband, though Herodias afterward dismissed her.

The right to divorce was not a major debate in Jesus' day because it was a common and acceptable practice. The heated discussions centered on the reason for divorce, focusing on the statement, *"some uncleanness in her."* During the time of the Gospel accounts, there were two schools of learning, Hillel and Shammai. The School of Hillel strongly disagreed with the School of Shammai. Hillel represented the liberal interpretation of the statement, *"some uncleanness in her,"* extending the cause to her burning or over salting his food. If the husband saw a woman whose appearance pleased him better than his wife, it was acceptable for him to divorce her. The School of Shammai represented the conservative interpretation of the statement, limiting divorce to a moral delinquency in the woman, mainly adultery.

We cannot find anywhere in the Word of God where the act of divorce is pronounced as a sin. From the beginning God never intended that divorce be an option. Jesus moved into the region of Perea beyond the Jordan, the territory under the jurisdiction of Herod Antipas. The beheading of John the Baptist was the raging controversy in this area. The problem behind this controversy was the adulterous affair and divorce of Herod and Herodias. Herodias was Philip's wife, the brother of Herod (Matthew 14:3-12). The Pharisees, desiring to trap Jesus, approached Him before a multitude with the issue of divorce. Their question to Him was, *"Is it lawful for a man to divorce his wife for just any reason?"* (Matthew 19:3). Jesus reminded them of their Scriptures. He quoted the intent of God from the beginning, which was that there was no provision for divorce (Matthew 19:4-6). God hates divorce, does not want divorce, and never intended that we dissolve a marriage by divorce (Malachi 2:16).

Jesus' response caused the Pharisees to see an opportunity to accuse Him. Was Jesus contradicting the commandment of Moses? No! Moses did what God wanted, but,

"Moses, because of the hardness of your hearts, permitted you to divorce your wives, but from the beginning it was not so" (Matthew 19:8). God made the allowance of divorce because of the self-centeredness of man's heart. Although divorce may not be the primary intent and desire of God, it may not be voluntary disobedience against His known will for your life. The overwhelming proof of this position is that while God hates divorce, He declared divorce against Israel, *"Then I saw that for all the causes for which backsliding Israel had committed adultery, I had put her away and given her a certificate of divorce; yet her treacherous sister Judah did not fear, but went and played the harlot also"* (Jeremiah 3:8).

Now we come to our passage (Matthew 5:31-32) where the issue is not "divorce" or "no divorce." Jesus does not address the sinfulness of divorce. He embraces the hurt and pain produced by the self-centeredness of the carnal nature. He is aware that sometimes divorce is necessary, which was also accepted by His culture. The issue for debate concerned the proper cause for divorce in that culture. Was the liberal approach of the School of Hillel correct? Can you get a divorce for just any reason such as burnt food or over-salted meat? Or is the conservative approach of the School of Shammai correct? Who is right? Jesus said, *"Furthermore it has been said, 'Whoever divorces his wife, let him give her a certificate of divorce'"* (Matthew 5:31).

How does Jesus answer the question? A major problem I have with Jesus is that He never stays with the subject I want to discuss. He does not address the question that I want answered. Jesus responds with, ***"But I say to you that whoever divorces his wife for any reason except sexual immorality causes her to commit adultery; and whoever marries a woman who is divorced commits adultery"*** (Matthew 5:32). It is easy to misread what Jesus said in our translation and in other interpretations of this verse. We are so focused on the question we want answered that the purpose of Jesus' statement is lost. Do we really want to know what Jesus said? Can we come with an open mind to the revelation of His Spirit?

I want to know when it is right for me to get a divorce? What is the proper basis for divorcing my spouse so I know that I am right and she or he is wrong? From Jesus' perspective the fact that we ask this question reveals we do not have the proper spiritual insight. Perhaps the crisis in your marriage does not warrant divorce, but that is not the issue. Whether I am right or wrong in seeking a divorce is not the issue either. If I focus on this question, I will miss the purpose for which God allowed this marriage crisis to happen in my life.

What is the truth concerning divorce from our passage (Matthew 5:31-32)?

Context

Divorce is the third illustration out of six given by Jesus to highlight a new righteousness in the Kingdom of Heaven. It is not a discussion Jesus held at a special time in a designated location. He progressed in His sermon to a contrast between the righteousness of the present Jewish religion (***"righteousness of the scribes and Pharisees"***) to the "righteousness exceeding" (Matthew 5:20).

Jesus' first illustration was "murder" (Matthew 5:21-26). ***"Those of old"*** limited their discussion to an outward activity of

Part Three: Fulfillment of the Kingdom - The Application: Marriage

murder, never considering their feelings and emotions, focusing on a stagnant deed. Their righteousness asked, "Did you murder?" The Kingdom's righteousness refused this question because the activity of the deed is not the problem in the Kingdom. The Kingdom asks, "Did you get angry, call him names, have an attitude of contempt, and demean him to the level of a fool?" These questions express a self-centered nature at the core of our being. This self-centeredness is the real issue!

Jesus' second illustration is "morality" (Matthew 5:27-30). "Those of old" limited their discussion to an outward activity, "adultery." Their sexuality was a body drive that needed to be limited to an acceptable standard, the seventh commandment. Their righteousness asked, "Did you commit adultery? Did you lust? Do your eyes see with the perspective of self-centered flesh and the satisfaction of selfish desires? These questions search out a self-centered nature at the core of our being. This self-centeredness is the real issue. This is such a serious issue that Jesus surrounds it with the subject of "hell!"

Now we come to the third illustration, "marriage" (Matthew 5:31-32). He begins this illustration differently. Neither of the previous illustrations begins with a conjunction but the third does, and it is the conjunction "de." This conjunction is ignored by many translations, but our translation (New King James) interprets it to mean *"furthermore."* The primary translation for "de" is the contrasting conjunction "but." Although this may not always be a proper translation, "de" is consistently used as "continuation." In other words, Matthew links this third illustration directly with the second.

In the first illustration, Jesus shifted the issue of murder proposed by *"those of old"* to the inner self-centered motive of anger, and He shifted adultery to the inner self-centered heart in the second illustration. Will this third illustration be any different? In the previous two illustrations, Jesus internalized the issue from outward activity to inner motive. Will he not continue to do so with divorce? The context of this illustration will not allow us to interpret Jesus' statement as instruction for proper divorce proceedings. His discussion does not include the issue of when it is proper to get a divorce.

Jesus calls us to examine our inner heart. Is self-centeredness the determining element of our desires? Will I allow the circumstances of my marriage to reveal the core value of my heart? The pressures I experience, the stress raking my system, and the anxiety I endure are all symptoms of a heart condition. What is that condition? Self-centeredness is the problem; it is verified by the context of our passage.

Continuation

What did Jesus teach about marriage and divorce? He references divorce four times in the Gospels (Matt 5:32; 19:3-9; Mark 10:2-12; Luke 16:18). Jesus' statement in Luke's Gospel is a duplication of our passage from the Sermon on the Mount (Matthew 5:32), and His statement in Mark's Gospel is a duplication of the Pharisees attempts to trap Jesus (Matthew 19:3-9). This means there are only two occasions when Jesus addressed divorce. However, Paul quotes Jesus on this subject in his letter to Corinth (1 Corinthians 7:10-15). No new insight is given to us in this passage.

The remarkable thing in each occasion recorded in the Gospels is Jesus' perspective on the issue being addressed. While the Pharisees highlight divorce, Jesus declares the **"the hardness of your hearts"** (Matthew 19:8). In each instance Jesus is not giving a seminar on divorce, and He is not trying to settle the debate between the two opposing schools. He calls His disciples to bleed, suffer, and die. This calling applies to the disciples' relationship with other disciples and their link with others.

Matthew records three major events in chapter 19. The

first is "marriage and divorce" (Matthew 19:1-12), the second is "mother's and dependents" (Matthew 19:13-15), and the third is "materialism and the depressed" (Matthew 19:16-30). The lesson Jesus teaches in each setting does not seem to address the apparent issue. He called His disciples *"to come after Me, let him deny himself, and take up his cross, and follow Me. For whoever desires to save his life will lose it, but whoever loses his life for My sake will find it"* (Matthew 16:24-25). How does this apply to "marriage and divorce?" How does this apply to "mother's and dependents," those who are less than you are? How does this apply to "materialism and the depressed?"

Because Jesus continually speaks to the destruction of self-centeredness in His teachings, why would He be different in our passage (Matthew 5:32)? Do not approach our passage to find the proper procedure for divorce and remarriage because that is not the focus of Jesus' teaching! We must examine the heart to find any residue of self-centeredness. The fact that we want to argue the issue of marriage and divorce declares the abiding presence of self-centeredness.

Conclusion

So what is the conclusion? If we attempt to find solutions to the major social problems of our day, we must look beyond the apparent need. What shall we do about divorce? What is the answer to "same-sex marriages?" How do we solve the crisis of homosexuality? What is the solution to a teenage boy who feels as if he should be a girl? Jesus declares that these things are not the problem! They are symptoms of the problem. We find the problem in the heart filled with self-centeredness. We have not lost our lives to Jesus. It appears even our involvement with Jesus is for our benefit. We continually use Him for what we want. It is time to lose our lives to Him; He wants to use us!

Matthew 5:31-32

KINGDOM MARRIAGE

> *"Furthermore it has been said, 'Whoever divorces his wife,
> let him give her a certificate of divorce.' But I say to you
> that whoever divorces his wife for any reason except sexual
> immorality causes her to commit adultery; and whoever marries
> a woman who is divorced commits adultery"*
> *(Matthew 5:31-32).*

Jesus is the answer! He is the truth of life! However, this statement leaves most people unmoved because they cannot fathom how He could be the answer. They view the problems and negative circumstances of their world and think the answer is a magical removal of these things however necessary. But Jesus does not use magic. Although we are amazed at His miracles, we continue to live with the obstacles and difficulties that mold and shape our lives. Jesus wants to be the answer to all of our circumstances, but it appears to us that He does nothing about them.

Wait! Jesus really is the answer! But the answer is not in what He does; it is in who He is! It is difficult to explain this to those who have not experienced Jesus. He does not tell you the truth; Jesus is the truth. Truth is not in the data and information He gives you. Truth is in the revelation of who He is in you. We find knowledge and new perspective in intimacy with Him. Our need is not that He remove or change our circumstances, but we need an ever-deepening oneness with Him.

Part Three: Fulfillment of the Kingdom - The Application: Marriage

In our studies we call this deepening oneness with Jesus "saturation." Saturation is not a technique or method but a principle of relationship. Will you commit yourself to saturate in the presence of Jesus? Will you develop "a God awareness" in your life, allowing Jesus to invade all aspects of your living? He wants to move from your morning devotions, your prayer before meals, your cry to Him in the moment of crisis to a consistent, moment by moment, interaction between you and Him. What if you relied on Jesus for every involvement of your life, large or small? Instead of figuring out how to source your actions, allow Jesus' mind to be in you.

Allowing Jesus to source your actions will change the focus of your living. Instead of seeking to make it through the day, solving a problem, or achieving a goal, you seek intimacy with Him. Your driving desire becomes Jesus! This new desire will be the one thing you "do." Christianity will cease to be a series of activities and become a relationship with Jesus. You will no longer source your Christian life because He will become your energy. You will saturate in Him!

Saturating in Jesus will change your approach to the Scriptures. The Bible has been a curriculum for specialized students. Many people have made the Bible their roadmap to heaven, an instruction manual for constructing the proper life, or a theological book to support a persuasion. Now the Scriptures become the whispers from the Lover of my soul. As I saturate in His presence, His Word becomes Him speaking to my soul. He takes me beyond the intellectual, academic understanding to the knowledge of His heart. I am no longer studying a book. I am in fellowship with a Person. I saturate in the Living Word by saturating in the Written Word.

My saturation in Jesus is happening in our investigation of the Sermon on the Mount. Our purpose is not to learn data or facts from the passage. We discover Jesus' heart, His tone, and how He thinks. In our previous study, we investigated the concept of our passage (Matthew 5:31-32). This concept is important in life, and we must carefully consider it again. Saturation is not a discovery of facts but a revelation of a concept.

These two verses highlight the subject of marriage and divorce. Many people investigate these verses to reveal the proper procedure for divorce. Arguments arise from the different interpretations of the facts in these verses, causing many questions. What are the grounds for divorce? If I get a divorce, may I remarry? If I marry someone who has been divorced, am I living in adultery? The debates about the answers to these questions continue endlessly. The tragedy of the situation is that we miss the purpose of the passage. Jesus does not answer these questions because they are not the issue He addresses! We do not see or understand it because we did not saturate. Our high intelligence or academic pursuit is not how we understand these verses. Our understanding comes from the presence of Jesus in the context of His Word. The Living Word and the Written Word become real in our lives.

Please allow me to again take you through the concept of Jesus' message in the Sermon on the Mount. Jesus' message (three chapters) shook the world of the disciples. Matthew said that it "knocked them out of their senses," **"the people were astonished at His teaching"** (Matthew 7:28). Jesus was radical from His first word to His last on the Kingdom of Heaven.

Jesus began with a series of "Beatitudes," "The Formation of the Kingdom" (Matthew 5:3-12). His words form congratulations, good fortune, and completeness. This is not something you receive but what you have. The Beatitudes are not a perspective of a heavenly future, but a view of your present state. You do not earn, merit, or achieve this reward because Jesus provides it for you. What all other religions offer as the result of discipline, achievement, and faithfulness, Jesus congratulates you for having now. This state is the Kingdom of Heaven. If you say that you do not live in the Kingdom of Heaven, it is not because it is not

Part Three: Fulfillment of the Kingdom - The Application: Marriage

yours. Everything associated with the Kingdom is yours. You may refuse to embrace it, but God always provides.

The Kingdom of Heaven is a state of embracing the absolute poverty of your inner spirit (Matthew 5:3). You recognize your helplessness. It is not that you are helpless in mastering certain skills in your physical world, but it is the poverty at the core of your being where your life is sourced. You are to embrace your helplessness as one who "mourns" (Matthew 5:4), like one who lost their dearest loved one. Grief so overtakes your inner being that your life expresses it. Embrace your helplessness with the passion or fervor that affects your perspective on life. If you do, you will be filled with the comfort of Jesus' presence (Matthew 5:4). You will find the Spirit of Jesus merging with your helplessness. When you and Jesus unite, the Kingdom of Heaven is formed. Out of this formation comes all that really matters in life: meekness (Matthew 5:5), inheriting the earth (Matthew 5:5), fulfillment of righteousness (Matthew 5:6), mercy (Matthew 5:7), purity (Matthew 5:8), seeing God (Matthew 5:8), peace (Matthew 5:9), relationship (Matthew 5:9), and intimacy with Him (the Kingdom of Heaven) that rises above all adversities (Matthew 5:10-12). You are not "in" the Kingdom; you have "become" the Kingdom!

Next, Jesus explains the "Function of the Kingdom" (Matthew 5:13-16). How does this Kingdom operate in our world? He uses the imagery of **"*salt*"** and **"*light*,"** "being" and "doing." The presence of the Kingdom of Heaven influences your world. What you are in the merger with Jesus transforms everything around you. Your world sees the Father and will stand in awe of Him (Matthew 5:16).

This transformation must have sounded radical to a culture of legalistic religion. The Pharisees developed six hundred and thirteen oral traditions based on the Old Testament. Their righteousness existed in their oral traditions, which they carried out in their temple activities. Their interpretation of the Scriptures demanded this righteousness. Did Jesus propose a new religion? Was He rejecting the Scriptures on which they based their righteousness? Is His proposed Kingdom different from what their promised Messiah would establish?

Jesus answers their question by proclaiming the "Fulfillment of the Kingdom" (Matthew 5:17-48). We have divided it into two sections: "Acknowledgment of the Fulfillment" (Matthew 5:17-20) and "Application of the Fulfillment" (Matthew 5:21-48). Jesus boldly declared His relationship with the Scriptures. He said, **"Do not think"** (nomizo). Do not let the pattern of thinking you have always embraced determine your thoughts now. Twice He said, **"I did not come to destroy."** Our perspective on the Scriptures is so contaminated that Jesus takes us back to what God intended in the Scriptures. The Kingdom of Heaven is what God desires for us and announces in the Scriptures. The Scriptures of the Old Testament find their completion in this new Kingdom relationship.

Jesus' fulfillment of the Kingdom produced a new level of righteousness. The scribes and Pharisees were doing the best they could do. Their source of righteousness was their helplessness. They were self-sourced! Now your helplessness can merge with the righteousness of God! What kind of difference will this make in your life? Even the beginner in this new relationship will far exceed anything self-sourcing can produce (Matthew 5:20).

Jesus knew they did not understand this because they had never experienced it, so He gave them some examples (Matthew 5:21-48). He presented six illustrations. The first one deals with "murder" (Matthew 5:21-26). **"Those of old"** considered their inner helplessness, which was filled with emotional upset, hatred, and bitterness. Anger surfaces when self is challenged. We must not allow these feelings to possess our lives and limit our expressions. The Ten Commandments offered a solution: **"You shall not murder."** This commandment is the best self-sourcing, my helplessness, can exhibit.

Part Three: Fulfillment of the Kingdom - The Application: Marriage

The Kingdom of Heaven offers another level of living. If my helplessness can be embraced by God's nature, I can experience a new expression of righteousness. Jesus did not offer a new rule to curb the expression of anger. He proposed an elimination of the anger itself! What if your source of living changes? How will you live if the nature of God were the source of your expression? This change is not "anger management;" this is "anger elimination." It is not a new rule; it is a new Source!

We must see this illustration in light of the idea Jesus proposes. In the "Formation of the Kingdom" (Matthew 5:3-12), we enter into a new state of living. It is a merger between the Spirit of God and our helplessness. This new Kingdom of God will be **"salt"** and **"light"** in our world, the "Function of the Kingdom" (Matthew 5:13-16). It will look like Jesus! He will hang on a cross and cry, "Forgive them!" He will communicate redemption in every encounter. Sin will not survive the atmosphere of this forgiving nature. It will be the "Fulfillment of the Kingdom" (Matthew 5:17-48). Everything God proposed in the Old Testament Scriptures will be completed in this new Kingdom person! It will be a righteousness far exceeding the righteousness of the scribes and Pharisees.

The second illustration is "morality" (Matthew 5:27-30). **"Those of old"** considered their sexuality a body appetite to give pleasure but not abuse. In viewing their helplessness, they saw their core self-centeredness as filled with the desires of the flesh. Lust, uncontrolled urges, and personal satisfaction managed their lives and needed to be limited in its expression. They found the boundary in the Seventh Commandment of the Ten Commandments, **"You shall not commit adultery."** This limitation was the best they could do sourced by their helplessness, and even this was difficult.

The Kingdom of Heaven offered a new level of righteousness. If my helplessness can be embraced by His Divine nature, a new righteousness can be experienced. Jesus did not offer a new rule to curb the raging desire of the body appetite but proposed a new source for the sexuality of my person. His sourcing will not eliminate my sexual desires but will transform them with a new perspective. The helpless self-centered heart looks through the physical eyes and sees what caters to its desires. What if my helplessness is embraced by His Divine nature? I will have a new perspective! The expression of my sexuality in every area will become the expression of Jesus. The way I walk, the way I dress, the interaction with the opposite gender, and how I view others will all be sourced by this new nature filling my helplessness. Even my sexuality will become *"salt"* and *"light"* in my world. My selfish helplessness will be transformed into a redemptive empowerment.

How will this affect my marriage? OH! "Marriage" is the third example (Matthew 5:31, 32). ***"Those of old"*** could not endure the normal irritations of marriage. With their helplessness dominated by self-centeredness, they considered benefits only for themselves. When two helpless self-centered people live together the result is conflict. Moses granted using a ***"certificate of divorce."*** Helpless self-centeredness requires the choice of divorce, and Jesus communicated the one reason for such a provision was our self-centered helplessness (Matthew 19:8).

"Those of old" never questioned the right of divorce. They asked only, "When may we divorce?" They debated the issue of cause, physical circumstance, or justification. The conservative school proposed the only justification for divorce is adultery while the liberal school proposed any unfavorable thing is a basis for divorce. Bad breathe, bad cooking, and finding someone more attractive justified divorce. Self-centered helplessness always looks for the boundary within which to be self-centered. In the emotional anger of life, it is murder; in self-centered sexuality, it is adultery. In marriage, divorce is acceptable, but what is the justifiable cause?

Part Three: Fulfillment of the Kingdom - The Application: Marriage

The Kingdom of Heaven offers a new level of righteousness. Jesus does not offer a new rule justifying divorce. Wait! He said, ***"for any reason except sexual immorality"*** (Matthew 5:32). You must see His statement in light of the second illustration. Sexual immorality is not a matter of physical activity but a matter of the self-centered helplessness of the heart. Because ***"all have sinned and fall short of the glory of God"*** (Romans 3:23) are we not all guilty of sexual immorality in the self-centered heart? Should we not all hang our heads and cry for deliverance from the self-centeredness of our lives that refuses to embrace our helplessness? Would not embracing and empowering our helplessness by the nature of Jesus enable us in the oneness of marriage?

We must see this illustration in light of the concept Jesus proposes. In the "Formation of the Kingdom" (Matthew 5:3-12), we enter into a new state of living, a merger between the Spirit of God and our helplessness. This new Kingdom of God will be ***"salt"*** and ***"light"*** in the world, the "Function of the Kingdom" (Matthew 5:13-16). It will look like Jesus! Paul said that it would cause me to love my ***"wife as Christ also loved the church and gave Himself for her, that He might sanctify and cleanse her"*** (Ephesians 5:25, 26). The redemptive nature of Jesus will fill the atmosphere of my home instead of the selfish demand of my desires! Where do we find divorce in that kind of oneness in marriage? This kind of marriage unity will be the "Fulfillment of the Kingdom" (Matthew 5:17-48). Everything God proposed in the Old Testament Scriptures will be completed for the Kingdom person in the marriage! It will be a righteousness far exceeding the righteousness of the scribes and Pharisees. My helplessness cries for His filling!

Matthew 5:31-32

THE MAIN SUBJECT

"Furthermore it has been said, 'Whoever divorces his wife, let him give her a certificate of divorce.' But I say to you that whoever divorces his wife for any reason except sexual immorality causes her to commit adultery; and whoever marries a woman who is divorced commits adultery"
(Matthew 5:31-32).

The context of our passage is of the utmost importance. Over the years, people have made assumptions creating issues affecting our understanding. Some of these assumptions come from the Jewish cultural environment of biblical times, while the language of the New Testament generates other assumptions. Jesus proposed a new spiritual perception of the Kingdom person, and His proposal also caused assumption. These assumptions are essential to our understanding of the spiritual concept Jesus relates to in our passage.

Design

Jesus' words in our passage are focused on and addressed to men. He follows the biblical idea for the structure of marriage, relating directly to the sexuality of the people involved. We could approach the subject from the psychological view and discover essential facts, but we are interested in seeing sexuality only through spiritual eyes. God gave male and female different sexuality for creating "one flesh." **"And the Lord God said, 'It is not good that man should be alone; I will make him a helper comparable to him'"** (Genesis 2:18), giving us God's purpose for female sexuality. The English word "complement" best conveys the meaning of this position. The wife is a **"helper"** who "complements" her husband in every way. A helping role does not imply inferiority because the husband also complements his wife.

In these complementary roles, **"the husband is head of the wife"** (Ephesians 5:22). The context of his position is, **"as also Christ is head of the church; and He is the Savior of the body. Therefore, just as the church is subject to Christ, so let the wives be to their own husbands in everything"** (Ephesians 5:23-24). God intended the husband to have a redemptive position with his wife, but his self-centered heart controlled his sexuality. He did not see his leadership position as redemptive, but allowing his selfishness, he dominated his wife for his satisfaction and desires. Self-centeredness is always destructive and never redemptive.

The Jewish culture of Jesus' day was a male-dominated society, and man's sexuality was self-centered. There were no women disciples. During the last six months of Jesus' life, women joined the disciples, providing financial aid for Jesus (Luke 8:1-3). They were faithful at the cross when the disciples fled in fear. These women met every requirement of a faithful disciple, yet they were never included in the role. In the Jewish tradition of marriage, the bridegroom had to pay a stipulated price to the bride's father for the privilege of marriage to his daughter. Because the husband paid a price for his wife, this seemed to give him liberty to exercise arbitrary power over her. The husband could renounce or divorce her whenever he chose, but the wife did not have the same privilege. Thus, in our passage (Matthew 5:31-32), Jesus directs His remarks to the self-centered man, not the woman.

Detail

Jesus focuses His remarks, clarifying that focus with the statement, *"except for sexual immorality."* Jesus is not talking about the husband who finds his wife unfaithful to him, committing adultery. This is evident when Jesus gives insight by saying, *"causes her to commit adultery; and whoever marries a woman who is divorced commits adultery"* (Matthew 5:32). If the wife has chosen to commit adultery, the reason for the divorce, then the husband's response is not the cause of the adultery.

Therefore, the spiritual truth Jesus communicates does not include the situation where adultery has occurred in the marriage. In Jesus' second illustration about "morality," He proposed a description of adultery in the spiritual world. *"Those of old"* considered adultery only in the physical. There was no provision in the Old Covenant for the cleansing of the self-centered nature that controlled sexuality. The Old Covenant did not have that power. The best *"those of old"* could manage was to put a limit on the expression of their sexuality, *"You shall not commit adultery"* (Matthew 5:27). Jesus moves man to the higher standard of the New Covenant where a man is not to "look" at a woman with lust in his heart. If a person's heart is changed from the nature of self-centeredness to God's nature, what they see, and their perspective of others also changes. Under the New Covenant, what adultery is in the physical world, lust is in the spiritual world.

Jesus' third illustration reverts to the Old Covenant view of adultery. Jesus aggressively moves us into the spiritual perspective. He does the same in His discussion of marriage. We have to maintain the spiritual view of the subject being discussed. Jesus uses an interesting combination of words to express this. The statement under consideration is, "for any reason except sexual immorality." This phrase is translated from "parektos logos porneia." Our words "porn" and "pornography" come from the Greek word "porneia." Jesus used the word "logos," which, on occasion, is used as a "cause" or "reason." So, what is the idea? "Logos" is the idea or thought being expressed and encourages us to consider the spiritual realm instead of the physical. Jesus' reference is to the idea or thought of sexual immorality.

Donation

Jesus' statement concerns what is "caused" in the woman. He speaks to the husbands and not the wives, desperately concerned about the spiritual view of the issue, the husband's contribution to his wife. If the husband's role is spiritual leader, he must be the redemptive source for his wife. The issue under discussion is, "what are you causing in her?"

The Greek word "poieo" is translated as "causes." The word is used for trees "bearing" (poieo) fruit, referring not just to the action but also to the action's nature and motive. The nature is driving the expression. Jesus is concerned about the husband, who is spiritual leader is the redemptive force in the home. The husband filled with self-centeredness becomes a manipulative, destructive, damning force in influencing his wife. Jesus is not talking about just the physical act of adultery.

The husband is responsible for creating a state or atmosphere in which the wife is drawn into submission, yielding, and surrendering Christ's life. The self-centered husband establishes a state or atmosphere in which she is drawn to self-centered expression. Instead of pulling her to Christ, he pushes her to a self-centered demonic nature. His self-centered actions cause her to seek to save her life, and instead, she loses it. He should be living in an atmosphere of holiness that draws her to lose her life so she will find it. Jesus was concerned about what "those of old" were producing in others. The husband who is focused on himself loses perspective of his wife's needs, and he ceases to be the spiritual leader and redeemer in his home. He aids in the production of self-centered sexuality in his wife.

Divorce

Now we need to review. Jesus does not speak to the women of His day, but He speaks to the men. The wives did not have the right to divorce. The husbands were the spiritual leaders of the "one flesh" marriage. He set aside any thought of justification for divorce, such as the wife involved in adultery. He does not discuss the adulterous wife in this illustration. Jesus' primary concern is what the husband is stimulating in the heart of his wife. The husband is to be the spiritual leader responsible for producing an atmosphere in which his wife can surrender to Jesus.

Two Greek words we must examine are paramount to understanding this passage. The Greek word "apostasion" is a legal, technical term for the relinquishing of legal rights. When used concerning marriage, it means "divorce." When we hear that someone is "divorced," we know that they were once married, but that marriage is no longer binding, and they are now single. No one gets confused or misunderstands, using the word "divorce." If a married couple separates but does not legally dissolve the marriage, they are not divorced. The English word "divorce" and the Greek word "apostasion" always mean a marriage's legal dissolution.

The Greek word "apostasion" is used only three times in the New Testament. Each time "a certificate of" is used, the word "divorce" is included. This phrase emphasizes the technical and legal aspects of the word's meaning. One of those three uses is in the understanding of *"those of old."* They proposed, *"let him give her a certificate of divorce"* (Matthew 5:31). Moses

Part Three: Fulfillment of the Kingdom - The Application: Marriage

established this legality, and it has been in effect for hundreds of years (Deuteronomy 24:1).

The second Greek word is "apoluo," a general term used sixty-six times in the New Testament for various situations. It means "releasing, dismissing, sending, away (as a crowd or individual), liberating, discharging, releasing from debt, releasing a prisoner, dismissing a servant, forgiving or pardoning a debt or action, releasing from sickness, sending demons from a person, or sending apostles." In our passage, it means "for a husband to send his wife from his house." This is the Greek word equivalent to our English word "separation." "Separation" is never to be confused with "divorce" but is understood as the prelude to divorce, which may or may not occur.

In our passage (Matthew 5:31-32), "apoluo" (separation) is used three times, and "apostasion" (divorce) is used once. The Greek word "apostasion (divorce) is used in connection with ***"it has been said"*** (Matthew 5:31). "Apostasion" is not used at all in connection with, ***"But I say to you"*** (Matthew 5:32). Jesus is NOT discussing the subject of divorce. He is talking about separation! He does not give the biblical grounds for divorce; He does not discuss or describe divorce.

There may be a time to talk about the issue of divorce, but not from this passage. Is divorce applauded and exalted by God in the Scriptures? Absolutely NOT! Jesus is strong on the fact that from the beginning, God did not provide for divorce. Divorce was never the intent of His heart. He placed Adam and Eve together in "one flesh," and there was never a divorce provision. Self-centeredness so possessed the human heart that it destroyed the "one flesh" of marriage. God allowed divorce in such cases. He needed to divorce Israel. "Then I saw that for all the causes for which backsliding Israel had committed adultery, I had put her away and given her a certificate of divorce; yet her treacherous sister Judah did not fear, but went and played the harlot also" (Jeremiah 3:8). Is it God's desire and choice? NO! But occasionally, it is necessary.

Can a person remarry after being divorced? Perhaps the sin is not in divorce but in remarrying. The intent of God's provision through Moses for divorce was remarriage. After declaring the provision of giving a certificate of divorce (Deuteronomy 24:1), God made the stipulation, *"when she has departed from his house, and goes and becomes another man's wife"* (Deuteronomy 24:2). There is no guidance or condemnation about remarriage in this passage. The provision of divorce was for the possibility of remarriage, which would protect the woman. But these are all issues not discussed in our passage! Jesus addresses none of these issues in the Sermon on the Mount.

What is Jesus' concern? Will you and I embrace our helplessness and allow His person to fill and source us? Will we become dependent instead of independent? Will we recognize the destructiveness of our self-sourcing and discover the full potential in His sourcing (Matthew 5:13-16)? We promoted a self-centered, self-sourced, legalistic, religious clique instead of becoming the Kingdom of God fulfilling the Scriptures (Matthew 5:17-20).

We joined *"those of old"* in trying to manage our anger instead of being delivered from it. We limited the expression of our self-centered wrath and did not commit murder, but in the spiritual world, murder was committed (Matthew 5:21-26). We viewed our sexuality as a body appetite to be controlled by a rule, *"You shall not commit adultery."* All the while, in the depth of our being self-centeredness, mastered our sexuality, and expressed itself in *"lust."* We strut with pride in our walk, demand our rights in relationships, and grab for ourselves in our materialism. We con each other for self-satisfaction, manipulate others for our benefit, and continually parade our joy over others' failures. Our self-centered sexuality determines our perspective that becomes lust (Matthew 5:27-30).

Our self-centered sexuality appears in our marriages.

Part Three: Fulfillment of the Kingdom - The Application: Marriage

The old provision was "tired of your wife, divorce her." If you find some unfavorable, unclean thing about her, then legally remove yourself from her. Do you see that the real problem is self-centeredness? Jesus speaks to the husbands who are the spiritual leaders of their marriage. He highlights what happens in the spiritual realm because of self-centeredness. You separated yourself, pushed your wife aside, for your self-centered desires. Instead of drawing her into the fullness of Jesus in her life, you pushed her aside. You left her dangling, emotionally, and spiritually deprived of all that would make her the godly wife she could be. She found herself without spiritual leadership and reverted to self-centeredness as you taught her.

Jesus addressed the situation common in His culture. Husbands would easily separate from their wives, leaving the women with no means of support. If they could not return to their father's home, they were homeless. These separated wives' only possibilities were prostitution or another marriage, which created an adulterous situation because they were not legally free from their previous marriage. Why would a husband put his wife in such a position? The reason is the self-centeredness of his inward heart!

Even though I might be proud that I have never done such to my wife, have I lived out of myself, failing in the spiritual leadership of my home in the spiritual realm? Although my wife has not had an adulterous affair, have I failed to meet her emotional and spiritual needs, causing her to commit spiritual adultery? Am I not responsible for my "one flesh?" If "she is me" (Genesis 2:23), am I destroying myself when I do not allow Jesus to source me?

Matthew 5:31-32

SPIRITUAL SEPARATION

"Furthermore it has been said, 'Whoever divorces his wife, let him give her a certificate of divorce.' But I say to you that whoever divorces his wife for any reason except sexual immorality causes her to commit adultery; and whoever marries a woman who is divorced commits adultery"
(Matthew 5:31-32).

There are people who are spiritually sensitive and desire the presence of God in their lives. We know what it feels like to live in the violation of His will, and this rests heavily on us because we are guilty. We understand that the violation of His will in our lives destroys our relationship with God. The only chance for any peace in His presence is forgiveness. The forgiving heart of God is the theme of the Scriptures. Jesus said, **"Therefore I say to you, every sin and blasphemy will be forgiven men"** (Matthew 12:31). We can draw assurance from John when he wrote, **"If we confess our sins, He is faithful and just to forgive us our sins and to cleanse us from all unrighteousness"** (1 John 1:9).

Jesus is **"the image of the invisible God"** (Colossians 1:15). Jesus' characteristics, as highlighted in the Gospel accounts, reveal the mind and nature of God. Jesus always forgives, even in the worst of circumstances. Enduring the suffering of the cross, He said, **"Father, forgive them"** (Luke 23:34). Amid a pressing crowd, Jesus said to the paralytic lowered in front of Him, **"Son,**

be of good cheer; your sins are forgiven you" (Matthew 9:2). The only thing Jesus will not tolerate is a self-centered rebellious attitude that will not embrace forgiveness.

Although I have never been divorced, it seems to me that the difficulty is forgiveness. I can imagine it would be a struggle to forgive the spouse who repeatedly injured the offering of your heart, but it may be an even greater hurdle to forgive yourself for your part in the destruction of your marriage. We are often haunted by our failure in the context of our relationships. Is divorce like the death of a spouse, only they never go away? How do you forgive yourself and the others involved to move on?

It is not my intention to increase guilt regarding divorce. Whatever your situation, this is a call to learn the spiritual lessons for which God allowed this to happen. Was my divorce right or wrong? Divorce is never right! We recognize the cause of every divorce is the heart of sin, which is self-centeredness. You must allow what happened to cause your surrender to Jesus and never again allow self-sourcing in your life!

Our study of this passage leads us to discover that Jesus is not addressing the issue of divorce. Although most translations interpret this passage with Jesus using the word "divorce" three times, I oppose these interpretations. The Greek word "apostasion" is a legal, technical term for the relinquishing of legal rights. When used in relation to marriage, it means "divorce." When we hear that someone is "divorced," we understand they were once married but that marriage is no longer binding, and the people are now single. The word "divorce" and "apostasion" always mean a legal dissolving of marriage. The word "apostasion" is used only once in our passage and refers to "a certificate of divorce." The Greek word "apoluo" is a general term used sixty-six times in the New Testament for a variety of situations. This is the Greek word equivalent to our English word "separation." "Separation" as applied to marriage is never confused with "divorce." We understand that a "separation" is often a prelude to a "divorce,"

Spiritual Separation | **Matthew 5:31-32**

which may or may not occur. Jesus is NOT talking about the subject of divorce but about the subject of separation! He does not give biblical grounds for divorce. He does not describe a state of adultery for those who remarry after divorce. He is not talking about divorce at all. Every time *"divorce"* appears in these two verses except for *"a certificate of divorce,"* the word should have been translated "separates."

In the Sermon on the Mount, Jesus continually exposes the self-centered heart. These two verses are a continuation of His theme. The scribes and Pharisees separated from their wives at the slightest upset, and according to Jewish law they should have given her a certificate of divorce. However, the sexuality of the husband dominated by self-centeredness would separate from his wife and not bother with the certificate of divorce. Separation without divorce meant the marriage was not dissolved. The woman was left helpless without support, forcing her into adultery, either prostitution or remarriage even though she was still legally married. The problem was not in the legal divorce but in the separation.

Jesus does not speak to the *"woman"* but forcefully exposes the self-centered husband. The Bible defines the role of the husband as *"head of the wife"* (Ephesians 5:23). The self-centered heart hears those words and interprets them as "boss, use, and manipulate," but that was never the spiritual intent. Paul clearly speaks to this in his letter to the Ephesians. *"Husbands, love your wives, just as Christ also loved the church and gave Himself for her, that He might sanctify and cleanse her with the washing of water by the word, that He might present her to Himself a glorious church, not having spot or wrinkle or any such thing, but that she should be holy and without blemish"* (Ephesians 5:25-28). The biblical role of the husband is a spiritual role!

My responsibility as a husband is to provide an atmosphere in which my wife can flourish spiritually in intimacy and oneness with Jesus. I am to protect her from every evil power and influence that would drag her into self-centeredness. Marriage is the commitment of death to self-centeredness. I am giving myself to my wife in a spiritual, physical, and legal sense, losing my life to my wife. Loving my wife in this manner is the principle of the Kingdom that Jesus expressed when He said, ***"For whoever desires to save his life will lose it, but whoever loses his life for My sake will find it"*** (Matthew 16:25). When I lose my life to my wife and seek only to meet her needs, my needs are met! When I use her to meet my needs, neither her needs nor mine are met.

Jesus talks about the problem of self-centeredness in our passage. The new righteousness of the Kingdom that exceeds the righteousness of the scribes and Pharisees is a righteousness of death to self-centeredness. In the self-centeredness of the old righteousness, the man separated from his wife in the marriage relationship, instead of giving her a certificate of divorce. He did not legally divorce but mentally and spiritually separated from his wife, most often dismissing her from his home. Even if he allowed her to remain in his home his, self-centeredness produced an atmosphere that left her alone and without support, and in each situation he was not following the biblical principle of marriage.

Security

Understanding the culture of Jesus' day is of utmost importance. The culture was a male dominated society; the woman was slightly above the category of slave. The bridegroom paid a fee to the father of the bride for the privilege of marriage to her. The self-centered male developed an attitude of ownership of his wife. Only the husband had the right to divorce. The woman had no means of support outside marriage. Her security

Spiritual Separation | **Matthew 5:31-32**

was in her husband. With this attitude the debate focused on the "grounds for divorce." If the wife committed adultery, the husband was obviously justified in giving her a certificate of divorce. However, the husband could commit adultery, but the wife was without the same option.

The School of Shammai taught that physical adultery was the only grounds for divorce. The School of Hillel disagreed with that position, and they gave a liberal interpretation of the statement *"some uncleanness in her"* (Deuteronomy 24:1). Her "uncleanness" could include burning his food or merely over salting it. If the husband saw another woman whose appearance pleased him more than his wife's, divorce was acceptable. In this atmosphere the woman lived in a state of physical insecurity.

We have been looking at the physical security of the wife in Jesus' day. What about the emotional and spiritual security of her life? In female sexuality God placed the need for security and stability in intimacy. Although the physical provisions of life contribute to her security, they are not the final answer. In illustrating the righteousness exceeding the righteousness of the scribes and Pharisees (Matthew 5:20), Jesus moved from a physical accomplishment to the spiritual realm. A person cannot murder in the physical realm and be righteous (Matthew 5:21). However, anger in the spiritual realm is spiritual murder (Matthew 5:22). The focus of male sexuality was reduced to a body drive. Therefore, abstaining from adultery accomplished righteousness in the physical (Matthew 5:27). But Jesus explained that our hearts determine our sexuality, how we see things (Matthew 5:28). Our core selfishness in the spiritual realm is equal to the act of adultery in the physical. This same principle was applied to Jesus' view of marriage. Remember, He is not discussing divorce in our passage. In the spiritual realm, masculine sexuality lives for itself and deprives feminine sexuality of spiritual and emotional security. She no longer experiences the purpose of her creation, *"bone of my*

bones and flesh of my flesh" (Genesis 2:23). The husband ceases to embrace the wife with the security of "she is me!"

The self-centered husband can neglect his role as the figure of Christ to his wife in the spiritual realm. He might feel justified that he has not physically divorced her or separated her from his home, but instead of enveloping her in stability, intimacy, and security he uses and abuses her for his physical satisfaction. When Jesus discussed this attitude with His disciples, their response was astounding! ***"If such is the case of the man with his wife, it is better not to marry"*** (Matthew 19:10). They thought if you cannot use your wife for your benefit, why would you want to marry? To the self-centered heart, marriage is beneficial only when my needs are met.

Jesus was speaking to the masculine sexuality of His day. The role of the husband in the Kingdom was to provide an atmosphere of security in which his wife could experience spiritual intimacy with Jesus. The husband is the "Christ-figure" to his wife. This was the failure of the first sin (Genesis 3). Adam failed to provide the spiritual leadership in his home. Eve played the role of spiritual leader and sin was born. Sin appeared in a conversation between Eve and the serpent. Adam refused to take part in this spiritual discussion. When God came walking in the garden, He was looking for Adam (Genesis 3:9). Although Eve experienced the consequences of sin with all creation, it was Adam that God confronted first! He failed to give spiritual security in his home.

Stability

Providing "stability" for his wife is another aspect of the spiritual atmosphere of the husband, the key to security. There is no security unless stability is present. Security comes with consistency. A variety of men came to Jesus with good intentions of discipleship. They were captivated by His message and miracles. Jesus radically called them to consistency. He said to one person, *"No one, having put his hand to the plow, and looking back, is fit for the kingdom of God"* (Luke 9:62).

Jesus is not discussing divorce in our passage (Matthew 5:31-32). He highlights the "separation" happening in the marriages of His culture. The problem with the marriages was not divorce but separation without a certificate of divorce. Jesus sees the problem not just as a physical separation, leaving the wife with no support, but separation in the spiritual realm. The physical separation was possible only because of the spiritual separation that preceded it. The physical separation and divorce is a product of spiritual separation. The role of the husband is to provide security that is possible only because of consistency in the spiritual atmosphere of the marriage.

In Jesus' culture, self-centered masculinity produced an atmosphere of instability. The wife did not know what her husband might do next. If the physical standard was do not murder (Matthew 5:21), he was free to vent emotionally in the home to express his upset. The husband determined the quality of the day and the atmosphere of the home, and there were days when everything was wonderful, but other days were filled with anger. When the circumstances of his life outside of his home caused his emotional upset and he could not vent on the people there, he then chose to lash out at home. The husband was responsible for the stability of the spiritual atmosphere of his home. This stability provided a security in which his wife could grow.

If the physical standard was do not commit adultery (Matthew 5:27), the husband was free to engage in lust, flirtations, and emotional affairs. His wife was not the focus of his love; one flesh marriage became dissolved in self-centered desires and activities. The emotional and romantic security of the wife was destroyed, and stability was not present.

Security and stability are impossible to maintain because we have up-and-down experiences. How may we not be affected by our world and our circumstances? That is Jesus' premise in the Sermon on the Mount. He calls us to embrace our helplessness (Matthew 5:3). He will come in His fullness and source our lives. We become the Kingdom in our home. Self-centeredness can never produce security or stability. The atmosphere in which the wife can grow and find spiritual maturity in Jesus is destroyed by the self-centeredness of the husband.

Spirituality

The husband cannot save his wife. Jesus is our Savior. However, if the intent of every Christian is to be the light of the world and the salt of the Earth that displays good works and glorifies our Father in heaven (Matthew 5:13-16), how much more must this happen in our homes? This mandate is the responsibility of the husband for his wife. The spiritual atmosphere of the home is the responsibility of the husband. He is to create a home where his wife can experience spiritual growth in Jesus, without obstacles.

Jesus calls us to the marriage of the New Covenant. Losing our lives to each other is the chief ingredient. We are to embrace our helplessness in the mourning manner that allows the Spirit of Jesus to source us. Meekness, fullness, mercy, purity, seeing God, peace and rejoicing amid of adversity will flow from this (Matthew 5:3-12), which does not produce separation but intimacy with each other and Jesus.

PART FOUR
MATTHEW 5:33-37

Fulfillment of the Kingdom –
The Application:

MORALS

Matthew 5:33-37

MORALS

"Again you have heard that it was said to those of old, 'You shall not swear falsely, but shall perform your oaths to the Lord.' But I say to you, do not swear at all: neither by heaven, for it is God's throne; nor by the earth, for it is His footstool; nor by Jerusalem, for it is the city of the great King. Nor shall you swear by your head, because you cannot make one hair white or black. But let your 'Yes' be 'Yes,' and your 'No,' 'No.' For whatever is more than these is from the evil one" (Matthew 5: 33-37).

Our passage begins with the Greek word "palin," which is translated *"again."* It is a continuative particle connecting circumstances that refer to the same subject, meaning "once more" or "further." Jesus does not give us a new concept, but He applies the same concept to another area of our lives.

The premise rests on the establishment of the Kingdom of God. Something new is happening in the world. Jesus is birthing the Kingdom! "The Formation of the Kingdom" is clearly stated in the Beatitudes (Matthew 5:3-12). The Kingdom is a merger between my helplessness *("poor in spirit")* and His great resource *("shall be comforted")*, a relationship with Jesus. All the necessary qualities of the Kingdom are found in this merger, this new creature. Jesus was the first of this new species!

How does this manifest itself in practical life? "The Function of the Kingdom" (Matthew 5:13-16) is described as *"salt"* and *"light."* We cannot do *"salt"* and *"light;"* they simply are! Although each accomplishes something, it is not a formula to follow or duties to perform; it is the essence of their existence. This is true of the new Kingdom person.

Let no one propose this as a new idea. This new creation is "The Fulfillment of the Kingdom" (Matthew 5:17-48). Let us begin by establishing the present tense reality of this fulfillment, "The Fulfillment Acknowledged" (Matthew 5:17-20). Jesus, as the first Kingdom person, fulfilled the Old Testament Scriptures! All the dreams of the Old Covenant law were accomplished in this new creation, a Kingdom person. My helplessness merged with Jesus' nature produces a person whose *"righteousness exceeds the righteousness of the scribes and Pharisees"* (Matthew 5:20).

The quality of this statement must be explained because inconceivable anyone could exceed the righteousness of the scribes and Pharisees. Jesus boldly proclaimed six illustrations or applications of this new righteousness, "The Fulfillment Applied" (Matthew 5:21-48). His proposition in these illustrations is preposterous. No man can achieve such a high standard unless there is additional resource given to him. We discover the heart of Jesus' teaching in this truth! We are helpless to achieve such high standards. But the Spirit of Jesus comes to fill us, then become Kingdom people who live out of the nature of God.

Jesus' first illustration is "murder" (Matthew 5:21-26). The best man can accomplish in his self-centeredness is not to kill. Controlling his anger, disciplining his urges, or dominating his emotions is the best man can expect. However, Jesus proposed not the elimination of murder, but the elimination of anger. This proposal demanded a new nature, a new resource.

Jesus' second illustration is "morality" (Matthew 5:27-30). Those of old viewed their sexuality as a body drive to be controlled. The highest standard was not committing adultery. No one could expect more than that. Jesus proposed a new view at the core of the heart. Sexuality dominates the expression of our lives. If self-centeredness controls the heart, sexuality will express nothing but self. If a new nature, the nature of Jesus indwells the heart, what will be expressed through every avenue of sexuality? A righteousness that exceeds will be expressed.

The same is true in Jesus' third illustration on "marriage" (Matthew 5:31-32). The highest standard of the Old Covenant proposed ending marriage with a certificate of divorce. Jesus was more concerned with what we "cause" in our marriage. If I am to focus on my spouse rather than on myself, I will need a new nature.

Now we come to the fourth illustration, "morals" (Matthew 5:33-37). Our purpose in this study is to expose this illustration.

Involvement

In each previous illustration, Jesus agrees with *"those of old."* Jesus is not discrediting their statements. *"Those of old"* said, *"You shall not murder and whoever murders will be in danger of the judgment"* (Matthew 5:21). Is this not true? God gave this to us as the sixth of the Ten Commandments (Exodus 20:13). Jesus' intent was not to dismiss the "letter of this law" but to give the spirit of God's desire. This commandment is fulfilled in the New Covenant and is of little concern in the Kingdom of God. The indwelling Spirit eliminates anger in our lives.

"Those of old" said, *"You shall not commit adultery"* (Matthew 5:27). Was Jesus saying that adultery is allowed in the New Covenant? Absolutely not! This commandment is the seventh of the Ten Commandments (Exodus 20:14). However, as murder is of little consequence in the New Covenant, so is adultery. Jesus proposed we capture God's heart and be filled with His nature. This changes the perspective of our sexuality

from the heart. The core of our life's source will now be the mind of Christ!

Divorce was a social problem in Jesus' day. Two thousand years later we face the same dilemma. The Old Testament standard said, *"Whoever divorces his wife, let him give her a certificate of divorce"* (Matthew 5:31). God made provision for divorce in the Old Testament (Deuteronomy 24:1-4). Jesus did not contradict this provision. The concern of the New Covenant regards what a man *"causes"* in his wife (Matthew 5:32). If the core of my life changes from self-centeredness to Christ-centeredness, I will be redemptive. How may I redeem my wife, my home, and my children?

Jesus agreed with *"those of old"* regarding oaths. They said, *"You shall not swear falsely, but shall perform your oaths to the Lord"* (Matthew 5:33). The Greek word "horkos," is translated *"oaths."* It comes from the Greek word "herkos" meaning "a fence, and suggests a limit or restraint." Therefore, using an oath is to place a fence or restraint around a promise. The writer of the Book of Hebrews stated clearly the Jewish tradition of taking an oath, *"For men indeed swear by the greater, and an oath for confirmation is for them an end of all dispute"* (Hebrews 6:16). An oath is a solemn affirmation appealing to God as a witness to the truth of what is being said. It includes a curse of His vengeance or a renunciation of His favor, if what is affirmed should be false or what is promised is not performed.

In the statement of *"those of old."* the oath under consideration invokes the interaction of God. This is based on God's instruction, *"You shall not steal, nor deal falsely, nor lie to one another. And you shall not swear by My name falsely, nor shall you profane the name of your God: I am the Lord"* (Leviticus 19:11-12). God carefully restated this, *"When you make a vow to the Lord your God, you shall not delay to pay it; for the Lord your God will surely require it of you, and it would be sin to you. But if you abstain from vowing, it shall not be sin*

Morals | **Matthew 5:33-37**

to you. That which has gone from your lips you shall keep and perform, for you voluntarily vowed to the Lord your God what you have promised with your mouth" (Deuteronomy 23:21-23).

The issue Jesus suggested for *"those of old"* was giving oaths only that involved God. Obviously when it is you and me, there is no concern for honesty. Stretching, manipulating, or embellishing the truth is of no concern unless God is involved. Because God is omniscient, we must be careful about promises. We cannot hide or escape His knowledge. The psalmist David understood this.

> *"O Lord, You have searched me and known me.*
> *You know my sitting down and my rising up;*
> *You understand my thought afar off.*
> *You comprehend my path and my lying down,*
> *And are acquainted with all my ways.*
> *For there is not a word on my tongue,*
> *But behold, O Lord, You know it altogether"*
> (Psalms 139:1-4).

When God is involved in the promise, it is foolish to lie. Jesus does not dispute this in any degree. The Old and New Covenants demand honesty when God is involved. When we involve God honesty is demanded because of the greatness of His person, knowledge, and presence.

Involvement Complete

Although Jesus agreed with *"those of old"* about oaths involving God, what if God was always involved? Jesus described a righteousness (New Covenant) that exceeded the righteousness of the scribes and Pharisees (Old Covenant). Obviously this increase is not in quantity of deeds but is in quality of internal character. Something must happen in the heart nature of man and can be completed only in the fusion of man and God. Jesus died not to just forgive our sins, not to just give us eternal life through the resurrection, and not to ascend to the right hand of God and rule as King (as great as all those provisions are), but He died to pour out the Spirit of God on us (as revealed in His own life!). God has come to be involved completely in our lives.

Therefore, we do not need to swear at all (Matthew 5:34). What *"those of old"* considered true when they gave an oath is now true all the time. If God is involved, we dare not lie. When is the time He is not involved? An oath summons the presence of God as a fence around what is said. When is the believer not captured by His presence, under the influence of His Spirit, or being directed in attitude and word by His influence? This influence is the state of the New Covenant!

Why would a Spirit-sourced person swear by heaven? Jesus said, *"for it is God's throne"* (Matthew 5:34). Is God not involved in His throne? In fact, has not the New Covenant Christian become the throne of God who rules in him? Our helplessness merged with the presence of the King creates a Kingdom over which He rules. Is He not King over all of our statements? Therefore, *"do not swear at all"* (Matthew 5:34).

In fact, do not swear, *"by the earth, for it is His footstool"* (Matthew 5:35). When Solomon's great wealth is described in the Old Testament, the wonder of his throne is highlighted. *"Moreover the king made a great throne of ivory, and overlaid it with pure gold. The throne had six steps, with a footstool of gold, which were fastened to the throne; there were armrests on either side of the place of the seat, and two lions stood beside the armrests. Twelve lions stood there, one on each side of the six steps; nothing like this had been made for any other kingdom"* (2 Chronicles 9:17-19). The footstool was necessary, both so the person might ascend and to support the legs when he was placed in it. If heaven were the throne of God, would not His footstool be the earth? If He reigns in us in the New Covenant, would we not be His footstools as well? Therefore, is He not involved in every expression of His footstools?

Jerusalem is *"the city of the great King"* (Matthew 5:35). Its citadel is the temple, the dwelling place of the King. The city was under the control and influence of the mighty King. In the New Covenant, am I not the temple of the Holy One? **"Do you not know that you are the temple of God and that the Spirit of God dwells in you"** (1 Corinthians 3:16)? How could I swear by any part of my body, especially the head (Matthew 5:36)? *"And He is the head of the body"* (Colossians 1:18). I cannot swear by anything greater than Jesus. Nothing is in my life apart from Him by which I can swear. Therefore, *"do not swear at all"* (Matthew 5:34).

Involvement Complement

Jesus made a concluding statement, *"For whatever is more than these is from the evil one"* (Matthew 5:37). Jesus was plain in His meaning. In the New Covenant, any addition to God's involvement is sin. If the Spirit of Jesus sources the believer, every aspect of his life is involved in that sourcing. He becomes the visible expression of the invisible God. If anything is added beyond this sourcing, it is from the evil one.

We can easily compartmentalize our Christianity. We allow God in some areas of our living but not in all. We think God must notice when someone commits murder, but when that person is angry, He does not care? We want God to have influence in our isolated sexual drive, but we do not allow Him to flow through every expression of our sexuality. We understand that God dictated the legal expression of divorce, but we do not allow Him to have input into what we cause in our homes. Certainly when God is involved, I cannot lie. When I lie, the risk of calling on God to verify my oath is far too great. Therefore, I isolate God from my oaths and swear by those things that are not as risky. The involvement of anything outside His influence comes directly from the evil one.

His unlimited involvement in my life is the righteousness that exceeds the righteousness of the scribe and Pharisees. This is the New Covenant person! His poorness of spirit is embraced with the richness of the Spirit. A merger between God and man has taken place. Man no longer serves God in his meager doing, but lives as a new creature revealing the mind and resource of Christ. If anything is added to this merger, it is sin and from the evil one. This merger should be the totality of man's existence. Therefore, ***"do not swear at all"*** (Matthew 5:34). Never allow anything outside His presence to influence your life. Live captured by His grace, fenced in by His wisdom, and absorbed in His resource!

Matthew 5:34

NEVER SWEAR

"But I say to you, do not swear at all: neither by heaven, for it is God's throne" (Matthew 5: 34).

In previous studies we looked at the three illustrations of murder, morality, and marriage. **"Those of old"** held to the law, but Jesus' focus of these illustrations went much deeper. As we now move into the illustration of morals, Jesus begins His insight in the same way He did the previous three. Jesus said, **"But I say to you, do not swear at all: neither by heaven, for it is God's throne"** (Matthew 5: 34). Jesus has the authority to make this statement, establishing a contrast between **"You have heard that it was said to those of old"** and **"I say to you."** The contrast is suggested by the contrasting conjunction **"but,"** translation of the Greek word "de." Jesus did not directly quote the Old Testament though He could have used significant verses from the past. For instance, God commanded, **"And you shall not swear by My name falsely, nor shall you profane the name of your God: I am the Lord"** (Leviticus 19:12). Was Jesus contradicting God's Old Testament commandment? Is He suggesting a new and better commandment?

Jesus is the base of authority for this new instruction. His statement has a double focus on the word **"I."** Two Greek words are used in His statement, the Greek verb "lego," translated **"I say,"** and the subject "ego," translated **"I."** Furthermore, for the first time Jesus speaks His instruction in the negative, emphasizing this illustration differently. Two Greek words for "not" are possible, "me" and "ouk." The difference between these two words is the authority of "not." "Me" is dependent on the person speaking; it is an opinion. "Ouk" is independent of the person speaking, suggesting a universal understanding. Jesus said, ***"Do not* (me) *swear at all."*** He uses the dependent "not," expressing His opinion.

Jesus stated His authority in the beginning of the other three illustrations. He did not contradict what was spoken in the Old Testament but boldly stated twice that He ***"did not come to destroy but to fulfill"*** the Law or the Prophets (Matthew 5:17). The issue was not the Law or the Prophets but their interpretation of the Law or the Prophets. Both in the Old and New Covenants reproach must not be brought on the name of the Lord. A person was not to swear by God's name falsely. But in the New Covenant, the relationship of God and man is drastically different. Jesus merges with us; Jesus produces our lives. He is involved in every word we speak not just when we call on His name. Jesus speaks to us as a Spirit-sourced Man. He said that swearing by the name of God has value only when God is not consistently present in a person's life. If God is involved only when you swear by His name, then oaths take on value. If God sources every word we speak, then oaths have no place because we will be honest! Swearing an oath when God is involved is the basic concept of this illustration. Let's step into the illustration and experience three sections or elements of the passage.

Ludicrous

The English dictionary defines "ludicrous" as "so foolish, unreasonable, or out of place as to be amusing." This idea is the basis of many jokes. The reason a joke is funny is because it is ludicrous. Was Jesus expressing a sense of humor in this illustration? If He was, the local Jewish population did not understand His humor. They did not have the spiritual depth to grasp how ludicrous the Old Covenant standard was in light of the New Covenant.

For instance, it is ludicrous to treat a 40-year-old man as you would treat a 2-year-old boy. You do not plead with grown men to eat their green beans. "If you do not eat your green beans, you cannot have any ice cream." This statement fits in dealing with children, but it is ludicrous in the context of grown men. No one instructs a grown man, "Hold my hand and look both ways before you cross the street." That instruction for a grown man is ludicrous.

These examples of Jesus illustrate the difference between **"the righteousness of the scribes and Pharisees"** and the righteousness of the Kingdom of God (Matthew 5:20). The scribes and Pharisees did not grasp the wonder of the Kingdom Jesus proposed in the Sermon on the Mount. My helplessness (***"poor in spirit"***) is filled with His Comfort (Holy Spirit). This merger forms a new creature, the Kingdom. The Kingdom of God is not a location in which I dwell (that is heaven). The Kingdom is a relationship with the fullness of the Spirit of Jesus, moving from self-sourcing to Spirit-sourcing. Their resources limited the scribes and Pharisees. A Kingdom person is limited only by the resource of God, and God's resources have no limits.

Jesus is the demonstration of the Kingdom person. He was the first Kingdom Person, a Man filled with the Spirit of God. You might suggest that before the fall of man, Adam was the same way, and that would be true. It seemed the purpose of man's creation. God created a physical, visible world. In all of the beauty of nature and the strength of the animal kingdom, God was not seen. ***"No one has seen God at any time"*** (1 John 4:12). Therefore, God created man. He did not create man as the animal kingdom. He formed man out of the dust of the ground with His own hands, and He breathed into him the breath of life, His own Spirit! The Trinity God said, **"Let Us make man in Our image, according to Our likeness"** (Genesis 1:26). Man would **"have dominion over the fish of the sea, over the birds of the air, and over the cattle, over all the earth and over every creeping thing that creeps on the earth"** (Genesis 1:16). Man is the visible image of the invisible Trinity God.

Jesus is described as the first Kingdom person and is **"the image of the invisible God, the firstborn over all creation"** (Colossians 1:15). When you see Jesus, you see His Father. He is not the Father, but He looks exactly like Him. Jesus is **"the brightness of His glory and the express image of His person"** (Hebrews 1:3). Jesus fulfills the destiny of man's creation. An invisible Trinity God became visible to a physical world. Anyone at anytime could look at Jesus and know what the Trinity God is like. But God does not want just one Son; He wants **"many sons"** (Hebrews 2:10). Through Jesus, we are born from above (John 3:1-8).

Jesus is the picture of God and defines the New Covenant person's scope of life. The New Covenant person is a representative, the visible image of God in his world. His function is not to display talent, manifest intellectual knowledge, or perform feats. His destiny is to look like Jesus, the visible image of God. In fact, Jesus **"is not ashamed to call them brethren"** (Hebrews 2:11). Brothers are individuals born from the same life source. The Spirit of God in Jesus is now in us! This indwelling is the New Covenant.

Anything outside of this demonstration is "sin." In other words, sin has at its core the letter "I." Anything sourced by self is sin. When I tell a lie, I say that God is a liar and cannot be trusted. I was created by God to reveal who He is; God says, "I am not a liar and I cannot have you telling people I am." When I steal, I say that God is a thief. God says, "I am not a thief, and I cannot have you telling people I am." When I hate, I misrepresent God who created me. Sin is misrepresenting God to our world. We are Kingdom people, the demonstration of His Person! This revelation is the righteousness that exceeds the righteousness of the scribes and Pharisees.

Jesus began His illustrations with the subject of "murder." ***"You have heard that it was said to those of old, 'You shall not murder, and whoever murders will be in danger of the judgment"*** (Matthew 5:21). How ludicrous to say this to a Kingdom person! The Kingdom person does not get angry (Matthew 5:22) and does not need to be told not to murder. This law or commandment is ludicrous to him. However, it is also true that those in the Old Covenant considered even the possibility or suggestion of not getting angry as ludicrous. They laughed saying that not having anger was ridiculous. To not be angry was idealistic and an impossible standard.

"Those of old" proposed ***"You shall not commit adultery"*** (Matthew 5:27). How ludicrous to suggest they could live without lust. They isolated their sexuality into a body drive they had to control. They did not see that their self-centeredness controlled their sexuality and expressed itself in all areas of their lives. The Spirit of Jesus living at the core of life and flowing through their sexual expression was a ludicrous idea. The Spirit-filled Kingdom person does not need to be told not to lust because he is filled with the Spirit of Jesus!

God made provision for the self-centered Old Covenant person to divorce his wife by giving her a certificate, a legal act. The Kingdom person's major concern is what is he "causing" in his wife (Matthew 5:32). If the husband is the head of the home, where is he leading his wife? To say to the Old Covenant man that he should be deeply concerned about his daily influence on his wife is ludicrous. Whereas, to say to the New Covenant man that he can dismiss his wife for any reason by a legal act is ludicrous.

In our present study, it is ludicrous to indicate that you have to be honest only when God's name is involved. The New Covenant person is merged with the Spirit of God and knows continuance intimacy with His presence. He is always involved with God's name; therefore, honesty is without question. The New Covenant person does not need the commandment, ***"You shall not bear false witness against your neighbor"*** (Exodus 20:16). No one is proposing this commandment is false; instead, it is just unnecessary for the New Covenant Spirit-filled person to whom lying is ludicrous.

Levels

The rest of the illustration has an emphasis on levels. When we focus on commandments or "doing," we inevitably promote levels of achievement. We have a need to compare ourselves with others to measure how we are doing. We compare how well we do with how well others are doing, which allows us to excuse our misbehavior. Although I may not do the right thing in one situation, I keep commandments in other realms. I am not perfect, but I am better than most people. I am a Christian, but I may not be a very good one. We can easily to justify our behavior if we can find someone we think is not doing as well as we are.

Jesus described the process of levels in the rest of this illustration. The Old Covenant allowed the Jews to establish levels of honesty. If a person took an oath and included God, they were obligated to fulfill their vow. However, if they swore by heaven, the obligation for fulfillment was reduced because God was not involved in the oath. If you swear by the Earth, it would be less binding than heaven. Jerusalem was the city where God dwelt. The rabbis distinguished between swearing toward Jerusalem, which was binding, and swearing by Jerusalem, which was not. Even the issue of one's head was mentioned. It suggested the issue of aging where we have no control. But still it is not on the level of taking an oath on God's name.

When we bring this thought into the New Covenant (fullness of the Spirit), the issue of levels is removed. Jesus rightly said, **"Let your 'Yes' be 'Yes,' and your 'No' be 'No'"** (Matthew 5:37). If you do not want to live in the realm of God's presence, which dictates the honesty of every statement, you must live in the realm of being a liar. Liars cannot be in the Kingdom of God. The reason is the difference between the Old and New Covenants. "Doing" is the heart of the Old Covenant where the performance of activities is the gauge. But the New Covenant is the merger with God's nature, producing a new creature. This new creature finds it impossible to lie. We are not judged by the activity of lying; we are judged by the integrity of our nature.

Perhaps we should clarify that there are levels of maturity, baby humans, young adult humans, and senior humans. But no category describes those half human or partial human. Babies are as much human as senior adults. Although there are levels of maturity, there are not levels of being human. There are no levels in being Christian, having the nature of God, commitment, or surrender. All New Covenant Kingdom people are surrendered to Jesus, because He is Lord. The baby Christian may not have experienced all of the avenues to express God's nature. In the humanity of a person, the nature of God may be hindered because of a lack of understanding. But the driving force of God's nature fills the Christian, and they give expression of this nature. With this consistent flow of God's nature, swearing is ludicrous. We live on the level of His consistent presence.

Lucifer

Because there are no levels in being Christian, and it is ludicrous to swear by the name of God, there is only one conclusion. God is the source of every word. Anything beyond the borders of God's presence is an expression of the *"evil one."* Listen to the words of Jesus, *"Let your 'Yes' be 'Yes,' and your 'No' be 'No.' For whatever is more than these is from the evil one"* (Matthew 5:37).

The leaders of Israel lacked the understanding of the New Covenant, which caused the conflict between them and Jesus. They were not open to the new revelation coming through Christ rather than being incapable to understand. As the controversy raged, they claimed Abraham as their father. Jesus replied that it was false. If Abraham were their father, they would not have sought to kill Jesus. They responded that they were not like Jesus, born of fornication. They claimed only one Father – God. Jesus said, **"You are of your father the devil, and the desires of your father you want to do. He was a murderer from the beginning, and does not stand in the truth, because there is no truth in him. When he speaks a lie, he speaks from his own resources, for he is a liar and the father of it"** (John 8:44).

No wonder Jesus declared that swearing by the name of God was ludicrous. Any attempt to make levels of honesty and excuse lying is ludicrous and is the expression of the nature in you. You were "birthed"; someone "fathered" you. If Jesus "fathers" you, your word is good enough. If the devil "fathers" you, you make excuses and allow dishonesty.

As in all of Jesus' other illustrations, the issue is not "murder," "adultery," or "divorce," and it is not "lying." Jesus is the issue. Am I the Kingdom of God? In embracing my helplessness, has His Divine presence filled me? Am I merged with Him?

Matthew 5:34

SUBSTITUTES FOR GOD

"But I say to you, do not swear at all: neither by heaven, for it is God's throne" (Matthew 5: 34).

Jesus illustrated the contrast between the righteousness of the Old Covenant and the New Covenant. He is the first representative of the New Covenant; therefore, He is contrasted with the scribes and the Pharisees. God carefully stated the premise of the Old Covenant. **"You shall not steal, nor deal falsely, nor lie to one another. And you shall not swear by My name falsely, nor shall you profane the name of your God: I am the Lord"** (Leviticus 19:11-12). When God is involved in my statements, honesty is necessary. When the boundary around my statement is God, any falsehood is a reflection on His character and name. I must maintain honesty in the presence of God.

You will notice only the end of the statement deals with oaths involving the name of God. God's intent is given in the first half of the statement. **"You shall not steal, nor deal falsely, nor lie to one another."** This requirement is for the people of God. The nation of Israel was called by God to be His people for a specific destiny. The standard for such a people is "do not lie." After establishing this standard, God proposed the involvement of His name in the honesty of His people. If this was true in the Old Covenant, how much more it is true in the New Covenant.

"Those of old" did not recognize the first half of the statement but focused on oaths that involved only God's name. In their division of the statement, they adopted a policy approving dishonesty outside using God's name. God never made such a provision. Thus, swearing by other things became their pattern. *"Heaven," "earth," "Jerusalem,"* and *"your head"* were less binding. A man may have intended to keep his word, but it was impossible because of his circumstances. Because God's name was not involved, the person was not bound by the oath.

The New Covenant does not recognize a division of this statement. The standard is *"Do not swear at all"* (Matthew 5:34). Can you swear by *"heaven"* and not involve God? Is it not *"God's throne"*? The Greek word "ouranos" is translated *"heaven,"* one of the most frequently used words in the New Testament, appearing 274 times. The singular and plural are used interchangeably and provide no difference in meaning. Physically, it is the overarching, all-embracing heaven with the Earth below, including everything contained in its realm. Heaven is used repeatedly as the dwelling place of God. Jesus descended from and ascended into heaven (John 3:13; Hebrews 8:1). *"Heaven"* also refers to the final dwelling place for Christians and involves the holy city, the New Jerusalem (Revelation 21:2).

In our passage, Jesus states the premise of the New Covenant. When our helplessness merges with His nature, we become the Kingdom of God! Because He is the constant source by which we move and have our being, God is always involved. He overshadows, influences, and dominates every thought, circumstance, or word. The intent of the Old Covenant becomes true in the New Covenant. *"Do not swear at all."* Swearing by *"heaven," "earth," "Jerusalem,"* or *"your head"* Jesus categorizes as *"from the evil one"* (Matthew 5:37). When we swear by these things we attempt to step outside the boundaries of God's presence.

Comparing Issue

Not one of the writers of the Scriptures attempts to prove the existence of God. Each writer simply assumes Him on every page. *"In the beginning God"* (Genesis 1:1) is the words that begin the Bible. Where did God originate? From the beginning to the end of the Scriptures, He is just there! If a person wants proof of His presence, there is none. You cannot prove God any more than you can prove love. You cannot explain God anymore than you can explain beauty. However, there is strong, even convincing evidence that is more for God's existence than for non-god. In fact, while is no evidence for non-god, there is 99 percent evidence for God. But it always takes a step of faith. By faith, I experience God within and need no proof.

The Psalmist cried, *"Even from everlasting to everlasting, You are God"* (Psalms 90:2). God did not have a beginning, and He will not have an end. If you are determined that God must have started, go back to that place. Stand tall and look beyond where you stand; you will discover more God! We live in the time zone, but God is eternal, beyond and above time. God is everywhere, so everywhere with God is here. God is all the time; therefore, all the time with God is now.

The temple that Solomon built in Jerusalem was beyond description. In his prayer of dedication, he said, *"But will God indeed dwell on the earth? Behold, heaven and the heaven of heavens cannot contain You. How much less this temple which I have built!"* (1 Kings 8:27). How great do you think God is? We judge everything in our world by comparison. People describe me as skinny because they compare me with others who weigh more. If everyone were my size, I would not be called skinny. We have an established measurement of one foot, and three of those measurements make one yard. When we have traveled 5,280 we have completed one mile. We can measure everything based on how it compares with that standard.

We view the world God created and cry, "God is great!" However, we have no way to measure how great He is! But that is determined by the measurement of our world. Some universes and multi-universes are beyond our comprehension. The scientists proclaim that there are millions, billions, trillions, quadrillions, quintillions, sextillions, septillions, octillions, nonillions, and decillions of stars, planets, moons, suns, solar systems, galaxies, and constellations in outer space. God spoke them all into existence. How big is God? What is the measuring rod? God is bigger than this world; this is by the measurement of this world. God is bigger than the whole universe; this is by the measurement of the universe.

God's power has no limit. His ability is not absolute; it is infinite. If we accumulate all the power of God that it took for creation and remove it from Him, He will have as much power left over as He had before the creation. If we multiply the power accumulated by 1000 and remove it from God, there would be as much power left in God as before the removal. God cannot be compared by any measuring rod.

Therefore, is heaven a measurement for God? If I substitute heaven as the fence or boundary for my honesty instead of God, am I not moving from the superior to the inferior? But is this not our pattern? We continually embrace the inferior instead of the superior. Instead of embracing a life in victory and living above sin, we advocate, "no one is perfect." "I can be the person I was created to be" is far too demanding; therefore, I propose, "I cannot help the way I am."

The New Covenant (my helplessness merged with His resource) is superior to the Old Covenant (my helplessness attempting to match His resource). Remaining inferior is much easier. Jesus challenged the scribes and Pharisees with the superior. "Controlling our anger so we never commit murder" is inferior to the elimination of anger. "Controlling our sex drive so we never commit adultery" is inferior to eliminating the self-sourcing at the heart of a life expressing its sexuality. "I can always get a divorce" is inferior to allowing God to spiritually influence my heart, "causing" good things in my home. It is inferior to adjust the truth of my words because I swore by heaven, not God's name. To realize God indwells and sources my life is superior. Therefore, all my words reflect Him.

The superior covenant, the New Covenant, calls me beyond myself. The inferior covenant, the Old Covenant, makes allowances and excuses. Jesus brings me to accountability. When I go my way, the evil one is thrilled. Living within the boundaries of God's presence demands consistency. The law allows enough righteousness to justify my lack. Destiny is found in God; chaos is the cancer of the soul dependent on itself.

Swearing by heaven is man's attempt to reduce God to a more manageable state, a "comparing issue."

Controlling Issue

Why would you swear by the lesser when the greater is pressing on you? If swearing *"by heaven"* lowers the standard of your life and is *"from the evil one,"* why would you make such a substitution? The issue of the choice focuses on Jesus' description of heaven, *"it is God's throne"* (Matthew 5:34), a control issue. The unquestionable motive of *"those of old"* in swearing by heaven instead of God was to reduce control. If God was involved in their oath, He became the fence, the boundary of their promise. There was no adjustment to truth; honesty was demanded. Who would openly risk the displeasure of God on their life? If you swear by heaven, there is flexibility in the oath. It becomes "I will do the best I can." The hope is that everything will work out so the promise can be kept but if not, all is well.

Part Four: Fulfillment of the Kingdom - The Application: Morals

This thought process of control springs from the Old Covenant and is an illusion. Control was not intended in the Old Covenant and would not be remotely possible in the New Covenant because of the infilling of the Holy Spirit. Most adjustments in our spiritual lives concern His Lordship and are expressions of our desire to be in charge. The cause is the old story of the fall of man (Genesis 3). Sin has always been and will always be the issue of dependency or independence. The self-centered carnal mind demands independence. Any deviation from Jesus being the fence and boundary of my existence is from the evil one.

Here is an amazing fact. The evil one is not bent on drugs, rape, and murder. He was quite content with the scribes and Pharisees who designed a religion they could control. They produced their righteousness from self. They were fully justified in their righteous standard in swearing by heaven and doing the best they could. They controlled honesty and dishonesty. Paying Judas 30 pieces of silver to trap Jesus did not seem strange to them (Matthew 26:48). They could have imprisoned Jesus any day while He walked and taught in Jerusalem (Matthew 26:55). During Jesus' resurrection they found no discomfort in giving the soldiers a large sum of money to spread the lie, **"His disciples came at night and stole Him away while we slept"** (Matthew 28:13). By the testimony of the soldiers, they knew this statement was a lie. But when God is not the fence or boundary of your life, you are free to control what is told as truth. So they swore by heaven and adjusted the truth to fit their need.

In the New Covenant, God moves us to a new level of righteousness. The new level is the awareness that He is always the fence and boundary of our words and lives. If we swear by heaven, there is no adjustment or flexibility from the truth. It does not create a lesser standard for truth. Is not heaven the throne of God? Therefore, we call on all the authority of God's ruling to surround our words. There is no adjustment to truth at His throne. Any adjustment results from foolishly listening to the lies or deception of the evil one. God's ruling authority is based on His sovereign Person. His righteous judgments are expressions of His inner character, His Person. To come to His throne is to come to Him.

The only conclusion is, ***"Do not swear at all"*** (Matthew 5:34). For the heart filled with God's nature, swearing is unnecessary. The mind of Christ is a mind of honesty. Allow your helplessness to merge with His Person. Become an expression of His integrity.

Connecting Issue

In the New Covenant, every circumstance involves Jesus. No flexibility, vacation, or non-involvement is available. The "exceeding righteousness" is a result of the merger of the one poor in spirit with the resource of the Comforter. A new creature is birthed in this merger. You cannot be this Kingdom person some of the time. Life is found in Him!

Christianity is not "a touch from above" or "a visit from the Divine." Christianity is a merger with a Person. Jesus is not a counselor giving advice to be considered, and He is not a Rescuer to save us from the pitfalls of life. He is not a bandage to bind up our wounds until they heal. He is not an inspiration for our down moments, and He is not a moment of rest from the stress of our lives. He is not a drink of water for the man who is thirsty. He is not a coach instructing from the sidelines, and He is not the director of the orchestra arranging the music you will play. All these imageries have one thing in common. They are temporary. They are not real connection; they are not merger.

Jesus' proposed standard of righteousness takes a new involvement between God and man. The Old Covenant was the proof; man cannot keep the law of a Holy God when he is separated from Him. A merger must happen. This merger requires the surrender of man to God. We cannot hesitate, give part of our time, or give only some of ourselves. Is not the cross of Jesus convincing evidence of the commitment of God to us? If this sacrifice is the level of His commitment to us, what will be the level of our commitment to Him?

The single element between victory and defeat is commitment. Who will give their life to Jesus without compromise or waver? Who will die to self-will or self-centeredness? Who will abandon themselves to His heart and mind? This personal commitment is the person who will know the merger of God and man. He will not need to be told not to murder. Self-centered sexuality will no longer dominate the heart of man. He will not need the restraints of the law, "do not commit adultery." The platform for ministry in intimacy will be marriage. The Spirit of Christ will cause redemption in the home. He will not need the restraints of oaths in God's name to pressure him to honesty. He is merged with the One who is Truth!

Matthew 5:34-35

A FOOTSTOOL

"But I say to you, do not swear at all: neither by heaven, for it is God's throne; nor by the earth, for it is His footstool" (Matthew 5:34-35).

The Jewish concept of the "footstool" was shaped by the description of Solomon's throne. The three-verse description of Solomon's throne ends with the words, **"nothing like this had been made for any other kingdom"** (2 Chronicles 9:19). This throne was extravagant, made of ivory overlaid with pure gold. There were six steps leading up to the throne with a footstool also of gold. The footstool was necessary to get into the throne. Twelve lions stood on each side of the six steps, and the armrests were made of two lions standing on each side of the throne. The throne was a magnificent sight!

However, Solomon's throne was meager compared to our God! Israel constructed the temple as an extravagant dwelling place for God, made of the things God Himself created. He asked, **"Where is the house that you will build Me? And where is the place of My rest?"** (Isaiah 66:1). There were no answers to these questions because God said, **"Heaven is My throne, and earth is My footstool"** (Isaiah 66:1). What He desired was not a place to dwell or throne to sit on, but one **"who is poor and of a contrite spirit, and who trembles at My word"** (Isaiah 66:2).

These statements in Isaiah come from God again in the Sermon on the Mount. ***"Blessed are the poor in spirit"*** (Matthew 5:3). Who will embrace their helplessness? Who will allow their helplessness to engulf them just as they do their grief in losing a loved one to death (Matthew 5:4)? Who will live conscious of their condition and become the Kingdom of God? God's Spirit merged with your helpless spirit forms the Kingdom. This is a call to embrace your poverty in spirit because we are ***"poor and of a contrite spirit."*** Should we not tremble at His word?

Jesus' use of the word ***"ge,"*** translated "earth," is significant in the Sermon on the Mount and used 250 times in the New Testament. "Ge" is translated "earth," "land," "ground," or "country," and is contracted from the word "soil." Soil is the substance from which the physical part of man's creation came; God formed him from the dust of the ground. ***"And the Lord God formed man of the dust of the ground, and breathed into his nostrils the breath of life; and man became a living being"*** (Genesis 2:7). God's involvement in the creation of man was different. The Hebrew word "yatsar," translated ***"formed,"*** means, "to mold into form." It gives the imagery of a potter whose skilled hand determines the shape of the vessel.

Perhaps, man's practice of swearing by the Earth is swearing by himself, bringing man full circle to repeat the first sin. Man chose to be his own god; he substituted himself for god. In swearing by himself, man justifies the adjustment of truth to fit his agenda. The person swearing becomes the boundary of his oath.

Provided

This is not the first time Jesus referred to the ***"earth"*** in the Sermon on the Mount. He first spoke of it in the Beatitudes. Jesus established our position according to creation in the first

Beatitude. We are *"poor in spirit"* (Matthew 5:3). We are to embrace this helplessness as *"those who mourn"* (Matthew 5:4). We are to allow this condition to envelop our lives; it must influence, dominate, and be constantly reflected in our living. In this condition we will be filled with *"Comfort,"* the Spirit of Jesus. The merger of our helplessness with His Spirit forms the Kingdom of God. A new creature is created through this relationship!

Flowing from this merger, the Spirit of Jesus sources the helpless one, and we experience meekness (Matthew 5:5). This meekness was a foreign concept to the culture of Jesus' day. The Jews expected a military Messiah who would restore the nation of Israel back to the pomp and glory of the days of Solomon (Acts 1:6). Because of the oppression of Rome, they longed for deliverance from domination. They experienced the miracle power of Jesus, and they expected Him to use His power for military victory. The idea of a meek Messiah leading meek people was far from their idea of the Messianic Kingdom. As Jesus expressed His meekness in terms of bleeding, suffering, and dying, Peter rebuked Him. It was not a rebuke of disbelief in His position as Messiah, but was unbelief in the type of Messiah Jesus proposed (Matthew 16:21-22). Peter could not conceive how the Messiah could be meek and be killed. He understood military and miracle power, but the power of meekness was incomprehensible.

In the Jewish mind, meekness would not conquer Rome or liberate Israel. Yet, Jesus said that the meek would *"inherit the earth"* (Matthew 5:5). We swear by our "dust" expecting to achieve our dreams. We take pride in what we physically achieve by work, effort, and sacrifice, yet our physical, earthly accomplishments do not satisfy; we enjoy less and less our accomplishments. Although we give all our efforts to have the physical, the physical turns on us like a tyrant. We become slaves to our physical drives and possessions. We do not own the physical; it owns us! What we have tried to earn pays us back with destruction!

The physical, earthly things are ours only when we inherit them. We do not earn an inheritance; an inheritance comes to us through someone's death. Inheritance is given to us as a gift! We can never experience the value of our physical world until we inherit it by Jesus' source, the cross. Our self-centered attempts to master, control, or dominate the physical realm only thwarts, hinders, and destroys the gift of the physical in our lives. The beauty and purpose of the physical realm for our lives eludes self-centered attempts. The grandeur of the physical realm is experienced in our helplessness being sourced by His Spirit; it is given to us!

Primary

Jesus describes this relationship in its daily function. He uses the imagery of *"salt."* However, it is not just *"salt;"* it is ***"the salt of the earth"*** (Matthew 5:13). You would think in using the salt imagery that He would link us with meat, vegetables, or some type of food. He links Kingdom people with the physical. Whatever we are in merging with Jesus affects the physical world. The value of the physical world is in the Kingdom of God. Think about this truth! The physical world has no value without the merger of my helplessness and His Presence forming the Kingdom. If the Kingdom is removed, the physical becomes valueless. In fact, the physical becomes an instrument of destruction.

You may carry many pieces of paper in your pocket with only one piece having value. The piece of paper called a "dollar" is valuable. Its value is not in the paper; money has value because people believe that they will be able to exchange this money for goods and services in the future. We are ***"the salt of the*** *earth."* We have heard the stories of those whose materialism is in abundance, but they are unhappy with life. Is this the old, old message that you may be the Rich Young Ruler and still not know life? If the physical world becomes the center of your love, you must rid yourself of it to find Him. Materialism has no value outside the Kingdom. The value of materialism is not in its accumulation but in its distribution. The value of our physical world is in the investment and contribution to the lives of others, a Kingdom principle. You are *"the salt of the earth."*

The creation story reveals this truth to us! Before the creation of man, God stated His purpose. *"Then God said, 'Let Us make man in Our image, according Our likeness; let them have dominion over the fish of the sea, over the birds of the air, and over the cattle, over all the earth and over every creeping thing that creeps on the earth'"* (Genesis 1:26). After creating man, God communicated this intention to man (Genesis 1:28). The physical world was made for us, given to us, and designed for us, deriving its meaning and completeness from us. The physical creation extended into the physical body God gave us. The physical flesh is the platform on which the spiritual reality of our intimacy with God is displayed, the display of our spirit.

Our circumstances, physical pressures, or materialism were not made to dominate us. Our physical appetites were not made to possess or dictate to us. God never intended us to be addicted to any physical appetite. The physical loses its value when we are addicted. We are *"the salt of the earth"* giving value to the physical existence around us. When we fail to do this we become foolish; it is the meaning of the Greek word "moranio," translated *"loses its flavor."* It is where we get our English word "moron."

Jesus instructs us in the progression of the Kingdom. I am helpless; if I will embrace and be embraced as the grief I experience over the death of a loved one, He will merge with me

(Matthew 5:3-4). As I am sourced by His resource, the physical world becomes dominant and is sourced by this new Kingdom person just as I am dominated and sourced by Him. The physical world becomes an expression of my merger with Him.

Permanent

Through the sacrifices and death of Jesus, I have inherited the physical world. The physical world was created to be a platform of demonstration for the merger between my helplessness and God's resource. The Kingdom person is given the physical, and it is permanent. *"For assuredly, I say to you, till heaven and earth pass away, one jot or one tittle will by no means pass from the law till all is fulfilled,"* (Matthew 5:18). In fairness to the passage, the focus is on the law being fulfilled. The law (Scriptures) is not destroyed at all. Even in the eternal age to come the law (Scriptures) will be maintained. The content and context of the Scriptures are permanent. Will we have a book called the "Bible" in heaven? Despite your answer to this question, the truth of the Scriptures will be displayed and lived everywhere in eternity.

Although this is the focus of the verse, the permanence of the physical is stated to verify the permanence of the Scriptures. Although verses indicate the perishing of the Earth (Psalms 102:25-27), the impact of our verse is the permanence of creation. We are sure our physical bodies are permanent. They will be changed from the natural to the spiritual, but they are permanent. Forever we will live in a physical body sourced by the Spirit of God. God created us as a dichotomy (Genesis 2:7). He was involved in the creation of man in several ways not included in the animal or plant kingdom. He formed man out of the dust of the ground; it was the physical creation. God breathed into man the breath of life; it was the principle of life, the spirit. Man became a living soul; man is a combination of the physical and the spiritual. Jesus rose from the dead with this combination, and He will return the second time with the same.

The purpose of this physical link is demonstration. The physical is the platform for the action of the spiritual. The physical does not dictate to the spiritual. The drives and cravings of the physical are not to control or shape the spiritual being. When this occurs, the spiritual condition of the person is manifested through the physical. When I yield my spiritual life to the cravings and drive of my self-centered flesh my helpless spirit is dominated and sourced by my selfish flesh.

My helplessness is to be filled with His nature so my physical being manifests the merger. People see God through my life. As Jesus is the visible image of the invisible Father, so I am the image of the same nature. This is the Divine plan for the physical. As I embrace my helplessness and the resource provided by His death, I inherit the physical in a manner never before possible. God PROVIDES my physical. Once again man, the new creature, dominates the physical. This Kingdom man becomes the PRIMARY not the physical. The physical is a platform for the action of God's Nature in the man. This is a PERMANENT design. Eternally we will display the glory of Jesus through our physical beings.

Perverted

Now we come to our passage, *"But I say to you, do not swear at all: neither by heaven, for it is God's throne; nor by the earth, for it is His footstool"* (Matthew 5:34-35). The Jews were deeply aware that honesty was necessary when God was involved. An oath sworn on the name of God involved dishonesty and would profane the name of God. God commanded, *"You shall not swear by my name falsely, nor shall you profane the*

name of your God; I am the Lord" (Leviticus 19:12). The Jews adjusted their oaths to swear by other things that did not involve God. They intended to keep their promise, but if it did not work out, they were not held accountable because they swore by the Earth instead of God.

This practice was false in the Old Covenant and is false in the merger of the presence of God with the Kingdom person. ***"Those of old"*** perverted the intention of God. God's purpose for the physical became a twisted perversion. In the New Covenant, the Spirit of Jesus merges with the helplessness of man. In this new combination, God is always involved in the expression of man through the physical. The speaking of God sources the speaking of man. The physical voice of man becomes an expression of God's intentions. Anything less than honesty is a perversion of our physical inheritance from His death!

This is true for murder as well (Matthew 5:21-26). The Jews recognized the evil of murder in the physical realm. Murder in the spiritual realm is as destructive to human life as physical murder! When I physically murder someone, I destroy life. When I hate in the spiritual realm, I destroy life! If we allow hate, anger, demeaning, and belittling in our family relationships, day after day our children are exposed to its toxic rays. The heart of the child is destroyed; we kill the capacity for love in him. Anger is profaning God's name in my physical world.

What about physical adultery (Matthew 5:27-30)? Adultery is a physical perversion of God's desire for the marriage relationship. You must not participate in such an activity. But in the New Covenant, my core sexuality expresses God's sourcing it. Would not every expression of my sexuality, the way I walk, think, solve problems, and dress be an expression of His mind? Would not demanding my selfish personal rights be spiritual adultery, perverting God's actions through my physical being?

In marriage, physically removing my wife in divorce is a provision of the Old Covenant (Deuteronomy 24:1). However, because the spiritual demonstrates itself through the physical, what have I caused in my wife throughout our time as one flesh? Perhaps the reason I decide to divorce her is a product of my selfish sexuality expressing itself in our physical relationship (Matthew 5:31-32).

    I swear by the Earth because it is does not demand honesty as does swearing by God (Matthew 5:34). Is the physical Earth not His footstool? Has He not given me the physical by inheritance to demonstrate Him through me in the physical? Am I filled with self-centeredness until every arena of my life is perverted in the demonstration of His presence? In every illustration the physical is perverted by the self-centeredness of my heart. I must embrace my helplessness and be embraced by His Person!

Matthew 5:35

INTO JERUSALEM

"Nor by the earth, for it is His footstool; nor by Jerusalem, for it is the city of the great King" (Matthew 5: 35).

Jerusalem is a city with an amazing history. We first learn of it in connection with the renowned high priest Melchizedek, called the King of Salem (Genesis 14:18). Melchizedek was to whom Abraham tithed his spoils around the year 2080 BC (Hebrews 7:1-3). Jerusalem and Salem are the same place; the Jews thought the name of the city of Salem was changed to Jerusalem. King David indicated the same when he wrote,

"In Judah God is known;
His name is great in Israel.
In Salem also is His tabernacle,
And His dwelling place in Zion"
(Psalms 76:1-2).

Jerusalem is the two thousand year-old city, over which Jesus wept (Matthew 23:37-38), now over four thousand years old.

God gave Abraham a testing command, - **"Take now your son, your only son Isaac, whom you love, and go to the land of Moriah, and offer him there as a burnt offering on one of the mountains of which I shall tell you"** (Genesis 22:2). In complete obedience Abraham built an altar on the mountain, and took a knife to slay his son, but God intervened and provided His own sacrifice. Josephus, the Jewish historian, wrote that this mountain in the land of Moriah was the mountain on which Solomon built the Temple and was also the location God offered His own Son. It is *"the city of the great King"!*

King David's desire was to construct the Temple in Jerusalem, but even though David designed the plans and accumulated the needed material, God did not allow him to do so. David said to his son Solomon, **"My son, as for me, it was in my mind to build a house to the name of the Lord my God, but the word of the Lord came to me, saying, 'You have shed much blood and have made great wars; you shall not build a house for My name, because you have shed much blood on the earth in My sight'"** (1 Chronicles 22:7-8). Solomon carried out the plans of his father, and the Temple was beyond description in its beauty, design, and costliness. At the dedication of the structure, Solomon prayed and **"fire came down from heaven and consumed the burnt offering and the sacrifices; and the glory of the Lord filled the temple"** (2 Chronicles 7:1). The celebration was beyond belief. Solomon offered a sacrifice of 22,000 bulls and 120,000 sheep. After 23 days of celebration, Solomon sent the people to their homes. God came to Solomon in the night hour and said, **"For now I have chosen and sanctified this house, that My name may be there forever; and My eyes and My heart will be there perpetually"** (2 Chronicles 7:16). As the Israelites gathered in concentric circles around the tabernacle of old, so the temple in Jerusalem was the heart of Jewish life. The knowledge of the presence and blessing of God on them was secure because of His dwelling place, the Temple. No wonder Jesus called Jerusalem *"the city of the great King"* (Matthew 5:35). This comes from the words of the psalmist,

> **"Great is the Lord, and greatly to be praised**
> **In the city of our God,**
> **In His holy mountain.**
> **Beautiful in elevation,**

Part Four: Fulfillment of the Kingdom - The Application: Morals

> *The joy of the whole earth,*
> *Is Mount Zion on the sides of the north,*
> *The City of the great King.*
> *God is in her palaces;*
> *He is known as her refuge"*
> (Psalms 48:1-3).

Direction

An oath was sworn connected to Jerusalem. The oaths sworn by *"heaven"* and *"earth"* were not as binding as an oath to the Lord. However, an oath connected to Jerusalem had a complication attached. That complication is suggested in the language of our passage. Jesus said, ***"But I say to you, do not swear at all: neither by*** (en) ***heaven, for it is God's throne; nor by*** (en) ***the earth, for it is His footstool; nor by*** (eis) ***Jerusalem, for it is the city of the great King"*** (Matthew 5:34-35). The Greek word "en" is often used regarding "means or an instrument," and therefore is properly translated ***"by."*** Jesus changed the preposition in speaking of ***Jerusalem***. The Greek word "eis" means "into" and directly relates to direction.

The rabbis debated about the binding quality of an oath sworn "as Jerusalem" or "by Jerusalem." They proposed that there was no binding of an oath "by Jerusalem," but a binding was in effect with an oath "toward Jerusalem." An oath "by Jerusalem" required that a person must face toward Jerusalem, or the vow was worthless. Jesus indicated this worthlessness by the change in the preposition. Do you see how ridiculous it is to think a person needs not be truthful unless they are facing Jerusalem? Facing any other direction allowed dishonesty and deception.

Jesus' premise of the Sermon on the Mount was that we are ***"poor in spirit,"*** helpless (Matthew 5:3). If our helplessness is possessed by the demonic nature of self-centeredness, we will go to desperate means to deceive ourselves and justify our self-centered adjustment of truth. Honesty through our self-centered perspective becomes whatever caters to our selfish desires in the moment. Jesus proposed a new and radical change! The self-centered nature attached to our helplessness is a parasite surviving from our helplessness. If this could be replaced by the nature of God, everything would be different. As self-centeredness permeates and affects every area of our lives including our honesty, the Spirit of Jesus will also permeate and affect us!

Refraining from murder is not the issue (Matthew 5:21). If we allow God to remove the spirit of anger, we will become an expression of His redemptive heart. The elimination of physical adultery is not the standard (Matthew 5:27). When we allow the nature and character of God to flow through us we express His design through our sexuality. When we allow self-centeredness to use our spouse for ourselves we are brought to divorce, but the nature of Christ causes godliness and oneness in our marriage (Matthew 5:31-32). If we are honest, we are an expression of the continuous presence of Christ in our lives, and we do not require an oath involving His name to force the truth. His name will always be involved, which produces consistent integrity.

In the heart of a Jew making an oath, invoking the name of God would have been more binding than merely looking toward Jerusalem. Many modern day people feel the same, always looking toward God. Crisis circumstances force their attention to helplessness and the need for His presence. They willingly pause in their busy lives to correct an unbearable circumstance. They adjust their schedules to include a momentary encounter with God. A "touch" from God is acceptable, and they welcome Jesus passing by. They want to look at Jerusalem and recognize the dwelling place of God, but they do not want to dwell there.

Jesus proposed a merger between God and man. The helplessness of man must merge with the Spirit of God. Just as self-centeredness sources, influences, and dominates our lives, Jesus wants to do the same. Moments of looking toward God occur in everyone's life, but it is not the relationship Jesus proposed for the Kingdom person. We allow self-centeredness to maintain its dominance in our lives as we use God to aid us. Multitudes attach themselves to the church to look toward God but never embrace Him. The righteousness of the scribes and Pharisees was a product of that view. The Old Covenant kept us outside the Holy of Holies. Only one man dared to enter into the presence of God and only once a year.

The New Covenant insists that we are the **"temple of God"** (2 Corinthians 6:16)! We no longer look toward; we have fully embraced. Jesus is no longer the answer in a needy time; He is the Lover of my soul. He does not counsel me when I am upset; Jesus is the mind by which I think and the nature by which I live. I no longer do things for Him as I look toward Him; He is the source of my every movement. I no longer worship Him from afar as He sits on His throne; I am His bride dwelling in His bedroom chamber. He no longer comes down to Mount Sinai giving me commandments; He writes His desires on the tablets of my heart. I am lost in His arms; His presence envelops me. My petitions are no longer forced on Him with a hope He will answer; I desire only what He wants. I do not attempt to be Christlike in actions; I am the visible image of the invisible Jesus. I no longer look toward Jerusalem; I am Jerusalem, the dwelling place of God!

Deflection

Matthew referred to Jerusalem as **"the holy city"** (Matthew 4:5), as indeed it was. However, when you search through the pages of Matthew's Gospel, Jerusalem is presented as a city of hostility. The profound announcement of Jesus' birth took place in Bethlehem not Jerusalem, which begins Matthew's account (Matthew 2:1). When the wise men came to Jerusalem seeking the new King, the response was one of disruption and upset; **"When Herod the king heard this, he was troubled, and all Jerusalem with him"** (Matthew 2:3). The holy city did not embrace the birth of a new King!

Jesus referred to Jerusalem as the scene of His betrayal, suffering, and death. In the first and third predictions of His death, He clearly said He must go to Jerusalem to experience the cross (Matthew 16:21; 20:18). The heart cry of Jesus is expressed in His weeping. He cried, **"O Jerusalem, Jerusalem, the one who kills the prophets and stones those who are sent to her! How often I wanted to gather your children together, as a hen gathers her chicks under her wings, but you were not willing!"** (Matthew 23:37). In Galilee Jesus was confronted by scribes and Pharisees from Jerusalem (Matthew 15:1). They traveled eighty to one hundred miles to check on His activities. Jerusalem is the location of the crucifixion, the place of death.

Is this the reason I want to only look toward Jerusalem instead of embracing and entering? Does oneness with God demand a cross? I can look away from Jerusalem or even look toward Jerusalem and manipulate the truth. But to enter Jerusalem and live in the nature of God means joining Him in His death and resurrection. I want to *"know Him and the power of His resurrection,"* but do I desire to know Him in *"the fellowship of His sufferings"?* (Philippians 3:10).

Truth that results in hostility is not found only by dwelling in Jerusalem. We also see it in a Philippi jail (Acts 16:16+) and the raging threats of the Sanhedrin (Acts 4:13+). To embrace truth is to embrace conflict from a hostile world. I do not refer to being unkind or mean. Love amid the hate often produces conflict. Truth amid deception is salt in the wound of a world. Looking toward truth is so much easier than embracing the Truth!

But Jesus is relentless in His premise. I am helpless (Matthew 5:3). I must embrace this helplessness and allow Him to embrace me in a merger with His nature. The fallout of this merger is not my concern. Anger may be eliminated (Matthew 5:22), and demeaning or belittling may be removed (Matthew 5:22), but that does not mean there will not be adversaries (Matthew 5:25). I will never be an adversary, but I will have adversaries. This does not mean I may escape divorce (Matthew 5:31), but it does mean I will never cause it (Matthew 5:32). My speech will involve God until my "yes" is "yes" and my "no" is "no" (Matthew 5:37). My integrity shall be a result of His resource saturating my helplessness. Anything outside of this is from the evil one (Matthew 5:37).

Dictation

I will not just swear by or look toward Jerusalem; I will march into Jerusalem and fully embrace this city, **"the city of the great King"** (Matthew 5:35). In embracing the city, I embrace the King. I must keep the premise of Jesus' sermon in mind as He moves me to the new level of a relationship, and I merge with the King. The King of the Kingdom is the Man filled with the Spirit. God became a helpless baby in the incarnation. He was dependent on the Spirit of God. The Spirit of God did not aid Jesus; the Spirit was not just a counselor giving advice. The Spirit was not even a boss who told Him what to do. The Spirit of God merged, infiltrated, and fused with Him. Jesus was the first One in the new merger of God and man. He is the King of this new species of humanity called sons of God. It was through His merger with the Spirit and the empowering of the Spirit that Jesus became the Redeemer. He opened the way for many sons to become the Kingdom of God. Jesus is King of the Kingdom.

Jerusalem became the physical symbol of the great King. As we dwell in Jerusalem, the city, so we dwell in Him. As the atmosphere of the city surrounds us, we are surrounded by the atmosphere of His Spirit. If the city is the place of crucifixion, it is also the place of resurrection. As I dwell in the city, His death, I dwell in His life, His resurrection. His life is my life!

Dwelling in Jerusalem is absolute. My helplessness is empowered by His invasion. I cannot visit the city; there are no tourists. Looking toward the city or living on the outskirts is no possible. The gates of the city are open; I am either inside or outside. The parables of the Kingdom of Heaven highlight this truth. A person either has on the provided wedding garment or he does not (Matthew 22:11). The door was shut, and five foolish virgins came too late (Matthew 25:10). Each servant received a number of talents; each servant either engaged his investment or he buried it (Matthew 25:24). Each nation is either a sheep or a goat (Matthew 25:32). Dwelling in both worlds or having two masters is impossible. *"No one can serve two masters; for either he will hate the one and love the other, or else he will be loyal to the one and despise the other. You cannot serve God and mammon"* (Matthew 6:24).

Will you merge with Him?

Matthew 5:36

MY OWN HEAD

"Nor shall you swear by your head, because you cannot make one hair white or black" (Matthew 5: 36).

Jesus gives six illustrations in this section of the Sermon on the Mount. We must know the premise of the sermon to understand each illustration. If we do not continually focus on the premise we may develop misconceptions about what Jesus said. The Sermon on the Mount begins with the Beatitudes (Matthew 5:3-12) as Jesus presents the "Formation of the Kingdom of Heaven." He began the "Kingdom language," and although the concept of the Kingdom is in prophecy, the language of the Kingdom is absent in the Old Testament.

There are two responses in the premise of the Sermon on the Mount. The first is our helplessness, **"poor in spirit"** (Matthew 5:3). This helplessness is extreme and complete. No resource resides in the human life apart from the God's presence. We must embrace this condition as in mourning (Matthew 5:4). The grief in the loss of a loved one overwhelms us, and we live in the constant awareness of that loss. We are to embrace our helplessness as we are embraced by our helplessness. Congratulations! This opens the door for God's nature to merge with our helplessness. This is the second response. The Spirit of God becomes our source, and in our union with God we become the Kingdom of Heaven. God is not the Kingdom; I am not the

Kingdom. A new creature is created in the merge of the two.

When our helplessness merges with God's resource, the Beatitudes become a reality in our lives. Meekness creates a new relationship with the physical world (Matthew 5:5). The righteousness of God's nature fills the hungering, thirsting, and helpless person (Matthew 5:6). Receiving and giving mercy is characteristic of a helpless person filled with God's nature (Matthew 5:7). Intimacy with God and purity of heart are natural for a Kingdom person (Matthew 5:8). A Son of God is another name for the Kingdom person; he is a peacemaker (Matthew 5:9). Rejoicing in persecution is a common experience of this merger (Matthew 5:10-12).

Jesus contrasted Kingdom righteousness with the righteousness of the scribes and Pharisees (Matthew 5:20). There is no comparison because it is not a contrast of duration or quantity, but of quality. It is the difference between never physically murdering and victory over anger and hate (Matthew 5:21-26). In the realm of sexuality, it is the difference between physical adultery and inward purity (Matthew 5:27-30). In marriage, it is causing your spouse to be godly instead of divorce (Matthew 5:31-32).

Quality also applies to integrity and honesty (Matthew 5:33-37). Those of old agreed that when God was involved you must tell the truth. It was serious to swear an oath in God's name. The act of calling on God to back up the truth of your statement demands total compliance. Who would want the wrath of God to come upon them? Who would want to slander the name of God by involving Him in dishonesty? Who would dare testify they had intimacy with God and drag His character into deceit or say they dwelt in the same place with God and demonstrate a demonic nature? No one in his or her right mind would do that! ***"You shall not swear falsely, but shall perform your oaths to the Lord"*** (Matthew 5:33). If this were true for the righteousness of the scribes and Pharisees, what would the new

Kingdom righteousness demand? The concept of the illustration is consistent with all other illustrations. If total honesty were required when God is involved, what would we do if God were always involved? The Kingdom of Heaven is a merger between man and God, helplessness and Divine Nature. If I embrace my helplessness, God becomes the source of every attitude, speech, and expression. There is no place for dishonesty in this new level of relationship.

Confinement

"Those of old" would not swear on the name of God, but they would swear by heaven because it was less threatening than the presence of God. A person may intend to keep his word, but sometimes changes in circumstances demand adjustment in a promise. Swearing by heaven gives one a safe way to adjust an oath to accommodate unexpected circumstances. How ridiculous this is; heaven is the throne of God. Is He not involved in His own throne? In the New Covenant do you not become the throne by which He flows His authority into the world? There is no adjustment here!

One might consider swearing by the earth even less threatening because it is far beneath heaven. Its size and expanse is inferior to heaven. Can truth be manipulated based on a comparison between heaven and earth? Isn't earth the footstool of God? Earth is the platform on which God walks and demonstrates His love and power. Earth is the physical existence into which God breathed life. Is not our physical life the platform for His Divine expression? Should we not be the demonstration of the One who is Truth!

How foolish of us to think we can swear by Jerusalem and eliminate God's involvement. If we look away from Jerusalem while swearing an oath is that less binding than looking toward Jerusalem? God brought a glorious new level to us in the New Covenant. We are the temple of God located in the great city of the King. He rules within and through us. In light of His consistent presence and sourcing in our lives, truth is always demanded!

Would you consider your head superior to the heavens? King David didn't think so. While he watched his sheep, he gazed at the stars and cried,

> *"When I consider Your heavens, the works of Your fingers,*
> *The moon and the stars, which you have ordained,*
> *What is man that You are mindful of him,*
> *And the son of man that You visit Him?"*
> (Psalms 8:3-4).

Has your mind captured the complete knowledge of the earth? Is not its very existence beyond the "head" of humanity? While our minds may conceive the great city of Jerusalem, did we think into being the descending presence of God who dwells there? It is not our city; it is the *"city of the great King."* Our heads dwell only on the surface of the earth's truth. Our knowledge and travel are limited in comparison to the expansions of outer space. We *"cannot make one hair white or black."* Do we think swearing by our heads will be less demanding of truth than all the others?

Jesus proposed the logic of *"those of old"*. When God is involved you must tell the truth. The answer is simple; do not swear by the name of the Lord. *"Heaven"* would be a little closer to His presence than *"earth." "Jerusalem"* is further removed in size and quantity than the rest. But your *"head"* is the least of all. The foolishness of this thought process is beyond expression. The New Covenant places God in the midst of the human life, the *"head."* Why would they consider such a concept?

Part Four: Fulfillment of the Kingdom - The Application: Morals

Creation

Those of the Old Covenant did not consider God involved at all in the *"head."* They could not conceive that God would be involved in man's thinking. Certainly there were prophets of old who conversed with God, but the average person had no contact with Him. Man's involvement with God in the temple was strictly ceremonial. God was in the Holy of Holies; He was not accessible to man. Since they had no intimate relationship with God, they considered the inner part of man removed from the watchful eye of God and did not need to worry about what was within. They thought that God could see only their outside actions. This was the battle Jesus had with the scribes and Pharisees, which eventually brought about His crucifixion. Their concern focused on the exterior; Jesus was concerned with the interior. His example of comparing them to *"the cup and dish"* cleansed on the outside, *"but inside they are full of extortion and self- indulgence"* (Matthew 23:25) illustrates the difference. He said, *"For you are like white-washed tombs which indeed appear beautiful outwardly, but inside are full of dead men's bones and all uncleanness. Even so you also outwardly appear righteous to men, but inside you are full of hypocrisy and lawlessness"* (Matthew 23:27-28). Jesus returns to the premise of the Sermon on the Mount. The Kingdom of God is a merger. It is a new creature created by man's helplessness and God's power. It is an absolute fusion of these two until they act and become as one. The "helpless" element always remains helpless. Helplessness is united with the resource of the God's nature. What does a helpless man sourced by the God's nature look like? The answer is Jesus! Jesus is the first Kingdom Person!

If I try to adjust the truth with a lie to swear by my *"head,"* I have a gross misunderstanding of my *"head."* The problem is a sourcing issue, because there is nothing about my *"head"* that I source. I had no choice in the color of my hair or eyes, and the size and shape of my nose were completely out of my control. My intellectual ability is not determined by my will power. You and I are not in charge; we are helpless. Our *"head"* proves the point!

Jesus highlighted the concept of man's inability to source anything about his *"head"* in the words he used. He said, ***"Because you cannot make one hair white or black."*** The word *"make"* is a translation of the Greek word "poieo," a familiar Greek word in our studies. "Poieo" is the Greek word translated "bear" and is used in reference to trees producing fruit. It can be translated "doing" but has the connection to "nature." It describes the action of the doing produced by the nature of the producer. The action of the *"head"* must take the form of the nature of the *"head."* Therefore, the *"head"* responds to the nature within it.

The idea of action taking the form of the nature that produces it is strengthened by the word *"cannot."* Jesus says, ***"Because you cannot make one hair white or black."*** There are two Greek words involved in the translation of *"You cannot,"* "ouk" and "dunamai." "Ouk" is an independent negative compared to "me," a dependent negative. "Me" depends on the opinion of the one speaking. However, "ouk" is a universal negative that is understood by everyone. The act of ***"making one hair white or black"*** is impossible. Everyone understood this truth. The Greek word "dunamai" expresses "to be able" or "to have power by one's own resource." The focus of Jesus' statement is on sourcing. We are helpless to source anything connected to our *"head."*

Therefore, since God is the source of everything connected to your head, how does swearing by your head separate Him from your oath? Swearing by heaven involves Him because it is His throne. Swearing by earth involves Him because it is His footstool. Swearing by Jerusalem involves Him because it is His great city and He dwells there. Swearing by your **"head"** involves Him because He is the source of everything connected to the **"head."** Since God is involved in all of these physical things, why should you swear at all? ***"But let your 'Yes' be 'Yes,' and your 'No' 'No.' For whatever is more than these is from the evil one"*** (Matthew 5:37).

Everything changed with the New Covenant. We are wrong if we think God is only interested in outward activities. When someone attaches his or her eternal destiny to a physical activity, we should be suspicious. It is wrong to allow ceremonies to become more important than relationships, and physical baptism is never more valuable than the spiritual baptism in His Spirit! Being a Christian is never determined by an experience in the past or participating in a particular ceremony. If you are a Christian you have an intimate relationship with Jesus as He sources your life!

Connection

With this understanding of a Christian, we come to Jesus' concluding statement. The New Covenant is not a physical accomplishment, but is determined by a spiritual relationship. Those of the Old Covenant interpreted righteousness as, ***"You shall not murder"*** (Matthew 5:21). Those of the New Covenant focus on murder in the spiritual realm. ***"Whoever is angry with his brother shall be in danger of the judgment"*** (Matthew 5:22). The attitude of demeaning or belittling your fellowman places you in danger of hell (Matthew 5:22). Again we see the sourcing issue. If I am helpless and merged with Jesus, how can this attitude come from me?

Those of the Old Covenant considered their sexuality a body appetite. In their minds they were righteous because they did not physically commit adultery (Matthew 5:27). But righteousness is never about a physical activity; righteousness comes from an inner sourcing. If sexuality is in the core of man's life (*"in his heart"*), what is the source of his heart? If self-centeredness is sourcing your life, spiritual adultery will happen in every area of your being. If Jesus sources your life, His mind will be expressed in every arena of your living.

In the Old Covenant marriage, man believed he could separate from his wife legally (Matthew 5:31). In the New Covenant marriage where Jesus sourced my life, I must consider what I am causing in my wife. Will I allow Him to flow through me to produce an atmosphere of His presence in my home? Will my wife and children experience security, unconditional love, and peace? Am I creating a "safe place" for them?

In the Old Covenant honesty and integrity were only required when God was involved. Thus, an oath based on the name of the Lord must be honored (Matthew 5:33). But swearing based on something other than God allows for flexibility in the truth. The New Covenant righteousness will not tolerate such a standard. The New Covenant exists in a connection between God and man. It is the embraced helplessness of man and the great resource of the Person of God that merges into a new creature. This means God sources the life of the man.

God does not connect with man to advise, aid, or assist him. Man does not connect with God for service, ceremonial allegiance, or law obedience. The connection of God and man is for merging. Man cannot become god for he is helpless. But God invited man into His nature. It was the destiny of our creation from the beginning. While we lost this in the fall, God restored it to us in the death, resurrection, ascension, and infilling of Jesus. We live in Truth, and Truth lives in us. Therefore, *"let your 'Yes' be 'Yes,' and your 'No' 'No.'* Anything outside of this sourcing *"is from the evil one"* (Matthew 5:37).

Matthew 5:37

LOGOS

"But let your 'Yes' be "Yes,' and your 'No, 'No.' For whatever is more than these is from the evil one" (Matthew 5:37).

The Gospel of John differs from the Gospel of Matthew in that John did not include the details of the birth of Christ. John referenced the pre-existent second member of the Trinity becoming flesh: **"And the Word became flesh and dwelt among us, and we beheld His glory, the glory as of the only begotten of the Father, full of grace and truth"** (John 1:14). John gives a spiritual and philosophical approach to the incarnation. In the preceding verses of this first chapter, John presented Jesus as **"the Word,"** using the phrase three times in the first verse. **"In the beginning was the Word, and the Word was with God, and the Word was God"** (John 1:1). He presented content to this **"Word,"** insisting Jesus was with God and responsible for creation in the beginning (John 1:2-3). The essence of life contained in this Person manifested itself as **"the light of men"** (John 1:4). The forerunner, John the Baptist, verified the same (John 1:6-9). Although men resisted Jesus' presence, the explosive power of birthing for our new life came through Him (John 1:10-13). The concept of **"the Word"** forms the foundation for all these thoughts.

The **"Word"** is a translation of the Greek word "logos." "Logos" has several uses in the Greek language that do not reference Jesus. However, John gave such a strong identification of this word with Jesus, it is difficult to separate them in Christian thought. "Logos" is an expression of an intelligent, reasoning thought; it is the act of speaking and what is spoken. In the intelligent thought of the Trinity, there was and is an idea. This idea contains all that is in the human being. Jesus is the expression of this idea.

In etymology, a study of word origins, the root sense of "logos" seems to mean, "back," referring to the background, content, or meaning of what is said. The content of the words spoken stands for the idea originally in the speaker's mind. The idea takes on the historical element in the spoken word. The word contains a thought. It makes a thing known, so to grasp the word is to grasp the thought or idea. Although the word is a thought or idea, it is also dynamic. The word is filled with a power felt by those who receive it. The truth may start as a thought, but when stated it embraces the individuals engaged in its expression. However, the word is present independent of any acceptance.

The idea of humanity is in the reason and intellect of the Trinity. Jesus is the full revelation of this idea! He is **"the Word."** He is the full expression of the idea and is also the idea. Everything the Trinity dreams for humanity is fulfilled in Jesus. Jesus is the intent of God for you and me. If it is in Jesus, we are to experience it. The resource God produced in the life of Jesus is intended for each of us in quality and quantity. We are to lack nothing that is in Jesus. The pivotal issue is surrender. If we embrace Jesus as Jesus embraced the Father, the full resource revealed in Jesus will be ours. He is **"the Word."** He is the idea of humanity in the mind of the Trinity and the expression of this idea in our world.

What does Jesus being **"the Word"** have to do with our passage? ***"But let your 'Yes' be 'Yes,' and your 'No,' 'No'"*** (Matthew 5:37). There are two words in the Greek text of our passage not translated. The Greek text reads, "esto" (let be) "de" (But) "ho" (the) "logos" (word) "humon" (your) "nai" (Yes) "nai" (Yes) "nay" (No) "nay" (no). The two words not translated are "ho" (the) and "logos" (word). A full translation could be: "But let your (the) word be 'yes' 'yes,' and 'no' 'no.'" Jesus did not speak only of keeping a promise. He placed the communication of our words on a higher level than not just lying. What is your idea? What has your imagination? Who are you deep in the core of your being? You express what is in you daily. You can never cover it constantly. You will reveal who you are. In other words, the core of your life expresses itself in your daily living!

Jesus again stated the premise of the Sermon on the Mount, the essence of **"the Word."** He created us **"poor in spirit,"** and He congratulates us on it (Matthew 5:3). We must embrace our helplessness as we experience mourning (Matthew 5:4). Our constant surrender allows the merger of the Spirit of Jesus with our helplessness. We become the Kingdom of God. I am not the Kingdom; God is not the Kingdom. The merger is what creates a new creature, the Kingdom person. This Kingdom person is the idea in the mind of the Trinity. Jesus was the first to experience it; He was God who became man to display the mind of God. For the first time we know the purpose and plan for the creation of the physical world and the destiny of man!

Contrast
"But"

Jesus gave illustrations to reveal the reality of this new life, the New Covenant. Each illustration presented a contrast. Our statement begins with the contrast, **"But"** (Matthew 5:37). **"Those of old"** understood the severity of involving God in their speaking. An oath involving God was binding and could not be adjusted. To escape this strong pressure of honesty, a person must eliminate the presence of God from their speaking. Thus a series of additional oaths based on **"heaven," "earth," "Jerusalem,"** and the **"head"** were established. These were not as binding; you can maintain the appearance of honesty and still not keep your word if God is not involved.

"But" (here is the contrast) God is always involved in the New Covenant, and He is the core. Our helplessness demands that God constantly indwells and sources our lives. If we are helpless, we do not need help, aid, or assistance; we need Him! We must experience the continual merging of His nature with our being. The moment we deviate from merging with Him, we are lost. One split second without Him, and we are devils again. All the failures of the past become present. We are hopelessly lost. Our salvation is not in doctrinal belief. We do not embrace our helplessness through church ceremonies or traditions. We do not experience salvation through a physical response such as baptism, communion, or kneeling at an altar. We only find salvation through merging with His nature.

Jesus must be the single focus of our lives. Everything other than Jesus is a minor detail. Laws and regulations are secondary to His presence. Ministry performance is a minor detail without the flow of His nature. The moment Jesus is not sourcing my life, I move from His righteousness to self-righteousness. Heaven becomes hell when He is not in me. I must have no other passion than Him. I must set aside all desires; the one goal for my life must be Jesus. My helplessness demands it. The New Covenant is founded on it.

The Trinity has a dream for humanity. This idea in God's mind is expressed in Jesus. He is the Word (Logos). He is the idea and the expression of humanity. Does this not also give expression to who we are? Do we not become the "word" (logos)? All the Spirit of God does in Jesus, He wants to do in us. Therefore, we become the idea of humanity from the mind of God to achieve and reveal that idea. To claim the name of

Christ (Christian) and not be the "logos" would be to profane His name. We would be lying. **"But let your word** (logos) **be 'Yes' be 'Yes,' and 'No' 'No.'"** In this sense, you are the "logos" of God to your world. The New Covenant is not concerned with merely an oath. The Kingdom is concerned about the statement of your life!

Condition
"let be"

The first word in the Greek text is the verb of the sentence, translated **"let be."** The Greek verb "esto," a form of "eimi," is the word. Using this word is significant because it is a state of being. "Eimi" is the verb in God's name, which was given to Moses at the burning bush. God said, **"I am Who I am"** (Exodus 3:14). This is the core of who God is. We cannot go deeper than this! God produces all His actions from this center, and all His attitudes flow from there as well. He cannot deviate from this. If God were to change His actions He, would have to change Himself. Paul wrote, **"in hope of eternal life which God, who cannot lie, promised before time began"** (Titus 1:2). The base of this statement is the nature of God. It is impossible for God to lie!

Now Jesus applies this word to us. He does not restate the ninth commandment: **"You shall not bear false witness against your neighbor"** (Exodus 20:16). Although this verb (esto) is an imperative in our verse, it is not a command concerning performance. It directly relates to the core of our being. Jesus' concern is not the honesty of our statements but the honesty of our inner state of being that produces our statements.

Involving God in our speaking requires honesty, the contrast of our passage. **"Those of old"** were focused on performance. Involving God forced them to maintain honesty in their performance of an oath. But if God was not involved, they were free to be dishonest. Their actions would continue to give self-comfort. Thus they developed other bases for oaths. But the New Covenant's concern pertains to the core of our being, state of existence. Have we embraced our helplessness? Does God fill our inner need? Are we the Kingdom of God, a new creature? This alone places us on a new level and expression of righteousness.

Never diminish the practical aspect of involving God in your speaking. His involvement applies to business dealings, relationships, and financial obligations. But Jesus never begins there! He is always more concerned about my core, state of being. Ultimately the external actions of my life will match the inner state of my being. I can only cover, control, and manipulate this inner being for a brief time. Who I am will manifest itself!

Therefore, Jesus calls us to be "logos" for our day. Our helplessness merged with His Divine person will form in us a new core. We will become the Kingdom of God. This Kingdom will give new expression for our lives. What *"those of old"* could not anticipate becomes a reality in us. Congratulations! What all other religions require we earn, merit, and deserve is now given to us. We are helpless and can never deserve such a level of living. In the embrace of His nature, we become the Kingdom. This idea is the mind and heart of God and gives expression in the fullness of the Spirit of Jesus. The dream of the Trinity is fulfilled in us. Jesus is the visible image of the invisible God. He is the idea from the mind of the Trinity giving full expression in the flesh. He is the first One in the Kingdom; He established the means for us to enter this relationship. We live in the state of being of this relationship.

Connection
"No"

Jesus illustrated this new life in the practical aspect of integrity. Our *"No"* should be *"No,"* and our *"Yes"* should be *"Yes."* In other words what is inside us should match what we express on the outside. This was the opposite of *"those of old"* understood and was the argument between Jesus and the Pharisees, which caused the Pharisees to arrange the crucifixion of Jesus. They could not tolerate the continual revelation of their hypocrisy compared to their external activities. What we are inwardly must eventually correspond to what we are outwardly. The division between the two cannot be tolerated forever.

All Jesus' illustrations highlight this truth. ***"Those of old"*** could only maintain ***"You shall not murder"*** (Matthew 5:21). The hate, anger, demeaning, and belittling of others is tolerated and covered. We cannot help it because it is the way we are. When we acknowledge humanity in the heart of the Father, we see our hypocrisy. He has come to unite with our helplessness to eliminate the spiritual murder in our state of being. The outward elimination of murder must come from the core of love.

If we consider our sexuality a body appetite, we miss the reality of the heart. Our sexuality must be filled with Him. In this merger He manifests Himself through our outward expression of sexuality. Our perspective will become His. We become the expression and the idea of humanity in the mind of the Trinity. It will flow into our marriage. We will cause in each other the "logos" of God's design. Because God is always involved in the expression of our lives, honesty and integrity are naturally expressed. What is in us will now be seen without! We are the "logos" of God to our world.

Jesus' use of the Greek word "ouk" for *"No,"* is significant. He contrasted "ouk" with another Greek word often used for the negative, "me." The difference between these two is that "ouk" is an independent negative, whereas "me" is a dependent negative. "Ouk" expresses the reality view; "me" expresses an opinion. "Ouk" gives no room for argument; it expresses universal truth. "Me" is based on the opinion and perspective of the individual expressing it.

When I swear by the *"earth,"* I swear on myself because I am created from dust; it is my opinion. When I swear by *"Jerusalem,"* I swear on something I have built; it is my opinion. When I swear by my *"head,"* I express my opinion. Jesus calls us to a new relationship, the Kingdom of God. I am to embrace my helplessness and be embraced by my helplessness. This embracement will open the door to His invasion of my life. In the merger between His nature and my helplessness, I become an expression of His mind. I am "logos." I become the idea in His mind and the expression of that idea. I no longer live out of my opinion. I express the universal, reality of God's dream for humanity. I cannot express God's dream for me without Him. The expression of His dream in me is not just His input, touch, or instruction but is my submergence in Him. The only element hindering this merger is the embrace of my helplessness. He accomplished all that is necessary in Christ to produce the Kingdom in and through me. Will I really be His? My destiny will be the "logos" of God!

Matthew 5:37

A NEW LANGUAGE

"But let your 'Yes' be 'Yes,' and your 'No,' 'No.' For whatever is more than these is from the evil one" (Matthew 5:37).

The Sermon on the Mount is not a sermon for the "entertainment church." It would not appeal to the "feel-good crowd" or those who adhere to the prosperity gospel. The legalistic Pharisee did not embrace this sermon because the practical application of its truth was far beyond the reasonable laws of religion (Matthew 5:21-48), and no one could possibly accomplish its standard. If you desire religious ceremonies, the Sermon on the Mount proposes none. No sacrificial lambs to offer, no ritualistic observances, or meetings to attend are involved. Even the spiritual disciplines such as charity, prayer, and fasting are taken to a level of relational intimacy (Matthew 6:1-18). The activity of prayer becomes meaningless in light of intimacy. If you think you are spiritually superior to others, this sermon is not for you. The Sermon on the Mount does not tolerate judgment of others (Matthew 7:1-5). This sermon is too narrow for the broadminded (Matthew 7:13-14).

The Sermon on the Mount is only for the helpless (Matthew 5:3). The poor in spirit must embrace their poverty like one who mourns (Matthew 5:4). We must constantly realize and embrace our helplessness, and we must never step outside its boundaries. The Spirit of God moves in those who embrace their helplessness (Matthew 5:4), sourcing a new creature. The Kingdom of Heaven is created in the merger of the helpless man and the resourcing God. Jesus who became a helpless man filled with the Spirit provides this new creation. God is not the Kingdom on His own nor is the helpless man. The union of these two forms the Kingdom of Heaven.

We should expect a new life-style to flow from such a fusion. Where defeat was once acceptable in man's helpless state, it is acceptable no longer. Where sin once mastered a helpless man, he is now mastered by righteousness. Attitudes change; actions are altered; desires are radically transformed. What or who can hinder a helpless man filled with God from transforming his world? Jesus proposed, **"For I say to you, that unless your righteousness exceeds the righteousness of the scribes and Pharisees, you will by no means enter the kingdom of heaven"** (Matthew 5:20). The beginning stage of the new creature, the Kingdom of Heaven, far overshadows the best man can produce in his helplessness.

Jesus gave six illustrations of exceeding the righteousness of the scribes and Pharisees (Matthew 5:21-48). Every aspect of man's helplessness is contained in these six illustrations. Each illustration contains the fundamentals of life. Jesus presented them in a contrast between *"those of old"* and *"But I say to you."* He did not speak from the authority of being God. He testified as the new creature, the Kingdom of Heaven. He is the first visible example of the merger between God and a helpless man. This merger is the picture of Jesus. Everything in Him is now in us because we are filled with the same Spirit of God.

The fourth illustration concerns "morals." *"Those of old"* understood honesty when God was involved. If they used the name of God, they must be honest. Anything outside of this standard profaned the name of God with severe consequences. The solution was simple; do not involve God in your promises. *"Those of old"* easily sidestepped honesty by swearing on a variety of things other than God; heaven, earth, Jerusalem, or your head were all good options. Each was less binding in the pressure for honesty.

"But I say to you" changed the equation. What if God was involved in everything you say? God cannot lie (Titus 1:2). Any merger with God requires honesty. This standard is impossible to maintain; no one is perfect. People can do only their best; an expectation of more than this effort is unreasonable. After all, we are human beings. But these statements prove only the premise of the Sermon on the Mount. We are helpless! Our self-efforts can never achieve the righteousness of the Kingdom of Heaven. The Kingdom must be a merger between God's nature and our helplessness. When this fusion occurs, the possibilities are expanded. Everyone understands the limitation of human resource. Who has exhausted the resources of the Divine?

The closing statement of the "morals" illustration is climactic. Jesus said, ***"But let your 'Yes' be 'Yes,' and your 'No,' 'No.'"*** (Matthew 5:37). In a previous study, we discovered the Greek word "logos" is not translated. The actual translation is, "But let your (the) word be 'yes' 'yes,' and 'no' 'no.'" In light of Jesus being the "Word," and His proposed merger with us, this statement takes on new meaning. The Greek word "logos" contains two merged ideas. One is the "idea" contained in the heart and mind of God. The Trinity has a plan and dream for the human being. The "idea" of humanity is as God determines us to be! The second aspect is the actual expression of this idea, which is Jesus. Jesus is the idea and the expression of the idea of humanity found in the heart of God. Everything God wants us to be, Jesus is!

Now in this illustration about oaths, Jesus said that we are to be the "logos" of God's heart through merger. The Kingdom person is the idea and the expression of God's nature in the world. Because we are helpless, this expression demonstrates God's nature and His sourcing of our lives. After stating this fact, Jesus continued, ***"For whatever is more than these is from the evil one"*** (Matthew 5:37). This statement directly relates to the idea of "logos" just expressed. "Logos" is the ***"these"*** in the statement. In other words the life of the Kingdom person is an expression of God's nature, which must be one of honesty. This honesty is not in the fact of not telling a lie but in expressing God's nature. Because the nature of God is love, we must be the expression of His love. The Kingdom person fulfills the call of God to ***"Be holy, for I am holy"*** (1 Peter 1:16). There is no hypocrisy between the nature of God and the expression of the Kingdom person.

Boundary Language

Jesus expressed this truth in "boundary language," the language ***"those of old"*** used to express their proposal of truth. In other words Jesus said, "I am going to speak your language." For instance, ***"You have heard that it was said to those of old, 'You shall not murder, and whoever murders will be in danger of the judgment'"*** (Matthew 5:21). ***"Those of old"*** were filled with anger, hatred, temper, and emotions. In their helplessness how were they to manage such feelings? They established a boundary they were not to go beyond. They controlled and managed their emotions so they never stepped over that boundary into murder. In maintaining this boundary, they considered themselves righteous.

The same kind of language was used for the second illustration, "morality." In their sexuality, they experienced a natural appetite, a sexual body drive. In their helplessness what could they do with their passion? They established the boundary of ***"You shall not commit adultery"*** (Matthew 5:27). This boundary was their attempt to manage and control the sexual desires necessary for marriage relationship and family life. In maintaining this boundary, they considered themselves righteous.

This kind of language is again repeated in the third illustration of "marriage and divorce." Jesus said, *"Whoever divorces his wife, let him give her a certificate of divorce"* (Matthew 5:31). Conflict in marriage is inevitable. What is the proper response to conflict? They needed a boundary to deal with marriage conflicts. If a man wanted to separate from his wife, he had to give her a certificate of divorce so she could remarry. In maintaining this boundary, they considered themselves righteous.

Now Jesus moves to this fourth illustration, "morals." A helpless person finds it difficult to always be honest. You can make a promise, but circumstances change; therefore, we may need to adjust our promises to fit the necessity of our circumstances. What is the boundary for honesty? *"You shall not swear falsely, but shall perform your oaths to the Lord"* (Matthew 5:33). When you involve God in your promise, you must maintain honesty. But if you do not involve God, you have room for adjustment. In maintaining this boundary, they considered themselves righteous.

In each illustration Jesus established a new boundary. *"For whatever is more than these is from the evil one"* (Matthew 5:37). Although this statement is related to the fourth illustration, it can easily be applied to the other three. A helpless person can maintain only the boundary of not committing murder. If we merge with the nature of God, what can that nature do through us? Can anger, demeaning, and belittling be eliminated? Can the idea of the God's mind be expressed through our lives? Anything outside of God's thoughts, we must eliminate!

If you are helpless, and your boundary for sexuality is "do not commit adultery," can a merging with God's nature find new perspective in your sexuality? Can your sexuality be engulfed by a boundary that changes your expression? Your dress, your walk, your life's perspective, and your mannerisms are all an expression of your sexuality. Can I be filled with Jesus so God's ideas and expressions are mine? Anything outside this boundary is not acceptable. The same is required in marriage. Although I may get a divorce, should I consider what I cause in my spouse? Helplessness sees impossibility. Could His nature cause a new thing in my marriage? Is His nature the new boundary?

In the fourth illustration on morals, the boundary is in "the presence of God." We must maintain honesty when God is present. If He is always present, the boundary must still be maintained. We must eliminate anything outside of the expression of "logos." We are the idea and the expression of what God intended every person to be. Live within the boundary of His presence!

Birthing Language

Jesus expanded the "boundary language" to the "birthing language." He said, *"For whatever is more than these is from* (ek) *the evil one"* (Matthew 5:37). Two Greek words are translated *"from,"* "ek" and "apo." They are never used interchangeably but can each be translated "from." "Ek" indicates that the original location was in another object; "apo" is used to indicate that the original location was nearby another object. In our passage Jesus highlighted birthing. Anything beyond the boundary of the "logos" is sourced and birthed from the devil's nature.

This principle is true in all six illustrations. Murder was viewed as sourced by *"the evil one."* In merging with the Spirit of Jesus, I experience a new sourcing. What was anger now becomes understanding; what was hatred now becomes compassion; what was revenge now becomes love. Anything beyond the boundary of His presence is a result of the birthing or sourcing of *"the evil one."*

Adultery is sourced by the devil. Sexuality is more than a body drive; therefore, what sources the other expressions of my sexuality? If I merge with Jesus, will He source my expressions? What will He cause in my marriage? Can His presence through me create security, love, intimacy, safety, and godliness in my home? Anything outside this boundary means I participate in the effects and desires of *"the evil one."*

Honesty and integrity are no different. If God's nature is involved in every word and intent of my heart, will He not birth honesty in me? From where will anything outside this boundary come? My helplessness filled with my self-centeredness is the demonic nature. I deceive myself by viewing my helplessness as an adequate source. Our language testifies to our helplessness. I am not perfect; I cannot live above sin; I cannot love everyone; I am doing the best I can. These are all statements verifying our helplessness. Does not honesty demand that I embrace the adequate resource of God's nature?

Being Language

"What should I do?" This is the wrong question and is an expression of self-centered helplessness. You can do nothing; you are helpless. You must "become" a new Kingdom person! Anything produced by you is only a product of *"the evil one."* Jesus said, *"For whatever is more than these is from the evil one"* (Matthew 5:37). *"Whatever"* is the subject and is a translation of "tou" in the nominative case. It can be translated as the definite article "the." The adjective "perissos," translated *"is more than,"* modifies the subject. Thus, the subject is translated *"whatever is more than."* The verb of the sentence is "eimi," translated *"is,"* although sometimes translated "comes from." "Eimi" is a verb of being. The focus is not on what you do, but what you are!

Now we come to the most difficult part of the concept.

When my focus is on being rather than doing, I envision laziness or inactivity. We say, "Because I am helpless, I will let God do it all." Although this may be true, there is a fact we have not considered. God will do it through us! Although we are in action, we dwell in a state of being. The tension, stress, and pressures of self-production are gone. We rest in the activity of Divine movement! But we cannot conceive of a state where we do nothing yet accomplish everything. How can I rest yet experience the exhaustion of Kingdom exertion?

No one advocates that we become "God." We propose the opposite! We must embrace our helplessness. Anything beyond this boundary is *"from the evil one."* We live within the boundary of His presence where our emotional responses, the expression of our sexuality, the atmosphere of our marriage, and our integrity are all expressions of His nature. The content of the word "our" is the merger of His nature and our helplessness. He lives through us. We are the "logos," the idea and expression of God's dream for humanity. What Jesus is, we have become; we are brothers with Christ. The same Life Source birthing Jesus births us. Anything beyond this boundary is an expression of *"the evil one."*

Fulfillment of the Kingdom – The Application:

MALICE

Matthew 5:38-42

THE REDEMPTIVE IDEA

"You have heard that it was said, 'A eye for an eye and a tooth for a tooth.' But I tell you not to resist an evil person. But whoever slaps you on your right cheek, turn the other to him also. If anyone wants to sue you and take away your tunic, let him have your cloak also. And whoever compels you to go one mile, go with him two. Give to him who asks you, and from him who wants to borrow from you do not turn away"
(Matthew 5:38-42).

The Sermon on the Mount is a masterpiece! There is no equal to it. Lesser thoughts must not diminish it; its standard must not be lowered by human excuses. In Matthew's Gospel the timing of the message highlights its importance. Although multitudes may have been present, Jesus gave this sermon specifically to His disciples. The typical person would have discovered no meaning or had little interest in such a ridiculous standard of living. Disciples were called to the new kingdom and rejoiced in its message. Jesus proclaimed this truth at the beginning of His ministry not at the close. Jesus began His ministry in Galilee (Matthew 4:12-17) and called His disciples to follow Him (Matthew 4:18-22). They needed to know the content of the Kingdom in which they would minister. The Messiah was establishing something new. The Sermon on the Mount is a "manifesto" of the Kingdom of God!

Part Five: Fulfillment of the Kingdom - The Application: Malice

Jesus started with the premise of the Kingdom, and if we do not understand His premise, all will be lost. The premise is a radical approach in the Beatitudes (Matthew 5:3-12). We are called *"Blessed"* in each beatitude. Jesus gives congratulations because we have arrived. We are fortunate because we have received. This receipt is a reversal of all religious thought. The Jewish approach to Old Testament teachings followed the ordinary thought of all religions. We must earn, merit, and achieve the favor of God. We can only achieve the benefits of the Kingdom through discipline, strenuous effort, and much sacrifice. But Jesus proclaimed a new Kingdom. What all other world religions require us to earn, Jesus gives freely. Congratulations! You are *"Blessed."*

In the first beatitude, Jesus declared this to the *"poor in spirit"* (Matthew 5:3). We do not merely lack resources at the core of our lives; we are empty. We have no resource in ourselves to produce anything close to the Kingdom. This lack is not because of sin in our lives; rather, sin is a product of all our attempts to produce life out of our helplessness. God created us to be helpless. We were destined to be dependent not independent. We are to embrace this helplessness like grief over a loved one who just died (Matthew 5:4). We are to live in the awareness of our helplessness. Never step out of the boundaries of helplessness. If you live in helplessness, He will "comfort you"! He is the "Comforter"! The Spirit of Jesus will merge with you. In this fusion a new creature is created! He is not this on His own; I am not this on my own. But when Jesus and I merge the Kingdom person becomes a reality. God is not my boss, telling me what to do. He is not my counselor, giving me advice. He is not my Savior, doing something for me. He is my life; He is my destiny; He is my completeness! Merging does not mean assisting; it is the creation of a Kingdom person. Congratulations on your helplessness! In embracing my helplessness and being embraced by my helplessness, I experience the New Covenant Kingdom!

The Redemptive Idea | **Matthew 5:38-42**

If my mind merges with His mind, how will I think? If my emotions merge with His emotions, how will I feel? If my will merges with His will, what will I choose? A helpless person without Jesus must grasp every resource available to survive. He or she lives in constant desperation trying to exist, never relaxing or feeling secure. They are in a constant battle, barely hanging on. What about being redemptive to others? Redemption of others is a foreign thought to those living out of their helplessness. They must use all resources coming their way for themselves. But consider the abundance of resource in Jesus! The helpless individual who merges with Jesus' resource will flow with the intent and desires of His resource. That person will always be redemptive because Jesus is always redemptive!

The remaining beatitudes come from the same perspective. I become a minister of meekness (Matthew 5:5). The Roman culture of Jesus' day knew nothing about meekness. They did not have even a word for it in their vocabulary. When there is a lack of meekness, redemption cannot exist. Self-centeredness sourced by helplessness dominates, demands, and conquers, developing a barbarous and brutal culture. Meekness can exist only in a person whose abundant resource and power cannot be threatened. When helplessness merges with the abundance of our Sovereign Lord, meekness flows in redemption.

The fullness of redemptive ministry can be experienced only in the *"hunger and thirst for righteousness"* (Matthew 5:6). If a person is not dominated by openness, he cannot be filled. If we are not filled with the Spirit, we cannot be redemptive. ***"Hunger and thirst for righteousness"*** comes only from embracing one's helplessness. A ministry of mercy comes only from obtaining mercy (Matthew 5:7). Redemptive ministry is sharing obtained mercy with someone else and is possible only when I embrace my helplessness and merge with Jesus. The ministry of holiness comes only when we see God; we cannot see God without purity of heart (Matthew 5:8). God cannot share His nature of purity

Part Five: Fulfillment of the Kingdom - The Application: Malice

with you unless you embrace your helplessness. We cannot be redemptive to others unless they can see God in our helplessness. Peacemakers are people filled with peace; they are sons of God (Matthew 5:9). Only those who embrace their helplessness find peace in Jesus' merger with their spirit. They are free from the stress of conflict and can minister peace. Redemptive ministry brings peace to the human soul. Who can possibly rejoice amid persecution (Matthew 5:10)? Only the person who embraces his helplessness and merges with Divine purpose! No redemptive ministry happens unless a person lives above the consistent persecution and demonic pressure of their world. This lifestyle is the foundation for all redemptive ministries. It is the "Formation of the Kingdom."

How does the "Formation of the Kingdom" demonstrate itself in my world? Jesus presented the imagery of salt and light. These imageries promote the "being" aspect of the Kingdom. But how can it be otherwise? We are helpless! There are good works produced through our lives (Matthew 5:16). Jesus does not promote inactivity. But He is the source. In the merger of God and man, the life of Jesus is produced. I am Christlike because the oneness Jesus had with the Father, I now experience with Him. Salt is the imagery of preservation and taste. Light is the imagery of creation and fulfillment. The image of salt and light is always redemptive. Such ministry is not contained in "doing." Redemptive acts never produce redemption! Redemption is a state of "being" experienced in the merger. This is the "Function of the Kingdom" (Matthew 5:13-16).

After establishing "The Function of the Kingdom" as the base, Jesus proclaimed the "Fulfillment of the Kingdom" (Matthew 5:17-48). He began with the introduction (Matthew 5:17-20) presenting what was happening in His own life. He did not come to eliminate the Scriptures (Law and Prophets) but to fulfill them (Matthew 5:17). Everything discussed in the Old Testament became a reality in the merger between God and man. The shadow became reality. Jesus was the first man to experience it. The Law of the Old was brought to completeness in the merger with Jesus. He made a way for us. This is the "Fulfillment of the Kingdom, Acknowledged" (Matthew 5:17-20). It is a call not a condemnation. The scribes and Pharisees may have been the best a helpless person could be on their own, but they did not begin to display the Kingdom person. ***"For I say to you, that unless your righteousness exceeds the righteousness of the scribes and Pharisees, you will by no means enter the kingdom of heaven"*** (Matthew 5:20). Therefore, Jesus presented redemption, not judgment or condemnation. He calls us to the fulfillment of all God dreams we can be. We can merge with Him and be the Kingdom!

Jesus gives six illustrations of this truth (Matthew 5:21-48). At the heart of each illustration is this simple principle: it is impossible for a helpless man to be redemptive unless He merges with the Divine Person. The best a helpless person can accomplish on his own is to curb his self-focus. Redemption flows only through the abundance of resource. The purpose of each illustration is redemption. Redemption was the dream proposed in the Old Covenant, but it is a reality embraced in the New Covenant. The Old Covenant pointed to it, but it is the usual lifestyle in New Covenant. The best in the Old Testament saw moments of its reality but could only prophesy about it. Those least in the New Testament experience its reality! Redemption is birthed in the New Kingdom!

Jesus exposed this principle in the illustration of "murder" (Matthew 5:21-26). The best a helpless man can accomplish is to discipline his outward actions, so he does not commit murder. Changing his attitude and motive is beyond man's ability. The focus of the helpless man's life must be himself. He must pour all his self-energy into controlling his outward activity. Man is without resource to be redemptive toward others. Not committing murder is his highest achievement. Jesus elevated the

Part Five: Fulfillment of the Kingdom – The Application: Malice

standard from outward righteousness to inward purity. He calls us to not be angry with, demean, or belittle others. The focus is not on maintaining proper activities but is embracing others in redemption. This focus is impossible in our helplessness. The life of the New Covenant flows from the merger of God and man. Only the new creature can experience God's nature, a redemptive nature that does not live for itself. It goes beyond curbing physical expressions for decency; it is an expression of God's heart. The issue is not about being angry; it is about pouring out our lives for others. We must seek reconciliation with others (Matthew 5:24).

Jesus progressed from "murder" to "morality" (Matthew 5:27-30). The rules within the boundary of marriage require a specific level of faithfulness. ***"You shall not commit adultery,"*** the seventh of the Ten Commandments. It focuses on maintaining sexual desires in the marriage relationship. I must control my sexuality for the sake of self-benefit. We have family, children, and society to consider. My self-respect is also at risk. This is not the heart of God. The New Covenant is my heart merging with His heart. The sexuality at the core of my life influences and determines the expression of my life. The way I walk, talk, and approach life expresses my sexuality. Sexuality controlled by self-centeredness manipulates every facet of life for self. Sexuality in the heart core must be filled with Jesus; therefore, it becomes a redemptive flow for others. Instead of curbing a body drive, my masculinity or femininity expresses the nature of God; it constantly draws people to Jesus. The strength of masculinity expresses the love of the Father's heart. Instead of masculinity expressing self-centered dominance in the home, it becomes a redemptive force of love in my family. Instead of masculinity finding pride in its muscles and strength, it discovers delight in compassion and caring. Masculinity is now an avenue for redemption!

How does this appear in "marriage" (Matthew 5:31-32)? The

"certificate of divorce" was established ***"because of the hardness of your hearts"*** (Matthew 19:8). Divorce was provided in light of using marriage for selfish desires. Self-centeredness creates a marriage "meeting my needs." Jesus proposed the redemptive element at the heart of marriage. The central issue is, "what am I causing in my spouse?" Am I being redemptive? Redemption is the heart of God! Anyone living out of his or her helplessness will grasp every advantage for self. Self-protection, self-fulfillment, and self-pleasure become the driving force of the marriage. This is the best people can accomplish in their helplessness. If the nature of Jesus merges with us, we reach a new level in marriage that is always redemptive. How may I cause godliness in my spouse? Am I drawing them into Jesus? In the oneness of marriage, am I imparting Christ into them?

The issue of "morals" is vital in the New Covenant (Matthew 5:33-37). The helpless man alone in his defense must lie, forcing truth from his life. Therefore, oaths are necessary. Even then, he will develop levels of truthfulness whereby he can adjust the truth to fit his needs. In the Old Covenant, the only possibility of truth was to involve God in the oath. Truth was forced from the individual because of fear. All other levels provide a manipulation of the truth. What would occur if the helpless person merged with the Spirit of God? The One, who is Truth, would project truth throughout the helpless person's life (John 14:6). Levels of truth would cease. Why does a helpless person manipulate truth? Manipulation of truth is the only means available to advance and protect self. Self must be saved at any cost! The nature of God merged with a person focuses on redemption Jesus sets us free in truth. Imprisonment in our lies simply binds us tighter in the trap of our lies. We are not free to redeem; we are too busy protecting self.

How will this redemptive style be seen in a world filled with helpless people? A person living out of helplessness must use every advantage he or she has for his or her self. "Malice" is the result (Matthew 5:38-42). *"You have heard that it was said, 'An eye for an eye and a tooth for a tooth'"* (Matthew 5:38). Those soaked in helplessness praise in this high level of fairness and justice. This is far above the evil paganism of the wicked world. This code of conduct is an attempt to limit personal vengeance and retribution, the best helpless people can do. It is more than fair in their sight. After all, people should not be allowed to continue in their evil ways. I deserve to be protected from their evil; when I experience their evil, adequate retribution is only fair.

"An eye for an eye" never produces a cross of redemption. It was a Man merged with the heart of the Father who willingly gave Himself to the cross of redemption. Do not view Jesus' Garden of Gethsemane experience as a struggle with redemption (Matthew 26:47-56). You can see this clearly as Jesus embraced the cross. His cry was, *"Father, forgive them, for they do not know what they do"* (Luke 23:34). Even the leaders of Israel recognized His redemptive heart and sneered in rejection. The sneering was the expression of helpless people who could not see beyond *"an eye for an eye and a tooth for a tooth."* They had no inclination for redemption. They cried, *"He saved others; let Him save Himself if He is the Christ, the chosen of God"* (Luke 23:35). No one can live for his or her self and be redemptive to others.

This is not a call to perform redemptive activities. This call is to and from the heart of God. Jesus painted the portrait of God's heart. God's heart is always redemptive. When we have God's heart, we will always pour our lives out for others. God's heart is not about resisting murder but reaching into the lives of people to be redemptive. His heart is not about controlling a self-centered sexual drive, but about allowing our lives to be governed by a redemptive principle. Every expression of our sexuality becomes redemptive to others. Sexuality expression is not about what we can gain from our marriage but is about what we can give. It is not about bending the truth to fit personal needs but is about being the expression of truth that releases others to be free. This expression is not about getting treated fairly, but it is about others being changed at the core of their lives. We must be redemptive.

Matthew 5:38

REDEMPTIVE PRINCIPLE

"You have heard that it was said, 'An eye for an eye and a tooth for a tooth'" (Matthew 5:38).

The Jewish tradition of Jesus' day had a long-standing concept of justice. Traditional justice was ***"An eye for an eye and a tooth for a tooth"*** (Matthew 5:38). This principle of proportionate retribution can be found in a variety of quotes from the Mosaic Law:

"But if any harm follows, then you shall give life for life, eye for eye, tooth for tooth, hand for hand, foot for foot, burn for burn, wound for wound, stripe for stripe" (Exodus 21:23-25).

"If a man causes disfigurement of his neighbor, as he has done, so shall it be done to him - fracture for fracture, eye for eye, tooth for tooth; as he has caused disfigurement of a man, so shall it be done to him" (Leviticus 24:19- 20).

"Your eye shall not pity: life shall be for life, eye for eye, tooth for tooth, hand for hand, foot for foot" (Deuteronomy 19:21).

Although this law was strongly proposed in the Mosaic Law, it was older and more widely recognized than the Law of Moses. This law is found in the "Code of Hammurabi," existing in the eighteenth century before Christ with the same examples of "eye" and "tooth." Even in that day, its proposal was a great advance. It meant evenhanded justice without respect of persons. However great the offender, he could not escape just punishment, and no matter how small his offense, no more could be exacted of him than his offense merited. It took punishment out of the realm of private vengeance. Therefore, its intention was not to sanction revenge, but to prevent excessive blood feuds by stating that the legal punishment must not exceed the crime. You should recognize that by the time of Jesus physical penalties had generally been replaced with financial damages.

Those of old proposed that punishment must precisely match the crime. The purpose of this principle was to establish a sense of fairness. No one should be allowed to commit a crime against another without some kind of retribution. This retribution was only "fair." A society that does not punish crime becomes a society that approves crime. The purpose of this principle was to curtail further crimes. If *"an eye for an eye and a tooth for a tooth"* is required *"those who remain shall hear and fear, and hereafter they shall not again commit such evil among you"* (Deuteronomy 19:20). Not abiding by such a principle would be unfair to the innocent and law-abiding.

However, this principle also prevented excessive punishment based on personal vengeance and angry retaliation. The punishment must not exceed the crime; this is fair. Anger and hatred must not be allowed to cloud the judgment in determining the punishment of a crime. A person who judges the crime cannot allow feelings to dictate the punishment; if they do, they disqualify themselves as a judge. This qualification is why we must have an impartial judge to decide. He has no advantage to gain or emotional involvement to influence the decision of justice. Therefore, this principle is applied, and justice is served. Then the judgment is fair!

Surely Jesus was reasonable and would see the logic of such a principle. All our senses are alert to hear His answer. *"But I tell you"* (Matthew 5:39). As noted in the preceding illustrations, the reference to *"I"* is given twice in the statement. The Greek word "ego" is translated *"I."* However, it was not necessary to

Part Five: Fulfillment of the Kingdom - The Application: Malice

give this word because the verb also indicates the first-person, singular pronoun. Because Jesus was a Spirit-filled person, He assumed the right to express the heart and nature of the Father. The Greek word "lego" is translated *"I tell."* This word originally meant to lay or let lie down for sleep, to lie together. Therefore, it began to mean, "to collect." It evolved into the idea of "to lay before" or relate, recount something collected. Thus, it came to be used for speaking with an emphasis on content.

Jesus was not merely quoting an Old Testament verse or restating the "Code of Hammurabi." He expressed the nature of God. He was a helpless Man filled with the nature of God. If the nature of God views the crime scene, what is His judgment? Remember, this merger is the premise of the Sermon on the Mount. We are helpless in our spirit. We have no resource available in us. If we live in this consciousness, He fills us with Himself. In the combining of these two natures, a new creature is birthed. This newly birthed child is called "the Kingdom of God." He lives on a new level that is utterly impossible to the person being sourced by his helplessness.

How does this new creature view crime and its punishment? The best we can expect from a person sourced by his helplessness is fairness. *"An eye for an eye and a tooth for a tooth"* is fair. What could be better than being fair? The answer is "be redemptive!" Jesus takes us from the "fairness" of the self-centered helpless person to the "redemption" of God's nature. This redemptive life makes no sense to the person sourced by his helplessness. He must guard, protect, grab, and accuse in order to gain any advantage. The Spirit-filled person needs no advantage. His perspective is the heart of God. His resources are extravagant; he does not need to protect or guard. He can afford to be redemptive. He can give mercy because he has received mercy.

Jesus proposed, *"But I tell you not to resist an evil person"* (Matthew 5:39). The Greek word "antistenai" is translated *"to resist."* This word occurs 14 times in the New Testament and always in the middle voice. In other words, Jesus does not describe just an action in which we must participate. He describes an attitude, a feeling, or an emotional response we must have. Jesus' concern focuses on the personal preference of our motive. How do you view the *"evil person"* who offended you? Can you look beyond their evil offense and consider the value of their person? Can you view them with a redemptive heart and experience with them the terrible consequences of evil in guilt and destruction? The Greek word "poneros" is translated *"evil person,"* and is used 26 times in the Book of Matthew. Matthew uses it in the moral sense. In our passage a person becomes the agent of the evil activity; therefore, a person must be considered. However, the Greek word "poneros" is a focus on the moral trait; the actual word *"person"* is not included in our passage. Can you and I embrace the evil person? Can redemption flow from us to the person in the grips of evil?

Concept
"Fairness is determined by my standpoint."

Consider the idea of the self-centered person who must guard and protect. He has no resource and must hang onto every advantage he can find. "Fairness" is the highest approach he can make toward an injustice against him. Fairness is determined by the injured, the suffering one who experiences hurt, pain, and loss of his person. Self-focus is the standard for his fairness. We take what has happened to us; we impose it on them. This response is fair!

Someone punched out my eye; is it fair for him to be living his life with two eyes while I have only one? They should feel the pain I feel. My disability should become his disability; after all, he is to blame. I deserve to be compensated for what I have suffered. He should be responsible for my compensation, even if it is only the satisfaction of knowing he did not get by with it. He needs to suffer as I have; he needs to know how I feel. For him to get by when I have to live with one eye is unfair. I should not have to suffer the consequence of his evil while he does not!

God's heart is redemptive. Maybe life is not about being fair but about being redemptive. How may I save the day? How can the life of the man who took my eye be changed forever? How can he be delivered from all that causes him to be as he is? Think of all the hate and bitterness in him that caused him to lash out and to injure me. Think of all the broken relationships his anger has left. View what his anger has done and is doing to his family. The long-range view of the consequences is unbearable. How may we redeem him?

You must not consider the words of Jesus in our passage to be idealistic or merely philosophical. The Gospel accounts are filled with illustrations of Jesus' application of this teaching. Perhaps He did not apply it as a mere activity; the demonstration of this reality flowed spontaneously from His life. He was the combination of the poverty of the spirit of man filled with the nature of God, the Kingdom person! Imagine the thoughts of a self-centered person in the Garden of Gethsemane. Jesus confronted the evil of every person in every generation. Nothing was fair about One who never sinned becoming sin for us. The one who sinned should bear the consequences of his decisions. The person who lives by the self-centered principle of fairness must grab a sword and defend his position (Matthew 26:51). The One who is filled with the nature of redemption must insist that swords be put aside (Matthew 26:52). Self-centered fairness will forsake and flee the scene of redemption (Matthew 26:56). The redemptive heart yielded Himself to the will of the Father and carried the suffering of the world's sin.

It simply is not fair! But this suffering is not about fairness; it is about redemption. Redemption is not about getting even; it is about changing lives. How will you reach into the life of the man who slaps you on the right cheek in an act of redemption (Matthew 5:39)? How do you redeem the man who sues you to take away your tunic (Matthew 5:40)? How does the man who compels you to go one mile experience the love of God (Matthew 5:41)? How is the man who wants to borrow from you ever going to embrace the love of Jesus (Matthew 5:42)?

If we respond in redemptive ways, will we not get the "raw end" of the deal? Are we to live our lives allowing others to take advantage of us? How will we ever prosper? Those questions spring forth from the helpless person who lives out of their poverty. The only way the person who has nothing can gain anything is that if he holds onto everything that comes his way. He cannot afford to be forgiving or generous in any realm. But the one who embraces their helplessness and experiences Jesus' resource can afford to be extravagant. This person does not worry! Jesus illustrated this with the lilies of the field. They make no effort at all, yet they are clothed in beauty beyond Solomon in all his glory. *"Now if God so clothes the grass of the field, which today is, and tomorrow is thrown into the oven, will He not much more clothe you, O you of little faith?"* (Matthew 6:30).

Listen to the Beatitudes again: I can be meek in my relationships because I have inherited the Earth (Matthew 5:5). I can be generous because I am constantly being filled (Matthew 5:6). I can lavishly extend mercy because I have obtained mercy (Matthew 5:7). I can be pure in the face of evil because I see God (Matthew 5:8). I can extend peace always because I am a son of the Peacemaker (Matthew 5:9). I can rejoice, even in persecution, because I am a Kingdom person, one merged with God (Matthew 5:10).

Circumstances
"Fairness is determined by my situation."

Jesus said, *"An eye for an eye and a tooth for a tooth"* (Matthew 5:38). Someone took my eye; for the rest of my life I will experience only half the sight I deserve. He has each of his eyes. This inequity is not fair. He should know my pain. The circumstance in which I am because of his sin is the same circumstance he should have to experience. My circumstance should be his circumstance; it is only fair. No doubt this is true! However, it is the viewpoint of a helpless person living out of his helplessness. He is focused on himself. "Look what he did to me! See how I have suffered. View the circumstances of my life because of him!" Fairness is determined by his circumstances.

The person who thinks another should suffer like them does not have a redemptive view. Jesus is the demonstration of a helpless person filled with the nature of God. What a helpless person cannot produce by his or her helplessness must merge with the Spirit of God and be radically changed. Jesus consistently demonstrated this in His life. Jesus fed 5,000 men besides the women and children (Matthew 14:13-21). Giving all that food to such a large crowd and receive nothing from it was unfair. Jesus will soon have to pay the temple tax (Matthew 17:24). Jesus was in such need that Peter went fishing and took a coin from the mouth of a fish to meet their obligation. Jesus should have taken an offering from that large crowd. They should have paid for their meal. In fact, this crowd was the one that soon demanded Jesus' death on a cross. He fed them and healed them of all their diseases. Their response was not fair!

Jesus' early death at age thirty-three was not fair. His life was cut short. He could have become a great author. His books on philosophy and theology could have become the core of many universities in the world. He never had a family; He did not have an opportunity to grow old. The hatred, vile plotting, and vicious anger was not fair. Jesus took your sin on Himself and experienced your penalty of hell. This suffering was not fair!

But Jesus revealed the heart of God when He suffered your penalty to be redemptive. You and I can remain in our circumstances and view them through self-centered eyes. We have pity-parties for ourselves, because we are not treated right. Others should have to suffer as well. But how far will you go to be redemptive? Will you give yourself away? Will you be filled with the nature of God and allow Him to flow redemptive resource into your circumstances?

Concerns
"Fairness is determined by my suffering."

My suffering quickly becomes the focus of my life. I have suffered the loss of my eye; I am missing a tooth. Do you know what I have suffered because of what someone did to me? My jaw swelled to twice its usual size when they knocked out my tooth. The roots of the tooth remained; it was painful to have them pulled. It quickly caused infection. I did not deserve this, and it is not fair! But is this a self-centered view of a helpless person? As I try to live out of my helpless resource, I find no capacity to extend mercy. I can only bemoan my suffering, because is not fair.

Can you imagine being filled with God's nature? The infilling of the Spirit of God provides the abundant supply of His heart. In the abundance of His supply could I ask, "Can I suffer for them?" This is redemption. Is it possible that the role of Jesus on the cross could be extended through me in some small manner? As He took on the sin of the world and suffered for all mankind, redemption was birthed. Every person received forgiveness; access to the resource of God's nature was extended. Can my circumstances bring this to light? Does this explain what Paul meant when he said, *"I now rejoice in my sufferings for you, and fill up in my flesh what is lacking in the afflictions of Christ, for the sake of His body, which is the church"* (Colossians 1:24). I am to extend the sufferings of Christ to my world by being redemptive amid of their evil.

Matthew 5:39

INSULTS

"But I tell you not to resist an evil person. But whoever slaps you on your right cheek, turn the other to him also" (Matthew 5:39).

"An eye for an eye and a tooth for a tooth" (Matthew 5:38) was proposed prior to the Law of Moses. The "Code of Hammurabi," existing in the eighteenth century before Christ, contained this proposal. The proposal was an advance toward fairness, meaning "evenhanded justice without respect of persons." However great the offender, he could not escape just punishment. However small the offense what was extracted from him could be no more than his offense merited. The law was an acceptable judicial code, taking punishment out of the realm of personal vengeance.

"But" was the reply of Jesus (Matthew 5:39). The Greek text begins with the word ***"I"*** (ego). Because this word is indicated in the verb of the statement, it does not need to be included except for emphasis. The focus is on the Spirit-filled Jesus. He speaks the mind of the Father. ***"But"*** (de) suggests a contrast between the "Code of Hammurabi" and the New Covenant. Fairness from the perspective of the judicial law is different from the heart of God! The redemptive heart of God proposes a redemptive approach!

Jesus tells us ***"do not resist."*** In a previous study, we discovered the Greek word "antistenai," translated "to resist." This word occurs 14 times in the New Testament and is always in the middle voice. Jesus describes an attitude, feeling, or emotional response. Jesus focused on the personal preference of the motive. We are not to resist *"an evil person"* (poneros). This Greek word is masculine not neuter. Jesus does not forbid the resisting of evil as such, evil in the abstract, nor "the evil one," meaning the devil (James 4:7). He proposed not resisting "an evil person" or "the person who wrongs you."

Jesus described four life situations to clarify exactly what God desires. He begins with "insults" (Matthew 5:39). The focus is not on physical injury but the violation of one's honor or pride. Jesus quickly moved into the area of "insecurity" (Matthew 5:40) with materialism and the comfort of living in relationship to others as the focus. "Inconvenience" (Matthew 5:41) is the next issue. How do the needs of others affect my schedule and comfort? Jesus ends the discussion with "inclusion" (Matthew 5:41). Who really does own your possessions?

Let's begin with "insults"! The contrast *"But"* appears again. *"But I tell you not to resist an evil person. But whoever slaps you on the right cheek, turn the other to him also"* (Matthew 5:39). The first *"but"* is a translation of "de"; the second *"but"* is a translation of "alla." One might refer to "alla" as an extended contrast. It is a contrast plus! The word is an emphatic antithesis after a full negation. Jesus stated what we are not to do; we are *"not to resist an evil person."* Jesus then says the opposite of resisting by telling us what we are to do! "Alla" is an adversative particle. This word is etymologically derived from "allos," a combination of a verb, "separate," and a conjunction, "but or rather." Therefore, it means "differently" and refers to whatever is "different, to contrasts, separations, and new beginnings."

If I am not to resist an evil person, how am I to respond? What is the extreme antithesis of resisting an evil person? Jesus boldly stated the first area, "insults"! *"But whoever slaps you on your right cheek, turn the other to him also"* (Matthew 5:39).

This refers to an injury of insult, not of violence. In Jesus' day the most insulting physical blow that one could give another was a slap with the back of the hand against the right cheek. Jesus used the Greek word "rhapizo." It means to hit with an open hand and is distinguished from "kolaphizo," meaning "to punch, hit with a clenched fist" (Matthew 26:67). Many Bible scholars seize on Matthew's use of *"right cheek."* A right-handed person using the dominant hand and facing the one being struck would have to deliver the blow with the back of the hand. If this is the scene, the insult is more important than the physical injury or hurt itself.

Each example Jesus gave is concerned with our response to an initiative first taken by another. In each situation Jesus highlighted the proper response of the Kingdom person. The realistic view is that we do live in a world of evil. The Kingdom person is going to consistently find themselves in unfair circumstances. We do not provoke or initiate such situations; it is simply who we are and where we dwell. Christianity does not focus on the removal of unfair treatment; it dictates the response to such.

The proper response is always to be redemptive! We are to save the day and rescue the situation. If someone slaps you on the cheek, he or she is challenging you. They are "picking a fight." Do not engage in such activity. Do not physically or verbally move into their level of self-centered assertion. Do not allow the self-centered assertion of another control how you respond. They slap you; must you in turn slap them? Embrace your helplessness; be filled with His resource and become an expression of His heart. De-escalate the situation with redeeming love. Be redemptive!

Who is the stronger? Is it the one who flares out in retaliation? Is it the one who has the moral and inner strength of the Spirit of God's resource who can forgive and redeem? Psychologists tell us that violence is born of weakness not strength. The strong man can love and suffer hurt; the weak man thinks only of himself and hurts others to protect self. He hurts others then runs away for his protection. Jesus highlighted this to His disciples in the Garden of Gethsemane. Jesus' superior strength was exhibited in that He could, **"now pray to My Father, and He will provide Me with more than twelve legions of angels"** (Matthew 26:53). He was not submitting to the insults of betrayal out of weakness but out of strength! The Greek word "rhapizo" is used by Matthew to describe the Sanhedrin's treatment of Jesus during the mock trial, **"Then they spat in His face and beat Him; and struck Him with the palms of their hands, saying 'Prophesy to us, Christ! Who is the one who struck You?'"** (Matthew 26:67-68). These examples took place at the close of Jesus' life and ministry. He instructed His disciples about this response at the beginning of His ministry, the Sermon on the Mount. The Sermon was an invitation for them to participate in what was happening in His heart. What Jesus so vividly portrayed in His trials and crucifixion were present and active throughout His life. This portrayal was His heart. We must apply this instruction to our hearts. This is not a new rule or an act for us to accomplish. Jesus calls us to respond with our hearts.

Heart's Response

Jesus consistently returns us to the issue of the heart. The Greek word is "kardia," appearing 157 times in the New Testament. It never refers to the physical organ of the heart. The core of a person, the source producing his life, is the focus of the term. Jesus focused on the heart in the Sermon on the Mount. The Jewish faith of Jesus' day focused on the physical. All oral traditions were based on physical accomplishments, and there was no concern for the heart. The New Covenant, the Kingdom person, is the opposite.

Let us return to the premise of the Sermon on the Mount. Jesus began by congratulating us on being *"poor in spirit"* (Matthew 5:3). We are helpless in the core of our being. We must allow this helplessness to embrace us as grief embraces us when we lose a loved one. We are to mourn (Matthew 5:4). If we live in our helplessness, the Spirit of Jesus merges with our helpless nature. In oneness with Him, we become the Kingdom of Heaven. Jesus becomes the source for our living! Our lives express the nature of His presence. This is not keeping a set of rules, and we do not achieve it by performance. We become an expression of God's nature as He dwells in our hearts. We are helpless; therefore, the Kingdom of Heaven can never be what we accomplish.

Now Jesus calls us to have His heart's response when our honor, dignity, or person is insulted. He does not call attention to the physical act of "turning the cheek." How you respond at the moment of insult is an expression of your heart. What is the attitude of the heart? If the heart refuses to embrace its helplessness, it becomes filled with self-centeredness. After insult, the heart gives immediate expression to self-protection. All the expressions of hurt, bitterness, retaliation, revenge, and anger escape in my physical actions. I say, "This is not fair. I have my rights; I am hurt." When someone attacks my honor, I want to attack in return. That attack is an expression of my heart. When we are reminded of this principle of "turn the other cheek", we reply, "How many times do I need to turn the other cheek?" In other words, does this principle have a limit? Surely enough is enough! But even the question is an expression of your heart. You declare that you have not understood the real issue. You have not embraced your helplessness and been filled with Him!

What if the heart is filled with Jesus? A person embraces their helplessness and merges with the nature of Christ. That person's heart response will be an expression of Jesus. The same attitude in which He lives is our attitude. Listen to the heart's response from a cross, ***"Father, forgive them, for they do not know what they do"*** (Luke 23:34). We might want to dismiss this example because it was Jesus. But do you know about the young man named Stephen. The crowds did not crucify him but stoned him. As he was dying, he knelt and cried with a loud voice, ***"Lord, do not charge them with this sin"*** (Acts 7:60). What was in the heart of Jesus was in the heart of Stephen! Jesus calls us to this heart response! Be very clear. The response is not a physical one as in a new rule we must develop. This is a heart's response. What is in your heart?

Heart's Rage

Let us understand the heart is always in a rage because that is the nature of the heart. The heart is in a constant stage of response, and this response is always in rage. In other words, the heart is never quiet, silent, or nonresponsive; it is always declaring its personal state. This declaration is expressed through the personality of the person. How you feel in your heart will be known; it cannot be silenced because it is a rage.

We can see this in each of Jesus' illustrations. Those of old limited the heart's rage by the boundary of ***"You shall not murder"*** (Matthew 5:21). Jesus did not question the rage but the source of the rage. Although a person controls the self-centered heart's rage by eliminating murder, that heart will rage in demeaning, belittling, and degrading (Matthew 5:22). If the source of the heart's rage changes from self to the Spirit of Jesus, what will be its expression? We will seek redemption and reconciliation. Although a person continues to have adversaries, his heart will not allow him to be an adversary (Matthew 5:23-26). Those of old considered their sexuality a simple body drive they could control. The rage of sexuality must not go beyond the boundary of ***"You shall not commit adultery"*** (Matthew 5:27).

Although that expression of the heart may be eliminated, the rage continues. If the heart is filled with self-centeredness, its rage will express itself in looking, walking, lusting, and all areas of life (Matthew 5:28). If the heart is filled with Christ's nature, the rage of the heart will give the sexuality of life a new expression.

The rage of the heart is also true in marriage (Matthew 5:31- 32). Those of old discussed the right to divorce; Jesus discussed the rage in the heart that causes (poieo) your marriage. The heart filled with self-centeredness causes anger, bickering, and divorce; the heart filled with Jesus causes peace, spiritual maturity, and love. The rage of the heart produces integrity or the lack of it (Matthew 5:33-37). A self-centered heart rages with cover-up, personal advantage, and deceit; a heart filled with Jesus rages with honesty and integrity. The heart is always raging.

The self-centered heart rages with revenge and personal retaliation (Matthew 5:38). A person must control the heart's rage with the boundary of, **"An eye for an eye and a tooth for a tooth."** This limits the expression of the rage to fairness. But if the heart is filled with the nature of Christ, how will it rage in response to insults? When our dignity is offended, Jesus not only suggests we do not avenge our honor by retaliation, but that we indulge the offender further. We freely offer our other cheek (Matthew 5:39). Perhaps when someone insults my honor, I disconnect and no longer associate with him. I no longer stay within the range of their abuse, their insulting heart's rage. But Jesus did not suggest running away; instead, he said to stay within the range of their insult. Why would He make this suggestion?

The heart will rage! Jesus did not propose that we be passive; this is impossible for the heart. Our heart must rage with His passion; we must be redemptive. How may we be redemptive if we disconnect from those who insult us? Are you open to the heart's rage of Jesus? As Isaiah predicted of Him, Christ gave

His back to those who struck Him and His cheeks to those who plucked out His beard (Isa. 50:6). Peter summed up our Lord's example,

"But when you do good and suffer, if you take it patiently, this is commendable before God. For to this you were called, because Christ also suffered for us, leaving us an example, that you should follow His steps:
'Who committed no sin,
Nor was deceit found in His mouth'
who, when He was reviled, did not revile in return; when He suffered, He did not threaten, but committed Himself to Him who judges righteously"
(1 Peter 2:21-23).

Frank Laubach, a great preacher in his day said, "It is true that people may deserve criticism but we are not trying to give them what they deserve - we are trying to get them saved from what they deserve. The criticism they deserve will only do them harm. Only prayer will do them good. So, here is a good rule; if we feel like condemning, pray." We must be redemptive with a raging heart filled with Jesus.

Heart's Rate

Amid conflict, the heart rate accelerates. But there is a normal heart rate. If you do an amazing amount of physical exercise, it will lower your normal heart rate. In our passage, Jesus does not refer to the unusual circumstances. In each of these illustrations, He highlighted the average, normal situations of His culture. The principle applies in our lives and culture as well. In discussing this with His disciples, Jesus said, **"Woe to the world because of offenses! For offenses must come, but woe to that man by whom the offense comes!"** (Matthew 18:7).

In other words, the circumstance of insult is going to happen; it is normal, not abnormal. You can expect it; please do not be surprised. Jesus gave the same emphasis in the Sermon on the Mount. In His opening statement (Beatitudes), He gave beautiful insight into the virtues of the human life. A person experiences the warmth of these virtues but is amazed as Jesus thunders to a climax with "persecution" (Matthew 5:10-12). He treats this subject as absolute meaning it is going to happen in your life. He said, ***"Blessed are you when they revile and persecute you, and say all kinds of evil against you falsely for My sake"*** (Matthew 5:11). He is not suggesting this might take place; He says, ***"when!"***

Jesus does not call us to high moments in our lives where we respond in a redemption way. This is the normal heart rate of the individual filled with Jesus. One can understand this reality in contrast with what is normal for the person filled with self. The heart filled with self-centeredness has a consistent heart rate of selfishness. Even when it seems he is being generous, he is doing so for selfish reasons, for this person to step beyond their selfishness is impossible. The Spirit filled person can respond only as Jesus responds. When we embrace our helplessness, Jesus merges with us, and we become a constant expression of His heart rate. This is the core of our existence. The question is, "for what does your heart beat?"

Matthew 5:40

INSECURITY

"If anyone wants to sue you and take away your tunic, let him have your cloak also" (Matthew 5:40).

In the crisis moments of life, it is impossible not to defend, protect, and guard what is ours. However, there is one exception to this truth! Redemption is our goal. If we are to react in a redemptive manner, we must step out of the boundaries of our self-centered nature and live in a new nature. When we are possessed by the carnal mind, self-centeredness, we will always have the need to defend. Self will always guard and protect its self-interest. Self will overlook the interest of others of self.

The premise of the Sermon on the Mount is a death to self-centeredness. Jesus said, **"Blessed are the poor in spirit, for theirs is the kingdom of heaven"** (Matthew 5:3). All truths of this sermon are based on this reality. We are helpless in the core of our lives. Any attempt to deny it expresses self-centeredness. All self-expression is a helpless person acting as if they are not helpless. They defend because they consistently deny they are helpless. Jesus proclaimed that we must embrace our helplessness until we live in the boundaries of our helpless reality. In this state is when the comfort of the Spirit comes to our lives. His resource merges with us. We become the new creature, the Kingdom of God!

We must always realize and verify that we are helpless.

Jesus does not deliver us from our helpless state because in the dying we live and is in the losing we win. The moment we step out of embracing our helplessness, we are filled with the self-centered need to protect. We must never slip back into, "I can handle it!" Cockiness and arrogance have no place in the helpless person. Our total resource is now Jesus! He is all in all! Only in this reality is the possibility that we, **"Do not resist an evil person"** (Matthew 5:39).

What does this mean? James uses the same word in his epistle. **"Therefore submit to God. Resist the devil and he will flee from you"** (James 4:7). The order of the steps in the statement becomes important. First, we submit to God. Second, we resist the devil. The act of submission is the embrace of our helplessness. If this submission does not happen, we embrace evil in its raw nature, self-centeredness. Merged with Jesus, we present a barricade of opposition to all self-centered evil. Therefore, we are encouraged to resist evil but not the person through which evil may come. What is our attitude toward the person who insults us? We must be redemptive! This attitude is impossible unless we "submit to God" and "embrace our helplessness."

In two ways it is impossible. First, in our self-centeredness we join the nature of evil that we should oppose. We become an additional avenue for evil with the person being used by evil to confront us. Second, we cannot look beyond the evil opposition and see the need of the person being used by evil. We must live in the nature of God to view the value of a person possessed with evil. How can we look beyond our suffering to cry, **"Father, forgive them, for they do not know what they do"** (Luke 23:34). This cry is from a person who sees others through the nature of God's heart. This way of seeing is the call of Jesus!

Practically, Jesus applied this truth to "insults." **"But whoever slaps you on your right cheek, turn the other to him also"** (Matthew 5:39). No one dwelling in a self-centered state can fulfill this. We must dwell in the redemptive nature of God.

Part Five: Fulfillment of the Kingdom - The Application: Malice

Living in the boundaries of our helplessness, we can see the helplessness of the person who insults us. Does our heart not break for his painful entrapment of evil over which he has no victory? He is being used as an instrument of expression for the demonic nature. How can we be redemptive?

Jesus' second application is "insecurity." According to Jesus, security is focused on materialism. The statement of Christ is plain, **"If anyone wants to sue you and take away your tunic, let him have your cloak also"** (Matthew 5:40). I tried my best to adjust the words in this passage. I searched through all the commentaries to find acceptable interpretations. But I am afraid that it is even worse than you might expect. Jesus does not describe how to respond when the act is complete. Once a person has taken your tunic, how should you respond? The imperative of this passage focuses on the response before the act. He described a person who **"wants."** The Greek word "thelo" expresses active volition and purpose. This person is someone who has already decided and plans to sue you.

The person who plans the forceful act of suing you is not begging or requesting but has planned to take your possessions by force. The Greek word "lambano," translated **"take away,"** generally includes the action of force. Jesus described a person planning to take from you the security of your materialism. What makes this more pointed is what they plot to remove from you. They do not plot to take the patio furniture in the backyard, which you could live without. The plan is not even to take the living-room furniture without which you could survive. Their plot is to take your **"tunic"** (chiton), your undergarment. This undergarment or tunic is made from a simple sack-like garment. It took various altered forms and styles but was either worn against the bare skin or over a linen shirt. The tunic was made of linen or wool, reached to the ankles or knees, had long or half-sleeves, and was worn by rich and poor. Jesus described someone determined to take the basic physical possessions from you.

Jesus' statements in the Sermon on the Mount are severe. He forces the extreme in every illustration. Murder becomes the issue of anger (Matthew 5:21-22). We might adjust to this somehow, but Jesus speaks of demeaning and belittling people (Matthew 5:22). Then He demands that I should never be an adversary. Although I do everything not to have adversaries, I must never become one (Matthew 5:23-26). This demand is so extreme! Jesus continued the same approach regarding sexuality. The issue is not about just looking at women. The issue is what is in my heart that determines the expression of my sexuality. Jesus' focus shapes my thinking, determines my identity, and forms my viewpoint of the opposite sex (Matthew 5:27-30). I thought Jesus would highlight the proper procedure for securing a divorce, but He wants to discuss what I am "causing" in my spouse (Matthew 5:31-32). He wants me to consider the reality that I contribute to the problems causing the divorce. I certainly believe in honesty, but realistically there are occasions when we need to make adjustments. Complete, honesty in all dealings would be severe (Matthew 5:33-37)! We would never be able to create an advantage for ourselves. Jesus presented a righteousness that exceeded the righteousness of the scribes and Pharisees (Matthew 5:20). The severity of Jesus is apparent; it is an impossible standard unless there is a complete nature change from self-sourcing to Christ-sourcing.

Again, we see Jesus' severity. How are we going to respond to the evil person? Showing redemptive love to the person who insults you is extreme. When someone wants to rip away your material security. He is not taking just superficial things but also the clothing next to your skin. This cannot be judged as fair. What if this is not the issue Jesus addresses? What if He is doing in this illustration what He did in all the others? We want Him to tell us what the rule is or what our limited action is. He wants to reveal the heart of our being!

Part Five: Fulfillment of the Kingdom - The Application: Malice

Foundation for Security

Jesus again strikes a blow at the foundation of our living. He takes the spiritual sword of His Word and cuts us wide open. He reveals the heart! This revelation does not produce an action issue. He does not establish a new rule. The purpose is not to correct old responses and establish new ones. He does not counsel us or offer techniques to alter our patterns. This revelation is not an encouragement "to work on it." He exposes the filth of our self-centered hearts.

The Sermon on the Mount refers directly to the physical, materialistic world. Jesus begins with the third Beatitude (Matthew 5:5). The meek inherit the earth! In previous studies we discovered the *"earth"* reflects our physical lives. Jesus proposed that those who embrace their helplessness (Matthew 5:3) are filled with the resource of God's Spirit (Matthew 5:4). These are people who discover the full expression and purpose of the physical life. Their physical lives become tasteful (Matthew 5:13). The goodness of their spiritual lives is expressed in the goodness of their physical lives!

Jesus offered the premise that our heavenly Father *"knows the things you have need of before you ask Him"* (Matthew 6:8). Because of this reality, we should pray, ***"Give us this day our daily bread"*** (Matthew 6:11). In full confidence all we need in the physical flows from our merger with Him. Because of this reality, a strong instructional imperative is offered, ***"Do not lay up for yourselves treasures on earth, where moth and rust destroy and where thieves break in and steal; but lay up for yourselves treasures in heaven, where neither moth nor rust destroys and where thieves do not break in and steal"*** (Matthew 6:19-20). These verses are not an indictment against material things. Jesus did not indicate that materialism was wrong because the physical aspect of something was evil. Rather, ***"For where your*** *treasure is, there your heart will be also"* (Matthew 6:21). Jesus quickly gives the rationale behind this thought. *"No one can serve two masters; for either he will hate the one and love the other, or else he will be loyal to the one and despise the other. You cannot serve God and mammon"* (Matthew 6:24). These thoughts became the reason Jesus urged, *"Therefore I say to you, do not worry"* (Matthew 6:25). This admonition is focused on food and clothing (Matthew 6:25-32). Those who merge with Jesus simply *"seek the kingdom of God and His righteousness"* (Matthew 6:33).

The preceding is the context in which we find our passage, *"If anyone wants to sue you and take away your tunic, let him have your cloak also"* (Matthew 5:40). Jesus' concern is for the heart of the person. He cares about the evil person who wants to take materialism from us, and He cares about us from whom the materialism will be removed. He cares about the heart of everyone!

Heart Issue
"Love"

In all the Scriptures we just read, and the illustrations of Jesus about exceeding righteousness, the issue is the heart's love. The Gospel according to Jesus is never about materialism or physical things being evil. God created the physical and called it *"good"* (Genesis 1:4, 10, 12, 18, 21, 25, 31). The emphasis of Jesus is on the priority of materialism in the context of your life. Listen to the admonition of Paul to Timothy. *"Command those who are rich in this present age not to be haughty, nor to trust in uncertain riches but in the living God, who gives us richly all things to enjoy"* (1 Timothy 6:17). The Scriptures never indicate that materialism is wrong, or riches are sinful. The focus is on the love of your heart!

Jesus proposed two masters, and it is impossible to love them both. *"For either he will hate the one and love the other, or else he will be loyal to the one and despise the other"* (Matthew 6:24). The heart's love is always the emphasis. This was the answer to the lawyer's question, *"Teacher, which is the great commandment in the law?"* (Matthew 22:36)? Jesus' answer is equally amazing, *"You shall love the Lord your God with all your heart, with all your soul, and with all your mind"* (Matthew 22:37). This was a quotation from the Old Testament (Deuteronomy 6:5). Every Jew listening to Jesus' answer had memorized this verse. Although this was the first and great commandment the second is like it, *"You shall love your neighbor as yourself"* (Matthew 22:39).

Loving your neighbor is the core of our passage. *"But I tell you not to resist an evil person"* (Matthew 5:39). This must be evident in our relationship with materialism. We must love with the heart of Jesus the person who threatens our materialism. When it comes to a choice between embracing materialism and the evil person, we must be driven by the love of the Kingdom merger. We are one with His nature. His love is now our love. We are an extension of God's redemptive heart!

Heart Issue
"Lordship"

The lordship of the heart is the issue in all these Scriptures and in all the illustrations about exceeding righteousness. The interaction and relationship between the physical world and the spiritual world are consistently recognized in the Scriptures. Paul said, *"For the flesh lusts against the Spirit, and the Spirit against the flesh; and these are contrary to one another, so that you do not do the things that you wish"* (Galatians 5:17). The Greek word "sarx," translated *"flesh,"* refers to the physical. However, it is the physical under the lordship of the evil, self-centered nature. The issue is not the physical, which is good; the issue is lordship.

None of the illustrations found in the Sermon on the Mount indicate that materialism is evil. Evil is determined by the allegiance of the heart. The idea, **"No one can serve two masters,"** highlights the issue of lordship. **"You cannot serve God and mammon** (materialism)**"** (Matthew 6:24). Jesus interweaves this into the premise of the Sermon on the Mount. God created us "helpless." We will depend on someone or something. If Jesus is not Lord of our lives, something else will take His place. The natural that the things of the physical, which we can see and feel, naturally become the controlling issue of our lives.

Our helplessness is the core of our passage. **"But I tell you not to resist an evil person"** (Matthew 5:39). How should I respond to someone who threatens my materialism? Should I be more concerned about my materialism than about the person? This question is not really about materialism or even the person; it is about Jesus. Will I feel as He feels? Will I care for what He cares? Will His nature reign supreme in my life and dictate my response to everyone around me? Will He be Lord?

Heart Issue
"Living"

The living experience of the heart is the issue in all these Scriptures. The practical life expression of the heart is the issue in all the illustrations about exceeding righteousness. What controls the heart of a person controls the expression of their physical life. Jesus highlighted this in the illustration of our sexuality (Matthew 5:27-30). What dominates my heart will determine my viewpoint. My heart determines what I like or dislike.

The heart is the core of our passage. **"But I tell you not to resist an evil person"** (Matthew 5:39). Jesus is so practical in

Part Five: Fulfillment of the Kingdom - The Application: Malice

His application of this truth. He applies it to the area of "insults" and now to the area of "insecurity." My security or insecurity is determined by what dominates my heart. If self-centeredness dominates the heart, materialism will be of greater value than the person who threatens our possessions. We can advocate the value of human life, while we demean and belittle others by valuing materialism more than them. We devalue ourselves by valuing physical pleasure more than our eternal souls. We sell ourselves in the market of the physical for such a cheap price. We do the same thing to others unless we are Kingdom people. We need call to be filled with His nature, have His perspective, and be merged with His nature!

Matthew 5:40

FREEDOM FROM INSECURITY

"If anyone wants to sue you and take away your tunic, let him have your cloak also" (Matthew 5:40).

As Jesus gave a spiritual discourse on the Kingdom of Heaven, He spoke about the physical. This discourse was a consistent reality throughout His ministry. **"An eye for an eye and a tooth for a tooth"** (Matthew 5:39) was the old standard for justice from the "Code of Hammurabi," which was in the eighteenth century, before Christ. This code was before Moses and the Ten Commandments, which God gave to Israel. This standard ushered in a new level of physical justice in retribution.

Jesus brings us into the Kingdom of Heaven with a new spiritual standard. He said, **"But I tell you not to resist an evil person"** (Matthew 5:39). This was not a new rule or code; instead was an expression of a new attitude in the spiritual realm of our lives and focuses on a person spiritually possessed by evil! The obvious intent of Jesus was that we resist evil in our lives. But this truth is a focus on the person possessed with evil. This physical emphasis is so interesting! As Jesus applied this truth in each illustration, He focused on the physical aspect.

Concerning insults, the focus is physical, **"But whoever slaps you on your right cheek, turn the other to him also"** (Matthew 5:39). This is about insults and the focus is on the physical. Jesus again makes a connection between the spiritual

Part Five: Fulfillment of the Kingdom - The Application: Malice

and the physical. The evil person expresses his spiritual attitude by slapping with the back of his hand. He does not intend to physically hurt you but desires to spiritually insult you. If you respond with a physical strike in return, your action will escalate the spiritual condition inside the evil person. We never redeem when we participate in the physical expression of their evil.

Jesus' second illustration equally expresses the physical, ***"If anyone wants to sue you and take away your tunic, let him have your cloak also"*** (Matthew 5:40). Jesus described how we are to respond to someone who wants to sue us. They do not intend to forcibly remove insignificant things from us, but they want to take the clothes off our backs. The undergarments (chiton) or tunic represents the basic physical possessions, our security. This is a difficult truth to apply to our lives. Jesus calls us to reexamine our security.

Although Jesus presented this truth in sermon form, the principle was expressed in living reality. The Rich Young Ruler came to Jesus requesting guidance. ***"Good Teacher, what good thing shall I do that I may have eternal life,"*** he asked (Matthew 19:16). Because his request focused on "performance," Jesus suggested the Ten Commandments. The young man boldly said that he kept them all but still felt a need. The answer was simple. The young man's security was his riches. If the security for eternal life were to be his, he would have to give up his materialism, his security. The young man did not respond positively to this truth (Matthew 19:22). Jesus was profoundly affected by this rejection. He took the initiative to share with His disciples, ***"Assuredly, I say to you that it is hard for a rich man to enter the kingdom of heaven. And again I say to you, it is easier for a camel to go through the eye of a needle than for a rich man to enter the kingdom of God"*** (Matthew 19:23-24).

What a statement! Notice Jesus states the same thing twice. Each statement ends with a reference to the Kingdom. The Kingdom is a relationship involving a merger between my nature (helplessness) and His nature (Holy Spirit). He must be my only security. Material possessions are not a blessing from God; they are an obstacle or hindrance to the Kingdom merger. Material or physical things are not evil in themselves. Physical things become evil when they occupy the priority position in our lives. When the claims of Kingdom relationship confront a person, their security based on materialism cannot adjust. The illustration of a camel, the largest animal in Jewish culture, going through the eye of a darning needle is absolutely impossible. The disciples' response verifies this, **"Who then can be saved"** (Matthew 19:25)? Jesus responded, **"With men this impossible, but with God all things are possible"** (Matthew 19:27). The Spirit of God can birth this transformation in the heart of a person!

In our passage, Jesus proposed the circumstance where a person wants to forcibly remove the basic material possessions from the Kingdom person's life. How should the Kingdom person respond?

Foundation of Security

Let us begin with the truth from our previous study. Materialism, the physical, is not the basis of our security. We are not shaken or disturbed when the threat comes to remove material things from our lives. Material things do not hold us secure, rather we hold them. We do not measure God's blessings by the materialism we have. This assessment is true in every realm of the physical! Wealth or prosperity is not the measure of our relationship with God. If so, then God did not bless Jesus, a homeless man. The call of the Sermon on the Mount is **"do not worry"** (Matthew 6:25)! The focus of this statement is materialism being the security for your life. Jesus focused on the essentials of life – what we eat, drink, and wear. The Gentiles sought these things, but not the Kingdom people. **"But seek first** *the kingdom of God and His righteousness, and all these things shall be added to you"* (Matthew 6:33).

Just as the foundation of our security is not in physical possessions, it is not in physical activities either. Jesus highlighted the three fundamentals of all religions. "Charitable deeds" are a valuable response to God's heart. But if material possessions secure your spiritual position, they are an expression of pride; their value is nullified (Matthew 6:1). Isn't prayer important? Communication is the pulse beat of the merger of who I am with who He is. But when my spiritual security is based on the activity of "prayer," any value is nullified (Matthew 6:5). The setting aside from typical practices of life for my relationship with Jesus is of value. Yet when I "fast" to be secure in Him, I nullify my reward (Matthew 6:16). We often base our spiritual assurance on the activities of ministry instead of His presence. I have encountered numerous elderly people who could no longer physically minister in the church as they had in their youth. A sense of guilt and emptiness plagued their spiritual lives, often causing them to doubt their salvation. Their spiritual security was based on their ministry activities instead of Jesus!

Freedom of Security

Listen again to our passage, *"If anyone wants to sue you and take away your tunic, let him have your cloak also"* (Matthew 5:40). This is a person who *"wants to sue you."* The Greek word "thelo," translated *"wants,"* is a participle expressing a desire or wish. The Greek word "krino," translated *"to sue,"* is an infinitive expressing the act of taking legal action against someone in a court of law. The Greek word "lambano," translated *"take away,"* is also an infinitive expressing purpose. In other words, the purpose of his desire and wish is to take you to court and to remove from you by force the most fundamental things of your physical existence. Does this not produce fear in your life? Questions immediately arise, how will I live? What will I wear? What will I eat? My inner soul is immediately gripped by fear!

But listen to the instructions of Jesus! *"Let him have your cloak also"* (Matthew 5:40). The Greek word "aphiemi," translated *"let have,"* is a significant word and the main verb in the sentence, in the imperative mood, making it a command! This verb is not a suggestion from Jesus. He does not paint an ideal picture for our achievement. This is the required standard of the Kingdom person! The statement is even stronger when we realize the emphasis of the Greek word "aphiemi," which gives the sense of releasing, letting go, or repelling. But most often it is used with the sense of force. He commands that we take the most significant physical possessions of our lives and push them on the person who wants to take them from us. We are to insist that he not only receive our undergarments but also the coat on our back. We are not to hold onto, release with great reluctance, or begrudge the giving of our materialism.

This verse is so radical that I searched the passage carefully to find another interpretation. My selfish heart cried that this could not possibly be the meaning. Yet when I search the Scriptures, it appears to be the fiber of commitment to Jesus. The best example of this is in the "faith chapter" of the Book of Hebrews (Hebrews 11). Abraham is one of the great heroes of faith. Abraham *"went out, not knowing where he was going. By faith he dwelt in the land of promise as in a foreign country, dwelling in tents with Isaac and Jacob, the heirs with him of the same promise"* (Hebrews 11:8-9). Listen to the testimony concerning Moses, *"By faith Moses, when he became of age, refused to be called the son of Pharaoh's daughter, choosing rather to suffer affliction with the people of God than to enjoy the passing pleasures of sin, esteeming the reproach of Christ greater riches than the treasures in Egypt"* (Hebrews 11:24-26). The close of this chapter consists of a general report of how many others pushed aside physical possessions and comfort for Christ. *"Still others had trial of mocking and scourgings, yes, and of chains and imprisonment. They were stoned, they were sawn in two, were tempted, were slain with the sword. They wandered about in sheepskins and goatskins, being destitute, afflicted, tormented - of whom the world was not worthy. They wandered in deserts and mountains, in dens and caves of the earth"* (Hebrews 11:36-38).

The Scriptures present a picture of men and women who are freed from the bondage of materialism and physical comfort. They pushed from themselves physical advantages for redemption. It appears not to be a disciplined action but a love action. They were so in love with Jesus that materialism had no hold on them. This is the picture given of the early church. *"Now all who believed were together, and had all things in common, and sold their possessions and goods, and divided them among all, as anyone had need"* (Acts 2:44-45). Even after the Sanhedrin threatened their lives, it is reported, *"Now the multitude of those who believed were of one heart and one soul; neither did anyone say that any of the things he possessed was his own, but they had all things in common"* (Acts 4:32). This sounds so radical, *"Nor was there anyone among them who lacked; for all who were possessors of lands or houses sold them, and brought the proceeds of the things that were sold, and laid them at the apostles' feet; and they distributed to each as anyone had need"* (Acts 4:34-35).

The severity of this persuasion is illustrated in the death of Ananias and Sapphira. What a story! They were husband and wife in the early church who *"sold a possession"* (Acts 5:1). They held back part of the proceeds for themselves. They presented the rest to the apostles as if they had given it all. As the apostles confronted each individually, they died. According to Peter's confrontation, the issue was not the amount of the materialism but the lying to the Holy Spirit (Acts 5:3-4). Although the physical is not evil, materialism as the basis for your security will create such deception and evil in the heart that it will produce death in the physical life.

A clear understanding of the Sermon on the Mount's premise becomes essential in this discussion. I must embrace and live in my helplessness. In this helpless state the resource of God's nature can fill me, bring me to a new level of living, and we become the Kingdom of Heaven. Jesus illustrated the change from self-centered sourcing to Christ-centered sourcing. Self-centeredness always focuses on physical comfort, and security is found in accumulation of materialism. A helpless person acting as if they are not helpless will automatically cover their helplessness with the power of materialism. When Jesus becomes the total resource for living, we are freed from such dominance. Materialism no longer dictates our actions. The person is free to be redemptive despite the physical cost! When materialism is already released, the one wanting to sue you is not a threat; you have already given it away!

Because you already released materialism, it has no hold on you. Materialism is no longer the source of your security, because in your poverty (Matthew 5:3) you live in the resource of Jesus' sovereignty. You are free to lavishly, abundantly, and aggressively risk everything physical in your life as He directs you. Your security in Him gives you freedom.

Freedom of Security
"Redemption"

In view of this freedom, the focus becomes redemption! With self-centeredness as the source of life, the focus is on protecting, guarding, and controlling. Now we are free from such a focus. We are free to be redemptive. In our passage, the overarching premise is redemption. Concerning insults, be redemptive. Concerning insecurity, be redemptive. Jesus did not give a new set of rules to obey. He exposed a human life that is now merged with the heart of God. This life is always redemptive.

Redemption is the core mission statement in the life of Christ. Did He come for any other reason? Before He was born, the angel announced, *"And she will bring forth a Son, and you shall call His name Jesus, for He will save His people from their sins"* (Matthew 1:21). During His conversation with Zacchaeus, Jesus said, *"for the Son of Man has come to seek and to save that which was lost"* (Luke 19:10). This means that the central issue in our passage is not about how to handle insults or someone wanting to sue. The main idea is how can I be redemptive. The new creature, the Kingdom person, is captured by one driving desire, to be redemptive. The Kingdom person will quickly sacrifice materialism and physical comfort for redemption. Physical things have no hold on this new creature proposed by Jesus!

Freedom of Security
"Redeemer"

If God's heart is redemption, He must express this by some means. He chose to sacrifice everything comfortable to extend redemption to His created world. Although Jesus was equal to God, He *"made Himself of no reputation, taking the form of a bondservant, and coming in the likeness of men. And being found in appearance as a man, He humbled Himself and became obedient to the point of death, even the death of the cross"* (Philippians 2:7-8). The redemptive heart of God became flesh (John 1:14); Jesus became the instrument of redemption, demanding He sacrifice everything physical in His life. It determined His birth, life, and death. It determined economy, friendships, and His physical comfort. He released it all; His security was in His Father. He became a physical manifestation of the redemptive heart of God.

His message now calls us to the same. You and I are to be the instruments of redemption. Self-centeredness as our security will not allow us to set aside our pride to receive insults for the sake of redemption. Self-centeredness as our security will not allow us to set aside our materialism and physical comfort to be an instrument of redemption. We must release materialism and physical comfort if we are to be instruments of redemption.

Freedom of Security
"Reconciliation"

The premise of the Sermon on the Mount is the merger between who I am (helpless) and who God is (holy nature). This merger provides a resource that produces a righteousness exceeding the righteousness of the scribes and Pharisees (Matthew 5:20). Jesus gives six illustrations of the new life of such righteousness. At the heart of each illustration is the redemptive principle. However, He also illustrates the heart or purpose of this redemption. The purpose is not to produce museum pieces or statistics of accomplishment. The heart of God is not interested in how many; He is concerned about the reconciliation of each person to Himself. He wants the merger to happen in every life.

Although the old were concerned about "murder," the new are not concerned about "anger" in the same manner as they should be (Matthew 5:21, 22). The Concern is about reconciliation. The result of not being angry is an attitude of reconciliation. If I bring a gift to the altar and have someone with whom I am not reconciled, I must go to that person and seek oneness. If someone drags me into court, I must seek reconciliation on my way (Matthew 5:23-26). The two

Part Five: Fulfillment of the Kingdom - The Application: Malice

illustrations on sexuality are about relationship with the opposite sex, and your heart will determine how you view them. What if you and I view the opposite sex with eyes of redemption? When separation occurs in marriage, I must consider what I have "caused" in my spouse (Matthew 5:27-32). My goal becomes redemptive and ultimate reconciliation. Even in the taking of an oath, the issue is relationship (Matthew 5:33-37). The issue is not simply deception involving God; the deception affects others. If I am to be redemptive toward others, integrity really matters.

Jesus fully expressed this in our illustration (Matthew 5:38-42). In the old standard of *"an eye for an eye and a tooth for a tooth,"* there was no redemption and therefore no reconciliation. When I merge with His nature, I resist evil through the method of redemption, and I am determined by the motive of reconciliation. Amid insults and receiving a backhanded slap on my cheek, I will be redemptive for the purpose of reconciliation. If someone wants to take the basic physical necessities from me, I will not only offer him what he wants but I will offer additional items as well, for the purpose of being redemptive and reconciled.

Being redemptive in my response is an impossible standard! It does not seem practical and is idealistic. In a perfect world, it might work. But if the world were perfect, we would not need to be redemptive and reconciliation would not be necessary. Only the person lost in the love of Jesus, captured by the sovereign control of God's heart, and full of His Spirit can attempt such a lifestyle. This lifestyle is the Kingdom person.

Matthew 5:40

FORGIVENESS IN SECURITY

"If anyone wants to sue you and take away your tunic, let him have your cloak also" (Matthew 5:40).

Forgiveness is amazing! Finding forgiveness between two human beings is a wonder, but to think of God's forgiveness is beyond comprehension! Forgiveness demonstrates the correlation between the physical and the spiritual. When you forgive your offender, that forgiveness alters your physical expression. Forgiveness changes your spirit toward that person. You cannot treat your offender with disdain once forgiveness has been granted. Thus, forgiveness is in attitude and physical action, the spiritual and the physical.

In our passage, forgiveness is the undercurrent of this truth. **"If anyone wants to sue you and take away your tunic, let him have your cloak also"** (Matthew 5:40). The Greek word "aphiemi," translated **"let have,"** displays this attitude of forgiveness. A forgiving attitude is required if we fulfill the command of this passage. "Aphiemi" is used in the sense of "to allow, to permit the presence of, or permit an activity without opposing or prohibiting it." When Jesus finished preaching, He **"sent the multitude away"** (Matthew 13:36). "Aphiemi" here is translated, "sent away." At the crucifixion, Jesus **"yielded up His Spirit"** (Matthew 27:50). "Aphiemi" is translated here as **"yielded up."** The primary meaning of the word is "to send forth or away, to let go from oneself."

Part Five: Fulfillment of the Kingdom - The Application: Malice

The idea of releasing is more often related to debt or possessions. In the Parable of the Unforgiving Servant, the servant was forgiven an insurmountable debt and would not forgive a small debt. Regarding his forgiveness Jesus said, *"Then the master of that servant was moved with compassion, released him, and forgave* (aphiemi) *him the debt"* (Matthew 18:27). This word is often used for the forgiveness of sins. In the Sermon on the Mount, Jesus used it in His teaching on prayer, *"And forgive* (aphiemi) *us our debts, as we forgive* (aphiemi) *our debtors"* (Matthew 6:12). Jesus told the Pharisees, *"Therefore I say to you, every sin and blasphemy will be forgiven* (aphiemi) *men, but the blasphemy against the Spirit will not be forgiven* (aphiemi) *men"* (Matthew 12:31).

The consistent use of "aphiemi" for forgiveness in the New Testament helps to shape the concept. The idea begins with "embracement." Forgiveness cannot be offered unless the person offended recognizes and acknowledges the sin of the offender but beware of the self-centered attitude of how wrong the offender was or how much they hurt you. In other words, I am not to embrace the consequence of their offense in my life; it is not self-centered condemnation or criticism. I am to acknowledge the result of the sin in their life. I embrace the plight, misery, damnation, and destruction they experience. Jesus did this for the Trinity God. Did He not become one of us to embrace sin with all its aspects? Without such an embrace, there is no forgiveness. Listen to Paul's explanation, *"For He made Him who knew no sin to be sin for us, that we might become the righteousness of God in Him"* (2 Corinthians 5:21). We are not expected to embrace the sins of others toward God because we have no power to do so, but what about those sins against us? How can we possibly forgive others if we dwell in self-centered hurt and self-pity?

When we embrace the sin in the offender, we can move from "embracement" to "elimination." To forgive sins is not to disregard them and do nothing about them. God did not choose to forget we did wrong! His love moved Him to eliminate sin in our lives as He paid the consequence of our sin. Again, listen to the apostle Paul, ***"And you being dead in your trespasses and the uncircumcision of your flesh, He has made alive together with Him having forgiven you all trespasses, having wiped out the handwriting of requirements that was against us, which was contrary to us. And He has taken it out of the way, having nailed it to the cross. Having disarmed principalities and powers, He made a public spectacle of them, triumphing over them in it"*** (Colossians 2:13-15). Jesus' crucifixion did not guarantee that all would experience forgiveness. Jesus' death and resurrection provided the "embracement" and the "elimination" of forgiveness for every person.

Jesus calls the Kingdom person to this heart's physical response! If I am to forgive the person who insults me or plots to take my necessities, I must embrace the consequences of his sin. I must not be their "caretaker" or allow them to abuse me physically, verbally, or emotionally. However, my forgiveness replaces their self-centered consequences with love. Although I am not capable of or expected to forgive another person's offense against God, can I do it for their offense against me?

This forgiveness is our only means to evangelize our world. Jesus proposed redemption! "Embracement" is the first step. In the style of the cross, I embrace the person who offended me, as I am deeply aware of the destruction in his or her life. I am not to focus on what is happening to me because of their sin, but I am moved by what is happening to them. This viewpoint enables me to act; my action is "elimination." In forgiveness, I do not forget what they did, but I embrace the consequences of their sin to eliminate it in their life. This approach is what Jesus did for me! He embraced the consequences for my sin in Himself to eliminate sin in my life. His redemptive act revealed the love of God and opened the door for me to know God's forgiveness. To forgive others does not mean to separate myself from them, but through my contact with them I allow them to know God who can free them from their sin. Thus, we should do everything in our power to see that the sins of others are removed from them through the grace and power of Jesus Christ, which we make known to them. We participate in the redemptive action of God! That is evangelism!

So, we might not miss the impact of Jesus' message, let us step back and view His message in its totality. We can see the strength of what He said in the context of the Scriptures.

Concept of Redemption

In the first words of the Sermon on the Mount, Jesus calls for a merger between God and man. Any contact with Him outside the merger is trite and does not redeem. I am to bring all that I am and all that I have to this merger; God will do the same. What resource have I to contribute? Jesus proposed, **"poor in spirit"** (Matthew 5:3). I have no resource! I am needy or lacking in some areas because I am helpless; I have nothing to bring to the merger. God created me this way; it was a result of His Divine plan in creation. I am created to be dependent not independent. In mourning (Matthew 5:4) or fully embracing my helplessness, He will merge with me; a new creature is created called "the Kingdom of Heaven." The rest of the Beatitudes flow from this merger. The human life is taken to a new level, righteousness exceeding **"the righteousness of the scribes and Pharisees"** (Matthew 5:20).

This merger is God's nature united with the helplessness of man. When the helplessness of man yields to the resource of God's nature, His focus becomes my dominant expression. If **"God is love"** (1 John 4:8, 16), and **"No one has seen God at any time"** (1 John 4:12), His love will be known through us because, ***"we abide in Him, and He in us, because He has given us of His Spirit"*** (1 John 4:13). Redemption will become my distinction just as it is His! The expression of the merged hearts is redemption. Any deviation from this purpose strays from God's heart. We dare not become "program centered," "career centered," "statistic centered," "success centered," or even "ministry centered." We must be redemption centered. Although every ministry will have programs, career involvement, records and statistics, desires to accomplish, and ministry activities, the moment these become central we are "self-centered."

Jesus highlights the value of this expression in the imagery of salt and light (Matthew 5:13-16). He chose salt and light because it expresses imagery not dependent on activity, and it always redeems. You cannot "do" salt nor can you "perform" light. In the context of the picture Jesus gives, these imageries are always redemptive. They give value to physical life and reveal the redemptive heart of God. The Scriptures are fulfilled in the expression of God's redemptive heart (Matthew 5:17). Everything the Trinity God wanted to express in the Old Testament is in the pure expression of His nature, redeeming love. Fulfillment of the Scriptures is not in keeping the activity (law) but in the expression of God's redeeming heart.

Murder in the physical realm is the same as anger in the spiritual realm (Matthew 5:21-26). Therefore, the redeeming heart cannot tolerate anger. The redeeming heart cannot have relationship with God and not be reconciled with his brother (Matthew 5:23-24). Although the redeeming heart may have adversaries, he can never be one (Matthew 5:25-26). The redeeming heart cannot allow his sexuality to exist for his own pleasure. His viewpoint influenced by his sexuality is always redemptive not self-consuming (Matthew 5:27-28). The focus of marriage is redemptive (Matthew 5:31-32). The primary concern of the redemptive heart is "what do I cause?" Deception is always self-centered (Matthew 5:33-37). Truth is redemptive; we are expressions of ***"'Yes' be 'Yes,' and your 'No,' 'No'"*** (Matthew 5:37).

This redemptive idea continues into our present illustration of "malice" (Matthew 5:38-42). If someone ***"slaps you on your right cheek,"*** the question of God's heart is, "How can I be redemptive?" ***"If anyone wants to sue you and take away your tunic,"*** the heart of God asks, "How can I be redemptive?" This is the driving concept in every situation.

Concern of Redemption

The old standard was, ***"An eye for an eye and a tooth for a tooth"*** (Matthew 5:38). This was a step toward fairness and limiting self-centered retribution. Self-centeredness will always exaggerate its expressions and desires unless kept in check. Limiting the expression of self-centeredness was the best approach of those of old. But Jesus suggested a death to self-centeredness and "living" in the nature of God. He struck a blow at the heart's concern. What is it that you and I really want? Will I be concerned about others or myself? What about my feelings? Feelings are not the concern of the redemptive heart! But he slapped me; how do you think that makes me feel? Feelings are not the concern of a redemptive heart! What he is doing is not fair. He has no right to do that to me. This attitude is not the beat of the redemptive heart.

In one of his books, Watchman Nee wrote of a true event. A man had a rice field on the side of a mountain, and a neighbor had a rice field just below his. The man with the rice field above his neighbor's was a Christian and regularly attended the Wednesday evening prayer service. One evening he shared with the group a problem he was having with the neighbor just below him. Each morning the Christian pumped water into his rice field to help the rice grow. He built banks around the field to help contain the water. When he returned one afternoon, he found that his neighbor had poked holes in his banks, which allowed the water to leave his field and run into his neighbor's field below. This occurred repeatedly. It simply was not fair and must cease. What should the Christian do? As they prayed about it at the altar a fellow believer knelt beside him and asked, "What do you want, really want?" The answer was obvious. I want my neighbor to stop stealing the water from my field. "No," the fellow believer said, "What do you really want?" After prayerful consideration, the Christian replied, "I want my neighbor to know Jesus!" He went home and pumped water into his field and into his neighbor's field. He did this day after day until his neighbor, through this process, began to come to church and encountered Jesus!

"What do you want, really want?" This is the question of our passage. When a person wants to take from you the necessities of life, "What do you want, really want?" Are you more interested in your material possessions or his spiritual state? When he insults you with a backhanded slap, "What do you want, really want?" Are you more interested in your pride, appearance, and cultural honor or in his eternal destiny? Perhaps this reflection reveals your spiritual state and eternal destiny! If someone tries b to remove the necessities of life from me, I respond, "But this is all I have!" What does this indicate? My security is based on what I have. You might respond, "But I am not speaking about my spiritual life, I am referring to my physical life, all I have in the physical." To divide the physical from the spiritual is a tragedy. Jesus teaches us the bare necessities of life (tunic) are not all we have in the physical or in the spiritual. If they are all we have, we are of all men most miserable. We are not free to be redemptive unless our necessities of life are in Him!

Consequence of Redemption

This freedom is the consequence of our redemption. Have you ever felt trapped in the prison of reaction? What others do to you seemingly forces you to respond likewise. You despise what they do to you, yet you respond in the same awful way. It seems the same evil force working in the person who slaps your right cheek causes you to slap them in response. The same selfishness that causes them to sue you, demanding the necessities of your life is now working in you. You justify it in the name of fairness. Yet there is the haunting reality of imprisonment. You are not free but mastered by those around you. Your action is dictated by their action.

Circumstances control us in the same way. When we have a good day, we are happy and joyful. However, when we have a bad day, we respond similarly. We spend our lives responding to the master of our circumstances. The witness of the New Testament church was pronounced. They were not controlled by their circumstances; Jesus was Lord of their lives. Amid persecution they were free to rise to a new level of victory. They praised when surrounded by unfair treatment and misunderstanding. This freedom in the Spirit of Jesus ushered redemption into their surroundings repeatedly.

Jesus proposed this in our passage. When our fellowman insults us, we are free to be redemptive. Although you may control the outward response, it is impossible to control the inner response. Jesus did not refer to a controlled action, but a change in the inner nature. When insulted, we are free to forgive and embrace (Matthew 5:39). When the necessary elements of our physical lives are threatened, we are free to be generous (Matthew 5:40). When the actions of our fellowman produce anger, we are free to love (Matthew 5:22). We never lower ourselves to demeaning or belittling (Matthew 5:22). We will never become an adversary though we have adversaries (Matthew 5:25).

Jesus proposes the same regarding our sexuality (Matthew 5:27-30)! When our sexuality is mastered by self-centeredness, we express and view sexuality from self-satisfaction. If our sexuality was filled with the nature of Jesus, could it be used for redemption? We are not to be mastered by our sexuality; it should be a flow of redemption to our world! If the purpose of marriage were not self-gratification, what would be its purpose (Matthew 5:31-32)? The man should be the savior of his wife (Ephesians 5:23)! We are to redeem! The integrity of our word is not to be dominated by circumstantial pressure (Matthew 5:33-37). The need to protect, guard, and deceive does not control us. Our integrity is a flow of redemption through the control of Jesus' nature in us!

If this seems impossible, it is! We prove the premise of the Sermon on the Mount. We are helpless (Matthew 5:3). He must merge with us. It is only the nature of the Trinity God who can source in us such freedom. This will produce redemption in those around us. We never redeem through argument or debate. We find and give redemption through the cross style. Will we join Jesus in the redeeming process?

Matthew 5:41

INCONVENIENCE

"And whoever compels you to go one mile, go with him two"
(Matthew 5:41).

Jerusalem is a great city. We come here yearly for the Feast of the Passover. This trip is essential for my two boys. We spend a week in religious celebration as a family. We also do some family outings. I must confess; I always schedule a few business appointments on the side to help pay for the trip. By the way I am Simon. We are from Cyrene (Matthew 27:32).

It happened on Friday. I had an early business appointment outside Jerusalem. I promised the boys we would do something special when I returned. Everything went well with the appointment, but trouble began as I returned and entered Jerusalem. The city is always crowded during the Passover week, but something unusual was happening on this day. I should have entered the city from another entrance, but the main entrance was closer to where we were staying. By the time I realized what was happening, the crowd trapped me. I stood back in the shadows of the entrance to one of the shops to wait for the crowd to pass. I remember looking at my watch knowing I would now be late to meet the boys.

It took longer than expected. Finally, the core of the parade passed. There was a man they called "Jesus," who had been mercilessly beaten. His blood and sweat mixed as He strained to carry His cross. Stumbling, He fell right in front of my hiding place. One of the Roman soldiers began searching for someone to help Him finish the journey to His death. There was no need for me to volunteer. I am not from Jerusalem; I have nothing to do with the politics behind this crucifixion. I knew about Jesus but never heard Him preach. I guess He is a good man; crucifixion is a terrible way for His life to end.

Suddenly, the Roman guard spotted me and thrust his sword in my direction. "You, come here and carry this Man's cross," he ordered! I did not have time for this. My boys are waiting for me. I was dressed in a new suit; it would be ruined if I got involved in this blood covered cross. I tried to slip away, but the guard blocked my path. The Persian Royal Post started this practice. They authorized their couriers to press into service any man or animal to guarantee the delivery of the King's message (Esther 3:13). The Romans adopted their model. Here I am thrust into a situation of service that has nothing to do with me. What an inconvenience this is. But what can I do? The law requires it.

As I look back on that situation, now I must correct my statement. Carrying that cross was the best thing that ever happened to me. I admit at the time it did not seem so. You must understand, this law compelled me to go one mile and brought me face to face with Jesus. Without it, I would have gone on an outing with my boys as planned. I would have finished the celebration of the Passover week and made my way home. However, this encounter changed my family and me. You will find that Mark mentioned my family in his Gospel account. ***"Then they compelled a certain man, Simon a Cyrenian, the father of Alexander and Rufus, as he was coming out of the country and passing by, to bear His Cross"*** (Mark 15:21). This inconvenience brought my family and me into an encounter with Jesus. In fact, in the early church Paul wrote, ***"Greet Rufus, chosen in the Lord, and his mother and*** *mine"* (Romans 16:13). I will forever be grateful for a barbarian Roman guard who commandeered my service beyond my will and desire. Redemption happened in me when he compelled me to carry Jesus' cross!

This is difficult to apply to my life! I have schedules to keep and places that I must go. Everyone thinks they need something from me. Thousands of circumstances interrupt my schedule and interfere with my focus. I cannot be inconvenienced with these things. Beyond all these things, the evil world wants to hinder the ministry I think I must accomplish. But maybe this hindrance is the point of the matter; it was the ministry "I" think "I" need to do! Suppose an inconvenience is not an inconvenience at all but the platform for redemptive embrace.

Providence

Jesus boldly said, *"And whoever compels you to go one mile, go with him two"* (Matthew 5:41). Although we have no specific knowledge of how this command was practiced in Roman Palestine, we do know that in Persian times it was customary and legal for those in authority to commandeer people or their animals for temporary service without notice. This practice is well documented. Those who suffered from this practice found this requirement irksome and resented it. If you were hostile to the atmosphere of Roman rule you would find such encounters extremely distasteful.

Jesus addressed this internal aggravation, emotional disturbance, and upset, without making a statement about the right or wrong of the compelling, but He highlighted the redemptive response of the person being compelled. A negative response can be interpreted only as an expression of selfish, self-centeredness. When a person is focused on their schedule, agenda, or pleasures, any disturbance produces a negative response. Impatience is born out of this same frustration. When my expectations, desires, and dreams are not fully met, I react with impatience and negativity.

Jesus described the Kingdom person as the helpless person who recognizes God's full resource merging with his life. This merger directs the external interferences of typical life patterns. Such divine control brings purpose and meaning to the commandeering imposed on the present situation. Therefore, no longer is it an interruption or inconvenience but the fulfilling of God's plan, "providence"!

Providence is defined as the protective care of God over a person. It brings meaning to this biblical statement. *"And we know that all things work together for good to those who love God, to those who are the called according to His purpose"* (Romans 8:28). *"My brethren, count it all joy when you fall into various trials, knowing that the testing of your faith produces patience. But let patience have its perfect work, that you may be perfect and complete, lacking nothing"* (James 1:2-4). Is Jesus really adequate to resource my life? Can I trust Him in all things? Have I embraced my helplessness completely and relied on Him for all things? When I get upset over the interferences pressed on my life, does that indicate a lack of trust in Him?

The statement Jesus made in our passage is inclusive (Matthew 5:41). For the disciples to apply this to their circumstances was not difficult. Although we find ourselves some two thousand years later, we can grasp this principle and apply it to our lives. "Going the second mile" fits the rich and the poor. We cannot segment this statement to a specific set of circumstances. We cannot say this applies to church board meetings but not the interaction between a husband and wife. This fits everyone everywhere! There are no exceptions.

God interacted in the lives of every biblical character with this truth. Joseph knew the distress of unwanted circumstances in his betrothal to Mary. Yet, those unwanted circumstances

Part Five: Fulfillment of the Kingdom – The Application: Malice

placed him in the middle of God's redemptive plan for a world. The angel said to Mary, **"Blessed are you among women"** (Luke 1:42), but that involved great inconvenience and risk. Did she not have to flee with Joseph and her Child into Egypt in exile (Matthew 2:13-15)? Think of the families who experienced the death of baby boys from two and under (Matthew 2:16). When evil men commandeer your life and the lives of your sons, can you trust the providence of God? Is He really in charge? Is there a redemptive plan? John the Baptist experienced great ministry (Matthew 3:5) however, though he was the forerunner of the Messiah, he was imprisoned and beheaded as a part of God's plan. As we stand on this side and see the complete story, we know God fulfills His providence in every circumstance of life.

Is this why Jesus urges us to **"rejoice and be exceedingly glad"** amid persecution (Matthew 5:12)? What else could we, who are helpless yet filled with the resource of God, do? Is there anything that can come to our lives that He does not allow and use for His glory? No inconvenience is outside of His Divine plan! There are no exceptions. God orchestrates every encounter to accomplish His divine purpose of redemption! He is intimately involved in our lives. Jesus explained that not one sparrow falls to the ground aside from the will of the Father (Matthew 10:29). Even the hairs of your head are numbered (Matthew 10:30). **"Do not fear therefore; you are of more value than many sparrows"** (Matthew 10:31).

Will you embrace your helplessness? Will you allow Jesus to control your life, including all you do, and all done to you? Will you place everything in your life under His caring providence as He works His redemptive plan through your life? Instead of rebelling against the commandeering of your service, the interruption of your schedule, and the interference with your plans, will you allow His redemptive attitude to permeate those around you? Will you see the big picture of His caring providence?

Personal

Jesus said, *"And whoever compels you to go one mile, go with him two"* (Matthew 5:41). *"Whoever," "you,"* and *"him"* are specific. Each word is singular. He did not refer to governments or institutions but to people! His reference is to an interaction between you and another person. This interaction is you setting aside your schedule and convenience for the need of someone else. They may be in the wrong and impose on you something unfair. However, through Jesus' sourcing of your life, He brings you opportunities that give the expression of His heart to that person.

The singularity of this statement is important. I have often heard people say, "The church has hurt me!" On investigation of the situation, I find it was not the church as an institution that produced the hurt. It was a conflict between two people with one imposing something on the other that brought the conflict. Normally, the person with hurt feelings can describe in detail exactly what was imposed on them. They expressed how unfair and intruding it was. They interpreted the motive of hate and ill will that caused the other person to be unfair. Blaming the institution is easier than it is the person, which leaves us without an avenue of reconciliation. However, the real issue is how one person took advantage of the other and how they responded to it. That negative response made them adversaries.

In Jesus' first illustration in this series (Matthew 5:21-26), He highlighted reconciliation. Although those of old were content with eliminating the act of murder, that was not the Kingdom standard. The focus of the Kingdom is on the attitude generated by the person's inner nature. Jesus did not suggest we control our anger, but that we eliminate the feeling of anger. He desires to change the demeaning or belittling attitude of the person. We must see every person through the nature of

God's heart; that nature caused Him to offer up His Son's blood to redeem us all. We are that valuable to Him. Jesus proposed that reconciliation with God could happen only when we have reconciliation with others. The Kingdom person must be reconciled with all people in his or her heart. However, not every person with which you attempt to reconcile may be receptive. If a person will not reconcile with you, they become your adversary. However, you must reconcile with them in your spirit and never be their adversary.

Now in this illustration (Matthew 5:38-42), Jesus proposed the need of reconciliation always. In other words, if we have the right attitude initially, we will not need reconciliation in the end. Therefore, when someone takes advantage of the situation and compels you, you must realize the presence of God's moving hand. Is the situation merely an inconvenience or is God giving you an opportunity of ministry? Could the opportunity of ministry to this person be possible outside this circumstance? Will you allow God's nature to flow through you to the person compelling you? Will you be an avenue of redemption in Jesus' name? This truth applies to each example in this illustration. Amid insult (Matthew 5:39), insecurity (Matthew 5:40), inconvenience (Matthew 5:41), and inclusion (Matthew 5:42), will you look beyond the evil present and embrace the person for redemption?

Pointed

Jesus said, *"And whoever compels you to go one mile, go with him two"* (Matthew 5:41). The Greek word "angareuo" is translated *"compels to go"* and is in the indicative mood, a simple statement of fact. It means "requisition." The main verb of the sentence is *"go."* A translation of the Greek word "hypage," an imperative, a command! If a person demands from you a service for his benefit, Jesus gives a command that supersedes their demand. The Kingdom person has a compulsion from within that overrides all other demands or requests. The Kingdom person must be redemptive; the indwelling heart of God demands it! How can the Kingdom person be redemptive to the person who is taking advantage?

Kingdom people will find themselves in a unique situation. They will be connected to the person compelling them in a way never before possible. This relational connection could not be except for the compelling. The redemptive heart requires not only complying with the required mile but also extending the opportunity of ministry by going the second mile. In this second mile, the expression of the God's redemptive heart is expressed. Opportunity is afforded to extend redemptive relationship in a way that could not be done outside of this situation. Is this situation an inconvenience in the believer's life, or is it a Divine encounter between the Kingdom person and the compelling person?

This response is Divine and is the typical, normal, and spontaneous response of the heart of the Kingdom person, not those extra sensitive to spiritual issues. They are mature in the faith, not the person desiring extra rewards in heaven. The response is the typical, everyday one of the Kingdom person merged with the heart of God. This means it is not forced; one does not do so under pressure. The one merged with the heart of God is watching carefully for such opportunities. He is prepared for such occasions. These are opportunities of redemption, carefully planned by the prevenient grace of God. The one merged with God's heart gets to be a part of His redemptive plan for another's life! Nothing could be more thrilling! This participation is the crowning event of knowing Him in the power of His resurrected life and participating in the fellowship of His suffering, bringing us into conformity with His death, the expression of His heart (Philippians 3:10).

This participation only happens when the merger of my

Part Five: Fulfillment of the Kingdom – The Application: Malice

helplessness and His nature occurs, the premise of the Sermon on the Mount. The formation of the Kingdom of God may be seen and expressed properly only in the second mile. One may ask, "Do I have to go a third mile?" If you ask, you declare you know nothing about the merger with His heart! You have missed the Truth, Jesus!

Matthew 5:42

INCLUSION

"Give to him who asks you, and from him who wants to borrow from you do not turn away" (Matthew 5:42).

"Give to him who asks you" (Matthew 5:42). What do we do with this statement? These are the words that someone who wants something aggressively pushes on me. In each illustration given by Jesus, someone initiates the activity. In the first illustration, a person backhanded me on my right cheek, trying to pick a fight. This is the ***"evil person"*** Jesus tells us not to resist. In the second illustration, this evil person tries to take legal action to obtain everything I own, even the necessities of life. In the third illustration, this evil person wants to use me for their advantage. They interfere with my schedule and demand inconvenient actions from me. This final illustration may be worse than any of the previous three. This person demands I give them what they think they need.

They are not called an ***"evil person"*** because they do evil deeds. They are evil, and their deeds are a consequence of this condition. Evil is their self-focus. They are ***"poor in spirit"*** (Mathew 5:3), helpless! If they do not live in the awareness of their helplessness, they act as if they are not. They use all their energy to grab for themselves. They use every situation to their advantage. They reach into the lives of others to sustain their own existence. No wonder they constantly want something from me!

Part Five: Fulfillment of the Kingdom – The Application: Malice

But the One proposing this statement is not *"an evil person;"* it is Jesus, and He has no personal agenda. He is a helpless Man filled with the resource of His Father. He lacks nothing. His only motive is redemption. His focus is on how to be redemptive. Evidently, Jesus views everything that a person has as a means or avenue for redemptive influence. His expression of the Father's heart is driven by this redemption. Material things are a platform for redemptive action.

Herein lies the problem, PRIORITY. Material things take greater importance than people. The dictionary definition of materialism is "a tendency to consider material possessions and physical comfort more important than spiritual values." Let me be very clear, physical and material things are never considered evil. In our definition of materialism, possessions and physical comfort are not the issue. How you view them becomes the element of destruction. What priority does physical materialism have in your life?

Paul wrote to Timothy, *"For the love of money is a root of all kinds of evil, for which some have strayed from the faith in their greediness, and pierced themselves through with many sorrows"* (1 Timothy 6:10). Money is never the problem; the problem is money's priority in the heart. The physical is always a platform on which the spiritual condition of the person demonstrates itself. The physical does not dominate and control the spiritual; the spiritual expresses itself through the physical. When the helpless person refuses to embrace their helplessness and be filled with Jesus, they can easily substitute material things for the resource and security of life. Jesus proposed the perspective of the Father's heart. Material things are to be instruments for redemption. The physical is to be a display of the "never think about yourself" cross style of the Kingdom person. Jesus revealed this to the Pharisees who criticized Him for healing a man with a withered hand on the Sabbath day (Matthew 12:9-14). He presented the fallacy of their priority. They openly admitted they would rescue a sheep that had fallen in the pit on the Sabbath day. However, they would allow a man with a withered hand to continue in that condition because it was the Sabbath day. Jesus challenged their materialistic view, ***"Of how much more value then is a man than a sheep?"***

Herein lies the problem, POINTER. Material things, the physical, become the measure of success. The person who accumulates the most things is the most successful. The helpless person who attempts to live out of their helplessness naturally has this fallacy. They scramble to establish security in their lives. Because their security is not in their spiritual resource, it quickly becomes a physical resource. This helpless person focuses their life on materialism. Do not fall into the trap of assuming all wealthy people are self-centered. The problem with materialism is not how much you have but having your focus center on how much you can obtain. A person can live in financial poverty and still be dominated by materialism.

Luke beautifully described this truth (Luke 21:1-4). After a day of controversy and trick questions from the leaders of Israel, Jesus wanted to leave Jerusalem. The disciples were admiring the great buildings of the city as if their spiritual security resided in these temple structures. Jesus told them what would happen to these structures soon. Where would they find spiritual security when these material things were gone? As they moved out of the temple, Jesus suddenly stopped. He ushered His disciples into the shadows as if some spectacular event was about to occur. As they waited an older woman moved slowly into view. This widow went to the offering box and deposited two coins and departed. Jesus seemed amazed. The disciples must have reported how they viewed a Sadducee who gave an abundance compared with the small amount of the widow. Jesus just shook His head at their lack of understanding. The focus was not on the amount given but, on the amount, kept. The widow gave everything she possessed!

Part Five: Fulfillment of the Kingdom - The Application: Malice

This is the problem with the religious rules that govern materialism. The Old Testament rule of tithing focused on amount, giving the sense of ownership and self-centered pride. I earned the money; I decide how to spend the money; I determine whether to be generous. I have not been embraced by my helplessness. I have not realized that all my material possessions come from Him! How is this displayed in the Kingdom person? In the Sermon on the Mount Jesus exclaimed repeatedly, *"do not worry"* (Matthew 6:25, 28, 31). This command focused on the materialistic essentials of life. *"But seek first the kingdom of God and His righteousness, and all these things shall be added"* (Matthew 6:33). That is the cry of the Kingdom person.

Herein lies the problem, POWER. Materialism offers a false sense of control and security. We deem everything solid and dependable based on the physical provisions and circumstances. Materialism becomes a covering for the helplessness of the inner spirit. Our material possessions provide power over others, a sense of superiority to those who express their need, and it dominates our spiritual lives. Instead of our spiritual lives controlling our physical lives, we become controlled by possessions. We try to measure how much God loves us by materialism.

People often see God's blessings in the physical instead of the spiritual. The disciples seeing a man blind from birth asked Jesus, *"Rabbi, who sinned, this man or his parents, that he was born blind"* (John 9:2)? The disciples viewed the spiritual condition of this family by the physical circumstances of their lives. After the rejection of the Rich Young Ruler, Jesus said to His disciples, *"Assuredly, I say to you that it is hard for a rich man to enter the kingdom of heaven"* (Matthew 19:23). The Greek word "dyskolos" is translated *"it is hard for,"* referring to "great difficulty." In other words, material things are not a blessing from God; they are a handicap or obstacle to spiritual victory. Materialism is something we must overcome to be a Kingdom person. Materialism provides a false sense of security and power; it hides our helplessness.

With this background, we are ready to investigate our passage.

The Command

The overall statement of Jesus about materialism is not an imperative. *"But I tell you not to resist an evil person"* (Matthew 5:39). The Greek word "anthistemi" is translated *"to resist" and* is an infinitive verb focusing on purpose. Jesus' focus is redemption; redemption is His purpose! Each illustration magnifies a response to a person filled with evil intent. The key response word in each illustration is an imperative. *"Turn"* (imperative) the other cheek to the one who slaps on the right cheek (Matthew 5:39). *"Let him have"* (imperative) your cloak, if he sues you for your tunic (Matthew 5:40). *"Go"* (imperative) the second mile with the person who compels you to go the first mile (Matthew 5:41). In our passage, *"Give* (imperative) *to him who asks you"* (Matthew 5:42).

"Give" is a translation of the Greek word "didomi," used 413 times in the New Testament. "Didomi" refers to an activity, which normally has a direct object. This word is never just a disposition or attitude of a person, giving always extends a gift. In John's Gospel, Jesus is what He is by God's gift! *"For God so loved the world that He gave* (didomi) *His only begotten Son"* (John 3:16). Jesus considered the, *"works which the Father has given* (didomi) *Me to finish - the very works that I do"* as gifts of the Father's giving (John 5:36). The Father gave the disciples to Jesus. *"All that the Father gives* (didomi) *Me will come to Me"* (John 6:37). According to John the Baptist, *"The Father loves the Son, and has given* (didomi) *all things into His hands"* (John 3:35). *"All things"* are a gift from the Father! The death

of Jesus on the cross is described as a gift resulting from the act of giving (didomi). Jesus said, *"Just as the Son of Man did not come to be served, but to serve, and to give* (didomi) *His life a ransom for many"* (Matthew 20:28).

We should note that this word, "didomi," serves the same purpose in writings outside of the New Testament. "Didomi" is traditional for the death of Jewish martyrs and Greek soldiers. "So he gave (didomi) his life to save his people and to win for himself an everlasting name" (1 Maccabees 6:44). The fathers and the prophets gave (didomi) themselves (Thucydides II, 43, 2). Having established this "didomi" is an act of giving, which points to a gift, we should also note that the disposition of "love" is most often expressed by "didomi." In all the above references, the gift given was motivated by love, either stated or indicated. This motivation is important in our passage. Jesus did not give a list of new rules in the Sermon on the Mount. The premise of the Sermon on the Mount demands we embrace our helplessness until the nature of God merges with us. The nature of God could not tolerate a sinful world without responding in redemption. He could not have a fleeting concern about sin and move on to other pressing needs. The commanding force of His nature demanded the gift of redemption through Jesus! If the merger of His nature and mine is the New Covenant, will this activity of redemption not continue through me? If this loving force is not present in the act of *"Give,"* it does not qualify in the context of Jesus' statement.

The Condition

Jesus gives further content to the act of "giving" when He qualified the one asking. *"Give to him who asks you"* (Matthew 5:42). The Greek word "aiteo" is translated *"who asks,"* expressing the simple idea of a request. However, this word presents a consistent situation, the inferior asking of something from the superior. Herod, the King, was angry with the people of Tyre and Sidon. **"But they came to him with one accord, and having made Blastus the king's personal aide their friend, they asked** (aiteo) **for peace, because their country was supplied with food by the king's country"** (Acts 12:20). The Greek word used consistently for begging. **"And a certain man lame from his mother's womb was carried, whom they laid daily at the gate of the temple which is called Beautiful, to ask** (aiteo) **alms from this who entered the temple"** (Acts 3:2). Jesus uses "aiteo" to describe a son asking his father for bread to eat (Matthew 7:9). "Aiteo" is used often for a man asking something from God. In each case it is the inferior asking for something from a superior.

The inferior asking of the superior gives us the context of what Jesus' said. The superior one is not coming to ask a favor from us. We would be honored to serve him, and he would be in our debt. If we gave to him, it would be to our advantage. This is not our best friend making a request. We always help each other; we give back and forth to the advantage of each. This is **"an evil person."** In some sense he is my enemy who tries to take advantage of me. This is true in the other illustrations. He is someone who initiates a fight by slapping me on the right cheek. He sues me attempting to take life's necessities from me. He uses legal powers to take advantage of me and compel my help. Now in his inferior position, he wants me to bail him out of some predicament his foolishness created for him, but this is not my responsibility. I cannot help everyone; I have all I can do to maintain my life and needs (I could go on and on with these kinds of statements!)

The Conclusion

None of the above statements should determine my decision to give when I am asked. Jesus did not make up a new rule. He wants you to see the presence and direction of God's heart in the daily occurrences of life. We are merged with His nature. I isolate myself if when confronted by evil people I build walls between them and me. Jesus cry is, "Be redemptive!" He did say we should give everything we have away for the sake of giving it. Redemption means we reach into the life of the evil person and bring him or her into the heart of God. We will not do this by responding to them as they respond to us. They want to pick a fight; so, we fight back. We become like them. They sue us; so, we sue them. If we build walls between us, they will never see the heart of God. They compel us, and we do the minimum to get rid of them; this does not demonstrate for them the heart of God. They ask something of us, but we show no concern and express no desire to help them. How will they ever know the love of Christ?

Could the purpose of your materialism be the redemptive process? Was not the physical established to be the visibility of Him invisible? John clearly stated this in his first epistle. **"No one has seen God at any time. If we love one another, God abides in us, and His love has been perfected in us"** (1 John 4:12). The Greek word "teleioo" is translated **"has been perfected,"** expressing the sense of finished or accomplished. God is invisible, and He merges with us in the physical so that His heart and nature can be demonstrated through us to our physical world. The purpose of our physical existence is to give visible demonstration to the nature of God. This is exactly who Jesus was in the flesh (Colossians 1:15).

Could the purpose of the physical things I possess be for the demonstration of the loving nature of God? Would anything less than spreading God's loving nature be a squandering of the material resources God granted me? Do I need to view each physical confrontation as an opportunity to manifest His nature? Each situation is different, and my response needs personal shaping from the inner presence of God. Will I allow Him to direct me?

Matthew 5:42

OWNERSHIP

"Give to him who asks you, and from him who wants to borrow from you do not turn away" (Matthew 5:42).

Ownership is a binding proposition, speaking of responsibility and liability. In a lawsuit against property, the owner of the property is liable. The owner is the person responsible for maintenance, insurance, and property taxes. In the last illustration of our passage, Jesus' focus is on ownership. In His statement, **"Give to him who asks you,"** it is assumed you "have" and therefore can "give." In the second part of the statement, **"and from him who wants to borrow from you do not turn away,"** it is assumed you "own" and therefore can "lend." If I do not own the item you seek, I do not have the right to lend it to you. Ownership is assumed.

To the lame beggar at the Gate Beautiful in Jerusalem, Peter said, **"Silver and gold I do not have, but what I do have I give to you"** (Acts 3:6). At first, you might think Peter was not telling the truth. He had funds available to him, which could be disbursed to the lame beggar. In describing the early church, the Book of Acts declares, **"and sold their possessions and goods, and divided them among all, as anyone had need"** (Acts 2:45). But Peter made a distinction between having silver and gold and having the life of Jesus.

Peter makes the distinction by using two different Greek

words. ***"Silver and gold I do not have*** (huparcho), ***but what I do have*** (echo) ***I give to you."*** The first word relates to materialism and the second to the fullness of the Spirit of Jesus. A person does not have materialism in the same way he has Jesus. What is the difference between these two? The Greek word "huparcho," translated ***"have,"*** is a compound word that relates to materialism (***silver and gold***), and, "hupo" expresses the idea of coming from under. "Archo" is the idea of being first; thus, it promotes the idea of ruling. It carries with it the same thrust as "eimi," translated "I am." It highlights the idea of "to be, live, or exist." A person exists in the state of materialism. You do not have materialism; it has you. Materialism is not something you carry in your wallet or contain in your bank account. Materialism carries you in its wallet. The amount of materialism is not the deciding element. You may have much or little money; it is a state of control and domination. It "has" you!

The Greek word "echo," translated ***"have,"*** is connected to Jesus; it paints a different picture. It defines something "one has in, or about him, including the idea of to bear, carries in oneself, as in the womb." Matthew described the natural Father genealogy of Jesus as, ***"she was found with child of the Holy Spirit"*** (Matthew 1:18). The Greek word "echo," translated ***"have,"*** is at the heart of this description. Having silver and gold is similar to a veneer covering, but having Jesus is more like pregnancy. What is present in you is not covering you, but shapes, manifests, and participates in your life! Although it is not always pleasurable, it contributes to purpose, life, and privilege. Pregnancy is the picture, the "merger," expressed by Jesus as the premise of the Sermon on the Mount.

Materialism can become the spiritual state of our being, our dwelling place. I ask you to picture materialism as a house in which you live. A house exists to meet your need. You arrange your living room and design your kitchen according to your desires. You set the thermostat in your house at a certain

Part Five: Fulfillment of the Kingdom - The Application: Malice

temperature to keep you comfortable. The house is not evil, but it does perform a function. Materialism is this way. No one proposes the elimination of material things because they are necessary. However, let us broaden the picture. Let us give the house life and make it an organism. Instead of a house existing for your sake, it begins to exist for its own sake. You exist to serve and minister to the needs of the living house. It sucks the life from you for its own survival. The house grows more powerful as you become much weaker. All your actions are determined by and contribute to the house. You are worse than a slave because the house feeds off you.

The Greek word "echo," translated *"have,"* has a dominant role in Christian understanding and is used 700 times in the New Testament in a variety of ways. The word is thoroughly and distinctively Christian. The basic meaning of this word is "to possess or own," and it distinguishes Christianity as a "religion of having." A long list of Scriptural references is present to describe the various spiritual aspects you could have. In John's account of the Gospel, he stressed repeatedly that we have (echo) eternal life here and now. This truth elevates the richness of the Christian life from the realm of hope to the realm of present possession. We have God's love (John 5:42), peace (John 16:33), grace (John 1:17), light (John 8:12), and life (John 3:15).

However, the most startling is we actually have (echo) God! Jesus is the heart of this possession. Two verses in John's epistles are paramount. **"Whoever denies the Son does not have** (echo) **the Father either; he who acknowledges the Son has** (echo) **the Father also"** (1 John 2:23). **"Whoever transgresses and does not abide in the doctrine of Christ does not have** (echo) **God. He who abides in the doctrine of Christ has** (echo) **both the Father and the Son"** (2 John 9). We must see "having Jesus" as Him "having us." His possession of us is understandable. He is the Creator and the Redeemer. He has every right to claim us as His possession. However, the only reason we can claim Him as our possession is because He gives Himself to us! In this interaction between "Him having us" and "us having Him," redemptive ministry takes place.

You can argue that the only reason we "have Him" is because "He has us." Jesus can "have us" without "us having Him." In fact, this argument is a picture of the devil and his relationship with us. He can possess us, but he never gives himself to us; we never possess him. Love is the only motive for God sharing Himself with us. Think of our unique position among all His creation. You and I are the receivers of such love. The old song says, *"Now I belong to Jesus; Jesus belongs to me. Not for the years of time alone, but for eternity."*

We must consider our passage in this reality! **"Give to him who asks you, and from him who wants to borrow from you, do not turn away"** (Matthew 5:42). An evil person initiates an act on us. They want to borrow something that is ours. What they want is not theirs. They have no investment in the object but want free use of its value. This approach is not fair. In the judgment of *"an eye for an eye and a tooth for a tooth,"* it is not fair for someone to gain using something for which I have worked hard to own and is valuable to me. However, do material things have you? When a helpless person acquires an asset, that thing owns them; it gives them value (hupacho). When I have (echo) Jesus, He has me. There is no room for any other ownership. The material things at my disposal come from Him. They are His not mine! No one can borrow anything from me because I own nothing. This solves the problem! This would be true if the statement was simply a new rule. But Jesus did not present a new rule, but He presented a merger. My helplessness must merge with the resource of God's nature. This new Kingdom person is an expression of the redemptive heart of God. I then view this evil person with God's eyes. I look beyond his offensive evil and see the tragic bondage, which traps him. How can I be redemptive?

Jesus says this strongly in our passage! *"And from him who wants to borrow from you do not turn away"* (Matthew 5:42).

Do not DISMISS

Jesus begins with *"and from him."* The focus is on the evil person who wants to borrow from you. The Greek word "apo," translated *"from,"* is specific in meaning. It basically means "the going forth or proceeding of one object from another." "Apo" indicates the separation of a person or an object from another person or the separation of an object from another object with which it was formerly united. Jesus did not propose a rule that requires me to fill every request someone demands of me. He boldly says to use of their contact with my life as a platform of redemption. Do not dismiss them! The emphasis is not to give him everything he wants but to be involved in his life to help him get what he needs. What he asks for may not be what he needs. Augustine rightly noted, Jesus said, *"Give to him who asks,"* not "give everything to him that asks," (De Sermon Domine en Monte 67).

How easy it is to dismiss the person who constantly wants to use you for his personal benefit. The fear is that they will continue to take advantage. If any consideration is extended to them, they will increase their demands. However, if dismissal is the policy, how does the redemptive heart of God reach them? If material things have you and are your primary concern, there is no room for sharing the power of Christ. This is the wonderful impact of Peter's encounter with the lame beggar as we discussed above (Acts 3:1+). The lame man was focused on material gain; he saw Peter and John as the avenue to fulfill his physical need. However, he did not know his real need; it was covered with 40 years of materialistic domination. Peter and John did not dismiss him. They gave him no financial aid but became the redemptive avenue for Jesus to touch his life.

We must see this truth in light of the Sermon on the Mount's premise. Jesus calls us to embrace our helplessness. We are *"poor in spirit"* (Matthew 5:3). We are to *"mourn"* in our helplessness. The reality of no resource is to embrace us as grief embraces one who experiences the death of a loved one. We must never ignore this reality. This presents the possibility of being filled with the resource of Jesus' nature. If we are not filled with His resource, we must live out of our helplessness. This causes us to guard, protect, and defend all that is ours. Material things become the resource of our lives. What else have we? We cannot risk what we have for the sake of others. It is not fair to lend them my things!

Jesus proposed the new Kingdom thought. This can happen only through the merger of His nature and mine. As a Christian, people consistently bombard me to leverage God for what they do not have. They want answers for their problems, finances in their bank accounts, health for their bodies, freedom from their bondages, peace in their turmoil, and on and on the list goes. They seek only what He can do for or lend to them instead of Him. They are willing to compensate Him with a few dollars or observe a few ceremonies at church. Think of the millions of people who have used this approach to God. How does He handle these evil people? He does not always give them what they want, but He never dismisses them as if they are unimportant. He goes past their self-centered use of Him to bestow grace and more grace upon them. If God does this for an evil person, how will He respond when He merges with me? Jesus urges us not to dismiss this person for the sake of redemption!

Dictate DIRECTION

Jesus continues, *"do not turn away"* (apostrepho). "Apostrepho" is a Greek word in the imperative, the command of the statement. Although Jesus may suggest that we should not dismiss the evil person who wants to borrow from us, He commands that we ***"do not turn away."*** This verb begins with "apo." Therefore, it contains the idea of dismissal and highlights this issue as a double emphasis. The second word involved in this verb is "strepho." Its basic meaning is "to turn." Although we might perceive the total meaning to be "do not be dismissal," using the word takes on a strange idea. It has to do with "causing" something in someone's life. When the evil person interacts with me, demanding to borrow something, my engagement with them shapes their life. I push them in a direction; I influence them for the Kingdom. Jesus raised the issue of "what I am causing in their lives."

This thought is unthinkable for the self-sourced person. The helpless person acts as if he is not responsible or concerned about how he influences the evil person. His concern is only for himself and how he is affected. This thinking is evident because this verb is in the passive voice, meaning the action of the verb is acting on the subject. Jesus did not command you to do something but to allow something to be done to you! In your helplessness will you allow the Spirit of Jesus to move through your life causing redemptive influence to flow to the evil person who wants to borrow from you? Will you become an extension of Christ's life that expresses the heart of the Father? Without the merger of your nature with His, this is impossible. He must do this through you!

Let me remind you again of the example of Peter and John in the Book of Acts (Acts 3). These men portray a picture of this truth. Peter and John are apostles of the early church with busy schedules. They do not have time to be interrupted by a lame beggar. They are headed into the temple to fulfill their religious duty during the hour of prayer and sacrifice. The disabled man is obviously an evil person with materialism on his mind. He is not allowed in the temple and is virtually banned from all redemptive influence. As the lame beggar begs for money, the worst Peter and John could do was ignore him. Many religious people in their service to God in temple worship did that. The best Peter and John could do was giving him some financial support, which would fulfill the Old Testament standard. But Peter and John are filled with the Spirit; they are Kingdom people, merged with Divine nature. They do not dismiss the lame beggar, although they did not give him what he asked, they caused something in his life he had never known before. His life was redeemed, physically and spiritually. Peter and John became the instruments to redeem his life.

Redemption is Jesus' challenge in our passage! What are we causing in the life of the evil person? ***"An eye for an eye and a tooth for a tooth"*** always approaches the evil person in view of what they are doing to me. The Kingdom person, merged with the Spirit of Jesus, approaches the evil person in view of what can I cause in them? Jesus highlighted this in the illustration of "marriage" (Matthew 5:31, 32). Those of old were looking for justification to divorce their wives. A helpless person sourced by that helplessness would use every means to protect and guard themselves. Their focus was strictly on themselves. Jesus proposed the question, "What are you causing in your spouse?" The Greek word He uses is "poieo." It is not rule focused or obligation sourced. The word is used for trees bearing fruit. What do I source or cause deep in the inner heart of another person? Do I push my spouse in the direction of prayer and dependence on Jesus? Do I surround them with godliness? The same principle is now being applied to the evil person who wants to take advantage of me. My response causes something in them.

Jesus insists that our interaction with the evil person will have an effect on them. Although they initiated the encounter for selfish ends, our interaction with them provides an opportunity for redemption. Although we may not give them what they want, could we give them what they need? This interaction is

Part Five: Fulfillment of the Kingdom - The Application: Malice

an impossible task without a merging with God's heart. Jesus presented a picture of the Kingdom person, a helpless person filled and merged with the Spirit of Christ. Every encounter presents the opportunity for redemption. We must look beyond the evil, which is to be resisted, and embrace the person who is trapped in their self-centeredness. It will not be difficult to find such situations! How will we respond?

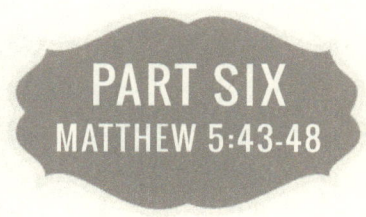

PART SIX
MATTHEW 5:43-48

Fulfillment of the Kingdom – The Application:

MOTIVE

Matthew 5:43-48

KINGDOM MOTIVE

"You have heard that it was said, 'You shall love your neighbor and hate your enemy.' But I say to you, love your enemies, bless those who curse you, do good to those who hate you, and pray for those who spitefully use you and persecute you, that you may be sons of your Father in heaven; for He makes His sun rise on the evil and on the good, and sends rain on the just and on the unjust. For if you love those who love you, what reward have you? Do not even the tax collectors do the same? And if you greet your brethren only, what do you do more than others? Do not even the tax collectors do so? Therefore you shall be perfect, just as your Father in heaven is perfect" (Matthew 5:43-48).

The final illustration in the Sermon on the Mount describes the exceeding righteousness of the Kingdom person focused on motive. In some sense, the motive is the underlying truth in each illustration, but it is most prominent in this paragraph. In the first five illustrations, physical action is involved: murder, adultery, divorce, swearing, and retribution. But this last illustration, from the viewpoint of what we have heard, is *"love your neighbor"* and *"hate your enemy"* (Matthew 5:43). The motive of God is the basis for Jesus' plea in the sixth illustration, and He challenges us to be like Him in our motive.

Having introduced motive in this last illustration, chapter six of Matthew expands it. This chapter begins with a discussion

Part Six: Fulfillment of the Kingdom - The Application: Motive

of the three fundamentals of all world religions: charitable giving (Matthew 6:1-4), prayer (Matthew 6:5-14), and spiritual discipline (Matthew 6:16-21). Although Jesus does not discourage any of these activities, His message is concerned with the motive of each event. Self-centered motivation destroys the reason for the activity. There must be a correct motive, or the proper effect of the action is lost.

What is the motive? According to the field of philosophy, there are three elements distinguishable in motive, the external object, the internal principle, and the state or affection of the mind, which results from the one addressing the other. For example, bread or food of any kind is the external object. The internal principle, appetite, requires sustenance; hunger or the desire for food is the internal feeling, which is excited by the presentation of the external object (bread) to the internal principle (appetite). The term motive applies to any of these three. However, strictly speaking in our general understanding, the internal principle of appetite is the motive.

A person might say, "It is my desire (motive) to go to heaven." However, heaven would have no appeal to the person unless there is an internal principle (appetite), which excites the mind with desire. One might say, "It is my desire (motive) to be holy." However, holiness would have no appeal to the person unless there is an internal principle (appetite), which excites the mind for holiness. Someone might say, "It is my desire (motive) to evangelize the world for Jesus." However, winning the world for Jesus would be at best a duty, unless there is an internal principle (appetite), which stimulates the mind with concern. In our passage, Jesus deals directly with this internal principle (appetite)! What is the internal principle of your life?

The internal principle of what they *"have heard that it was said"* is self-sourcing, self-centeredness. *"You shall love your neighbor"* was most often interpreted as nationalism. Their *"neighbor"* was another Jew. *"Your enemies"* were those outside the Jewish circle. *"Love"* and *"hate"* were dictated by the personal qualifications of the group or individual. The internal principle forming the motive is self-focus. Jesus calls for a new appetite! The structure of His presentation shows us the heart of God, His nature. This "bread" stimulates the appetite in us, creating desires for the merger with Him. The motive is the appetite of the heart.

The Proposition
Matthew 5:44

Jesus begins with a bold proposition, presenting four verbs: *"love," "bless," "do,"* and *"pray."* Each verb is in the imperative mood, a command of Jesus, equal in their intent and value. These verbs are an expression of the same internal principle, motive. Jesus contrasts the two appetites of the heart motive, which are the self-centered appetite expressed in those of old and the self-giving appetite of the new Kingdom person. The Kingdom person cannot manufacture the appetite (motive); he can only express it. Each verb is in the active voice, which is why we can see the appetite (motive) in the setting of *"enemies"* and *"persecution."* When persecuting enemies act on a person, the motive of the heart responds with *"love"* and *"pray.*

Jesus began the Sermon on the Mount with the premise, *"poor in spirit"* (Matthew 5:3). We are helpless at the core of our lives without resources. Acknowledging our helplessness removes the barriers to His comfort. He, the Comforter, merges with me (Matthew 5:4), and His nature becomes the source of my nature. I now have His appetite, motive. It is not reasonable to have a Kingdom person's appetite. Only in the merger with Him can my appetite change. If I do not embrace my helplessness, I live in emptiness. I use every situation for my resource to survive. I manipulate all circumstances for my benefit, guarding, and protecting for my safety. I cannot risk being redemptive. It is too costly. The quality of love Jesus requires for my enemy, I cannot give to my neighbor. I am helpless but act like I am not. My appetite does not hunger for what He hungers. What He commands is impossible. Indeed, it proves His premise. I am helpless and cannot possibly do as He commands. I must experience His appetite, motive!

The Purpose
Matthew 5:4)

Jesus began this statement with *"that"* (hopos), a purpose conjunction indicating the goal or aim of the action denoted by the word, phrase, or clause, which it joins. The purpose of our merger with His nature, to be an expression of His appetite or motive, is **"that you may be sons of your Father in heaven."** The purpose of Christianity is that I become a son. I want to be born of His life, sourced by His heart! I want His appetite. I want to think like Him and my life structure to be His. I want His nature to shape me in every way. But most of all, I want what motivates Him to motivate me! If I have His appetite (motive), will I not act like Him? If His internal principle is mine, will I not see like He sees, respond like He responds, and have His attitude?

But being like Jesus is idealistic. I am not motivated like Jesus; my selfish survival demands my attitude to protect, guard, and defend. The idealistic impossibility of being like Jesus proves His point! I can never be like Jesus. He must come and do this within me! Would this be the answer to the High Priestly Prayer of Jesus (John 17)? Just before the Garden of Gethsemane, Jesus revealed the depth of His concern in prayer to His Father. He knew that His hour had come. It was an hour of glorification when the Father gave Him eternal life. What is this eternal life? *"And this is eternal life, that they may know* (ginosko) *You, the only true God, and Jesus Christ whom You have sent"* (John 17:3). "Ginosko," the Greek word for "know," is the most intimate word for a relationship used for the sexual intimacy between husband and wife. It is a word that expresses "oneness." Jesus went on to pray, *"that they all may be one, as You, Father, are in Me, and I in You; that they also may be one in Us, that the world may believe that You sent Me. And the glory which You gave Me I have given them, that they may be one just as We are one: I in them, and You in Me; that they may be made perfect in one"* (John 17:21-22). Think of the intertwining merger of oneness between the Father and the Son. Jesus was *"the brightness of His glory and the express image of His person"* (Hebrews 1:3).

Is this not the heart of a son? All that the Father is in His nature indwells me. I hunger for what He hungers; His appetite is the same craving I experience. His life and my life have become one, fulfilling the statement of the Hebrew writer, *"For both He who sanctifies and those who are being sanctified are all of one, for which reason He is not ashamed to call them brethren"* (Hebrews 2:11). The heart of this verse is the phrase *"all of one!"* The word *"all"* refers to *"He who sanctifies and those who are being sanctified."* Jesus, who is the *"Captain of their salvation,"* is the sanctifying one. You and I are the ones He sanctifies. The writer says Jesus and you are *"of"* One. The Greek word "ek" is a movement term, always used for a movement originating from within something. The Man Jesus, as well as you and me, are birthed from the same life source. What produced Jesus produces us! We are out of *"One."* It is the Trinity God *"for whom are all things and by whom are all things"* (Hebrews 2:10). We are brothers with Christ, for we are from the same life source, having the same appetite.

Part Six: Fulfillment of the Kingdom - The Application: Motive

The Power
Matthew 5:45b-47

After presenting the purpose of this merger between you and Him, Jesus clearly states the basis or foundation for becoming sons. The nature of God, His Spirit, indwelling, and merging with us is how God births us. But Jesus, in this illustration, focused more specifically on motive. He introduced this section with the word *"for"* a translation of the Greek word "hoti." "Hoti" is a subordinating conjunction that expresses the basis or ground of action. Jesus commands us to *"love"* and *"pray"* to prove we are sons. We look like Him, have His DNA, and exhibit His mannerisms. But what is the power within God's nature that allows us to complete His commands?

Jesus demonstrates this power with two illustrations. God's activity in physical nature is one, and the second is the interaction of human relationships. God does not make any distinction between the good and evil or the just and unjust regarding the sun shining or the rain falling (Matthew 5:45). This lack of difference is explained only by the appetite of God. His motive is always to help. When He sees a need, His heart's response is to meet that need. The ungodly need both sun and rain as much as the godly. God has no appetite to punish or withhold goodness from anyone. Is this not the explanation for the power behind redemption? Is the Trinity God not one who *"so loved the world that He gave His only begotten Son"* (John 3:16)? Did His Divine love not flow on the evil and good, the just and unjust? He does not withhold His grace from anyone! **"But God demonstrates His own love toward us, in that while we were still sinners, Christ died for us"** (Romans 5:8). *"His own love"* is the appetite of His nature, His motive!

If this is God's appetite, will it not be His birthed son's appetite as well? Therefore, the power to love my enemies and

Kingdom Motive | **Matthew 5:43-48**

pray for every person is the appetite of God! Because God and I have merged, His motive empowers me in every expression of my attitude. The expression of God's heart motive within me is not a rule, duty, or discipline.

Jesus uses the illustration of human relationships (Matthew 5:46). The worst person in the mind of the Jews was the tax collector. But even the tax collectors mutually embraced each other against the world that hated them. If we express their appetite, how are we any better than them? If we withhold forgiveness and love from our enemies and persecutors, we express the appetite of the evilest people. In doing so, how can we consider ourselves *"sons of your Father in heaven?"* We do not have His appetite.

Again, Jesus forces us to remember the premise of the Sermon on the Mount. We cannot exhibit the motive of the Father if it is not our appetite. Jesus does not suggest a better way of life or reformation in living. He does not propose New Testament rules against the rules of the Old Testament, or offer a new approach to meditation and social reform. He says loving our enemies is an impossibility for any human. We are helpless and have no resource within ourselves to achieve this (Matthew 5:3). We simply do not have the appetite for it. We should mourn over this until the Comforter comes!

The Production
Matthew 5:48

The climax of this sixth illustration is startling! It is a troublesome statement over which most of us have struggled. We rationalize, ignore, and do not believe. The idea of *"Therefore you shall be perfect"* is incomprehensible. In the mindset of our culture, this is beyond anyone's ability. It is idealistic, especially when Jesus' required perfection is in the context of *"your Father*

in heaven is perfect." Suddenly we no longer compare ourselves to ourselves, but we compare ourselves to God. How ridiculous is this thought? I am to be perfect at the level of Divinity!

In the final illustration, we might consider perfection on the Divinity level, but Bible scholars agree we must apply the perfection to all six illustrations. The truth of the sixth illustration governs our interpretation of the other five. The Greek word translated ***"perfect,"*** related to us and God is "teleios." It comes from "telos," focusing on goal or purpose. Our word focuses on finished, that which reaches its end, term, limit; hence, "teleios" is complete, full, wanting in nothing. This definition does not help because if I were perfect in knowledge and wisdom, I would be omniscient like God, which will never happen in my lifetime or heaven. If I were complete in power and might, I would be omnipotent like God, which is never in the realm of possibility. If I were complete in presence, I would be omnipresent like God, although I might want it, I do not see it in my future.

You will notice in this sixth illustration there is no hint of perfection in any of the above areas. The single focus of the sixth illustration is the heart appetite of God, His motive. The Trinity God does not invite us to participate in what He has; He invites us to share in who He is, His nature! He wants to merge with us and create a new creature. This new creature demonstrates the appetite of God in the physical world. When we merge with God and show His appetite in our lives, we express completeness (perfection).

This completeness (perfection) is valid in each of the six illustrations. Although murder was not acceptable to those of old, God's appetite in the Kingdom person will not tolerate anger, demeaning, or belittling (Matthew 5:22) because it is not God's heart motive. Adultery was unacceptable to those of old. They had to control their sexual appetite and function within certain boundaries. Jesus speaks of sexuality that flows from the heart (Matthew 5:28). In the merger with God's nature, the heart's desire becomes one with God, controlling the perspective of the new Kingdom person. Those of old considered marriage from a selfish perspective, what they wanted. The heart of the Father is concerned about what is "caused" in one's spouse (Matthew 5:32). Oaths for those of old allowed manipulating the truth for personal benefit. The motive of God must maintain integrity and honesty. It is His appetite that increases, builds, grows relationships, and personhood (Matthew 5:37). Those of old guarded, protected, and managed all things for themselves. The Kingdom person sees everything intersecting his life as an opportunity for redemption. The sovereign hand of God allows adverse opportunities for the Kingdom person to extend redemption to the life of others (Matthew 5:39).

The theme permeating every illustration is the appetite of God. How can I desire what He desires? Legislated activities cannot change my heart's desire. I must have His motive. The premise of the Sermon on the Mount is that we are *"poor in spirit"* (Matthew 5:3). The fact we admit not having this inner appetite proves His point. We cannot manufacture such a motive. He must capture us! Outside the merger between His nature and my nature, I cannot reach this level. I consistently fail in my endeavor. I must merge with Him!

Matthew 5:43

AN EVIL APPETITE

"You have heard that it was said, 'You shall love your neighbor and hate your enemy.'" (Matthew 5:43).

We are engaged in a study of the Sermon on the Mount. Before we continue in our analysis of the sixth and final illustration of Matthew Chapter 5, we need to review some pivotal issues in this chapter. The Sermon on the Mount covers Matthew 5, 6, and 7. The final verse of chapter 7 gives us the reaction of the crowd listening to Jesus' message. **"And so it was, when Jesus had ended these sayings, that the people were astonished at His teaching"** (Matthew 7:28). The Greek word translated *"astonished"* is "ekplesso," meaning "to be or become astounded to such a degree as to nearly lose one's mental composure." They were astounded that His message lacked rules or instruction on personal discipline. All other world religions demanded performance and achievement at the highest level. Jesus offers us as a gift without meriting performance, something unheard of in the religious world!

We see the basis of this gift in the opening statements of the Sermon on the Mount, the Beatitudes (Matthew 5:3-12). Jesus proposes we are *"poor in spirit,"* without resource. We are helpless people at the core of our being. If we desire to be the godly people God created us to be, our resource must come from someone other than ourselves. Therefore, Jesus proposes the premise of the sermon. Jesus must come! We will be comforted by the Comforter, who merges with us (Matthew 5:4). If the nature of God becomes the source of our lives, what will be the level of living for us?

The proposal of God being our resource and Jesus' complete disregard for the "oral traditions" of the Pharisees, the multitude considered that Jesus was starting a new religion. The Pharisees formulated the "oral traditions" from their interpretation of the Scriptures. To them, it appeared that Jesus proposed dismissal of the Scriptures! Was He discounting the Old Testament? But Jesus said, **"Do not think that I came to destroy the Law or the Prophets. I did not come to destroy but to fulfill"** (Matthew 5:17). Jesus refused this thought or suggestion. His motive was not to release us from the Old Testament but to fulfill it. "To fulfill" is to take everything suggested in the Old and bring it to completion! If this happened in my life, how would it appear? It would complete the requirement of His statement before the six illustrations. **"For I say to you that unless your righteousness exceeds the righteousness of the scribes and Pharisees, you will by no means enter the kingdom of heaven"** (Matthew 5:20). The righteousness proposed is far beyond what we can imagine; it is impossible. We would have to exceed the best we can do; we would need to be supernatural. All of this proves the premise of the Sermon on the Mount. We are helpless to achieve this Kingdom life. We must merge with Him!

According to Jesus, this merger must be living and written. The Living Person of God wants to indwell us, but He also wants to speak to us. He fulfills the Scriptures in our lives through this combination. Jesus, a helpless Man, was filled with the nature of God (Matthew 3:13-17). It is the glorious experience of Pentecost (Acts 2:1-4) happening in the life of the believer. It is the merger between God and man! God sources us, and His speaking shapes our lives. How does He speak? He speaks through the Scriptures, the Written Word, and the Living Word,

Part Six: Fulfillment of the Kingdom - The Application: Motive

His presence, is never disconnected from the Scriptures. The Scriptures are not a manual for your life or a road map to heaven. The Scriptures are the whispering of Jesus' merging Spirit within you, the pillow talk of God in His merger with you. Anytime the Scriptures are removed from the expression of God's heart, misunderstanding and misdirection occur. Was this the explanation for the dominant mindset of the Jew? *"You have heard that it was said, 'You shall love your neighbor and hate your enemy.'"* (Matthew 5:43).

Read the Scriptures

"You shall love your neighbor and hate your enemy." Where would the Jews have found this statement in their Scriptures? Even though there was no statement, indication, or allowance for such an account, it was the accepted belief of Scriptural truth. Bible scholars agree this is a quotation from the Book of Leviticus. *"You shall not take vengeance, nor bear any grudge against the children of your people, but you shall love your neighbor as yourself: I am the Lord"* (Leviticus 19:18). The Jews of Jesus' day left off the crucial statement *"as yourself."* *"You shall love your neighbor and hate your enemy"* was a popular way in which the average Israelite considered the law of God. They regulated their lives concerning friends and foes based on this statement. It would be safe to assume since this teaching was so prevalent that Pharisees and scribes held it.

The Jews certainly could not plead ignorance of the phrase *"as yourself."* The scribe who quizzed Jesus about the first commandment was careful to include *"as yourself"* when He spoke about God's love and loving one another (Mark 12:32-34). On another occasion, a lawyer, an expert in Jewish law, questioned Jesus about inheriting eternal life. Jesus asked him, *"What is written in the law? What is your reading of it?"* So

he answered and said, 'You shall love the Lord your God with all your heart, with all your soul, and with all your strength, and with all your mind,' and 'your neighbor as yourself'" (Luke 10:26-27). Paul quoted this statement twice in his epistles (Romans 13:9; Galatians 5:14). If they understood the inclusion of this phrase, why did they ignore it?

Even worse than the omission of **"*your neighbor as yourself*"** was the addition **"*and hate your enemy.*"** There is no indication in the verse that enemies should be hated, yet this was the common understanding. In the context of the statement in Leviticus, **"*your neighbor as yourself*"** is highlighted. There is no instruction to hate your enemy in the Old Testament. By adding **"*and hate your enemy,*"** they shifted the emphasis away from the original intention of the law. The statement in Leviticus intended to emphasize love over against vengeance. This perversion drew a sharp contrast between "the neighbor" and "the enemy." This contrast brought much argument and debate concerning, **"*And who is my neighbor?*"** (Luke 10:29).

When Jesus said, **"*But I say to you, love your enemies,*"** His audience must have been amazed once again. He said something they probably had never before heard so succinctly and with such positive force. Jesus was the first who taught man to see every human as **"*neighbor.*"** He tells us to encounter every human in love! No one should ask the question, **"*And who is my neighbor?*"** Every person should prove himself neighbor to another in need, whoever they might be! Jesus in no way contradicted the Old Testament but brought to fulfillment all that the Scriptures intended.

How did they miss it? Perhaps it is easier to understand that they did not miss it! They misread the Scriptures. If this was the only occasion for such misreading, we might be sympathetic. Jews who traveled from Jerusalem to Galilee asked Jesus why His disciples did not wash their hands when they ate bread. It was a violation of the **"*traditions of the elders*"** (Matthew 15:1-2).

Part Six: Fulfillment of the Kingdom - The Application: Motive

Jesus asked the scribes and Pharisees why they transgressed the commandment of God, the Scriptures, regarding *"Honor your father and mother"*? They misread the Scriptures. It is plainly stated in the Scriptures how to honor one's parents, but they adjusted it in their reading to make it of no effect. Jesus called them hypocrites (Matthew 15:7) and proceeded to quote the prophecy of Isaiah, which was about them:

> *"These people draw near to Me with their mouth,*
> *And honor Me with their lips,*
> *But their heart is far from Me.*
> *And in vain they worship Me,*
> *Teaching as doctrines the commandments of men"*
> (Matthew 15:8-9).

John's Gospel records the heated debates between Jesus and the Pharisees. At the heart of a revealing explanation concerning the Pharisees' condition, Jesus said, *"You search the Scriptures, for in them you think you have eternal life; and these are they which testify of Me. But you are not willing to come to Me that you may have life"* (John 5:39-40). They misread the Scriptures. The Jewish nation clung to the Scriptures as the most sacred of their documents and said the Scriptures were the word of God to their lives, but they adjusted their reading to fit their need.

Are we not also guilty of the same? Without going into a long discourse describing the Scriptures we misread, can we challenge ourselves to correction? Can we have a new appreciation for the Scriptures as they are, bending our lives under its authority? As careful as we are about recording the numbers in our bank account, can we be as cautious when reading the Scriptures? Would you read the Scriptures to discover the truth? We read the Scriptures to win an argument, prepare a sermon, prove our theology, condemn those around us, and to justify our activity. Can we just read the Scriptures to discover Jesus? Better yet, can we allow Jesus to speak the Scriptures to us? If the Scriptures are the speaking of the indwelt Christ, will we listen to what He says? We dare not impose our thought process, educational achievements, or theological bias. We must come under His authority and bend our will to His spoken Word! We must read the Scriptures.

Realize the Scriptures

The urgency of this hour becomes clear! Let me remind you of the foundation Jesus established for these six illustrations. He came to *"fulfill"* the Scriptures, not *"destroy"* them (Matthew 5:17)! The Greek word translated *"destroy"* is "katalyo." It is a combination of "kata," which intensifies and "luo" meaning "to release or loose." It is the picture of a pack mule carrying the burdens of his owner, who in turn removes them from him at the end of the day. During the ministry of Jesus, the masses of people moved Him. Matthew describes His feelings with the word *"compassion,"* the strongest Greek word for "pity." It refers to a person profoundly disturbed and emotionally wrought deep within! Jesus saw the crowds as *"weary and scattered, like sheep having no shepherd"* (Matthew 9:36). The Greek word translated *"weary"* is "eklyo," meaning "to collapse due to fatigue." The crowds were utterly exhausted from the burden placed on them by the Pharisees, who based their requirements on the Old Testament. Jesus described the procedure as, *"For they bind heavy burdens, hard to bear, and lay them on men's shoulders; but they themselves will not move them with one of their fingers"* (Matthew 23:4). Jesus is not describing the Scriptures; He details the scribes and Pharisees misreading of the Scriptures.

Jesus came to *"fulfill!"* He was the first human to embrace the Scriptures in the power of the Holy Spirit, placing Him on

Part Six: Fulfillment of the Kingdom – The Application: Motive

a level of achievement beyond the scribes and the Pharisees. He viewed and interpreted His life experience in light of the Scriptures spoken to Him by the Spirit. In an upper room after His resurrection, He said, *"These are the words which I spoke to you while I was still with you, that all things must be fulfilled which were written in the Law of Moses and the Prophets and the Psalms concerning Me"* (Luke 24:44). Then He opened their understanding to the Scriptures that they might comprehend its reading. Why did He go to the cross? It was the instruction of the Scriptures. He said, *"Thus it is written, and thus it was necessary for the Christ to suffer and to rise from the dead the third day, and that repentance and remission of sins should be preached in His name to all nations"* (Luke 24:46-47).

Jesus, as a Spirit-filled man reading the Scriptures, completed the destiny of His life by fulfilling the Scriptures. Could this be the same for us? It may not be our destiny to hang on the cross as the Messiah, but is it possible that our destiny is written in the Scriptures as read to us through the Spirit? Therefore, the Scriptures are not a comprehensive book of instruction for all Christians but are a personal love letter expressed through the intimacy of our merger with God's nature. It is the expression of God's appetite becoming our appetite through the sharing of His thoughts, which shapes our lives! We cannot realize the reality of the Scriptures without His nature. We will misread and adjust His Word unless He speaks it to us as we embrace Him in the reading. It is not a scholarship or academic study; it is intimacy and embracing Him in relationship! Reclining in His presence in the merger of the Spirit, surrendering our heart to His, He whispers to us His Word, and we understand. We "realize" the Scriptures! Without this we misread the Scriptures, regardless of our education or knowledge.

Rationalize the Scriptures

Why has every generation misread the Scriptures? It is the premise of the Sermon on the Mount. ***"Blessed are the poor in spirit"*** (Matthew 5:3). We are helpless. If we refuse to acknowledge we are helpless and embrace our poverty, we manipulate every situation for our benefit. We must do so to have enough resource to survive. We use the Scriptures to justify and strengthen our self-centeredness; thus, we misread the Scriptures.

However, if the helpless person embraces his poverty, he can be filled with the appetite of God, His nature. The essence of God merges with us. Consider carefully the depth of communication now established with the Kingdom person. It will be different from the interaction of God and man in the Old Covenant. Clearly, we understand that communication. God established a meeting place where He could speak to His people. But the fear of the people was so great that they said to Moses, ***"You speak with us and we will hear; but let not God speak with us, lest we die"*** (Exodus 20:19). God granted their request and gave them prophets. But God wanted to communicate directly to His people.

God prepared for the day when He would indwell His people. This opportunity is now ours! We can merge with the nature of God; we can experience His appetite. Although He wants to source us internally, He wants to shape us externally. Our merger with God becomes complete when the Living Word in us merges with the Written Word of the Scriptures. The Spirit of Jesus merges with our thoughts and intently whispers His Word to us. We no longer misread the Scriptures for our benefit but experience the revelation of God in our lives. If this merger does not happen with us and with the Scriptures, we rationalize the Scriptures for our benefit.

The wonder of this experience takes place only when we embrace our helplessness. Jesus instructed us to live in this helplessness. We are never to step outside the boundaries of our helplessness. Do not get cocky, arrogant, or self-confident. Do not say, "I can handle this." We must embrace our helplessness and let our helplessness embrace us. Again, this relates to us that education, talent, or personality are not keys to understanding the Scriptures. It is not a book of rules or a manual of advice. It is the expression from the lips of Jesus to your heart as He merges with your nature.

The Jews of Jesus' day misread the Scriptures, searching for life only to find death. They studied to discover the will of God only to rationalize the Scriptures for their benefit. The Scriptures became the justification for their lives and a tool to judge others by, which can happen in our lives as well. We must embrace our helplessness, merge with His nature, and experience the expression of His heart in the Scriptures!

Matthew 5:44

LOVE YOUR ENEMIES

"But I say to you, love your enemies, bless those who curse you, do good to those who hate you, and pray for those who spitefully use you and persecute you" (Matthew 5:44).

The previous verse in this chapter is the cultural interpretation of the Old Testament approach. **"You have heard that it was said, 'You shall love your neighbor and hate your enemy'"** (Matthew 5:43). It is more accurately an explanation of the passage in Leviticus. **"You shall not take vengeance, nor bear any grudge against the children of your people, but you shall love your neighbor as yourself; I am the Lord"** (Leviticus 19:18). In all six illustrations, Jesus said, **"It was said,"** not "It was written." There is never an indication or quotation in the Law of Moses that says we should hate our enemies. How could the scribes and Pharisees miss this fundamental truth of the Old Testament?

The crucial issue here is, "who is my neighbor?" The scholars of Jesus' day debated and argued this often. This question prompted the parable of the Good Samaritan spoken by Jesus in Luke's Gospel (Luke 10:25-37). When a man was beaten and robbed by thieves, three passers-by saw his need firsthand. The priest and Levite passed by on the other side. But the despised Samaritan intervened in the man's need. Jesus proposed the question, **"So which of these three do you think was neighbor to him who fell among the thieves?"** (Luke 10:36).

Part Six: Fulfillment of the Kingdom - The Application: Motive

The answer is obvious. *"And he said, 'He who showed mercy on him"* (Luke 10:37).

How did the Jews miss the truth? In the passage found in Leviticus, the phrase *"the children of your people"* and *"your neighbor"* were equated. Jews considered only other Jews as neighbors, and they referred to Gentiles as "dogs." In Old Testament history, God commanded the Jews to eliminate the Canaanites. God commanded, *"that you will blot out the remembrance of Amalek from under heaven"* (Deuteronomy 25:19). Kindness was not the way to treat the Ammonites, Moabites, and Midianites (Deuteronomy 23:3, 6; Numbers 25:16-18). God never intended for these commands regarding foreign nations to be a rule of conduct between people! The Israelites took these commands and developed a nationalism. They restricted the word *"neighbor"* to those of their nation. Therefore, their *"enemies"* were anyone who was not a Jew. It is little wonder that the Romans criticized the Jews for being "haters of the human race."

Jesus consistently battled the traditions of the elders. Israel's leadership built and maintained strong walls and barriers between themselves and all other races of people. But Jesus broke down these walls and gave us a picture of the heart (appetite) of the Trinity God. The teachings of Jesus startled His audience (Matthew 7:28). He spoke a truth that had never before been so succinctly, positively, and forcefully stated! *"Love your enemies!"*

The Jews misread the intent of the Old Testament. There are abundant statements that verify this. For instance, in Deuteronomy, the Israelites were instructed to help their fellow Israelites (Deuteronomy 22:1-4). But they were equally taught to help their enemies in the same manner (Exodus 23:4-5). Job testified about his godly attitude towards his enemies: *"If I have rejoiced at the destruction of him who hated me, or lifted myself up when evil found him (Indeed I have not allowed my mouth to sin by asking for a curse on his soul)"* (Job 31:29-30). Listen to David's prayer: ***"If I have repaid evil to him who was at peace with me, or have plundered my enemy without cause, let the enemy pursue me and overtake me; yes, let him trample my life to the earth, and lay my honor in the dust"*** (Psalms 7:4-5). God's standard in the Old Testament does not change in the New Testament!

Explanation

We can see in Jesus the explanation for this standard. There is a re-occurring phrase, ***"But I say to you"*** (Matthew 5:44). Jesus established a contrast by introducing His statement with the Greek conjunction "de." Its first translation is the conjunction *"but."* The authority of the phrase rests on Him. *"I say"* is a translation of the Greek word "lego." But Jesus also included the Greek word "ego" in His statement, making a double emphasis on Jesus Himself. Jesus' authority is the case in all six illustrations. Jesus is the first Kingdom Person, and He set the standard for the motive.

To understand the content of *"love your enemies,"* we need only investigate the life action of Jesus. Luke was bold in his revelation of those involved in the crucifixion of Christ. He wrote, ***"both Herod*** (kings) ***and Pontius Pilate*** (rulers)***, with the Gentiles and the people of Israel, were gathered together"*** (Acts 4:27). This event included everyone. How did Jesus express His heart concerning His enemies? ***"Then Jesus said, 'Father, forgive them, for they do not know what they do"*** (Luke 23:34). There was no question about Jesus' intention when He said, *"love your enemies."*

The Pharisees and scribes were the prime movers of hatred toward Jesus. What was Jesus' heart motive expressed toward them? He said it best at the end of His final public message. He called them hypocrites (Matthew 23:13, 14, 15, 23, 25, 27, 29).

He declared they were blind guides (Matthew 23:16). We might conclude this was an expression of the hatred Jesus felt toward them. However, Jesus did not give this discourse in their presence. It was an address *"to the multitudes and to His disciples"* (Matthew 23:1). Jesus warned them about the influence of these leaders. He clearly expressed His heart at the end of the message: *"O Jerusalem, Jerusalem, the one who kills the prophets and stones those who are sent to her! How often I wanted to gather your children together, as a hen gathers her chicks under her wings, but you were not willing"* (Matthew 23:37). Jesus did not hate them but was expressing His broken heart for the dire spiritual condition of these leaders. It gives content to the statement, *"love your enemies."*

Surely this is the love motivation behind the brilliant close of Matthew's Gospel. Before the Garden of Gethsemane, Jesus instructed His disciples that after His resurrection, they were to meet Him in Galilee at the appointed place (Matthew 26:32). Mary Magdalene and the other Mary encountered the resurrected Lord before the disciples. He instructed these ladies to remind the disciples about the appointment (Matthew 28:10). Jesus met the disciples in Galilee at the mountain and revealed to them His throbbing love for the world. It was the "Great Commission." These disciples were to participate in winning the world, *"make disciples of all nations"* (Matthew 28:19). After His resurrection, but before His ascension, He expressed the scope of His love. *"Jerusalem, and in all Judea and Samaria, and to the end of the earth"* (Acts 1:8). Who would you say is not included in the love of Jesus?

Engagement

We must equate love with God and understand love in the context of His nature. Love is His appetite, the hunger of His heart! We must see this nature and embrace the person of Jesus, who is *"the brightness of His glory and the express image of His person"* (Hebrews 1:3). We must not mention or discuss love outside this reality! There are four Greek words translated "love" in the New Testament, "philia" is brotherly love and the love of friendship. However, "philia" is love limited by the connection between those we would call friends. "Storgo" is the love within the boundary of those who are family. The Greek word "eros" highlights romantic, sexual desire. There is some dispute concerning the origin of the Greek word "agape," a word seldom used in classical Greek. The New Testament, writers under the inspiration of the Holy Spirit, could not be satisfied to use the above three words for the love of God. Therefore, they adopted "agape" and gave it new content. It is a selfless, self-sacrificing, and "never think about yourself" kind of love. It is the motive of the heart that never focuses on self. It is an appetite that hungers for what is best for the other person. It does not focus on emotions, although emotions may be involved. "Agape" is the love from the inner core of a person.

The problem with "agape" is that human beings cannot produce this kind of love. One might conceive a loving family with the content of "agape" love. It might even apply to some friendships. However, the expression of love in these areas, especially in the focus of "eros," is self-focused. The appetite driving these loves depends on self-satisfaction, emotional appeasing, and self-benefit. But the love of the Trinity God as expressed through Jesus does not fit this category. God's love is beyond the human element contained in "philia," "storgo," and "eros." We cannot describe God's love using these three words. Thus, the Greek word "agape" with new content became the expression! Self-benefit is not within the boundaries of God's appetite. It is love that seeks and works to meet another's highest welfare. While elements or degrees of "agape" might be within the human effort of love, it is not humanly possible to accomplish this kind of love in the motive and appetite of God. Only the Trinity God loves on the "agape" level!

Carnal humanity tends to base love on their desire for the object of their passion. We love attractive people, enjoyable hobbies, great looking houses or cars because they please us. God's appetite is not like ours! As seen in Christ, the Trinity God, without self-benefit, sacrificed His convenience, safety, and resources to meet our needs. The Greek word "charis" also expresses this love, translated as "grace." "Grace" is "goodwill freely disseminated by God, especially to the benefit of the recipient regardless of the benefit accrued to the disseminator." Grace is the driving appetite of God's heart!

"Agape" love may involve emotion, but it must include action. Paul wrote to the Church at Corinth, giving fifteen characteristics of love, and they are all in verb form (1 Corinthians 13). Attitude is also involved in love because it begins in the heart. But it is best described, and best testified about by what it does. *"Beloved, let us love one another, for love is of God; and everyone who loves is born of God and knows God. He who does not love does not know God, for God is love. In this the love of God was manifested toward us, that God has sent His only begotten Son into the world, that we might live through Him. In this is love, not that we loved God, but that He loved us and sent His Son to be the propitiation for our sins"* (1 John 4:7-10).

Jesus' words, *"Love your enemies,"* must have been a knife cutting the heart of every person listening. In this illustration, Jesus compared the best humanity can accomplish to what God does, comparing the appetite and desires of humanity to the appetite and motive of God. Do you see how ridiculous such an imperative is? This standard can be accomplished only by God, BUT this is the premise of the Sermon on the Mount. We are *"poor in spirit"* (Matthew 5:3), an absolute state of helplessness. God created us to be dependent, not independent so that He could fill our core being with Himself. A merger between the nature of God and the nature of man must take place. This merger creates a new creature, the Kingdom person. Jesus was the first one. He was the action of God's love; He had the appetite of God.

"Because the love of God has been poured out in our hearts by the Holy Spirit who was given to us" (Romans 5:5). *"No one has seen God at any time. If we love one another, God abides in us, and His love has been perfected in us"* (1 John 4:12). Jesus expressed "Agape" love in washing the disciples' feet (John 13:1-17). He was a helpless Man merged with the Trinity God's heart! Jesus gave expression to the invisible heart of God, following this act of self-giving love with a new commandment. *"A new commandment I give to you, that you love one another; as I have loved you, that you also love one another"* (John 13:34). The disciples were self-centered men, quarrelsome, jealous of each other, and they argued with Jesus. Yet everything Jesus said to them and did for them was ultimately and without exception for their good. He called them and us to be this same expression. I must engage His heart as He engaged the Father's heart. I must merge with Him and have His appetite. Jesus validated this conclusion at the close of this illustration. *"Therefore you shall be perfect, just as your Father in heaven is perfect"* (Matthew 5:48). The appetite of God is His motive. He is love (agape)! We must and can be filled with Him, merged with His heart, and consumed with His appetite.

Enemies

Jesus, a helpless Man, merged with the Father, declared the appetite of the Kingdom person. He calls us to *"love"* (agape), the sole motive or appetite of God. Immediately the question arises, "Who am I to love?" The ordinary Greek words for love answer this question. In "philia" love, I am to love my friends (neighbor), brotherly love, or love in friendship. I can easily accomplish this love by eliminating those who are not my friends. The person who may have been my friend now ceases to be such, therefore, not requiring my love. There is also love for family (storgo). The family relationship may be in this focus; however, there are those we have disowned. The standard of the family connection must be maintained, or love is not required. "Eros" love is focused on sexual attraction, which limits my love focus on those who appeal to me. In each of these situations, the focus is on the question, "Who am I to love?"

"Agape" shifts the question. This love is selfless, self-sacrificing, and never thinks about itself. Within the boundaries of its expression, self-benefit does not dwell. It sees all the hatefulness and wickedness of a person, feels their stabs and their blows, and may even have something to do with defending one's self from them. Yet all of this fills the loving heart with one desire. How can I help, win, or rescue them from the bondage of their hate and sin? How can they become the godly people God created them to be? So, the question of "agape" love is not "Who am I to love?" It is, "How shall I love?"

We are to love everyone; there are no categories for the person who has the appetite of God's heart. This love is not feeling but about the expression of this love. God's love embraces the world (John 3:16). He loved each of us even while we were still sinners and His enemies (Romans 5:8-10). Jesus explained this in great detail in His first illustration (Matthew 5:21-26). Selfish humanity can only think in terms of managing hate and anger. The best management achieved was refraining from murder. But Jesus introduced the appetite of God's heart, the elimination of anger. It is not merely about the absence of anger but never demeaning or belittling anyone, a selfless heart that desires to reconcile with every person. We will have adversaries; certainly, Jesus had them, but we will not be an adversary. We are not to be enemies of those who may be enemies to us. From their perspective, we are their enemies; but from our perspective, they are our neighbors.

The Scottish Reformer, George Wishart, a contemporary and friend of John Knox, was sentenced to die as a heretic. Because the executioner knew of Wishart's selfless ministering to hundreds of people who were dying of the plague, he hesitated to carry out the sentence. When Wishart saw the expression of remorse on the executioner's face, he went over and kissed him on the cheek, saying, "Sir, may that be a token that I forgive you" (John Foxe, Foxe's Book of Martyrs, ed. W. Grinton Berry [Grand Rapids: Baker, 1978], p. 252).

There are so many illustrations of "agape" love throughout church history. The challenge is not to admire the expression of love but to be such an expression of His love. It is impossible for me unless I have God's heart. I must merge with His appetite and be an expression of His love. The opportunity may not be in the circumstance of execution, but in daily living with hurtful attitudes and selfish practices. Will I be the expression of the appetite of God?

Matthew 5:44

LOVE IS PRAYER

"But I say to you, love your enemies, bless those who curse you, do good to those who hate you, and pray for those who spitefully use you and persecute you" (Matthew 5:44).

To comprehend God, we must understand "love." The reverse of this is also true if we desire to comprehend "love," we must understand God. God is not more than "love;" God is "love" (1 John 4:8, 16). "Love" is not one of His many attributes like omnipresence, omniscience, or omnipotence. He does not have "love." "Love" has God! If "love" dominates and controls God, then God is not god, but "love" is God. Only "love" is not an influence or attitude, it is a person, and His name is God. It is the single explanation of the Trinity. How can three persons exist in the Godhead, and yet, there is only one God? How can the three be one? The explanation is "love." It is the welding that removes every impurity and makes them one. This welding happens in a real marriage. Two people, male and female, become one flesh. How is such a union possible? The explanation is "love."

God is "holy" (Isaiah 6:3). God is not two things; He is one. Therefore, "holy" and "love" must be the same thing. Holiness is a perfect heart motive, which is "love." Holiness is never about pure activities but is always about purity of motive and appetite. Legalism never accomplishes holiness. What is purity of motive? It is perfect "love." It is the agape love of God, which is selfless, self-sacrificing, and never thinks of Himself. "Love" is an appetite that hungers for what is right for someone else. Agape love is the essence of God!

Jesus expresses this appetite of God in the last illustration of His Sermon on the Mount. He gives a call to be **"sons of your Father in heaven."** God's appetite is contained in His making **"His sun rise on the evil and on the good, and sends rain on the just and on the unjust"** (Matthew 5:45). God is in control. The sun must shine in cooperation with the dictates of God; the rain must fall according to the desire of God. We can see the focus of God's appetite because He distributes sun and rain equally on His sons and His enemies. He hungers for goodness. He does good just for the sake of doing good. His appetite of love does not require a response to exist. His appetite knows no boundaries of friendship. If we stay in the limits of friendship, we will know the love of God, but limits are not how God functions. He loves because He is love! His love is unconditional; anything we do or not do does not determine God's love. We can never merit His love; therefore, we will never not merit His love.

God's unconditional love is the premise of the Sermon on the Mount. Discipline, spiritual growth, and the desire to do right can never produce the love of God in the human being. We are **"poor in spirit"** (Matthew 5:3). When we embrace our helplessness, we allow the Comforter to fill us with Himself. He does not fill me as you would fill a container, but two entities merge, God and me. Jesus wants to saturate my life with His heart. His nature and my nature merge, creating a new creature. In our passage, Jesus refers to this new creature as **"sons of your Father in heaven."** We feel like Him; we think like Him; we have His appetite! We cannot do, produce, merit, earn, or develop His appetite; we must encounter His life. We must merge with Jesus!

In our passage, Jesus comes to a climax with the sixth and final illustration. This illustration does not describe a physical activity such as murder, adultery, divorce, swearing, or determined justice. This illustration focuses on God's nature, a distinct description of this appetite (motive). God's nature is love, but not love in the conventional sense; "agape" love is only in the nature of God! This "agape" love is a selfless, self-sacrificing, self-giving love that never thinks of itself. The only possibility for humanity to know and express this love is to merge with God's nature. We must have Jesus' appetite.

Jesus gives the activity of this appetite to the worst of categories, "your enemy." There are no other categories beyond the enemy; therefore, everyone is to know this love from us. But that is impossible for us to carry out; thus, we prove His point. We are helpless and must have His nature. Jesus must merge with us and give us His appetite (motive). The Sermon on the Mount is not a list of rules or obligations we are to master. We are to have a relationship of intimacy with God.

Prayer Defined

Jesus linked the idea of *"love your enemies"* and *"pray for those who spitefully use you and persecute you"* (Matthew 5:44). Are these phrases not an expression of the same truth? Did Jesus substitute the word "pray" for "love," or *"those who spitefully use you and persecute you"* for *"enemies?"* Perhaps loving my enemies is the same as praying for them. The content of the command to *"love"* is *"pray."*

The Greek word "proseuchomai" is translated *"pray."* "Proseuchomai" is a compound word, "pro," a directional preposition pointing us forward or toward, and "euchomai," expressing the idea "to wish." "Proseuchomai" is the most commonly used word in the New Testament for prayer, an all-inclusive word, covering all aspects of prayer. It is devotional in its use, assuming a sense of intimacy between two people, God and man, so that God can offer the wish of the heart. How can humanity have the courage to express a desire to sovereign God? That can happen only in the atmosphere of love!

Within the scope of the word "proseuchomai," is ample room for "practicing His presence." "Practicing His presence" is a term from an ancient monk, Brother Lawrence, who found intimacy with God. In the monastery, his responsibility was kitchen chores. He reported that his superiors required him to pray at the altar. However, he insisted he could not tell any difference between prayer at the altar and prayer while washing dishes in the kitchen. God was present in both situations. Communication with God was real, regardless of the surroundings. Brother Lawrence fulfilled the cry of the Apostle Paul, *"pray without ceasing"* (1 Thessalonians 5:17).

"Practicing His presence" is prayer in which God and man are one. This oneness is a merger of man's nature with God's nature. The life of the person who lives in this oneness is in communication with God. He has the appetite of God; what God wants is what he wants. The life of the person merged with God communicates to *"those who spitefully use you and persecute you."* The reality of this is the state of "love" and the state of "pray." Does Jesus call us to more than reciting to God ideas about our persecutors? Is He calling us to be the expression of God's appetite for our lives?

What will this look like in life? Stephen was preaching to the Hellenistic Jews. The Holy Spirit so powerfully applied the truth he revealed, *"they were cut to the heart"* (Acts 7:54). Stephen was filled with the Spirit and was in such oneness with God that he saw Jesus standing at the right hand of God the Father. The Jews began to stone Stephen, and he prayed for them, *"Lord, do not charge them with this sin"* (Acts 7:60). His prayer for those stoning him was the expression of God's heart to them. The "agape" love of God flowed through the prayer of Stephen to his persecutors! He fulfilled the cry of Jesus to *"love your enemies"* and *"pray for those who spitefully use you and persecute you."*

Part Six: Fulfillment of the Kingdom - The Application: Motive

"Love" and *"pray"* were the same, so closely linked that *"love"* is the content of the prayer and becomes the physical expression of the *"love."* Prayer is defined by *"love."*

Prayer Demonstrated

We must see the *"love"* and *"pray"* commanded by Jesus in the context of *"enemies"* and *"those who spitefully use you and persecute you."* The Greek word "echthros" is translated *"enemies."* An enemy is a person who hates another and wishes him injury. It comes from the Greek word "echthos," meaning hostility, hatred, or enmity. There is no category worse than this. Jesus paralleled this with the person who spitefully uses you. It is a translation of the Greek word "epereazonton" and comes from the Greek word "epereazo," meaning threat, misuse, or revile. It expresses the sense of verbal abuse, insult, or the use of foul, abusive language against you. Peter used it as "accusing falsely" (1 Peter 3:16). The language is radical; it presents intense hatred and bitterness. Jesus speaks about the same person who is an enemy, describing a person who hates you. This spiteful person's sole objective is to inflict harm on you. Is there a better setting to demonstrate the appetite of God? Love is blaring amid hate. We must display forgiveness in bitterness!

Loving my enemies is not a philosophical or theological proposition. Jesus takes us to the marketplace of our lives. If religion does not work on the streets, it is merely platitudes. The Apostle Paul wrote an entire chapter on the reality of this truth (1 Corinthians 13). Great sounding messages spoken with the abilities of angels are hollow, empty words unless the throbbing appetite of God, love, is expressed (1 Corinthians 13:1). Our understanding of the mysteries of the universe, the scientific knowledge of the materialistic world, and the spiritual insight of a theologian are all superficial if the heart of God, love, is not demonstrated amid extreme persecution and hatred (1 Corinthians 13:2). All compassionate ministry consisting of shelter, food, and medical care is a bandage on the hurts of life, unless the healing oil of God's love, agape, is present (1 Corinthians 13:3). It is His appetite!

We see this demonstration in the life of Stephen (Acts 7:54-60). But this was a repeat of what we see in the life of Christ. Jesus prayed for His tormentors while they drove spikes through His hands and feet. *"Jesus said, 'Father, forgive them, for they do not know what they do'"* (Luke 23:34). The Greek word "lego," translated *"said,"* is in the imperfect tense, suggesting Jesus kept praying, kept repeating the expression of God's heart. The cruel torture of crucifixion could not silence Jesus' prayer for His enemies!

Jesus' prayer for His enemies is a picture painted in the extreme, but they saw it repeatedly in their daily encounters with Him. Did Jesus not feel the betrayal of Matthew, the tax collector? Matthew manipulated, cheated, and consistently lied for his selfish benefit. Surely Jesus understood the depth of sin in Matthew's betrayal. Why would Jesus cross the street to confront him? Why would Jesus disregard all that Matthew did, and in a simple invitation, suggest, *"Follow Me"* (Matthew 9:9)? Was not Matthew the enemy to everything God proposed for Israel? Jesus' call was not one of mere forgiveness or toleration. He invited Matthew into intimacy with Himself! His enemy became His traveling companion; His enemy rose to be God's instrument to portray the gospel account accurately! Is this the heart of God? Is this what it means to *"love"* and *"pray"* for *"those who spitefully use you and persecute you"*?

In response to Jesus showing Matthew the love of God, a Pharisee asked, *"Why does your Teacher eat with tax collectors and sinners?"* (Matthew 9:11). Jesus said the answer was in the appetite of God's heart. He said, *"Those who are well have no need of a physician, but those who are sick. But go and learn what this means: 'I desire mercy and not sacrifice.' For I did not come to call the righteous, but sinners, to repentance"* (Matthew 9:12-13). Is the appetite of God hungry only for mercy, not sacrifice? According to religious requirements, the activity of sacrificial offerings is not the passion of God's heart. Mercy drives God. Whether He says this in *"love"* or *"pray,"* is it not the same demonstration?

Jesus presented a chapter of teaching and spiritual training for His disciples (Matthew 18). He spoke to these men in the context of their seeking position in the kingdom and trying to make themselves look worthy by extravagant accomplishments. In the midst of it, Jesus told a simple parable. A shepherd discovers one sheep missing from his flock. He leaves the ninety-nine, risking his life in the night hour to rescue the missing one (Matthew 18:10-14). The rescuing of this one brought more joy to the heart of the shepherd than the ninety-nine who were secure. His action is an expression of the Father's appetite, His passion. We protect, fight, and promote ourselves; He risks, pours out, and dies for others, demonstrating *"love"* and *"pray."* Could I *"love"* like this without *"pray"* like this? Will this not dictate the content of my prayer life?

Prayer Determined

We are to view praying for someone as a personal expression of the heart. Prayer is not a ritual or physical activity we achieve. It is not an appointed time of day or part of a checklist that gives us pride upon completion, or an option to spare us from the responsibility of relating lovingly to our enemy. In other words, we are not to develop culturally acceptable physical practices as expressions of love. We are not to "walk away" from our enemy; we are to "embrace" him. God does not practice love by allowing the sun and the rain to come to those He likes and not to those who are His enemies. God expresses His sincere inward heart. He exhibits in the physical what is reality in His heart, His appetite!

This brings us back to the basic premise of the Sermon on the Mount. We must embrace our helplessness to merge with His nature. This is the Kingdom person! The Kingdom is a relationship of intimacy, a merger with the heart of God so we can become an expression of His nature. He does not remove our helplessness; we live in the constant awareness of our helpless reality. This constant acknowledgement is the response that allows Jesus to invade our lives. We become an expression of God's love nature. We have His appetite and share His hunger.

This merger determines *"love"* and *"pray."* If *"love"* is the appetite of His nature, this will express itself in the content and focus of our *"pray."* A person must not live in the state of "I am doing my best." Although we grow into spiritual maturity and knowledge, knowing His heart is an encounter with Him. We are without excuse, such as "I just had a bad day." "Agape love" becomes the craving of our existence, as it is for Him. If we miss this, we miss Him. **Love"** and *"pray* is not optional in Christian experience but is the foundation of all that is considered Christian.

Perhaps an adequate challenge for this moment would be to view the content of your prayers! Are your prayers self-focused? Do you pray for comfort either for yourself or for those in your care? Do you find anger toward others slipping into your prayers? Do you complain about others, or does your heart weep? Are you so motivated with love in your prayers that you find yourself becoming the answer to them? Do you join Jesus in the Garden of Gethsemane, overcoming physical comfort to participate in the will (appetite) of His Father (Matthew 26:36-46)?

Perhaps the place to answer these questions is to see your situation in relationships that involve conflict. How are you

Part Six: Fulfillment of the Kingdom - The Application: Motive

relating? Is your *"love"* and *"pray"* an expression of His nature in that situation? Allow Him to merge with you more intimately. Focus on Him and who He is. Allow Jesus to bring you into a level of oneness not yet experienced. He must do this in you; you cannot do it for yourself! Surrender!

Matthew 5:45

PURPOSE OF THE APPETITE

"that you may be sons of your Father in heaven; for He makes His sun rise on the evil and on the good, and sends rain on the just and on the unjust" (Matthew 5:45).

We must never lose sight of the premise of the Sermon on the Mount. Jesus' message opens with the Beatitudes (Matthew 5:3-12). "Merger" is the fundamental truth that profoundly echoes throughout the remainder of the sermon. The merger is the **"poor in spirit"** with **"shall be comforted."** The helplessness of man is merged with the resource of God, combining God's nature with our nature forming a new creature. Together we become "the Kingdom of God." God decided not to be the Kingdom on His own; we are incapable of being the Kingdom on our own. In Christ, we become the person God destines us to be. What an opportunity!

Jesus describes the life of the Kingdom person as **"exceeding righteousness."** This righteousness exceeds the righteousness within the boundaries of the old covenant, **"the righteousness of the scribes and Pharisees"** (Matthew 5:20). Jesus gave six illustrations to help us understand this thought. Every arena of life is covered and highlighted in these six examples. The first five are not the same as the final sixth. The biblical principle of our physical being as the platform for the demonstration of our spiritual life is clearly explained in the first five illustrations, each beginning with physical activity.

Part Six: Fulfillment of the Kingdom - The Application: Motive

The first illustration is ***"You shall not murder"*** (Matthew 5:21-26), an old covenant standard. ***"You shall not commit adultery"*** begins the second illustration (Matthew 5:27-30). The third speaks of marriage and ***"a certificate of divorce"*** (Matthew 5:31-32). The act of ***"swearing falsely"*** involving God in an oath becomes the physical act of the fourth illustration (Matthew 5:33-37). The fifth illustration, ***"an eye for an eye and a tooth for a tooth"*** (Matthew 5:38-42), concerns the standard of fairness involving revenge or justice.

In each of these five illustrations, the pattern is to examine the source causing the physical responses. Jesus internalizes man's response as an expression of his inner appetite. The solution to this problem is not that we change or manage our outward expression, but that we encounter the nature of God. When we acknowledge and embrace our helplessness, we become open to God invading our nature with His nature. We must express God's nature, His appetite, in our actions. Revealing His nature flows from the merger between God and man, the new creature called the Kingdom.

Although the sixth illustration in no way contradicts this premise, it does not begin with an outward activity. Jesus said, ***"You have heard that it was said, 'You shall love your neighbor and hate your enemy'"*** (Matthew 5:43). Each of the other illustrations reveals that we are needy in the motive of our lives. Jesus seems to say in this final illustration that we start with our inner motive. Have we learned His lesson? We must not defend our outward actions as fair and necessary, but go beyond the physical circumstances and look at the cause. Instead of saying, "I did the right thing" can we look at our appetite? Do we have the appetite of God? Can we cease to be rule-oriented to become heart oriented? Is God's purpose for us more than correct physical activity? He desires that we want what He wants! He wants sons!

Necessity

Jesus said, *"That you may be sons of your Father in heaven"* (Matthew 5:45). This phrase begins with the Greek word "hopos," translated *"that,"* a purpose clause. "Hopos" is a purpose conjunction indicating the goal or aim of the action denoted by the word, phrase, or clause to which is it joined. It is only in the New Testament with the subjunctive verb indicating the ultimate purpose, "to the end that" or "in order that." Therefore, *"love your enemies, and pray for those who spitefully use you and persecute you"* is intertwined with the premise of the Sermon on the Mount. The motive of God's nature, an appetite of love merging with the core of human life, is for birthing us as *"sons of your Father in heaven."*

The appetite of God is necessary for God to fulfill His purpose in your life. In light of the context of the first five illustrations, Jesus does not suggest a new rule. He does not propose the act of loving our enemies will put us in the position of being sons of God. He presents an impossibility; we are incapable of loving our enemies. Therefore, we must merge with God's nature to becomes sons of God who love their enemies. This act of love is an expression of God's appetite or hunger. We give expression to His nature.

Engrained in the proposition is the necessity of merging with God's nature. We cannot be sons of God without loving our enemies; we cannot love our enemies without being sons of God. In times past, people have asked the question, "What would Jesus do?" The error of such a pursuit is in the suggestion of "doing." Loving your enemies is not a discipline that allows a person to declare forgiveness for the enemy; it is a reality of investment in forgiving the enemy. To forgive my enemy, I must be involved in his or her life, which allows them to experience my forgiveness.

Part Six: Fulfillment of the Kingdom - The Application: Motive

In the fifth illustration (Matthew 5:38-42), Jesus gives four proposals regarding this involvement. When your enemy insults you (Matthew 5:39), you are to turn the other cheek, which invites interaction with him, allowing him to experience your forgiveness. The enemy who wants to sue you will never know the nature of God unless you express your love for him by giving him your cloak also (Matthew 5:40). The person who demands you go with him one mile will only know the love of God if you go with him the second mile (Matthew 5:41). Can the person who takes advantage of you experience God's nature through your embrace of his selfish act (Matthew 5:42)?

No human can learn, develop, or manufacture God's expression of love. We only receive it from being *"sons of your Father in heaven."* We must love our enemies; loving our enemies is birthed in us by God's nature as sons who love our enemies. Engrained in Jesus' proposal is the necessity of merging with God's nature. When we focus on the merger between God and us, that merger is the necessary expression of love in our relationships. We are never without our helplessness! We must embrace it.

Nurtured

Jesus said the purpose is *"that you may be sons of your Father in heaven."* The main verb translated *"may be,"* is the Greek word "ginomai," which means "to become." It has to do with entering or assuming a specific state or condition. Since it is in the subjunctive mood, it indicates it may be conditional. It is possible when we are dependent upon the nature of the Father, who enables us to express His love to our enemies.

The Greek word "ginomai" focuses on the origin or coming into existence. This verb is a middle deponent (adjective of a verb) indicated by the closing form "mai." The verb is middle in form because there exists no active form for a particular principle part in Hellenistic Greek, but whose meaning is active. Therefore, we must treat this verb as being in the active voice. Our response to the Father's appetite of love for His enemies expands and nurtures within us the state of being a son. As every son matures in the knowledge and ways of his father, so we are more and more embracing His nature. He is "fathering" us in His appetite! The issue is our response!

The verb "ginomai" is in the aorist tense. There is nothing like it in the English language. This tense does not focus on "when" the action of the verb occurs but on the occurrence. The nurturing of the Father in our lives does not happen in the past or future. We live in the constant occurrence of the Father's nature, spurring us into His likeness. His appetite hungers to love His enemies; as we respond to this appetite, we become more like Him. The Trinity God nurtures us!

There are passages throughout the Scriptures that highlight this process in Jesus. At the age of twelve, He submitted to His parents. He lived in Nazareth until the beginning of His ministry at age thirty. Luke records, **"And Jesus increased in wisdom and stature, and in favor with God and men"** (Luke 2:52). Was He not a boy who was nurtured by the nature of God in His son position? The writer of Hebrews relates insight into the life of Jesus. All Bible scholars agree he was obedient in the Garden of Gethsemane. The author writes, **"Though He was a Son, yet He learned obedience by the things which He suffered"** (Hebrews 5:8). They were not saying that Jesus went from disobedience to obedience. It is clear He was without sin (Hebrews 4:15). However, as Jesus faced the cross in the garden, He entered into a new circumstance that required additional response. This response to His Father nurtured Him in His position as son. He gave total expression to love your enemies!

The love chapter (1 Corinthians 13) ends with this concept. The qualities of God's loving nature are expressed vividly in this chapter. ***"Love suffers long, and is kind; loves does not envy; loves does not parade itself, is not puffed up; does not behave rudely does not seek its own, is not provoked, thinks no evil; does not rejoice in iniquity, but rejoices in the truth; bears all things, believes all things, hopes all things, endures all things"*** (1 Corinthians 13:4-7). Paul climaxes with the wonder of a child becoming a man. We must put away childish things. He pictures this as moving from seeing in a mirror dimly to encountering face to face. He contrasts this wonder as ***"Now I know in part, but then I shall know just as I also am known"*** (I Corinthians 13:12). Is this not the wonder of the Father's nurture? He fathers us into His image. We are more and more becoming an expression of His nature; we hunger for that which He hungers! We have His appetite. We respond to His desires, and He shapes us into His likeness! This is our destiny!

Native

"That you may be sons of your Father in heaven" (Matthew 5:45) is the purpose clause stated by Jesus. The focus of the purpose is ***"sons,"*** a predicate nominative, meaning that ***"sons"*** follows the verb and relates to the subject of the clause in equal manner. Therefore, ***"sons"*** and ***"you"*** are equated; they are the same. The Greek word "huios" is translated ***"sons."*** It is used 379 times in the New Testament and is only spoken of as related to man, contrasted with "nothos," which is an illegitimate son (Hebrews 12:8).

"Huios" is the strongest imagery used in the New Testament for the new creature, the Kingdom person. It relays the picture of the merging of the Father's nature with the son. The son possesses his distinct personality from the father, but the DNA of the father formed and shaped him. It pictures not only the forming of the person but also the nurturing aspect already discussed. It depicts a relationship unlike any other. It is beyond the idea of "brother," "servant," or "employee," and highlights a unique love connection between the two. We are *"sons!"*

John begins his Gospel account with a presentation of this intimate connection. ***"But as many as received Him, to them He gave the right to become children of God, to those who believe in His name: who were born, not of blood, nor of the will of the flesh nor of the will of man, but of God"*** (John 1:12-13). Notice the explosion of these words, ***"Behold what manner of love the Father has bestowed on us, that we should be called children of God! Therefore the world does not know us, because it did not know Him. Beloved, now we are children of God; and it has not yet been revealed what we shall be, but we know that when He is revealed, we shall be like Him, for we shall see Him as He is"*** (1 John 3:1-2). Paul echoes this cry, ***"For as many as are led by the Spirit of God, these are sons of God. For you did not receive the spirit of bondage again to fear, but you received the Spirit of adoption by whom we cry out, 'Abba, Father.' The Spirit Himself bears witness with our spirit that we are children of God"*** (Romans 8:14-16).

Again, we must remind you that this merger is the premise of the Sermon on the Mount. The merger of His nature with our poverty-stricken nature creates a new creature. This new creation is the new species of humanity called "sons of God." There has never been, nor will there ever be anyone like these men merged with God. They think like the Father, feel like the Father, have the appetite of the Father, share the desires of the Father, and the Father nurtures them. They are "sons!" There is no greater privilege; this is the destiny of our creation.

Need

Jesus placed the position of being a son in a unique context or atmosphere ***"that you may be sons of your Father in heaven."***

In light of the merger, the premise of the Sermon on the Mount, why would He place the essence of the Father in heaven? Why did He not picture the Father as in the spirit of our being or our hearts? *"Your Father in heaven"* is repeated throughout and is a pattern of reference for the sermon.

Jesus introduced this phrase in the "Function of the Kingdom." We are to let our light shine *"that they may see your good works and glorify your Father in heaven"* (Matthew 5:16). Jesus repeats the phrase at the close of the sixth illustration as the climax. *"Therefore you shall be perfect, just as your Father in heaven is perfect"* (Mathew 5:48). *"Your Father in heaven"* (Matthew 6:1) judges and rewards charitable deeds. As Jesus instructs us to pray, *"Therefore, pray: Our Father in heaven"* (Mathew 6:9). He establishes a link between what happens in heaven with what happens on earth (Matthew 6:10). The treasures we cling to must be *"treasures in heaven"* (Matthew 6:20). When He discussed worry, He reasoned in the generosity of *"your heavenly Father"* (Matthew 6:26, 32). Jesus exclaims the goodness of *"your Father who is in heaven"* for His children (Matthew 7:11). Jesus urges us to do *"the will of My Father in heaven"* (Matthew 7:21). Due to the frequency of Jesus' use of this phrase, we must view our position as sons in light of *"your Father in heaven."*

What is the significance of *"your Father who is in heaven"*? *"Heaven"* is a reference to authority regarding that which has power over humans and lies beyond their control. The idea of "below" and the things located there are defined in distinction or contrasted to "above." God and heaven belong together. Heaven shares in the inherent power of God, His authority. *"Heaven"* represents the sovereignty of God.

"Sons" are under the nurturing control and power of God. Whatever is going on in the Father must happen in the son! By the definition of being birthed as a son, we must come under the authority of His appetite. The Father's loving nature *"makes His*

sun rise on the evil and on the good, and sends rain on the just and on the unjust" (Matthew 5:45). The son does not dictate to the Father. God's nature and motive, his appetite, become the driving force of life.

Our most significant concern for the church movement in this hour is the reversal of this reality. Everyone embraces the greatness of being children of God. We sing the idea of being sons of God in our songs and repeat it in our sermons. But what kind of sons do we think we are? Have we become four-year-old children whining for a hot dog? Are we children who do not want to go to bed at night? Have we become self-centered in our sonship? Does our prayer life reflect a focus on ourselves and our comfort? We desire to use the gifts of the Spirit for our benefit. I should never get sick; I should never have a trial; I should always be successful; I should never have financial difficulty. All my enemies should receive the wrath of God; I should not because I am a son.

Matthew contrasts a son without any problems with a son coming to the Father in his work clothes. He wants to be a part of the Father's enterprise, and what the Father wants becomes the son's plan. If a cross is needed to accomplish the Father's heart, the son will volunteer. The son is under the controlling appetite of the Father, not the whims of his self-will. He has the perspective of the Father, longs for the things of the Father, thinks like the Father, and expresses the desires of the Father.

The picture of *"sons of your Father in heaven"* is beautiful, but it is imagery. The reality is that if you do not love your enemy, you do not qualify as a son. It is not a rule we must keep or a criterion to achieve. It is a quality of the Father's nature now sourcing your life. If you do not hunger for this, then you do not have the Father's appetite. Having the Father's nature is the atmosphere or position of a son. If we say we are a son but yet a prodigal, we admit our appetite is not His. We love the pigpen, not the righteousness of the Father, nullifying our sonship. We have squandered our right of inheritance.

Part Six: Fulfillment of the Kingdom - The Application: Motive

We are not to obsess on rules to obey; we have a nature of possession. Let us focus on Jesus; let us go after His nature; let us seek Him with our whole heart! In the fulness of Jesus' presence, we dwell as sons!

Matthew 5:45

I AM CAUSED

"that you may be sons of your Father in heaven; for He makes His sun rise on the evil and on the good, and sends rain on the just and on the unjust" (Matthew 5:45).

Jesus calls His disciples to a new level of righteousness in the Sermon on the Mount. All they have known is the righteousness of the scribes and Pharisees. **"For I say to you, that unless your righteousness exceeds the righteousness of the scribes and Pharisees, you will by no means enter the kingdom of heaven"** (Matthew 5:20). This new level is not a righteousness man can develop or eventually achieve. It is a righteousness that must be present, or we cannot cross the threshold of the kingdom.

Jesus gave six illustrations concerning this righteousness. He based His authority in each illustration upon **"But I say to you!"** The strength is the helpless Man filled with the Spirit, Jesus, the One living the reality of each illustration. No other argument is needed. If anyone wants to cry, "This is an impossibility for man," Jesus disputes this claim by His Person. He is a helpless Man filled with His Father. He is the first Kingdom person!

However, in the sixth illustration, Jesus adds strength to His challenge, **"love your enemies . . . and pray for those who spitefully use you and persecute you"** (Matthew 5:44). The purpose of Jesus' challenge is **"that you may be sons of your Father in heaven"** (Matthew 5:45). These two things are linked. No one can love their enemies without being a son of the Father in heaven, and no one can be a son of the Father in heaven without loving their enemies. Being a son and loving enemies is the heart of the Father. Being a son and loving enemies come from the Father's DNA; His appetite brings the reality of each! We dare not claim God as our Father while we hate our enemies; we dare not claim to love our enemies if we are not sons of our Father! Although the link between the two is secure, neither causes the other. Both are a product of something beyond us.

Jesus explains and highlights the truth in His next statement. The cause is, *"for He makes His sun rise on the evil and on the good, and sends rain on the just and on the unjust"* (Matthew 5:45).

Cause
Sovereignty of His Nature

The beginning Greek word "hoti," translated "for," is a causal subordinate clause, which expresses the cause of the related verbal action. Jesus stated the imperative of **"love your enemies."** The purpose is the expression of being **"sons of your Father in heaven."** But the reality is that no one is adequate to accomplish either of these things. I am incapable of loving my enemy as I am equally incapable of making myself a son of God. The hopelessness of this situation is in my helplessness. We are back to the premise of the Sermon on the Mount. I am helpless at the core of my being. I am created by God to be dependent, not independent. The poverty of my inner spirit convinces me of my helplessness (Matthew 5:3). I must embrace my helplessness and be embraced by it. Jesus likened helplessness to grief (Matthew 5:4). As I am overwhelmed by grief in the death of a loved one, my helplessness must envelop me. I must always be aware of my helplessness, live within its boundaries, consistently acknowledge its reality, which will allow Jesus to fill me with His comfort.

In my inadequacy to love my enemies, I must experience the sovereign nature of God. How does God respond to those who rebel against Him? We must not take the word *"enemies"* (echthros) casually. Jesus used it in the sense of a person who hates another and wishes him injury. It is not feelings of dislike but contains the intention of harm. The Greek word comes from the word group of "hate," "hostility," or "enmity," the opposite of the "loved one," or "beloved." How does God feel or respond to His enemy? He responds to them the exact way that He responds to His beloved. There is no difference. If this is true of extreme opposites, it must be valid for all that is contained in-between these extremes!

The Sermon on the Mount is the greatest sermon Jesus ever preached. He expressed it in heated preaching, sermonizing outlandish commands of love. He based it on the love of God, but the saying does not make it true. How do I know what God is like? Jesus goes to the fundamental experiences of nature. In His illustration of God's heart, He points to the unquestioned sovereignty of God's nature. God, who is the Creator of all things, is in charge of nature's expression. He decides to respond to the "beloved" and the "enemy" in the same manner regarding the crucial issue of sunshine and rain. The driving force of His nature will not allow Him to withhold from His enemy what He freely gives to His "beloved!"

God's manner of response to the "beloved" and the "enemy" is His appetite (motive). His sovereign nature hungers for everyone's best. In His sovereignty, there is nothing or no one beyond Him causing His response. This is who He is! His nature, which is His appetite, drives Him. He can respond in no other way. To deny this, we must alter the makeup of God's nature and produce a god of our choosing. God responds to the vilest sinner in the same way He responds to the most righteous saint. He makes no distinction between them!

If this is true in nature's underlying fundamentals, what is true in redemption's fundamentals in the spiritual realm? It is the heart and definition of "grace." God does not pick and choose those He will forgive based on their worthiness. He does not allow talent, success, merit, or achievements to determine His response. He does not decide to be closer to some than to others because He likes them more. All He wants for those we consider the best He aggressively wants for those we consider the worst. He does not distinguish between *"the evil"* and *"the good."* Nor does He make adjustments between *"the just"* and *"the unjust"* based upon who He is!

It is not hard to fathom this to be true of God. But what is unreal is that this can be true of me. Everything true about God's heart can become true about my heart. The only feasible means for such a reality is the merger between my helplessness and God's sovereign nature. Can I be filled with Him?

Condition
Significance of His Ownership

The sovereignty of God is an ownership sovereignty. Jesus said, *"His sun." "His"* is a genitive pronoun showing the relationship between the subject and the *"sun."* The relationship is possession due to creation. God began His revelation by saying, *"In the beginning God created the heavens and the earth"* (Genesis 1:1). The first ingredient of creative activity is *"Then God said, 'Let there be light'; and there was light"* (Genesis 1:3).

Though we do not have a complete understanding, it is easy to grasp the relationship between the sun and God. In the Book of Revelation, there is a reference to Jerusalem not needing the sun. *"The city had no need of the sun or of the moon to shine in it, for the glory of God illuminated it. The Lamb is its light"* (Revelation 21:23). Is there a correlation between God using the physical sun to display light in our world and the glory of His indwelling presence using us to shine His light to all individuals?

It is not feasible that the sun would act against its nature and refuse to shine. Science gives us the details of the sun's chemical structure and the reason it provides light continually. Jesus said, "Is this not true with God?" Does not the nature of God's loving heart demand His love for the saint and the sinner alike? Would not the structure of God's nature have to be altered for this love not to be extended?

If God created and owns the sun, does not His nature dictate the shining of its light? How much more is this true of you if you are His? The only possibility for you not to love your enemies is to reject God's ownership of your life. Perhaps we struggle with issues and questions already settled. Am I going to love my enemies? If you belong to Him, you have resolved this question. Your helplessness filled with His nature in the merger will love your enemies. Will I forgive those who offend me? If you belong to Him and are an expression of His nature, forgiveness is automatic. All six of Jesus' illustrations rest on this ownership.

Although creation is a strong argument for His ownership of our lives, is not His redemption even greater? Does He not have a right to "own" my life twice? Once through creation and again that He brought me back from the lost. Am I not His? ***"Or do you not know that your body is the temple of the Holy Spirit who is in you, whom you have from God, and you are not your own? For you were bought at a price; therefore glorify God in your body and in your spirit, which are God's"*** (1 Corinthians 6:19-20). If, in my helplessness, I am possessed, owned, by His Spirit, will I not demonstrate His nature? If His sun shines on the evil and the good, how much more my merging with His heart will shine His love on the evil and good? His ownership demands and causes such love! I must surrender every hesitation or deviation from the expression of God's love to His ownership of my life. I am His!

Consistency
Steadfastness of His Righteousness!

Jesus described the sovereign ownership of God as the steadfast actions from His heart. This means His sovereignty is righteous in nature. Jesus said, ***"for He makes His sun rise on the evil and on the good, and sends rain on the just and on the unjust"*** (Matthew 5:45). The two main verbs in this statement are ***"makes rise"*** (anatello) and ***"sends rain"*** (brecho). Each verb is in the indicative mood, meaning a simple statement of fact without argument. Each is in the present tense, a state of being without any sense of completion or end, continuing to happen. God does not weary in this well-doing. Evil does not push Him to His limit, changing His pattern of action. The consistency of His nature's expression is steadfast!

This flares in the face of my childhood teachings. Although God may be merciful and full of grace now, beware of the coming day when His coffers of wrath are full, and He brings judgment on His world. Does not this statement of Jesus demand a new view of such suggestions? God will not shift in His treatment of good and evil, just and unjust. The sovereignty of God is an eternal righteous expression!

The Father does not respond or determine His action by what someone else does or does not do. He is sovereign. His heart determines His response; He does not react to the actions of others. God's nature determines His actions. Therefore, He always allows it to rain on the just and on the unjust and the sun to shine on the good and evil ones. The world's evil does not affect His righteousness. We are not this way, but He is! ***"If we are faithless, He remains faithful; He cannot deny Himself"***

(2 Timothy 2:13). The Trinity God cannot give expression to anything other than His character and nature!

The self-centered nature of humanity finds *"love your enemies"* impossible in a continual manner. There will be times when it appears such love is being expressed, setting hatred aside for self-benefit, but allowing the sun to shine on good and evil is simply not going to happen. Thus, the premise of the Sermon on the Mount becomes paramount in understanding Jesus. We are helpless. We have proved His point repeatedly. We are not able to allow constant love to flow to our enemy; our response to his evil and unjust treatment flows from our selfish nature. Our enemy determines our actions.

We must merge with the nature of God. We must allow God to cleanse our self-centered motive; the hungering heart of God must become our appetite. The desires of God must drive us. Once my heart and His heart become one, will I not cease to respond to the evil around me? Will the driving force of my life not be the expression of His passion? His consistency will become my consistency!

Compassion
Sharing of His Heart

Now we come full circle in the truth of the Sermon on the Mount. We must share His heart. The new level to which Jesus calls us is to experience the nature of God. His sovereignty wills a heart involvement with you and me, the intent of all six illustrations, but particularly this last one. It is a focus on the motive of the individual. How do you feel about your enemies? How do you feel about those who persecute you? We must all hang our heads in shame, knowing we do not love our enemies. At best, we offer ritual prayers for those who persecute us. How can we ever do better?

Part Six: Fulfillment of the Kingdom - The Application: Motive

The nature of God revealed in the physical world around us demonstrates His holiness. Indeed, **"God is love"** (1 John 4:8, 16). He has not invited us into oneness with His attributes. We are not encouraged to be God, for this has been our persistent problem. In our helplessness, we ignore who we are and act in cocky arrogance as one who is lord. We have responded as Simon, the sorcerer (Acts 8:18-19). We would buy or earn God's power and use it for our benefit. From the beginning, Jesus has proposed our helplessness in all six illustrations, sealing His proposal. We are incapable of entering the Kingdom of God because we cannot meet the standard necessary. What is the answer? We must share His heart!

God has not invited us to participate in His omnipresence. The angelic host does not share this quality, nor is it ever proposed for us. The Trinity God never suggests we should share His omniscience. The all-knowing ability belongs only to God. Even in heaven, we will not achieve such knowledge. God has not invited us to share in His omnipotence, a power beyond our comprehension or ability to manage. He has not given us a power that would destroy us!

However, Trinity God has cracked Himself open at the core of His oneness and invited us into an intimate relationship with His heart. He offers His nature to us! No one could have invented such an idea. No world religion even comes close to such a radical concept. God, who is love (agape), has invited us to be filled with His nature, which is love (agape). It is self-sacrificing, self-giving, selfless love. He never thinks about Himself. Without hesitation, He allows it to rain on the just and the unjust and shines His sun on the good and on the evil. He hangs on a cross and cries, **"Father, forgive them, for they do not know what they do"** (Luke 23:34). When we were without strength and incapable of meeting His standard, Christ died for us (Romans 5:6). He not only opens His nature to us, He aggressively pulls us, wooing us to His heart. He is the relentless

I Am Caused | **Matthew 5:45**

Lover of the universe who will not let you go. He wants to share His nature, heart, and all He is in Christ with you. A simple response of "yes" will be enough. Please be His!

Matthew 5:46

LOVE LEVELS

"For if you love those who love you, what reward have you? Do not even the tax collectors do the same" (Matthew 5:46)?

Love is the biblical message God proclaims to the world. The most memorized verse in the Bible states this fact. **"For God so loved the world that He gave His only begotten Son, that whoever believes in Him should not perish but have everlasting life"** (John 3:16). This statement is in the middle of a conversation Jesus had with Nicodemus, a ruler, and teacher of the Jews. It follows an illustration from the Old Testament Jesus used to highlight His mission. Jesus said, **"And as Moses lifted up the serpent in the wilderness, even so must the Son of Man be lifted up, that whoever believes in Him should not perish but have everlasting life"** (John 3:14-15).

The mention of a snake on a pole brought the Old Testament story to the mind of Nicodemus (Numbers 22:4-9). Because of rebellion against God, snakes invaded the nation of Israel. Moses was instructed by God to erect a bronze serpent on a pole. Everyone who looked at this serpent would live. It was a symbolic Messianic prophecy about Jesus. Jesus is the snake on a pole who brings life to those who embrace Him! God expressed His love for the world through Jesus. The love of God is not an attitude or emotional feeling but is the nature of His being that consistently influences every decision and action He expresses towards us.

No wonder John cried, *"God is love!"* (1 John 4:8, 16).

The reality that God is love has been difficult for me to embrace. I have been jaded by many human relationships where love was expressed but not experienced. The words of a person may have shown love, but the actions of that person did not. What they said gave the appearance of love, but I felt no love from them. These experiences caused me to be suspicious of God's love. I cannot embrace Him in the flesh; I must embrace Him by faith. How can I trust that His love is not on the same level as the love expressed by the humans in my life?

Although this is a hurdle that each of us must conquer, we must not allow it to present an impossible barrier. The premise of the Sermon on the Mount proposes that we experience love on a new level. In each illustration, Jesus proclaims that our lives become an expression of God's heart. In our helplessness, we are to merge with the Trinity God. This merger creates a new creation who is the Kingdom person. It is this new person who loves like the Trinity God loves. In other words, Christianity is not a new rule that demands a new love expression from us. Since we are helpless, this is impossible. It is the new creature, the Kingdom person, who becomes the avenue of this love. The issue is not turning the other cheek or going the second mile. The problem is merging and becoming an expression of the redemptive loving heart of God. If we accomplish the criteria of ***"pray for those who spitefully use you and persecute you,"*** we would not fulfill the dream of God for our lives. It is in oneness with Him that we become an expression of His love. In this final illustration, Jesus proposes that we are to ***"love your enemies and pray for those who spitefully use you and persecute you"*** and become expressions of ***"sons of your father in heaven."***

In our passage, I wish Jesus would call us to ***"love our enemies"*** without additional details. The suggestion of such an endeavor would allow me to work out the details on my own. I could adjust the idea to fit my philosophical approach to life and then develop excuses as to why I cannot *"love my enemies."* The problem with the passage is that Jesus formulates this love within a context. Let us investigate that context!

Compulsion of Love

Our passage verifies the compulsion of love (Matthew 5:46). Everyone at every level of society loves. The issue is not will you love, or will you not love; you have to love. In our passage, even tax collectors love. They do not love everyone, but they need to love someone. Jesus calls for a new level of love; it is a call to love on His level. Human nature compels everyone to love someone, but what boundaries or limits are we going to place on our love?

The issue in every relationship is love, which is questioned by many non-Christians. Many relationships do not require or know any love expression. For instance, there is a relationship between employee and employer. A corporation made up of a group of people you do not know may employ you. You have no love in those relationships. You never interact with them nor have any emotional feelings about them, but in the heart of the Christian, this seems illogical. As a Christian, you are to operate within the relationship of employee and employer as if God is your employer. We are to express in our relationship with our employer the same love existing in God's relationship with Jesus,. It is not an emotional feeling of love as with the tax collector, but an expression of God's heart through the believer who expresses through his work ethic the selfless, self-sacrificing love of God.

Onesimus was a runaway slave who became a Christian. Paul sent him back to his owner with a letter in the Bible known as the Epistle to Philemon. Paul's appeal is that within this relationship of master and slave, the love of Jesus must be present. Is the master to love his slave as Jesus loves him? Is this an emotional attachment or a divine expression? It is love on a new level! The slave, Onesimus, had run away from his master. His path intersected with Paul while Paul was in prison. Onesimus was converted to Jesus through this connection and was ministering to Paul. Paul writes, **"Therefore, though I might be very bold in Christ to command you what is fitting, yet for love's sake I rather appeal to you"** (Philemon 8-9a). It is not about a command for love; we must become the expression of God's heart. The master-slave relationship must move to a higher level, **"a beloved brother"** (Philemon 16).

The only eternal issue is relationship. If you fight and argue, let it be for relationship. Material things will not outlast this life, only relationship. One hundred years from now, the physical will be gone, but relationship will remain. At the heart of our relationship is love, the heart of eternal life. Therefore, it is the crucial issue of the temporal. So, is there any area of life in which love is not the key issue?

On the highest level (God's level), love is the issue. On the lowest level (tax collector) love is the issue. It is the essential element of life, both godly and ungodly, the compulsion of all life. No one can say that love does not apply to them for you cannot survive without love. As we study the Scriptures to discover the will of God, we are driven to the eternal value of relationships. Paul consistently proclaims the issue of reconciliation, capturing the motive that brought the Trinity God to the sacrifice of the cross. **"For if when we were enemies we were reconciled to God through the death of His Son, much more, having been reconciled, we shall be saved by His life"** (Romans 5:10). But this is not a mere theological truth to be preached. Paul says, **"And not only that, but we also rejoice in God through our Lord Jesus Christ, through whom we have now received the reconciliation"** (Romans 5:11). We know love and relationship in the present moment. It is the passion of God's heart!

Paul thundered this truth to the church in Corinth. The motive behind the actions of the Trinity God in Christ is to bring us into a relationship that we, in turn, might be ministers of relationship to each other. *"Now all things are of God, who has reconciled us to Himself through Jesus Christ, and has given us the ministry of reconciliation, that is, that God was in Christ reconciling the world to Himself, not imputing their trespasses to them, and has committed to us the word of reconciliation"* (2 Corinthians 5:18-19).

Reconciliation is not new information to us as we discovered this in the previous five illustrations in the Sermon on the Mount. Jesus begins with murder (Matthew 5:21-26). Although those of old were content not to murder, Jesus calls us to examine how we feel about each other. He challenges every demeaning view, places reconciliation with those who have something against us above offering sacrifices to God, and wants us to agree with our adversary. Those of old were content not to commit adultery (Matthew 5:27-30). The issue is not an activity to do, but a selfless love we have in our heart for others. Those of old were concerned about separating from their wives (Matthew 5:31-32). Jesus' concern is what we cause in each other. Those of old kept their word when God was involved (Matthew 5:33-37). Jesus declared honesty and truth as the foundation for relationships. Those of old were concerned about fairness (Matthew 5:38-43). Jesus saw every circumstance as the platform to develop relationships through the expression of love.

Compensation of Love

Now Jesus speaks about loving others in the context of rewards. *"For if you love those who love you, what reward have you? Do not even the tax collectors do the same"* (Matthew 5:46). The Greek word "misthos," translated *"reward,"* can be used in a positive or negative sense. There is a reward for worthy acts and retribution for wrong deeds. We must understand it as a real wage or payment. The idea is that love always has consequences, which Jesus proposes as *"reward."* Prevenient grace introduces all love is a result of the direct intervention of God. If God left humanity to its own devices, there would be no love, not even self-love. The only reason the ungodly man can love his family is that the Spirit of Jesus intervened. The tax collector loves within his group, but this is only because of the Spirit of God. All love anywhere, or any place, is traceable back to God.

If the tax collector loved on his level, he received compensation. Jesus used this example because of the hated position of the tax collector. The tax collector was a Jew who betrayed his people for the sake of financial gain. He received the right to collect taxes for Rome by bribing the right people. The officials set the amount of the tax to be collected. Anything the tax collector gathered above that amount was his gain. He was shunned and hated by all. The only friendship or love possible in his life, he confined to his small group of fellow tax collectors. Within this little cluster of people, he was able to foster and justify his lifestyle. He justified cheating and lying because his best friends had the same practice. He practiced *"love those who love you"* (Matthew 5:46). He forced himself to find love in the small group like him.

Jesus expanded the idea of rewards in the next chapter of the Sermon on the Mount. When I do charitable deeds to be seen, praised, and appreciated by others, what is my reward? It is limited to the admiration and honor attributed to me by the small group that sees my charitable deed. Therefore, *"you have no reward from your Father in heaven"* (Matthew 6:1). When I pray like the hypocrites, what is my reward? *"For they love to pray standing in the synagogues and on the corners of the streets, that they may be seen by men. Assuredly, I say to you, they have their reward"* (Matthew 6:5). Their reward is limited to the appreciation and honor among those who hear them pray.

Part Six: Fulfillment of the Kingdom - The Application: Motive

When you fast, do not be like the hypocrites who put on a sad countenance and disfigure their faces so those around them will be aware of their sacrifice of fasting. *"Assuredly, I say to you, they have their reward"* (Matthew 6:16). Their reward is limited to the appreciation and honor bestowed upon them by their fellow men who see their fasting.

What would happen in our lives if we enlarged our boundaries beyond the limits of our select group to *"love those who love you"* (Matthew 5:46)? If we were *"sons of your Father in heaven,"* and experienced His boundary of love, what would be our reward? Regarding charitable deeds, Jesus said, *"But when you do a charitable deed, do not let your left hand know what your right hand is doing, that your charitable deed may be in secret, and your Father who sees in secret will Himself reward you openly"* (Matthew 6:3-4). In the matter of prayer, Jesus said, *"But you, when you pray, go into your room, and when you have shut your door, pray to your Father who is in the secret place; and your Father who sees in secret will reward you openly"* (Matthew 6:6). As to fasting, Jesus said, *"But you, when you fast, anoint your head and wash your face, so that you do not appear to men to be fasting, but to your Father who is in the secret place, and your Father who sees in secret will reward you openly"* (Matthew 6:17-18).

What reward will we receive if we live in the lightest level of love, which is *"love your enemies?"* Our boundaries will expand from our small group, which is to *"love those who love you."* This expansion includes loving everyone. Jesus pushed the limits of love to be all-inclusive. What will be the reward? We will be *"sons of your Father in heaven."* We have His design, DNA, or birthing to be a son. The nature of the Father becomes our nature! In reality, *"He makes* (poieo) *His sun rise on the evil and on the good, and sends rain on the just and on the unjust"* (Matthew 5:45). Our reward is being a son! Therefore, the issue is about your goal; what do you want for a reward? Is it Him?

Do you want to be approved in your limited group, or do you want to be accepted by Him as a son and become an expression of His nature?

Choice of Love

So, what are the levels of love? There are only two! There is the tax collector who loves those who love him and being a son of God who loves his enemies. I have tried to make the third level. I want to love those who love me and tolerate those who are my enemies. I want to love those who love me and ignore those who are my enemies. I do not hate them or even despise them; I eliminate them from my life. I establish the boundaries of my love, and if you are not in my circle, I do not include you. I do the same thing within the fellowship of the church. I have my group where I am accepted and relate. If you are not in this circle, you do not exist; you may attend the same church but are not within the realm of my love.

The difficulty with the establishment of this third level is motive, which expresses the nature. It is the same as *"love those who love you."* It is a selfish, self-centered love that contributes to my wellbeing and desires. I love people in Africa; I give to missions. I help with the homeless; I give money to a mother who does not have food for her kids. Let us analyze the motive behind such expressions of love. These are all in the limited love of the tax collector, which is the lowest level of love. He has his small cluster of people he embraces and helps. They are people who do not condemn him and are like he is. Why does he love this group that loves him? They meet his needs, make him feel good, and give him a sense of acceptance or importance. Why do I love the people in Africa and give to missions? It makes me feel good about myself and convinces me I am a good person. So, the tax collector loves his group because he loves himself, just as

I give because I love myself. Therefore, both are an expression of self-love, which limits my boundary of love.

Therefore, there are only two groups or levels of love. You either have self-love or the love of the Father. If we are to be **"sons of your Father in heaven,"** we must be an expression of His nature. It is not a rule or performance we are to achieve. It is a nature we express. I must have His mind and think as He does, giving expression in all my relationships. My boundary of love must be extended from self-love to loving my enemies, pushing the boundary to include everyone. It is the nature of the Father.

I am helpless, **"poor in spirit,"** the premise of the Sermon on the Mount. I must embrace this helplessness, allow God to fill me with His nature, and in the merger, He creates a new creature called the Kingdom of Heaven. The merger gives me the DNA of God's divine nature. I am a son of God, loving as He does!

Matthew 5:47

THE GREET SIN

"And if you greet your brethren only, what do you do more than others? Do not even the tax collectors do so" (Matthew 5:47)?

There is considerable confusion among Christians and non-Christians about the concept of sin. What is a sin? Can anyone in this life come to a position of not sinning? Is there forgiveness for all sin? These are questions we consistently ask in one form or another that shape the fiber of our life's character. If we take a moment to think carefully about the issue from a biblical perspective, we could quickly resolve the matter. To gain such insight, we must come to surrender and openness to Jesus. The difficulty is in releasing our need to adjust, protect, or cling to our traditions, activities, or attitudes.

Does God forgive all sin? Jesus answered this question in His discussion with the scribes and Pharisees when He said, **"Therefore I say to you, every sin and blasphemy will be forgiven men"** (Matthew 12:31). He made only one exception to this statement, **"but the blasphemy against the Spirit will not be forgiven men"** (Matthew 12:31). Jesus presents us with the two-fold aspect of sin consistently highlighted throughout the Scriptures. There is no problem with the forgiveness of the deeds of sin. Jesus' death is adequately, abundantly, and extravagantly more than enough for the forgiveness of all deeds of sin. In the New Testament, God already provided forgiveness, and it is ours for the asking. **"If we** *confess our sins, He is faithful and just to forgive us our sins and to cleanse us from all unrighteousness"* (1 John 1:9).

However, there is another category of sin. We sin because we have the nature of sin. Jesus entitled it *"the blasphemy against the Spirit."* In the Greek language. there are no capital letters. Therefore, in English translations, the capitalization of *"Spirit"* is an interpretation. In the final conclusion, it may not matter either way. If we capitalize *"Spirit,"* it is a reference to the Holy Spirit. It is a reaction of rebellion against the wooing of the Spirit of Jesus. If we do not capitalize spirit, it is a reference to the human spirit, the heart nature of man in rebellion against God. Forgiveness for the deeds of sin is never a problem for Jesus. However, the rebellious nature cannot be forgiven but must be radically changed.

Jesus highlights the deeds of sin with the nature of sin in each illustration in the Sermon on the Mount (Matthew 5:21-48). Those of old were concerned about the activity or deed of murder (Matthew 5:21). Still, Jesus' concern was about the nature of man expressed in anger (Matthew 5:22), demeaning or belittling others (Matthew 5:22), and division (Matthew 5:23-26). Those of old concerned themselves with the deed of adultery (Matthew 5:27). Jesus exposed the condition of the heart where the nature of sin resides (Matthew 5:28).

The rebellious nature of sin continues through each illustration in the Sermon on the Mount, even to our present study. Those of old concerned themselves with loving those who were within the boundaries of their standard, culture, and race (Matthew 5:43). Their attitude was a direct result of the rebellious nature of sin, protecting and guarding its value and comfort, which is not the nature of God! Jesus said that *"your Father in heaven"* does not respond like this, making it evident that it rains on the just and unjust, and the sun shines on the good and the evil. There is no possibility of being *"sons of your Father in heaven"* without sharing His nature.

When we live in the fallen nature of sin, we love only those who love us. We always love for self-advantage and cater to our self-benefit. In Jesus' day, the tax collectors lived on this lowest level of sin expression. Their fallen nature of sin could not be changed unless they became sons of God, knowing the nature of God. A person can curb the activities of sin, sometimes eliminating them, primarily if it caters to self-benefit. We can apply discipline to our deeds to increase self-comfort. Although we can control the expressions of the selfish, sinful nature, we cannot control or conquer the sinful nature. The biblical answer to this problem is crucifixion. Paul said, **"I have been crucified with Christ; it is no longer I who live, but Christ lives in me; and the life which I now live in the flesh I live by faith in the Son of God, who loved me and gave Himself for me"** (Galatians 2:20). God has to crucify the sinful nature; only He can bring it to death. God cannot allow the sinful nature to survive!

Position

Personal greetings seem like a small and insignificant issue in our culture, which was not the case in the culture of Jesus' day. The ceremony of greeting someone in the Jewish culture held high significance concerning position. Matthew records the final public message preached by Jesus (Matthew 23). He had endured a day of controversy with the scribes and Pharisees, where they engaged Him with trick questions hoping to discredit and embarrass Him. Jesus took charge of the conversation and asked them a question. **"And no one was able to answer Him a word, nor from that day on did anyone dare question Him anymore"** (Matthew 22:46). With that settled, Jesus proclaimed His final statement to the public.

Jesus' concern was not for the scribes and Pharisees but for His disciples and the people (Matthew 23:1). In His final message, He described the scribes and Pharisees. His intent was not to correct their actions but to expose their attitude or self-centeredness, which drove their actions. He labeled it hypocrisy. Jesus illustrated this with their desire to **"sit in Moses' seat"** (Matthew 23:2). He went on to say, **"all their works they do to be seen by men. They make their phylacteries broad and enlarge the borders of their garments"** (Matthew 23:5). Jesus pointed out that they loved to sit at the head table at the feast or demanded the best seats in the synagogues (Matthew 23:6). Among these illustrations, Jesus said they also loved **"greetings in the marketplaces, and to be called by men, 'Rabbi, Rabbi'"** (Matthew 23:7). The greeting, in the marketplace or on the street, was a distinction to which rabbis raised claim because of the dignity of their office. The rabbis wanted first greetings and, therefore, publicly recognized as superior. Jesus' instructions included a change in greeting because there is a change in attitude and nature. **"But he who is greatest among you shall be your servant"** (Matthew 23:11).

According to Jesus, this desire for position was not only true with the cultural status of the scribes and Pharisees seeking superiority, but it was also true with the heathen tax collectors. Who do the tax collectors greet? They greet their brethren who validate their value and worth (Matthew 5:47). The only person valuable enough in my perspective to greet is that person within the boundaries of my **"brethren."** Therefore, the driving motive behind "greeting" is the nature of sin within me.

The principal characteristic of the sinful nature is self-centeredness. Some scholars consider the sinful nature as separate from its expression, always one of selfishness. Other scholars believe the sinful nature to be self-sovereignty. Therefore, the expression of self-centeredness is the expression of the nature itself. Either way, we must agree that "always thinking about yourself" is the core nature of all sinful deeds. We are born with this natural tendency. Our first tears were for ourselves. We did not consider our mother's suffering to bring us into this world. We focused on our needs and comfort. As we matured, we chose to live for ourselves instead of living for others. In surrendering to our selfish will, we gave the sinful nature power over us, and it quickly became the dominating force of our lives. Even our good deeds become sinful deeds when they are an expression of the passion of our lives, ourselves.

Jesus revealed one more area of living that gives expression to this nature of sin. We see it in the activities of the most sinful people in Jewish culture, the tax-collectors. These men were so focused on themselves and their gain that they sacrificed their people for self-benefit. They collected taxes for the Roman Empire but stole from their fellow Jews by adding to the amount Rome required. Their sin was so blaring they became hated by the entire Jewish culture. No one would greet them or honor them or acknowledge they existed. Therefore, the only greetings the tax-collectors participated in was with their group.

But just like the tax collectors, the most righteous and religious people of their culture did the same. The scribes and Pharisees wanted everyone to greet them first to show their superiority. They were so focused on themselves they did not acknowledge others around them. Even when they did greet another person, it was to someone superior in position to them, thus elevating their status. The self-centered, sinful nature within the tax-collector was also in the religious Pharisee. How were they different?

In the sixth illustration (Matthew 5:43-48), Jesus calls us to **"love your enemies."** My self-centered, sinful nature will not allow me to do this. My enemy is not within the boundaries of what is beneficial to me. For instance, for a Pharisee to love and greet a tax-collector would be detrimental to his position. It would be entirely outside the boundaries of his self-love. He is only interested in "greetings" that bring meaning and verify his position. The self-centered person has no desire to validate anyone unless it contributes to his or her status.

I must embrace my helplessness, the premise of the Sermon on the Mount. I am ***"poor in spirit"*** (Matthew 5:3). I have no position to protect or status to guard. God must fill me with the nature of Jesus. I want to think like Jesus thinks and feel like He feels. His Spirit is the Spirit of cross style. "Never ever think about yourself" is the burning motive of His heart. Jesus lets it rain on the just and on the unjust; He allows the sun to shine on the good and on the evil. He has no boundaries of exclusion, but He sees everyone as valuable and loves them. Jesus does not recognize the categories of ***"neighbor"*** and ***"enemy."*** I must become a "son" of this nature!

Provision

There was another positive aspect of "greeting" in the Jewish culture and teaching of Jesus. The person greeting gave a spiritual blessing to the person he greeted. This spiritual blessing was more of an emphasis of Jesus than His culture because He knew the importance of blessing and peace contained within the "greeting." The ministry of Jesus expanded quickly until multitudes of people were coming from everywhere. Even the foreign countries surrounding the borders of Palestine were bringing ***"sick people who were afflicted with various diseases and torments, and those who were demon-possessed, epileptics, and paralytics"*** (Matthew 4:24). In fact, ***"great multitudes followed Him - from Galilee, and from Decapolis, Jerusalem, Judea, and beyond the Jordan"*** (Matthew 4:25).

Jesus realized the need to duplicate His ministry. ***"But when He saw the multitudes, He was moved with compassion for them, because they were weary and scattered, like sheep having no shepherd"*** (Matthew 9:36). Jesus called His disciples to pray that

He might send laborers into the harvest. Of course, they became the answer to their prayers; He sent them. Before He sent them out, Jesus gave an entire seminar on ministry. In this training, He spoke to them concerning the significance of bringing someone into the boundaries of fellowship through "greetings."

The disciples traveled from city to city following the instructions of Jesus. When they entered a house, they were to *"greet it. If the household is worthy, let your peace come upon it. But if it is not worthy, let your peace return to you"* (Matthew 10:12-13). They were not to enter a city or house without the accompanying word of salvation, in the form of a greeting of peace, or angelic greeting (Daniel 10:19). Anyone accepting the greeting becomes a "son of peace;" anyone rejecting the greeting remained excluded from salvation. Jesus did not tell His disciples to be friendly. The greeting was not to be a token jester of acknowledgment but was a genuine activity happening in the spiritual realm. They were to allow the spiritual state of their lives to encompass those they greeted. Something mystical occurred in the spiritual world through their greeting.

The idea of *"peace"* proposed in the greeting is not a blessing and or the absence of discord. It involves embracing the source of peace, the King of Peace. It contains the fullness of "salvation" in Jesus. The greeting is presented quite realistically as a "dynamis," a Greek word translated "power." The resource of Jesus' Spirit moved upon the person greeted. The greeting became a blessing or a curse on the person greeted based on their receptivity or rejection. The greeting is thus a power with which the disciples could spread blessing but the withdrawal of which has the force of a curse. *"He called His twelve disciples to Him, He gave them power over unclean spirits, to cast them out, and to heal all kinds of sickness and all kinds of diseases"* (Matthew 10:1). Therefore, the greeting is a sacramental action!

Jesus calls us to *"love your enemies."* If you extend your spiritual life only to those who are within the boundaries of your preferred friends, you exclude all others from the known wonder of His presence in your life. You consciously deprive them of the avenue of salvation through which God can change their lives. When you exclude your enemy from your love, you block the Father from fulfilling His dream through you. If you do not have the mind of the Father, how can you claim to be ***"sons of your Father in heaven"***?

The self-centered carnal mind protects, guards, and clings, only sharing the power of God to those considered worthy. Such a nature shares only when it is personally beneficial, even if such benefit is feeling justified or superior. How easy it is to pass another and mutter the greeting, "How are you?" If you are not sincere in wanting to know, there is no expectation to share in their heartache or their joys. Such a nature is so engrossed in its interests and desires that no spiritual life is shared. You might even say self-centeredness can only share spiritual death.

What an opportunity we have to greet everyone who walks through the front door of our church on Sunday morning. We have the possibility of impacting every person with the life of Jesus as we touch them and share the peace of His presence. Do you not want to bless all who come, your friends and your enemies? It is the nature of the Father who births us! We are His sons! But expand it beyond the church you attend on Sunday. At the job, in the grocery store, and on the street, we have the opportunity to bestow a "spiritual" greeting upon everyone we meet. We can address the stranger who ignores us with the Jesus who lives in us. We are the avenue for the extension of Jesus' presence to every life we contact. What a privilege! But we do not have time. How much time does it take to extend the spiritual blessing of His presence on someone passing by you? But we do not think about it. Why? It is because we are so engrossed in our own needs and concerns, which is not the nature of the Father who brings life to us!

Will I allow the Spirit of Jesus to extend the boundaries of my influence to include those who are the furthest removed, my enemies? Will we be ***"sons of your Father in heaven"*** and let the sunlight of His presence shine on the evil and the good? Will we allow the rain of His presence to bring moisture to the just and the unjust?

Matthew 5:46-47

DOING BUT NOT DOING

"For if you love those who love you, what reward have you? Do not even the tax collectors do the same? And if you greet your brethren only, what do you do more than others? Do not even the tax collectors do so" (Matthew 5:46-47)?

The Pharisees' belief in Jehovah God was from a physical, external view. They were committed to the law, which shaped their perspective on external obedience. They were strict in their observance of the ceremonies and feast days, which through the generations, became a physical activity causing them to lose the heart of the celebration. If every Pharisee had been present when the death angel passed over Egypt, and the blood of the lamb had saved their lives, their hearts would undoubtedly have grasped the wonder of it all. But now, several thousands of years later, they went through the ceremonies without feeling or heart involvement.

Without knowing the Jewish culture, we see that the conflict between Jesus and the Pharisees reveals the truth about their heart involvement. Jesus often broke their oral traditions. He healed a man with a withered hand on the Sabbath Day (Matthew 12:9-14). The compassionate heart of God valued this man more than sheep making it necessary to heal him; however, the Pharisees considered it a violation of the law. Jesus' disciples picked grain and ate it on the Sabbath Day, disobeying the Pharisee's external law (Matthew 12:1-8). But it was entirely proper for God to be more concerned about mercy (an internal condition) than sacrifice (external obedience).

There was undoubtedly a conflict between Jesus and the Pharisees. He had many discussions with them that revealed their need to be seen by men. He exposed their hypocrisy in giving of charitable deeds, their prayers, and their fasting practices (Matthew 6). Jesus' exposure of the Pharisees may have been the reason they sought to eliminate Him by crucifixion. When the Pharisees' external activities led them to be seen by men, this limited their reward to just that, and they received no real bonus from the Father. After one encounter with the Pharisees, Jesus had a private conversation with His disciples. He said, ***"Do you not yet understand that whatever enters the mouth goes into the stomach and is eliminated? But those things which proceed out of the mouth come from the heart, and they defile a man"*** (Matthew 15:17-18). Included in the last public message of Jesus, He vividly explained the heart of the Pharisees. He said, ***"For you cleanse the outside of the cup and dish, but inside they are full of extortion and self-indulgence"*** (Matthew 23:25).

A fundamental principle of the six illustrations Jesus gave in the first chapter of the Sermon on the Mount is this reality of the external versus the internal. Each illustration strikes a blow at the external physical approach and highlights the inner heart motive. The Pharisee was content with not murdering, but Jesus focused on anger (Matthew 5:21-22). They proposed the moral standard of not committing adultery, while Jesus spoke of eliminating the inner heart of lust (Matthew 5:27-28). They based a person's honesty on the physical object he used for his oath. Jesus declared it was a matter of evil in the heart (Matthew 5:33-37). The Pharisees measured fairness by physical circumstances; Jesus wanted to redeem the person through the compassion of the redemptive heart (Matthew 5:38-42). Now in this last illustration, Jesus proposes the climax of this truth (Matthew 5:43-48).

Part Six: Fulfillment of the Kingdom - The Application: Motive

The Pharisee could not conceive how he could love his enemies. His neighbor was someone within the boundaries of his fellowship and love. Outside those boundaries, there was no motive or resource to cause love to exist. Jesus consistently reminds us of the Father, who has no limitations of love. He allows the rain to fall and the sun to shine on both the good and the evil. Even the worst of sinners, the tax-collector, loves within the realm of his boundaries. He loves those who love him and accepts those who accept him. He greets those who greet him but excludes all others. If we claim to be the righteous ones and do the same as the worst of sinners, how are we any better than them?

It becomes apparent in these verses (Matthew 5:46-47) that Jesus is discussing the nature of the person. The tax-collector cannot love beyond his boundary because his nature cannot do so. He does not have the nature of the Father. In these two verses, Jesus uses the Greek verb "poieo" three times. The difference between the Greek words "poieo" and "prasso" is long-standing in our studies. The translation of both Greek words is "do;" however, they are not the same. "Poieo" is intimately tied to the nature of the source of the doing, consistently used for trees "bearing" fruit. The fruit is a direct result of the nature of the tree. "Prasso" is also doing but is focused more on duty or activity. "Prasso" is never used in connection with Jesus. Since the Father sourced Jesus, He always acted from the Father's nature.

Look at what Jesus declares in our passage. ***"For if you love those who love you, what reward have you? Do*** (poieo) ***not even the tax collectors do*** (poieo) ***the same? And if you greet your brethren only, what do*** (poieo) ***you do more than others? Do*** (poieo) ***not even the tax collectors do*** (poieo) ***so?"*** (Matthew 5:46-47). The tax-collectors were limited to the sourcing of their nature. They could not produce fruit that was not in the capacity of their nature. Loving people outside their limited boundary of those who love them was an impossibility.

They could not greet those who were not their brethren. It was not within their nature to produce such fruit. Jesus does not give us a new rule to do (poieo), something that we cannot do (poieo). He calls us to a change from our self-nature to having the nature of the Father. With the Father's nature, loving their enemy would not be a problem; they were within the extended boundary of the Father's sourcing nature!

Why?

To properly understand this teaching of Jesus, let us investigate several questions answered by the word and concept of "poieo." The foundational issue of Christianity is not what you do, but why you do what you do? Sin is never defined strictly by the action of the deed. If the action of the deed defined sin, we could make a list of all sins and avoid doing them. Every act or deed has the potential of being a sin. The best deed one may do on their best day could be the worst thing they have ever done. The real focus is not the action of the deed but on the motive or source behind the deed. What drives you? What causes you to do what you do? What is the inner nature of your spirit that can accept your activity?

Jesus reveals the actions of ***"your Father in heaven."*** He said, ***"for He makes His sun rise"*** and ***"sends rain."*** There is purposeful involvement in the action of the sun rising and the rain falling. The Greek word "anatello" is translated, ***"He makes rise."*** The prefix "ana" means "up," and the root word "tello" means "to set out for a goal" or "cause to rise." These actions do not occur by neglect or accidentally. Jesus intends to characterize the inner nature of God through the everyday work of the sun and rain. Carefully, Jesus describes the selfish nature of the worst of sinners, the tax collectors. They only love those who love them and greet those who are their brethren.

Part Six: Fulfillment of the Kingdom - The Application: Motive

In the case of the Father and the tax collector, it is merely an expression of their inner nature. This inner nature is the same logic and argument Jesus used repeatedly. At the peak of the conflict between Jesus and the Pharisees, they accused Him of having a demonic nature. They cried, *"This fellow does not cast out demons except by Beelzebub, the ruler of the demons"* (Matthew 12:24). The Pharisees did not criticize Jesus' act of casting out the demon. Everyone applauds the deliverance of a person from the clutches of an evil demon. The Pharisees' issue was the action coming from Jesus. He openly discussed the matter with them. His advice was, *"Either make the tree good and its fruit good, or else make the tree bad and its fruit bad; for a tree is known by its fruit"* (Matthew 12:33). We must not deny the correlation between the inner nature of the tree and its fruit. A tree with a good nature cannot produce bad fruit; likewise, a tree with an evil nature cannot produce good fruit. We cannot mix them.

Then Jesus applies it to the Pharisees, *"Brood of vipers! How can you, being evil, speak good things? For out of the abundance of the heart the mouth speaks. A good man out of the good treasure of his heart brings forth good things, and an evil man out of the evil treasure brings forth evil things"* (Matthew 12:34-35). It is an undeniable truth that a person speaks from the nature of his heart. In the Sermon on the Mount, Jesus proposed the question, "Why?" Answering this question requires sincerity and complete honesty. How easy it is to blame circumstances, others, or all kinds of pressures. All of these other things only set the stage upon which we reveal our real nature. Without honesty at the deep level of our life, there is no hope for change.

What?

Immediately, the question shifts from "why?" to "what can I do about it?" The first hurdle in answering this question is the sinful nature itself. If we do what we do because of our inner nature, the inner nature must change. But the sinful nature is not opposed to this. It will make all kinds of adjustments to survive. The Pharisees were the real proof of this factor. The worst of sinners, the tax collectors, indeed expressed the evil nature. They were content with cheating their fellow countrymen by charging taxes far beyond what Rome required. They felt no remorse in betraying their faith in Jehovah by cheating their fellow countrymen. But the Pharisees expressed this same attitude in the religious realm. The self-benefit that drove the tax collector also was the motive behind the action of the Pharisee. The Pharisee merely adjusted his self-centeredness to create a self-righteousness. It remained an expression of the same evil nature.

What can I do about it? Is it possible Jesus said that we could not do anything about it? A nature change must take place. The Father must replace the old sinful, self-centered nature with His selfless nature, which I cannot do. If I cannot do this to myself, someone else must do it to me! But this makes total sense. If I could do it for myself, then I would take pride in what I did, expressing more of my self-centeredness. If someone else does this for me, I have to rely entirely on them and praise them for what they did.

Jesus challenges us to be like the Father. However, the sinful, self-centered nature may interpret this to mean "imitation." I reduce Christianity to a list of rules or activities that self accomplishes, catering to and expressing the old sinful nature. The call of Jesus is *"that you may be sons of your Father in heaven"* (Matthew 5:45). Son of the Father is a new species, a new creation. It is the merger Jesus expressed at the beginning of the Sermon on the Mount. We must embrace our absolute helplessness (Matthew 5:3). My helplessness must so overwhelm me that I live in a state of continual recognition of it (Matthew 5:4). The Holy Spirit activates His work within us to merge with us. In the merger between God and man, God creates a new creature, a son of your Father in heaven. Our mind and His mind come together in a fusion. His heart and our heart begin to beat together. We begin to want what He wants. We "poieo" as the Father!

When?

The self-centered nature tends to make the Father's nature a goal we must achieve. We state phrases such as "I am working on it" or "God's not done with me." No one would question that growth and maturity take place when we merge with the Father. However, the self-nature of doing will make excuses. It will compare the self-improvement of the present with the activities of the past. "I am better than I was" becomes the standard, reducing Christianity to "improvement" rather than "conversion." It is "adjustment" rather than "transformation."

Jesus convinces us that loving those who love us has no reward (Matthew 5:46). Even the worst of sinners can accomplish this. When we greet those within the boundary of our friendship, we are on the level with everyone else (Matthew 5:47). Again, even the worst of sinners do this. Does not the language of these statements convince us that this attitude and response is not acceptable in any form? I cannot embrace any excuse in these statements. Any expression such as "I am having a bad day," or "they pushed me too far" does not excuse a violation of this call.

As Jesus moves to a conclusion, the strength of the call becomes even more substantial. He says, **"Therefore you shall be**

perfect, just as your Father in heaven is perfect" (Matthew 5:48). The translation of the Greek word "eimi" is ***"shall be."*** It is a state of being. It is in the future tense and the imperative mood. Some translators state this as ***"must be."*** If we are kingdom people, this is the state in which we must dwell. Becoming a kingdom person is not a challenge to accomplish; this is a nature to experience, not a standard to maintain; this is a state resulting from the birthing of the Father. The ***"poor in spirit"*** who embrace their helplessness in mourning ***"shall be comforted."*** The nature of the Father produces (poieo) through the son, the expression of His heart. What a relationship!

Paul developed this same idea in his contrast between the "works of the flesh" and the "fruit of the Spirit." He gave a list under the heading of the ***"works of the flesh"*** (Galatians 5:19-21). It is not an exhaustive list, but each deed listed is an expression of the nature of self-centered evil. In great boldness, Paul said, ***"Just as I also told you in time past, that those who practice such things will not inherit the kingdom of God."*** As he focused on the ***"fruit of the Spirit,"*** he contrasted it with ***"works." "But the fruit of the Spirit is love, joy, peace, longsuffering, kindness, goodness, faithfulness, gentleness, self-control"*** (Galatians 5:22-23). He reminds us that none of these things violate the law. The ***"fruit"*** is a "poieo" concept. It is the very expression of the nature of the Holy Spirit, the Spirit of Jesus!

Where?

The final question answered by the "poieo" concept is "Where?" In what areas of my life should the nature of the Father give expression to His heart. The answer is all-inclusive. Since it is a state of being at the core of the individual's existence, the Father's nature must influence every area. Certain religions have attempted to separate the physical from the spiritual. In some sense, this was the continual battle Jesus had with the Pharisees. They excluded the inner mind and heart and accepted only a token of the expression of God's law in physical practices.

Having the nature of the Father is the heart of Jesus' argument as He gives these six illustrations (Matthew 5:21-48). In this study of these six illustrations of life, I have desperately attempted to find one area not included in the six examples. I have not been able to find even one. The nature of the Father must give expression through the son in every area of life. There is no area not affected by His presence. Jesus does not propose reform or adjustment; He calls for a new creature who is produced (poieo) by the Father. This new creature is an individual who embraces his helplessness and allows the Spirit of Jesus to merge with him. The new creature is the fusion of the two. The issue is not, "will I do it?" The problem is, "will I allow Him?"

In this sixth illustration, Jesus described the expression of the Father's heart nature. Isn't it exciting? He selects the physical rain falling and the real sun shining on every individual, both good and evil. He does not isolate the expression of the Father's nature, to religious activities, miracles, or spiritual gifts. It is the most common, everyday activities in which we experience the core of the Father's nature. No doubt, the purpose of this illustration is to instruct us. When we merge with Him, will He not express His character through us in the everyday, ordinary, routine functions of our lives? Is this not the real test of our relationship with Him? We all love the high moments of religious experience. However, Jesus calls us to be consistent in everyday living in the presence of His Spirit. The expression of "poieo" must be in our lives!

Matthew 5:48

PERFECT?

"Therefore you shall be perfect, just as your Father in heaven is perfect" (Matthew 5:48).

The last verse of this chapter begins with the coordinating conjunction, **"Therefore"** (Matthew 5:48), translated from the Greek word "oun." **"Therefore"** conveys a deduction, conclusion, summary, or inference to the preceding discussion. There is no physical activity involved at the heart of the illustration; instead, the focus is on loving your enemies. Does the previous study refer to only the sixth illustration or all six illustrations? Either consideration brings us to the same conclusion. The challenge of Jesus in our verse climaxes His teaching on the Kingdom's righteousness exceeding that of the Pharisees!

Jesus boldly challenges us to be perfect as the Father is perfect, making it impossible to reduce the strength of perfection. When a person discovers the perfection of the Father in heaven, he knows the required state for his existence. This perfection is not a list to perform or something to do but is a state of inner nature. It parallels the preceding discussion of the Father's nature and challenges us to be sons (Matthew 5:45). Jesus does not require us, nor does the Trinity God invite us, to possess the Divine attributes of omnipresence, omniscience, or omnipotence. He opens His heart to us that we might share in His nature!

If we arrive at the state of **"love your enemies,"** we will know the reality of the other five illustrations. The invasion of the Father's nature in our lives allows the boundaries of our love to be unlimited. It will no longer be a struggle to love those outside the boundary of the ones who love us. Greeting those who greet us will no longer limit us. However, the nature of the Father merging with us will not only achieve this, but it will also eliminate anger in the heart (Matthew 5:22). Belittling and demeaning those considered beneath us will be as repulsive to us as it is to the Father (Matthew 5:22). We will never be an adversary to anyone, even though we have adversaries (Matthew 5:25-26). The Father infuses our helplessness with His nature, bringing us to the reality of both the first and last illustrations.

The lust of the human heart that determines our perspective of others will be altered as well (Matthew 5:28). Lust is a form we use to establish the boundary of self-centeredness, living only within those limits. If the nature of the Father fills us, we will eliminate using others for self-benefit. When the Father's nature fills us, He transforms our marriages (Matthew 5:31-32), and His redemptive love causes newness in our marriage. The Father's honest heart becomes our integrity, and oaths will be unnecessary (Matthew 5:33-37). I can only turn the other cheek to the evil person when the Father's nature causes me to love my enemies, and His nature flows in and through my life (Matthew 5:39). Being in the state of **"sons of your Father in heaven"** (Matthew 5:45), allows us to answer the call of each of these illustrations.

Jesus said the heart of the Father is more than just lovely feelings about someone but is an enlarged picture of love. We cannot live in a passive state, indifferent to the actions and attitudes of others. We must always see His challenge in the context of **"your Father in heaven."** Jesus defined this state of the Father as **"perfect"** (teleios). We can gain vital insight into this word's depth from its use in the Septuagint, the Greek translation of the Old Testament. **"You shall be blameless** (teleios) **before the**

Lord your God" (Deuteronomy 18:13). The word "blameless" is a translation of the Hebrew word "tamin," meaning "whole" or "entire." In the context of this statement in Deuteronomy, God called the Israelites to wholeheartedness and to lack compromise with pagan practices, to set aside involvement with all things outside the boundaries of their relationship with Jehovah. They were to be "perfect" in this focus! They were to be "tamin" (whole) or "teleios" (perfect) with Yahweh, the Lord your God.

The desire of God's heart for those who are His has not changed. What He wanted in the Old Testament He asks anew in the New Covenant. The righteousness that exceeds the righteousness of the scribes and Pharisees is the call to "tamin" or "teleios." It is the cry for an unalloyed commitment to the will or heart of God. The scribes and Pharisees had a shortsighted vision of God's heart and a distorted view of His desires. Jesus did not come to destroy the Law or the prophets. He came to take us beyond this distortion to the throbbing heart of the Father. We are to be God's sons and know how He thinks, bringing about an uncompromising, unquestioned commitment and surrender to all God is in His nature. It will mean a desperate, passionate desire to embrace who He is, eliminating all selfish agendas. The goal of the Christian is not heaven, righteousness, victory, fruitful ministry, or gifts; the goal is the pure, unmarred heart of the Trinity God!

In the past, I have been overwhelmed with the demands of such a challenge. How can we stand before a group of people and make such uncompromising statements? Who will understand the depth of such a commitment? But I have since realized that our world is consistent in its demand for such focus. My basketball coach in high school stood before forty young men on the first day of practice and yelled, "This team will be number one in your life, or there is the door!" Making basketball my focus would determine my schedule, including hours of sleep, hours of practice, and study of basketball formations. There was no other way to produce a winning team. On his team basketball would consume my life.

The successful businessman is focused on his success, giving tireless hours and relentless efforts, demanding the same from those he hires. His employees must sacrifice for the same success. We admire this dedication in the musician. The long tireless hours of practice, the total commitment to developing skills, and the fearless determination for perfection are all qualities necessary for achievement. The marine at bootcamp hears this same challenge. Not everyone will survive the stressful demands of physical and mental training. Success is only for those who give everything! Jesus calls us to "perfection!"

In a previous study, we referred to the verb Jesus uses to present the necessary perfection. It is "esesthe," which is the future indicative of "eimi," the verb that gives a state of "being." Since it is the future tense and the indicative mood, it becomes an imperative, translated *"shall be."* However, it is *"shall be"* in the sense of "must be." Jesus presents the Kingdom of God, a new level of relationship and involvement with the nature of God, which establishes the righteousness that exceeds the righteousness of the scribes and Pharisees in a remarkable way (Matthew 5:20). This new righteousness goes far beyond that required for entrance into the Kingdom and not a righteousness we develop as we mature. The patterns and practices of righteousness may grow in maturity, but this righteousness is required to enter into this new state of being, the nature of the Father. Jesus said this in the Beatitudes, the beginning of the Sermon on the Mount. In the poverty of our helplessness, we can know His significant presence; in the merger of our helplessness and His nature, we become "sons!"

Perhaps we will better understand this subject of "perfection" as Jesus presents it if we see it in action; how will that look?

Communication of Life
Jesus

In the Sermon on the Mount, Jesus described His life! His life communicates the standard of living in being *"sons of your Father in heaven."* Throughout the Scripture, Jesus is the first, the prototype of the new species called "sons." Paul calls Him *"the image of the invisible God, the firstborn over all creation"* (Colossians 1:15). The wonder of that is in, *"For it pleased the Father that in Him all the fullness should dwell, and by Him to reconcile all things to Himself, by Him, whether things on earth or things in heaven, having made peace through the blood of His cross"* (Colossians 1:19-20). Is there any wonder we praise Him?

Jesus was the first human to be the visible image of the invisible Father. We can see in Jesus the life God destined for us. Jesus' sacrifice in birth and death established the new category. We merge with the heart and nature of God to become an expression of Him. Jesus' heart spilled forth in redemptive love, and so should ours. Jesus loved His enemies because of oneness with the Father, and we must do the same. We can live in victory over our evil world because Jesus did. We can demonstrate the perfect heart of the Father, just as Jesus did, living in the power of the Father's nature. Paul summarized the focus and purpose of his ministry when He said, *"Him we preach, warning every man and teaching every man in all wisdom, that we may present every man perfect* (teleios) *in Christ Jesus"* (Colossians 1:28).

Christlikeness is not a dream, goal, or heavenly experience. To be like Christ is not beyond the typical Christian's life but is the reality of every Christian. The cry of the Christian's heart is, *"Oh, to be like You!"* The plea of the Christian's will is, *"Let the beauty of Jesus be seen in me!"* The mindset of the Christian is, *"Oh, I want to know You more. Deep within my soul, I want to know You, to feel Your heart and know Your mind!"* Christianity is not rules, ceremonies, rituals, a belief system, theology, or organizational structure. Christianity is Christlikeness! Anything less than this belittles and demeans the death of Christ. We cannot settle for less than, *"Therefore you shall be perfect* (teleois), *just as your Father in heaven is perfect* (teleois)*"* (Matthew 5:48).

Now let us return to our passage. The sixth illustration begins with the same contrast Jesus presented in the other five illustrations. Those of the past lived in an Old Covenant system and introduced a standard, *"You shall love your neighbor and hate your enemy"* (Matthew 5:43). Contrasted with this is the bold statement of Jesus, *"But I say to you, love your enemies and pray for those who spitefully use you and persecute you"* (Matthew 5:44). The phrase *"But I say to you"* is the same in all six illustrations. In the Greek language, *"I"* is included and indicated in the verb *"say."* However, Jesus, in His authority, gives a renewed emphasis with the word "ego" or *"I."* He says, "This is how I am!" The content of "loving your enemies" is the style of Jesus, which is a contrast between His life and the Old Covenant.

Completion of the Law
Fulfillment

What does *"love your enemies"* have to do with the law? During the days of Christ, there were many oral traditions (laws) based on the Old Testament, making it challenging to keep them all. Many scribes and Pharisees came to understand the necessity of prioritizing these laws. Long debates arose concerning the great commandment. In Jerusalem, the Pharisees *"plotted how they could entangle Him in His talk"* (Matthew 22:15). Other groups joined the scribes and Pharisees and designed trick questions to embarrass Jesus as a teacher. Jesus *"silenced the Sadducees"* (Matthew 22:34). The Pharisees regrouped and prompted "a lawyer," exceptionally skilled in debate, to confront Jesus. *"Teacher, which is the great commandment in the law"* (Matthew 22:36). Jesus quickly responded, *"'You shall love the Lord your God with all your heart, with all your soul, and with all your mind.' This is the first and great commandment. And the second is like it: 'You shall love your neighbor as yourself.' On these two commandments hang all the Law and the Prophets"* (Matthew 22:37-40).

Because he ignored the oral traditions of the scribes and Pharisees, many people listening to the Sermon on the Mount felt Jesus was forming a new religion with new rules. Jesus boldly said He did not come to destroy the Law or the Prophets (Matthew 5:17); in fact, He said it twice to make sure they heard Him. He proclaimed the fulfillment of the Law in Himself. Paul restated what Jesus said, *"Therefore love is the fulfillment of the law"* (Romans 13:10). If *"God is love"* (1 John 4:8, 16), if every desire He has for us comes from His loving nature, if now we have His nature and are *"sons of your Father in heaven,"* will we love our enemies as He did? Will we not express His heart? Jesus perfectly fulfilled the law, and we are to do the same.

Consuming Love
I Am

Our self-centered approach to Jesus' challenge is, "How can I do this?" But self-doing is the opposite of Jesus' suggestion. When a conversation turns to love my enemies, the same questions arise. *"Love your enemies,"* "turn the other cheek," and "go the second mile" are excellent ideas, but how far do I go with such principles? After all, there are limits to everything. How many times do I allow an enemy to take advantage of me or that I forgive their offenses? When do I take a stand and place the enemy outside of the boundary of my love?

Part Six: Fulfillment of the Kingdom - The Application: Motive

From the viewpoint of self-protection and self-centeredness, these questions seem legitimate. However, these questions arise from the framework of "doing." Loving my enemies is a rule to keep, but when does the rule no longer apply? But Jesus does not suggest we follow the rule or achieve the activity. He proposes we come into the New Covenant, the "Kingdom of God!" We need a "nature" change. If I embrace my "poverty of spirit" (Matthew 5:3), always aware of my helplessness, He will merge with me (Matthew 5:4), and a new creature emerges, the Kingdom person. Jesus is a son *"of your Father in heaven."* We can be *"sons of your Father in heaven,"* not something we do but someone we are! We think like He thinks and love as He loves.

As *"sons of your Father in heaven,"* we no longer react to the actions of those around us. How we respond to our enemies is not determined by them dwelling within our required boundary of love, or that they meet our standards. Our enemies do not control us. We are Kingdom people, driven by God's nature within us. The righteousness that exceeds the righteousness of the scribes and Pharisees is the Father's righteousness expressed through His sons. I know the merger of the Father and Jesus expressed through me as His son. I am an expression of God's heart. I am Christlike!

If Jesus' challenge is for us to DO something, we are lost. Jesus challenges us to surrender. Will we embrace our helplessness? Will we allow Him to merge with us and become who He created us to be? Will we become the new creature of the Kingdom? Will we be *"perfect, just as your Father in heaven is perfect"* (Matthew 5:48)?

Matthew 5:48

CHRISTIAN PERFECTION

"Therefore you shall be perfect, just as your Father in heaven is perfect" (Matthew 5:43-48).

John Wesley, the founder of the Methodist Church, was an influential preacher in the seventeenth century. He boldly preached an intimate relationship with Jesus, who would save a person from their sins. Jesus, the Savior, was the mission statement proposed by the angel of the Lord at the birth of Christ, *"And she will bring forth a Son, and you shall call His name Jesus for He will save His people from their sins"* (Matthew 1:21). With a heart desiring to know Jesus, Wesley searched the Scriptures to understand what this meant.

In His search of the Scriptures, John Wesley discovered forgiveness was the first step in an intimate relationship with Jesus. God could not engage the darkened heart of a sinful man because *"God is light and in Him is no darkness at all"* (1 John 1:5). But forgiveness is not a problem for Jesus. His sacrificial death provided abundantly for the sin of the world. He is *"faithful and just to forgive us our sins"* (1 John 1:9). Wesley believed in real and abundant forgiveness for all, but a tendency or nature toward sin resides in every human. All theological persuasions agree with this premise and that God must cleanse the sinful nature of man before he can enter heaven. Many believed the evil nature dies a little at a time until physical death happens. However, this leaves humanity in a constant inward battle against sin, with many failures needing forgiveness. The Scripture that says Jesus is **"faithful and just to forgive us our sins,"** continues **"and to cleanse us from all unrighteousness"** (1 John 1:9). If the atoning cross of Jesus is adequate to forgive sin, can it not cleanse even the inner nature of sin? While humans continue to live in a sinful, imperfect world, is it not possible to have a perfect heart? Yes, which means man's affections are no longer divided, and he has one focused love toward God. He aligns his being with the nature of the Father.

John Wesley proposed "Christian Perfection" is aligning with the nature of the Father. The term "perfection" repelled many people. It was unthinkable that anyone could be perfect. The only thing I know about perfection is that the person who thinks he is perfect is not! To those people who responded negatively and did not listen, Wesley explained what "Christian Perfection is not." It is not perfection in knowledge, perfection in our actions, or perfection in location, because we can never be omniscient, omnipotent, or omnipresent like God. All human shortcomings, frailties, and imperfections remain present in all humans born in a fallen world. We are in a constant battle with our inability to understand, the tiredness of our flesh, and our emotional frailties; thus, there is no absolute perfection in our human limitations. It is questionable as to whether perfection on such a level will exist in the coming world. We will never have perfect omniscience, omnipresence, or omnipotence, which belong to God only.

Then what are we to do? God promised us complete deliverance, the wholeness of heart, and perfect love! The perfect love He promised is necessary and was a command of Jesus. **"Therefore you shall be perfect, just as your Father in heaven is perfect"** (Matthew 5:48). The main verb **"shall be"** (eimi) is in the future tense and indicative mood. This combination creates an imperative, translated "must be." We must be perfect! Now you have a choice. You may do what many in John Wesley's day did, choosing not to be open and not to listen. They interpreted "perfection" according to their selfish definition and discarded the idea. But you can respond to Jesus with a desire to know the truth and to go beyond your present spiritual experience. We need to investigate the passage.

Standard
Father

No one can read our passage without the deep awareness that the Father is the standard for perfection. Jesus uses the Greek word "hos," translated *"just as,"* which is a comparative conjunction. *"Just as"* is a compelling comparison, which is foreign in our culture. We consistently compare ourselves to others but never to God, most often comparing ourselves to ourselves. In the competitive world, we measure ourselves by the standard of the person with whom we are competing.

Luke records a parable Jesus gave to those who trust in themselves (Luke 18:9-14). A Pharisee and a tax collector went to the temple to pray. The Pharisee stood and prayed with himself. The Greek word "pros" is translated *"with."* It is a preposition of location, which gives direction such as "towards." In other words, the Pharisee talked to himself and called it prayer. Judging himself, he said, **"God, I thank You that I am not like other men - extortioners, unjust, adulterers, or even as this tax collector. I fast twice a week; I give tithes of all that I possess"** (Luke 18:11-12). But the tax collector made no such comparison. He did not raise his eyes to heaven, but beat his breast and declared his sinfulness. Jesus said there is no justification in comparing ourselves to ourselves but is a means by which we exalt ourselves. Also, He promised that such a person would be brought down and humbled. Is it not a warning to us?

Part Six: Fulfillment of the Kingdom – The Application: Motive

Now we return to saturation in our passage (Matthew 5:43-48). If this last verse (Matthew 5:48) is a climatic statement bringing summary to all six illustrations (especially the sixth illustration), what is the focus of the perfection? Jesus did not say we should be God. The premise of the Sermon on the Mount eliminates that possibility. Our helplessness (poor in spirit) is the opening statement of the Beatitudes (Matthew 5:3). Helplessness is not a condition from which God saves us; it is a condition we are to embrace (Matthew 5:4) continually. While our helplessness merges with the Spirit of God, we do not become God. We continue in our helplessness, which is the essence of the relationship creating the Kingdom person. The inward growth in the new Kingdom person is the consistent deepening awareness of helplessness.

Since we will never be God, can we set aside all that God possesses? He does not discuss His omnipresence, omniscience, and omnipotence in this chapter. The practical discussion is God allows the sun to shine on the good and the evil and rain to fall on the just and unjust (Matthew 5:45). God allowing the same for the good and evil is a practical illustration of His love for His enemies. The call for perfection is in God's perfect love. The Trinity God calls us to join Him, not in what He has but in who He is! God wants to join us, merge with us, and diffuse His nature throughout our nature of helplessness. His thoughts can fill our minds; we can have the mind of Christ. We can express His emotions in the stressful moments of our living, and His concerns can be ours. We can have the appetite of God!

We can be perfect in love! Perfect love is love without alloy. The New Testament described this love by using a different Greek word for God's love. It is not "eros," sexual attraction, not "philo," brotherly love or friendship, and not "stergo," family love. It is "agape," which is selfless, self-sacrificing love. It is love that never thinks about itself but always about the beloved one. It is love that is not conditional because it receives something in return. It is love formed within the heart of its love nature. Therefore, we cannot deter it. This love we cannot earn and can never stop. In our helplessness, God fills us with His nature of love, and we express who God is to our world. We are perfect in love as He is perfect in love.

Substance
Father

If you see the "Standard" as unattainable, you would be correct. Jesus fulfilled Old Testament law in "love," but no one living in the old covenant was able to keep that "love." No matter how hard I try, how much I work, or how desperate I am in my efforts, I will never arrive at perfect love. But this is the premise of the Sermon on the Mount. I am helpless in my spirit, which sources my life (Matthew 5:3). I must embrace my helplessness at the beginning and the end of Christianity, living in the boundaries of this condition. I must never be cocky or arrogant and always live in the attitude of dependency.

Therefore, Jesus presents the substance of this perfection as the nature of God. Perfection is not in my helplessness; perfection is in His nature. Can my helplessness be filled with His nature? My helplessness is the fundamental proposition of the New Testament Scriptures! After highlighting the phrase *"in Christ"* or *"in Him"* numerous times, Paul thunders forth with the following statement. *"For by grace you have been saved through faith, and that not of yourselves; it is the gift of God, not of works, lest anyone should boast. For we are His workmanship, created in Christ Jesus for good works, which God prepared beforehand that we should walk in them"* (Ephesians 2:8-10). Grace is "unmerited" favor, a gift from God, not of our effort, for we are helpless. We become the workmanship of God. The Greek word "poiema" is translated *"workmanship,"* coming from the Greek word "poieo," a verb used consistently regarding trees "bearing" fruit (Matthew 7:17-20). It is the nature of the tree that births the fruit, not an assignment, rule, or duty; it is a result of nature. Paul proposed that the perfect nature of God indwells the helplessness of humanity and gives birth or bears the fruit of perfection. We were destined for this birthing beforehand!

In the Old Testament hour, God repeatedly said, *"I am holy"* (Leviticus 11:44-45). However, we are confused by such a statement because we have no framework in which to understand its content. What does it mean for God to be holy? God wrote it down in a book called the Old Testament, the holy nature of God in written form. God was saying, "If I were a human being, here is how I would act." In the New Testament, we see Jesus, the holy nature of God, lived in our world. The Old Testament was the written nature of God, and the New Testament is Jesus living the nature of God. Jesus is the visible image of an invisible God, and He invites us to share in His nature. Jesus demonstrates the written nature of God (the Law) in the living nature of God through us. Outwardly and inwardly, God shapes and produces us by His nature, the fruit of His perfection, perfect love!

Who could be against this? What denominational theology could say this should not be our deepest desire? Any other approach only engages self-pride in accomplishments of duty, ceremonies, and traditions. This self-centeredness is the heart nature of sin, refusing to embrace its helplessness. When self-centeredness manifests itself in the evil deeds of our world, we quickly recognize it. But we should equally accept it in the activities of religion birthed from the raging desires of self. It is not the activities of religion that we must eliminate but the appetite of the human heart not flowing from God's nature. Again, who could be against this? Would not everyone serious about spiritual reality embrace the wonder of belonging to Jesus, wanting to merge with God's nature and be His expression? Would this not eliminate sin (1 John 3:9)? Would we not dwell in perfect love?

We cannot contain Christianity in reform, New Year's resolutions, doing better, self-helps, or discipline. Paul contrasted the *"works of the flesh"* with the *"fruit of the Spirit"* (Galatians 5:19-23). The *"works"* we do contain the evil of our lives. It is a translation of the Greek word "erga," meaning "something that people do or cause to happen." But "fruit" is that birthed or produced by a plant or tree. "Works" is what one does, but "fruit" flows from the nature, the concept of "poieo" discussed earlier. If God merges His Divine nature with my helpless nature, what will I express? God will produce fruit from my life.

You will notice that "works" is plural because there is such a variety of expressions for the flesh. It goes from murders to outbursts of wrath, from sorcery to heresies, and the list is endless. The *"fruit"* is focused; it is love. Love is the substance of God's nature! The last expression of this focus in *"self-control."* It is not "self" controlling, but "Spirit" regulating self. The fruit is of the Spirit, not of self. Paul ended his presentation by saying there is no law against the fruit of the Spirit (Galatians 5:23)! Who can argue against perfect love? How can we not view the cross, Jesus dying to redeem others, with great admiration? Everyone exalts the person who risks his life for others in battle and scorns those who run in the face of conflict. All that I desire for my life is in the substance of the Father's nature. I am constantly reminded of my helplessness because I cannot achieve those desires on my own. His nature must fill me; I must know Jesus!

Specification
Father

The dictionary presents two views on the word "specification." The first is the act of describing or identifying something precisely or stating a precise requirement. Therefore, our passage is a specification (Matthew 5:48). Jesus described and defined the exact condition of being *"sons of your Father in heaven"* (Matthew 5:45). He described the fundamental expression of God's nature, having no boundaries on His love but allowing it to rain on the just and the unjust and the sun to shine on the good and the evil. Allowing the same for good and evil is an expression of the perfect love of the Father's nature. Treating all people the same is the specification, the precise requirement, of being a son of the Father!

The dictionary also describes "specification" as a detailed description of the design and materials used to make something. What does it mean to be *"sons of your Father in heaven"?* It is the perfect love of the Father's nature. If I present to you the makeup of *"sons of your Father in heaven,"* it would be the perfect love of the Father's nature. This climatic statement of Jesus is the blueprint of all He has described. It is not a goal or the final condition, but it is the beginning state. It is the righteousness that exceeds the righteousness of the scribes and Pharisees. Jesus said that without this new righteousness, *"you will by no means enter the kingdom of heaven"* (Matthew 5:20). Being filled with the nature of the Father is the entry-level into being this new Kingdom person.

Jesus began the sixth illustration contrasting the Old and New Covenants (Matthew 5:43-44). The Old Covenant embraced loving your neighbor but could not see the possibility of loving your enemy; therefore, hating your enemy was acceptable. The New Covenant does not allow hating your enemy. The boundaries of your love must be pushed to the furthest person from you, your enemy. After making this "proposition," Jesus extended to us the "purpose" for such a response. It is *"that you may be sons of your Father in heaven"* (Matthew 5:45).

Jesus closes with this climactic statement, concluding the matter, *"Therefore you shall be perfect, just as your Father in heaven is perfect"* (Matthew 5:48). In other words, if this specification or this conclusion is not right in your life, then you are not a son of *"your Father in heaven."* It is not an achievement to reach; it is a state in which to dwell. God fills helplessness with His resource, merging His nature with my nature and producing a new creature. We are like our Father!

Matthew 5:47-48

MORE!

"And if you greet your brethren only, what do you do more than others? Do not even the tax collectors do so? Therefore you shall be perfect, just as your Father in heaven is perfect"
(Matthew 5:47-48).

I fear there is a disconnect between what we hear from the pulpit and what we experience in our lives. The church teaches the message of love, victory, and forgiveness, but counseling sessions reveal we constantly battle guilt, hatred, and defeat. Everyone in the evangelical movement believes and promotes unity, and yet denominational divisions are strong. I might tolerate this in the general church world, but I do not want it in my life. I have a lot of religious involvement in my life, and I have to ask myself, "Is this the best religion can do?"

Jesus gave the marvelous picture of His role in our lives, picturing Himself as the Good Shepherd. The protection and daily care of a shepherd who values his sheep is His position in my life. He expanded the concept to include, ***"I am the door of the sheep"*** (John 10:7). He contrasts Himself with others who are thieves and robbers. He thunders to this conclusion. ***"The thief does not come except to steal, and to kill, and to destroy. I have come that they may have life, and that they may have it more abundantly"*** (John 10:10). The Greek word "perissos" is translated ***"more abundantly."*** "Perissos" means "over and above, beyond, and extraordinary." "Perissos" is superabundant! If Jesus' provision is superabundant, I look at my life and ask, "Is there more? What am I missing?"

The Scriptures tell me I am not alone in these feelings. There was a young man Matthew referred to as the Rich Young Ruler (Matthew 19:16-22). We do not know his proper name. In the materialistic realm, he lacked nothing. In health and physical life, he was at the peak of life experience. He had high self-esteem in his position as a ruler. Everything anyone could want to have had become his, yet, he confronted Jesus with a question that indicated he felt something lacking. He assured Jesus he had kept all the commandments of God, and still, he asked, **"What do I still lack"** (Matthew 19:20)? The Rich Young Ruler expressed the same thing I feel in my heart? Is there anything more?

The Parable of the Prodigal Son convinces us that there is something more than what we anticipate (Luke 15:11-32). After squandering the inheritance from his father, the son found himself living with the pigs. In Jewish tradition, this was the sign of total disobedience and the consequence of rebellion against God. The turning point in the story is **"he came to himself."** He expressed his recognition in a question, "Is there something more?" While he was filling his stomach with the pods the swine ate, his father's servants had plenty of bread. The only "more" he could conceive was to go home and become a servant. He had utterly violated his right to sonship; it would be generous of his father to allow him to be a servant of the household. There was something more in his father's heart because He gave his prodigal son the best robe, ring, and sandals. The father had the fatted calf killed, and there was eating and making merry **"for this my son was dead and is alive again; he was lost and is found"** (Luke 15:24).

The elder brother, working in the field for the father, came home after a long day to find a party for his long lost brother. When he heard the reason for such merriment, **"he was angry"**

(Luke 15:28). The father left the party and pleaded with his eldest son to rejoice and be glad. The elder brother responded, *"Lo, these many years I have been serving you; I never transgressed your commandment at any time; and yet you never gave me a young goat, that I might make merry with my friends"* (Luke 15:29). Was he not crying out, "All this time there was something more, and I missed it? While working in the fields and keeping the commandments, I never experienced the party!"

Jesus told many parables to describe the Kingdom of Heaven. He spoke of a tenant farmer who struggled every year to produce a crop (Matthew 13:44). His family was in great need; his home was in disrepair. One day as he worked his field, his plow struck an obstacle. Thinking it was another rock he would need to dig out and remove, discouragement overcame him. Questions arose in his mind. "Isn't there something more than this? Is this the best I can do for my family?" He uncovered the obstacle and found the answer. There was something more; it was a treasure!

Another parable of Jesus was of a merchant who traveled the world in search of beautiful pearls (Matthew 13:45, 46), finding many. Each pearl was beautiful and had some value, but wasn't there something more? Indeed, there was! *"When he had found one pearl of great price, went and sold all that he had and bought it"* (Matthew 13:46). He made many journeys, discovered many pearls, and found something more!

Finding something more in the spiritual realm flows through the Sermon on the Mount, the fiber that holds its truth together. When Jesus presented the Beatitudes (Matthew 5:3-12), He startled His listeners, causing them to imagine He was contradicting the Law or the Prophets. Jesus made it plain He was not eliminating the Law or the Prophets; He was fulfilling them (Matthew 5:17). While His proposal may seem new and startling, it is the intent of the Old Covenant, offering much more in the fulfillment. Jesus called them to a life exceeding anything they had known. He said, *"For I say to you, that unless your righteousness exceeds the righteousness of the scribes and Pharisees, you will by no means enter the kingdom of heaven"* (Matthew 5:20). The Greek word translated *"exceeds"* is "pleion," meaning "many, much, greater." It is used only one time in the English translation but twice in the Greek language, appearing before and after the word "righteousness." Is there anything more? Jesus stated it as "more and more."

In the sixth illustration (Matthew 5:43-48), Jesus used the word *"more"* (perissos). He said, *"And if you greet your brethren only what do you do more* (perissos) *than others"* (Matthew 5:47)? In this illustration, Jesus used "more" as a negative, making the answer to His question to be "no" or "nothing." If you greet only those who welcome you, you do nothing more exceptional or more extravagant than the worst of sinners. You meet the status quo. His statement intends that the New Covenant, the Kingdom person, lives beyond the normal or average. The Kingdom's life is superabundant and exceeding in love, off the charts! Jesus stated the Kingdom life in the strongest terms, *"perfect, just as your Father in heaven is perfect."* What else can you expect from one who is a son of *"your Father in heaven?"* He is *"more"* (perissos)!

Matthew Chapter 6 is the middle of the Sermon on the Mount, where Jesus presents the three fundamental elements of all world religions: charitable giving, prayer, and spiritual disciplines. Each of these elements demonstrates the usual pattern of the religious people of Jesus' day. They conduct their religious activities to be seen of men. It is a show! *"Take heed that you do not do your charitable deeds, before men, to be seen by then. Otherwise you have no reward from your Father in heaven"* (Matthew 6:1). Jesus says they also pray to be seen by men, which demonstrates a hypocritical spirit. *"Assuredly, I say to you, they have their reward"* (Matthew 6:5). The same hypocrites put on a sad countenance and disfigured their faces so all would know they were fasting. *"Assuredly, I say to you, they have their reward"* (Matthew 6:16).

The intent of Jesus' statements about charitable deeds, prayer, and fasting is that there is something *"more"* (perissos) for the Kingdom person! *"Your charitable deed may be in secret; and your Father who sees in secret will Himself reward you openly"* (Matthew 6:4). Communication with the Father's heart is the same as "more." Go to the secret place of your merger with Him, *"and your Father who sees in secret will reward you openly"* (Matthew 6:6). Spiritual disciplines are not to impress others, but to deepen intimacy with the Father. *"Your Father who is in the secret place"* (of the inner heart) *"who sees in secret will reward you openly"* (Matthew 6:18). All the critical involvements of religion take on new significance. Is there not something "more" than just doing good deeds, making beautiful prayers, and skipping a meal? Yes! There is something extraordinary, extravagant, and beyond in the merger with your Father who makes you His son. Becoming sons is the "exceedingly more" of the Sermon on the Mount!

While this may sound intriguing and even religious, what is this *"more"* that goes beyond what the sinful world entices us with, and religions can offer us?

Exceeding Righteousness
Matthew 5:20

Jesus demonstrates for us this "exceeding righteousness." The Trinity God presented it to us in the Old Testament Scriptures, but the scribes and Pharisees misread the Scriptures to cater to their level of righteousness. Now, Jesus, the helpless Man merged with the Father, expresses the *"more"* of the New Covenant. All Kingdom people will know the same intimacy that Jesus has with the Father. What is this righteousness that is "more?" *"For I say to you, that unless our righteousness exceeds the righteousness of the scribes and Pharisees, you will by no means enter the kingdom of heaven"* (Matthew 5:20). *"Exceeding righteousness"* becomes the springboard for six illustrations that demonstrate the "more righteousness."

There are common elements that flow through all six illustrations. One is the extreme emphasis on the INTERNAL. This righteousness is not a correction of an outward activity; it is an elimination of an interior motive or appetite. Jesus moves from the external act of murder to the internal feeling of anger (Matthew 5:21-22). Adultery changes because God alters the inward perspective of our hearts (Matthew 5:27- 28). God transforms the ease of physical separation from one's wife to a concern about what he is causing in her (Matthew 5:31, 32), and He replaces our methods of forcing honesty by oaths with inner integrity (Matthew 5:33-37). The redemptive heart of the Father overcomes our concern for equality and fairness in physical punishment or revenge (Matthew 5:38-42). Now in the final illustration (our passage), we focus on the righteousness of the Father becoming our appetite, motive, becoming His sons until we are perfectly like Him (Matthew 5:43-48).

Jesus INTENSIFIED another element in this righteousness. When we see each illustration as acceptable righteousness, we also see it as impossible. Each illustration leaves us breathless, in stunned silence, and startled by such a ridiculous claim. This intensification builds throughout each example, bringing us to the final blow. We are to **"be perfect, just as our Father in heaven is perfect"** (Matthew 5:48). Such a claim could be grounds for total dismissal because it seems beyond the realm of possibility. Yet, Jesus, a helpless Man merged with the Father, demonstrates it before us. If we can merge with the Father and become sons as Jesus was a son, can this righteousness be conceivable for our lives? The same Spirit of the Father that lived in Jesus fills you and me. Can this righteousness be found in us? Jesus presents a "more righteousness!"

Part Six: Fulfillment of the Kingdom - The Application: Motive

Exceeding Relationship
Matthew 5:45

The Sermon on the Mount begins with Jesus' presentation of a relationship with God, the premise of the sermon. God invades a person's helplessness with His nature and births a new creature. This merger, infusion, or saturation of God and man together in a relationship brings about the Kingdom person. Becoming a Kingdom person is the only feasible explanation for the "more righteousness" already discussed. While we must understand each illustration in light of this relationship or merger, Jesus does not distinctly state it in the first five illustrations. As Jesus comes to the last illustration, His focus is on the relationship! You are to be *"sons of your Father in heaven"* (Matthew 5:45). In this relationship, who He is will be who we are (Matthew 5:48). We are in such intimacy with Him that others see His nature in us. We are His sons!

Once more, let me clarify; we do not become God. We are helpless, our constant state, the boundaries in which we dwell. In this attitude of helplessness, dependency upon Him will flourish. It is the open door to intimacy with all that He is in His nature. We love our enemies as He does. We begin to understand this love for enemies is not a rare expression, occurring just when it is to our benefit. God was not trying to achieve something or create a historical moment of granting forgiveness through death on a cross. God expresses Himself every day through rain falling on the just and the unjust and the sun shining on the evil and the good. Jesus consistently reveals the nature of the Father, who is now intimate with us. When we embrace our helplessness, we release Him to merge with us and make us sons!

Is this not "more?" You might hear the actual voice of God once in your lifetime or sense His presence in worship on special Sunday services. In times of need, God might make Himself known to you, but who could dream of being intimate with Him so that you become the expression of His person. No wonder we place Jesus in a category of oneness with the Father that is "more" than we can imagine. Yet, this is the message of Christ to our lives. Jesus calls us to live in the "more!"

Exceeding Redemption
Matthew 5:48

This sixth illustration could easily be an extension of the fifth illustration. Who is the individual who insults us by slapping our right cheek? He is our enemy! Who is the individual filled with such hatred he wants to financially destroy us by suing us for our tunic (undergarments)? He is our enemy. Who is the individual who takes advantage of us and compels us to go one mile? He is our enemy. Who consistently uses us for his benefit by borrowing from us? He is our enemy. How am I to respond to him? I respond to him as the Father responds, for I am a son of my Father in heaven. I feel like He feels; I love as He loves!

In the practical activities of life, I allow the Father's nature to demonstrate love through me. I will enable it to rain on the just and the unjust; I will enable the sun to shine on the evil and the good. I am a son who is perfect as the Father is! The driving power of love is redemption, and the only redemptive force in the world is love. Love that is without a plan. In other words, it is not love that loves to be redemptive but is merely love. If love has an agenda, it is not like the Father. Love without a plan will be redemptive, but if we love to be redemptive, it is not love.

The Father's demonstration of love through me is the "more" of love! I experience a "more righteousness" in the Father's nature because of the "more relationship" of His intimate presence. I am perfect, just as my Father in heaven is perfect. It is enough to be His! His nature merged with my nature produces sonship, which is sufficient for me. In this fulfillment in my life, I experience redemption flowing to my world. It is not my agenda, but it is an expression of the Father's heart through my heart. I do not select some to love to redeem them. I am simply a demonstration of His love, which allows redemption for all. Redemption is the picture of Jesus who died for all, whether they respond or not. He died to forgive all, whether they repent or not. He is an expression of redemptive love. I have become His brother; I am redemptive love (Hebrews 2:11).

ABOUT THE AUTHOR

Stephen Manley has found through the saturation of the Word the message of the cross. It is beyond an event; it is a style. Thus, the cross is not a piece of wood or an emblem, but it is the heart of the person of Christ. Cross style is the Christ style. He must be central. As an international evangelist, Stephen has taken this message to the world.

After 41 years in itinerant evangelism, Stephen Manley felt a clear call from God to come off the road for the purpose of starting the Cross Style School of Practical Ministry. In 2009, Stephen launched and became the lead pastor of Cross Style Church in Lebanon, Tennessee to create the ministry platform for future students.

The Cross Style School of Practical Ministry was launched with a desire to not only train up men and women in the Word, but to give them practical hands-on experience in ministering to a lost and dying world.

Stephen's life, testimony, and preaching has been used throughout the last six decades to touch, influence, and transform the lives of countless people around the world. For Stephen, his life is wrapped up in a total saturation of Jesus and the Word of God. Time in the Word is more than an activity or duty to schedule in his day. It is the delight of his heart and the focus throughout his day because it draws him deeper into intimacy with Jesus Christ. He wants his "moment-by-moments" saturated with the Person of Jesus and the Word. He longs for Jesus to ever increase and expand in and through His life. As he once wrote:

"Jesus is present in every situation of my life. There is no conversation in which I do not feel His presence. He participates in all my recreation. He is everywhere I go. Who would want to be without Him? He is the protection for my life. He is the fragrance I constantly smell. He is the flow of my spiritual blood giving me life. He is my constant nutrition making me healthy. I cannot survive without Him. I am a Jesus pusher!!!!

I want to push Him on you.
I want you to join me in this obsession.
You do not have to work at it; it is not a discipline.
It is as natural as breathing.
Please let Him pull you to His heart."

Learn more about Stephen Manley
and the ministry of Cross Style at:
CrossStyle.org

www.ingramcontent.com/pod-product-compliance
Lightning Source LLC
Chambersburg PA
CBHW032012230426
43671CB00005B/58